PHYSICIANS' DI
OF TRUSTED REMEDIES

1,000+ Doctor-Approved Home Remedies for 145 Leading Health Concerns

By the editors of TrustedRemedies.com

YOUR 4 FREE EBOOKS!

Thank you for purchasing the **PHYSICIANS' DIRECTORY OF TRUSTED REMEDIES**. Use it in good health! Please accept these **Four Free Bonus eBooks** (pdf's) with our compliments; simply use the scan codes in the back of the book to access your free gifts. Each is also available as a paperback on Amazon for under $10.

PHYSICIANS' DIRECTORY OF TRUSTED REMEDIES

1,000+ Doctor-Approved Home Remedies for 145 Leading Health Concerns

IN CASE OF EMERGENCY, call 9-1-1 or safely go to the emergency room.

Cover design: Jason Velazquez, Quezart.com | Cover image: PurePNG, CC0
PHYSICIANS' DIRECTORY OF TRUSTED REMEDIES| 09232024
© 2024, 2023 Trusted Remedies Publishing LLC
ISBN: 979-8-9876969-3-4

CONTENTS

RASHES ... *"Dermatologists trust these remedies to soothe itchy skin"*
RAYNAUD'S SYNDROME ... *"These trusted remedies may help reduce or manage flare-ups"*
RECTAL ITCH AND ANAL FISSURES ... *Best remedies for the the pain, the bleeding, and the maddening itch*
RESTLESS LEGS ... *"Try trusted self-care remedies and get a good night's sleep."*
ROSACEA ... *Many "tips and tricks" on the internet claim to alleviate rosacea symptoms. What you really need are trusted, physician-approved remedies*

S-T-U – Page 217

SCARS ... *"Assist in your body's healing of scars or unwanted marks"*
SCIATICA ... *The pain can be excruciating; try these remedies before it gets that far.*
SCRATCHES, BITES, AND STINGS ... *These remedies can help can seemingly mundane events from becoming itchy, inflamed, or very serious*
SEASONAL AFFECTIVE DISORDER – SAD ... *"the healthiest way to increase serotonin levels"*
SHIN SPLINTS ... *5 trusted remedies to treat painful shin splints at home*

SHINGLES ... *"Self-care remedies can help you heal from shingles fast.*
SINUSITIS ... *"This self-care remedy can help clear your sinuses."*
SLEEPLESSNESS – see INSOMNIA
SNAKEBITES ... *"Do Not: attempt to suck the venom from the wound*
SNORING ... *Try these doctor-trusted remedies ... you just need one that works for you.*

SORE THROAT ... *These four delicious foods are known to help soothe and heal.*
SPIDER BITES ... *Call this national hotline for fast, free, personalized guidance*
SPLINTERS ... *These remedies get that small but offensive object out of your body f-a-s-t!*
SPRAINS ... *When it's okay resume mild exercise, which can help heal a sprained ankle*
STINGRAY STINGS ... *These remedies may help, but call Poison Control at 1-800-222-1222*

STOMACH FLU (VIRAL GASTROENTERITIS) – see NAUSEA AND VOMITING, DIARRHEA
STRESS ... *"Here are several trusted, evidence-based remedies for managing stress."*
SUNBURN ... *" Use these doctor-trusted remedies to treat sunburns and soothe the sting."*
TACHYCARDIA (HEART PALPITATIONS) ... *In most cases, these trusted remedies bring relief to the heart and help it operate normally.*
TEMPOROMANDIBULAR JOINT – TMJ ... *"If you have pain when you chew or yawn, you may find relief with some or all of the following therapies."*

TENDONITIS ... *"Here are five self-care remedies to help reduce tendonitis."*
TOOTH PAIN ... *Until you can get to the dentist, these remedies help calm the inflammation.*
ULCERS ... *Research supports these trusted remedies for managing a stomach ulcer.*
URINARY TRACT INFECTION ... *These ten physician-trusted remedies are often effective.*
URTICARIA – see HIVES

About Trusted Remedies Publishing | Mark E. Johnson, Publisher

I am not a doctor ... I am a tireless consumer advocate and health researcher, scouring the news for the latest breakthroughs to put you on the cutting edge of science and health – all so you can enjoy the very best of health for yourself and your family.

My readers count on me to review volumes of health and medical news daily so they don't have to. Anytime there's a major health discovery, I'm checking it out on behalf of my readers. If there's an emerging threat to my readers' health, I'm digging into that, too ... sharing how they can best protect themselves and their loved ones from harm while improving their lives with safe, doctor-approved remedies.

The personal health strategies I identify from trusted sources arrive in 8-10 million postal mailboxes each year. More than 150,000 health-conscious Americans subscribe to HeadlineHealth.com, my free health news service. 500,000 readers subscribe to a monthly medical newsletter in response to my invitation.

My life's work has been devoted to researching topics that impact the average American family and sharing findings with the potential to improve readers' lives. I started on Capitol Hill as a tax policy researcher and public affairs consultant working with the vice chair of the tax-writing United States House Committee on Ways & Means, U.S. Rep. Philip Crane. More than one million Americans actively supported the grassroots tax reform campaign I created with Rep. Crane and other members of Congress.

Next, I applied my interest in consumer affairs to the world of self-help publishing. My campaign for *Prevention* – already the world's largest health magazine – boosted readership from two million copies per month to three million. Harvard Health Publishing, Dr. Crandall's Heart Health Newsletter, Mayo Clinic (all consumer health publishers led by world-renowned physicians) and many more have provided my work to millions of consumers and grown their readership because of it.

The ***Physicians' Directory of Trusted Remedies*** represents my latest and potentially most impactful contribution to consumer health. All 1,031 remedies in the Directory are doctor-approved, so you've made a wise choice – you can place your confidence in everything here. | Photo: Donna H. Chiarelli Studio

PREFACE

Folklore remedies only put you at greater risk for dangerous diseases.

– Good Housekeeping, May 3, 2022 [1]

Dear Reader,

You've seen all the "weird tricks" that pop up daily on social media, viral videos, assorted blogs, and unwanted emails. Some of these "trending" cures are sales pitches disguised to appear as news from reputable sources. *"Try this tonight,"* they shout, expecting many to blindly go along.

But folklore remedies can be a real danger to your health. So says *Good Housekeeping*, the name families have trusted for home health and safety recommendations for over 135 years.

What you really need are trusted remedies backed by real doctors –
physicians, dentists, and other providers and scientists with health-related Ph.D.s.

That's what you'll find here in the *Physicians' Directory of Trusted Remedies* – more than 1,000 reliable remedies, each and every one backed by one or more respected doctors of medicine or a closely related field of human health. And no risky folklore.

Deep down, you probably know that searching the internet for health remedies is not safe. There's even a term for this inner feeling: *cyberchondria.* According to Prof. Vladan Starcevic, M.D., cyberchondria refers to the anxiety-amplifying effects of online health searches. [2]

Who needs all that anxiety and uncertainty when all you really want is to feel and look better, as quickly and affordably as possible! The *Physicians' Directory of Trusted Remedies* has you covered. With heart disease, diabetes, cancer, virus epidemics, sexually transmitted infections, mental health woes, drug side effects, and so many other dangerous diseases on the rise, none of us can afford to just trust our health and our future to risky folklore remedies anymore.

Sadly, many medical doctors can attest to the real danger of folklore remedies. They see patients who tried unproven remedies that only made their conditions worse and harder to treat. In other cases, folklore remedies simply have no effect – but people delay needed treatment in the false hope that an unproven cure and or "weird trick" will work.

Throughout this directory, you'll find trusted remedies you can implement on your own, at home. When appropriate, we also include remedies that you initiate, but that involve seeking out professional services – the best of both worlds.

---

[1] Goodhousekeeping.com
[2] Cyberchondria: Challenges of Problematic Online Searches for Health-Related Information

As it says on the cover, every remedy is doctor-approved – all 1,031 of them. In most cases, that means approved by a physician, but in all cases, by someone with a doctorate in a field of human health (the name of the degree may vary slightly by specialty or nationality).

What all these remedies have in common is a chance to improve your health – in some cases, dramatically. And often, you'll have an opportunity to save money, too, also very dramatically in many cases. It's all about living a better life; that means length of life, but first, quality of life.

The key is to decide once and for all that you will take control of your health, your life, your future, and your daily decision-making, based on trustworthy information only.

We kick off this directory of doctor-trusted remedies in Part I by tackling the top ten most common health issues facing Americans today, as given by the University of Rochester (NY) Medical Center. Every reader should read this portion of the book in its entirety.

After the top ten, Part II offers a full A-to-Z listing of 145 conditions and the best doctor-approved remedies available today for each. *It's your health, your future, and your life – make the most of it!*

Wishing you the best of health for years to come,

Mark E. Johnson, Publisher, Trusted Remedies Publishing

How to use this directory

This compendium of more than 1,000 doctor-trusted remedies is better than any "thriller" – it's about you, your future, your independence, your well-being, and maybe saving some money along the way. It just does not get any better than that. We truly intend for this to be one of the most important publications you've ever owned.

Read **Part I** in its entirety. This is your guide to reducing your risks for the ten leading causes of disability, sickness, and early death in America today. On each page, you'll find doctor-approved ways to cut your risks, and when appropriate, remedies for correcting the health consequences. *We suggest you reread **Part I** once each year on a date that's easy to remember, such as your birthday or New Year's Day.* Think of it as an annual present to yourself and your loved ones.

Any time you open this directory, you may discover a tip that turns out to be instrumental in helping you make it safely to your milestone in life. You'll also become your family's expert in home health and safety, able to help household members and loved ones avoid common causes of death and disability. *Imagine saving the life of a spouse, parent, sibling, son, daughter, neighbor, or even a total stranger. It would be one of the proudest moments of your entire life! (See the personal note from one of the editors on the next page.)*

Next, flip through **Part II** from A (Acne) to Z (Zoster), reviewing any entries that pertain to your current health concerns. Later, come back to **Part II** for any new concerns that arise for you or a loved one. Note that throughout the book, each remedy is backed by one or more physicians or the equivalent – individuals holding a medical degree (M.D., D.O., D.M.D.) or other type of doctorate in a field of human health. Their names appear in bold.

The editors of this book believe that when a doctor is willing to associate her or his professional reputation with a remedy at a public level, that remedy is more than worthy of your attention. And as noted in our disclosures, you should not rely solely on information published by any single source to evaluate any health remedy, product, or service; do your own research to confirm that the remedy suggested is sound and right for you.

Another quote you'll find in this book is worthy of special attention here. **Caldwell Esselstyn, M.D.**, author of *The New York Times* best-selling *Prevent and Reverse Heart Disease*, notes:

> ***"Some people think that the plant-based whole foods diet is extreme. Half a million a year will have their chests opened up, a vein taken from their leg and sewn onto their coronary artery. Some people would call that extreme."*** [3]

You do not have to go to the extent of committing yourself entirely to a plant-based, whole-foods diet in order to make this book useful to you. You may, however, find that many of the doctor-approved remedies in this book can save you from medical treatments like open heart surgery or a lifetime of taking various pharmaceuticals; doctors themselves confirm this to be true.

It's important to note that while these remedies may significantly improve the quality of your life and save you a great deal of money, *they are in no way intended to eliminate the need for*

---

[3] Exercise and Seniors, wholehealthdietitian.com

professional medical services. As aptly stated by *Financial Mechanic*:

> **"While basic self-care is important, it is critical that it does not become a substitute for proper medical care. My experience with acne made me realize how easy it is to try to use self-care to try to cure problems that are ultimately too big to treat alone."** [4]

This leads to one more key feature you'll find for each condition listed in **Part II.** Look under the **"Doctor, Doctor!"** subheadings to find guidance on when to seek professional medical advice for symptoms that call for more than a home remedy. Yes, for every health topic mentioned in this directory, there are times when calling a doctor is your best option. Many doctors' offices are prepared to ask screening questions over the phone to assess your need to see a doctor; *when in doubt, call.*

Finally, while we have strived to make this directory thorough and comprehensive, no single source can be exhaustive. Use the footnotes (nearly 700 of them in all) to read more from the same doctors, clinics, hospitals, universities, and sources we rely on throughout the directory.

Also see the state-by-state RESOURCES list of healthcare providers beginning on page 259. They may be able to provide personalized professional care close to home or online.

A personal note from the publisher ...

On the value of learning lifesaving techniques you may not need to use today ...

In my youth, I was required by my mother to take Red Cross swimming lessons [5] every summer from grade school through high school. Levels began with "Tadpoles," where the main skill to learn was blowing bubbles, and progressed yearly to Beginner, Advanced Beginner, Swimmer, Junior and Senior Lifesaving, and likely a few others that I'm forgetting. Lessons were held in the mornings in early summer, when the lake was quite chilly. Only a steady rain would cause postponement; sprinkles, gray skies, and goosebumps were the norm.

A certificate of completion was awarded at each stage through Senior Lifesaving. I never worked a day in my life as a lifeguard. I did not join the Coast Guard, the Navy, or the Merchant Marine. I did not become a fisherman or engage in any other water-related activity on a regular basis.

However, I did go to summer camp. Mornings meant lessons and chores, and afternoons were for recreation, which often included swimming. One afternoon, only a small number of us were in the water, including me, age 17, and some younger campers. I noticed one girl bob under the surface and come up struggling, then bob under a second time and come up gasping. I did not wait for a third bob. My right arm went over her shoulder, my right hip went under her lower back, and she was on the beach in seconds. The techniques the Red Cross taught me saved the day, and possibly a life.

If you learn something today that helps save someone's life in the future, you will never forget it. It's a really good use of your time and talents. Literally just turn the page and get started ...

---

[4] When Self-Care Gets In The Way – FinancialMechanic.com
[5] Swim Classes & Training | Red Cross

Part I: Doctor-Trusted Remedies for the
Top 10 Most Common Health Issues

The University of Rochester (NY) Medical Center sums up the **Top 10 Most Common Health Issues facing Americans** today in 25 words or less:

1. **Physical Activity and Nutrition**
2. **Overweight and Obesity**
3. **Tobacco**
4. **Substance Abuse (drugs, alcohol)**
5. **HIV/AIDS**
6. **Mental Health**
7. **Injury and Violence**
8. **Environmental Quality**
9. **Immunization**
10. **Access to Healthcare**

How did researchers arrive at their list of the top contributors to disability and premature death? [6] Quite likely by reviewing morbidity and mortality data; their list is very similar to one published by the United Health Foundation based on *CDC Multiple Causes of Death Files, 2019.* [7]

Genetics always play a role, of course, but note that these top ten health issues often involve personal choices and individual behaviors over which you have control. Make better choices and your health risks go down while your odds of a longer, healthier, happier life go *way up.*

Now turn the page and discover the top doctor-recommended trusted remedies we've found for these ten most common health problems.

---

[6] Top 10 Most Common Health Issues, University of Rochester (NY) Medical Center, urmc.rochester.edu
[7] Explore Premature Death in the U.S., 2021, America's Health Rankings, americashealthrankings.org

If you are reading the electronic version of this work, click any footnote to view the original source. If you're reading the print version, typing the content of the footnote into any browser should take you there.

1. PHYSICAL ACTIVITY AND NUTRITION

The La-Z-Boy recliner company boasts that sales have grown 8.5% annually over the past ten years.

Great for them, but here's the rub: Lazy boys, lazy girls, and lazy adults die from lack of physical activity. The remedy: get moving. Here's how:

Walking shoes: The best remedy we know for inactivity is a good pair of walking shoes, priced at $60 to $100 (*Why Doctors Recommend Walking Every Day*, **Southeastern Spine Institute physicians**, Mt. Pleasant, SC [8]). That's a fraction of the price of a recliner, and you can expect to recoup the cost of your new shoes many times over in future savings by reducing your risks for heart disease, dementia, high blood pressure, and other conditions tied to lack of exercise (there, we said it – 'exercise' needs to stop being a dirty word, at least if you seek to live a longer and healthier life).

Is $60 to $100 too much to spend? Then swim for free in any suitable body of water in your area. Benjamin Franklin, who excelled in many fields, was an avid swimmer. Franklin did not even have the expense of a pair of swimming trunks; the famous statesman, patriot, and publisher swam *au naturel*. He must have been on to something, as he lived the good life to age 84.

Mayo Clinic, led by CEO and President **Gianrico Farrugia, M.D.**, recommends these trusted remedies for increasing your physical activity:

Aerobic exercise: Moderate aerobic exercise includes activities such as brisk walking, swimming, and mowing the lawn. Vigorous aerobic exercise includes activities such as running and aerobic dancing. Strength training can include the use of weight machines, your body weight, resistance tubing or resistance paddles in the water, or activities such as rock climbing.

As a general goal, aim for at least 30 minutes of moderate physical activity every day. If you want to lose weight, maintain weight loss, or meet specific fitness goals, you may need to exercise more. Want to aim even higher? You can achieve more health benefits if you ramp up your exercise to 300 minutes (five hours) a week.[9]

The site FamilyDoctor.org (American Academy of Family Physicians, **Gary L. LeRoy, M.D.**, president [10]) has these physical activity tips for mature adults:

Adults age 65 and older should get at least 2.5 hours of moderate aerobic exercise (such as brisk walking) every week. That's about 30 minutes on most days of the week. Or you should get 1 hour and 15 minutes of vigorous exercise (such as jogging) each week. You should also do strength training at least 2 days a week. You can work on balance and flexibility every day.

You should incorporate physical activity into your daily routine. Examples of working more activity into your day include:

---

[8] Why Doctors Recommend Walking Every Day, Southeastern Spine Institute, southeasternspine.com
[9] How much should the average adult exercise every day? Mayoclinic.org | Image: CDJ, openclipart.org
[10] Gary Lewis LeRoy, MD, FAAFP | ABFM

- Taking the stairs instead of the elevator.
- Parking farther away from your destination.
- Walking or biking places instead of driving.
- Walking your dog.
- Working in the yard.
- Doing light exercises while watching TV. [11]

If you aren't used to exercising, check with your doctor before starting an exercise routine or if you have any medical conditions.

If this is all advice you've heard before, *it's probably because doctors know that these steps work* – and let's be honest, some of us need to hear it over and over again before it finally kicks in. The sooner it does kick in, the sooner you'll start to experience the benefits.

Follow the Mediterranean diet: As important as increasing your physical activity is improving your nutrition. This topic alone has filled many books, and if that's what you're looking for, pick up any book on the Mediterranean diet – the eating plan that many doctors agree is best.

At Amazon, you'll find many Mediterranean diet books written by doctors, such as:

- *The Mediterranean Method: Your Complete Plan to Harness the Power of the Healthiest Diet on the Planet – Lose Weight, Prevent Heart Disease, and More! (A Mediterranean Diet Cookbook)*, by **Steven Masley, M.D.** [12]

- *The Complete Mediterranean Diet: Everything You Need to Know to Lose Weight and Lower Your Risk of Heart Disease*, by **Michael Ozner, M.D.** [13]

- *The Super Easy Mediterranean Diet Cookbook for Beginners on a Budget: 250 5-Ingredients Recipes that Anyone Can Cook*, by **Dr. Belinda Mack.** [14]

These books can help transform your life, provided you open them, read them, and put them into practice. Leaving them on the shelf doesn't count!

Want practical nutrition advice without buying another book? Top doctors trust these remedies:

- *"Let food be thy medicine and medicine be thy food."* **Hippocrates, Greek physician**

- **Donald Hensrud, M.D.,** author of *The New York Times* #1 bestseller *The Mayo Clinic Diet*, says one of the easiest ways to improve your overall nutrition is to begin and end every meal with fruits and vegetables. He also suggests buying a bigger salad bowl. [15]

- *"I tell every patient who seeks to have weight loss surgery, above all, I want you to be the cook. I want you to be the one that when someone is having a party, they want you to do the cooking. I want to turn you into a food snob. I want you to find chain restaurants not*

---

[11] Exercise and Seniors, American Academy of Family Physicians, familydoctor.org
[12] The Mediterranean Method (A Mediterranean Diet Cookbook), amazon.com
[13] The Complete Mediterranean Diet, amazon.com
[14] The Super Easy Mediterranean Diet Cookbook for Beginners on a Budget, amazon.com
[15] The Mayo Clinic Diet, Third Edition by Donald D. Hensrud, M.D., M.P.H., mcpress.mayoclinic.org

as interesting as restaurants that serve made-to-order food." **Terry Simpson, M.D.** [16]

- *"The problem is we are not eating food anymore, we are eating food-like products."* **Alejandro Junger, M.D.** [17]

- *"Some people think that the plant-based whole foods diet is extreme. Half a million a year will have their chests opened up, a vein taken from their leg and sewn onto their coronary artery. Some people would call that extreme."* **Caldwell Esselstyn, M.D.** [18]

- *"About eighty percent of the food on shelves of supermarkets today didn't exist 100 years ago."* **Larry McCleary M.D.** [19]

- *"Moderation is the only rule of a healthful life. This means moderation in all things wholesome."* – **Herbert M. Shelton, N.D.** [20]

- *"We are a species with amnesia, who effectively forgot how to feed itself."* **Steven Lin, D.M.D.** [21]

- *"The three-fold increase in obesity in less than a quarter of a century cannot be the result of genetic change in the population. Rather, it is the result of increased availability and consumption of food, coupled with decreased physical activity."* **David Bender, Ph.D.** [22]

The American Medical Association [23] (**James L. Madara, M.D., CEO** [24]) has published a useful guide that offers nine diet-based trusted remedies. It may also sound like familiar advice, but that's because doctors keep seeing a steady stream of patients suffering from diseases that could have been prevented with wiser nutritional choices.

The AMA says that eating a healthy diet can help adults live longer and have a lower risk of obesity, heart disease, diabetes, and certain cancers. Healthy eating can even help people with chronic disease manage those conditions and prevent further complications. However, most of us are not eating a healthy diet and could benefit from some nutrition and lifestyle changes:

Avoid excess sodium: Most of the sodium in your diet comes from packaged, processed foods. Adults consume more than 3,400 mg of sodium per day – far more than the 2,300 mg limit recommended by the American Heart Association. Minimizing consumption of these foods can reduce sodium intake, lower BP, and prevent hypertension from developing in the first place.

Eat more fish: Fish oil supplements are beneficial, but they should not replace eating fish. The AHA recommends eating fish at least twice a week as it is a good source of protein and, unlike fatty meat products, is not high in saturated fat. Fish is also a good source of omega-3 fatty acids, which may help reduce the risk of heart disease and stroke.

---

[16] Myth: Doctors Aren't Taught Much Nutrition, yourdoctorsorders.com
[17] Titles By Alejandro Junger, M.D., New York Times bestselling author, amazon.com
[18] Caldwell B. Esselstyn, Jr., MD, Cleveland Clinic Wellness Institute, Lyndhurst, Ohio, dresselstyn.com
[19] Feed Your Brain, Lose Your Belly by neurosurgeon Larry McCleary, M.D. (retired), amazon.com
[20] Herbert M. Shelton, Doctor of Naturopathic Medicine (1895-1985), amazon.com
[21] Dr. Steven Lin, New South Wales, Australia, drstevenlin.com | The Dental Diet, amazon.com
[22] David A Bender, Professor of Nutritional Biochemistry, University College London, david-bender.co.uk
[23] 9 Diet Questions Patients Should Be Asking Their Doctors, ama-assn.org
[24] James L. Madara, MD, ama-assn.org

Fatty fish such as salmon, mackerel, herring, lake trout, sardines, and albacore tuna are high in omega-3 fatty acids. But some types of fish contain high levels of mercury and other contaminants. These are highest in older, larger, predatory fish and marine mammals. Shark, swordfish, king mackerel, and tilefish all have elevated levels of mercury, according to the AHA.

Limit red meat: Higher consumption of red meat is associated with increased risk of chronic disease and mortality. Current recommendations from the AHA, American Cancer Society, and U.S. dietary guidelines call for limiting red meats and processed meats.

Avoid diet soda: Drinking diet sodas will not help you lose weight. While diet soda is calorie-free, most cans still contain 40 mg of sodium. Diet soda also contains artificial sweeteners, which often confuse the body.

Avoid artificial sweeteners: Most people should avoid artificial sweeteners completely because they stimulate the appetite and encourage a sweet tooth, both of which make you pack on the pounds. This adds to the risk for obesity, type 2 diabetes, heart disease, and fatty liver. There is one exception, though; artificial sweeteners are preferable to real sugar for patients with diabetes.

Mind your total calories: Don't stake your nutritional hopes on fat-free foods. It takes more than limiting high-fat foods to lose weight. It is essential to watch how many total calories you eat. Extra calories – even from fat-free and low-fat foods – get stored in the body as fat. Low-fat options can help cut total caloric intake, but it also pay attention to caloric intake from carbohydrates and proteins.

Eat more nuts: While nuts are high in fat and calories, they are still incredibly healthy. Eating nuts is not associated with weight gain, which means patients can regularly eat nuts as part of a healthy diet. Nuts can even help with weight loss, but it is important to exercise portion control.

Limit alcohol: Over time, heavy drinking can damage your heart. For healthy adults, women who have more than one drink a day and men who have more than two drinks a day can see an effect on blood pressure. One drink equals 12 ounces of beer, 5 ounces of wine or 1.5 ounces of 80-proof liquor.

Dr. Sarah Leahy Granite [25] , a doctor who is also a mom, says your path to better nutrition begins when you grab an empty cart at the supermarket. Follow her three rules and you'll weed out the real foods from their not-so-real food-like-substance counterparts. [26]

> **Rule #1: Stay to the perimeter of the store:** Since most grocery stores are laid out in the same manner, this is one of the easiest to follow, she says. Staying to the perimeter of the store means that you primarily shop for produce, meat/fish/poultry, and possibly dairy. Venturing into the abyss that is the center of the grocery store is where things get complicated. Here you will find aisle after aisle of packaged products, many that, even by minimal standards, only pass as food-like substances rather than actual food. Try to enter into these aisles as little as possible.
>
> **Rule #2: If your great grandmother couldn't recognize it, you shouldn't be eating it.**

---

[25] Tips for a Healthy Shopping Cart | Granite Chiropractic
[26] Drs. Sarah & Adrian at Granite, Granite Chiropractic, Dedham, MA

Rule #3: Buy foods that contain as few ingredients as possible.

To reduce temptation in the grocery store, eat a full meal before shopping, and take a list of all the healthy foods you plan to buy. Make a list at home on your computer, and send a link to your phone to use in the store … easy to do in Google Docs if you use gmail. You'll find more fitness and diet tips related to specific conditions and symptoms throughout this directory.

COST-SAVINGS EXAMPLE:

Best-selling La-Z-Boy James Rocking Recliner	**$1,049.00**
Best-selling walking shoes, New Balance 608 V5	**$54.97**

A recliner makes you "lazy" … walking shoes used daily make you fit!

2. OVERWEIGHT AND OBESITY

Next on the University of Rochester Medical Center list of the **Top 10 Most Common Health Issues Facing Americans** is obesity – a true killer. Obesity puts you at substantially higher risk for heart disease, hypertension, diabetes, and the above-mentioned lack of physical activity – all conditions which in turn promote still greater weight gain.

According to the National Center for Chronic Disease Prevention and Health Promotion (**Karen Hacker, M.D., MPH**, director [27]) , if your body mass index (BMI) is 30 or higher, it falls within the obese range. That means you are at higher risk for obesity-related diseases if you are:

- A 5'6" adult weighing 186 lbs or more
- A 5'9" adult weighing 203 lbs or more
- A 6" adult weighing 222 lbs or more

It can feel pretty bad to learn that you are "clinically obese" when you only thought of yourself as being slightly fluffy. However, rather than having your ego bruised, take it as a strong hint that your health might benefit (a lot) from some changes in your lifestyle. Those changes could be as simple as going back to the preceding pages – trusted remedies to improve **Physical Activity and Nutrition**. Some other possible approaches specifically targeting obesity:

Pick up a Mediterranean diet book: The nice thing about the Mediterranean diet is that the food is delicious. Choose a Mediterranean diet book with a weight loss focus; at least three of them authored by doctors (**Steven Masley, M.D.,** [28] **Michael Ozner, M.D.,** [29] and **Dr. Belinda Mack** [30]) are named in the **Physical Activity and Nutrition** section directly above under

---

[27] National Center for Chronic Disease Prevention and Health Promotion (NCCDPHP), cdc.gov
[28] Dr. Steven Masley, St. Petersburg, FL, drmasley.com | Image: Gan Khoon Lay, The Noun Project
[29] Michael Ozner, M.D., Wellness & Prevention, Baptist Health South Florida, drozner.com
[30] Books by Dr. Belinda Mack, amazon.com

"Follow the Mediterranean diet" … just turn back three or four pages.

Commit to the Mayo Clinic Diet [31] (by **Donald Hensrud, M.D.** [32]): Many people have used this best-selling diet and seen dramatic results. The diet is designed by some of the world's best doctors and includes delicious meal plans created by Mayo Clinic nutrition experts to fully meet your body's needs while peeling off excess pounds. Not only is it medically approved, it's designed for a lifetime of success.

Join a gym or a fitness class: This may cost you a few dollars, but it's far cheaper than the financial burden and lost independence of long-term obesity. A free option is to find a walking partner or group you can meet up with several times a week. You can also use free or low-cost smartphone apps like *30-Day Fitness Challenge* to remind you to do your exercise and track your progress. It's one of several fitness apps recommended by family physician **David Rebedew, M.D.** [33]

Physical activity: Incorporate this directory's doctor-recommended physical activity guidelines – detailed just a few pages back – into your weight loss plan.

Use *Eat This, Not That!* weight loss tips: Beyond these, *Eat This, Not That!* [34] has created a useful guide to 25 doctor-approved weight loss tips (**Cedrina Calder, M.D.** [35]). Do not feel you have to do every item on this list, at least not initially. Start with three or four and build from there, adding a couple new changes each week. Soon these tips will become habits and you can expect to see those extra pounds come off:

1. Drink more water
2. Eliminate sugar-sweetened beverages and added sugar
3. Drink less alcohol
4. Monitor portion sizes
5. Cook at home
6. Prep your food for the day
7. Increase your protein intake
8. Eat more vegetables and fruits
9. Eat less starch
10. Get physically active
11. Start resistance training
12. Get adequate sleep
13. Focus on mindful eating
14. Try wheatgrass shots
15. Stock up on Greek yogurt
16. Cut back on caffeine (four-cup limit)
17. Eat more dark, leafy greens
18. Add chickpeas to your diet
19. Eat more eggs
20. Feel fuller with avocados
21. Add more nuts/nut butters to your diet
22. Avoid added sugar
23. Know your deli meat ingredients
24. Watch out for granola or "energy" bars
25. Choose when to have your "cheat" meal

COST-SAVINGS EXAMPLE:

People with obesity pay more out of pocket than others. Medical costs for people with obesity are $1,429 higher *each year*. Over a 20-year period, you can expect

[31] Weight Loss For Life. diet.mayoclinic.org
[32] Donald D. Hensrud, M.D., Mayo Clinic, Rochester, MN, mayoclinic.org
[33] Six exercise apps, aafp.org | Dr. David L. Rebedew, Monroe, WI, webmd.com
[34] 25 Best Weight Loss Tips Straight From Doctors, eatthis.com
[35] Dr. Cedrina Calder, Nashville, Tennessee, fitdocofficial.com

obesity to cost you $28,580 in medical bills, which would pay for a lot of gym memberships and healthy food. In all, obesity costs Americans $147 billion a year. [36]

Nutrisystem (www.nutrisystem.com) costs about $300 a month, which may be less than you're spending now on groceries and dining out. [37]

Verywellfit.com offers a useful resource that's totally free, their "Healthy Grocery Shopping List for Weight Loss." [38]

Why put yourself through all those costly medical procedures ... make the healthy choice and save $28,500 – and possibly your life!

3. TOBACCO

Tobacco is one of the few legal products that is fatal when used as directed. So just do it – *quit*. Millions have done it, you can too. *You can quit, and you must;* tobacco is a slow poison that infiltrates and attacks every cell in your body.

Smoking is toxic to your heart, lungs, brain, and oral health, not to mention its effects on your appearance, fellow household members, pets, employment prospects, and even the resale value of your home and auto.

Did you notice we mentioned oral health in that litany of the dangers of tobacco use? Besides staining your teeth and giving you very bad breath, tobacco smoke in your mouth starves your gums of oxygen. This is a key reason why experts say cigars are not a safe alternative to cigarettes. The oxygen starvation caused by tobacco smoke damages the gum tissues needed to keep your teeth strong for a lifetime.

Kicking nicotine addiction is hard, a fact that has made the tobacco industry billions of dollars. If you're a smoker, quitting should be #1 on your list of lifestyle changes; you can get back to **Physical Activity and Nutrition** and **Overweight and Obesity** later.

Maher Karam-Hage, M.D. [39] and **Diane Beneventi, Ph.D.** [40] of M.D. Anderson's Tobacco Treatment Program [41] offer these tips when thinking about trying to quit:

Stick to it: "Research has shown that people who have previously quit are more likely to achieve long-term success on their next attempts than people who have never tried. The important thing

---

[36] Obesity Facts, healthline.com
[37] Enter Your Height & Weight To Find A Weight Loss Plan For You, nutrisystem.com
[38] How to Make a Healthy Grocery List, verywellfit.com
[39] Maher A. Karam Hage, MD, mdanderson.org | Image: Webtechops, The Noun Project
[40] Diane Beneventi, Ph.D., MD Anderson Cancer Center, Dallas, TX, faculty.mdanderson.org
[41] Want To Quit Smoking? 5 Questions To Ask Your Doctor By Clayton Boldt, Ph.D. – mdanderson.org

is to keep working toward your goal to quit."

Take good care of yourself: "Get plenty of rest, relaxation, good nutrition, and exercise. All of these factors can contribute to your success."

Get medical help if you need it: "There are seven medications approved by the U.S. Food and Drug Administration to help people quit smoking. Some of these are available over the counter, while some are available by prescription only." Ask your pharmacist or your doctor for guidance.

Consider counseling: "The best combination when trying to quit smoking is medication and counseling."

Have alternative activities to turn to when you are tempted to light up: "You can practice deep breathing, progressive muscle relaxation, or mindfulness. You can also utilize substitutes to satisfy the urge such as sugar-free gum, chewy candies, or healthy snacks. If you can substitute an activity that is completely opposed to smoking, such as exercise (e.g., walking), that would be even better."

M.D. Anderson's Tobacco Treatment Program: This program offers tobacco-cessation services, including in-person behavioral counseling and if you need them, medication treatments. Clinical trials offering similar services for smoking cessation are sometimes open to the public. For more information, please call (866) 245-0862 or send an email to quitnow@mdanderson.org.

WebMD offers a list of thirteen effective doctor-recommended remedies to give up tobacco (reviewed by **Jennifer Robinson, M.D.**): [42]

Find your reason to quit smoking: To get motivated, you need a powerful, personal reason to quit. It may be to protect your family from secondhand smoke. Or to lower your chance of getting lung cancer, heart disease, or other conditions. Or to look and feel younger. Choose a reason that is strong enough to outweigh the urge to light up.

Prepare before you go "cold turkey": Line up support in advance. Ask your doctor about all resources that may help, such as quit-smoking classes, counseling, medication, and hypnosis.

Consider nicotine replacement therapy: Studies show that nicotine gum, lozenges, and patches improve your chances of success when you're also in a quit-smoking program.

Learn about prescription pills: Medicines can curb cravings and ease withdrawal symptoms. If self-help steps aren't enough for you, ask your doctor about this option.

Lean on your loved ones: Tell your friends and family that you're trying to quit. They can encourage you to keep going. You can also join a support group or talk to a counselor.

Give yourself a break: Once you quit, you'll need new ways to unwind. You can exercise to blow off steam, tune in to your favorite music, treat yourself to a massage, or make time for a hobby. Also, try to avoid stressful situations during the first few weeks.

Avoid alcohol and other triggers: It's well known that alcohol reduces inhibitions. Drinking makes it harder to stick to your no-smoking goal. Limit alcohol when you first quit. Likewise, if

---

[42] 13 Best Quit-Smoking Tips, webmd.com

you smoke when you drink coffee, switch to tea for a few weeks. If you usually smoke after meals, find something else to do instead – brushing your teeth, taking a walk, or chewing gum.

Clean house: Once you've smoked your last cigarette, eliminate all reminders of smoke and smoking. Toss all ashtrays and lighters. Wash your clothes, clean your carpets, drapes, and upholstery, and use air fresheners.

Try and try again: It's okay to try a few times before giving up tobacco for good. If you light up, don't lose hope. Instead, think about what led to your relapse – your emotions or the setting you were in. Use it as a chance to step up your commitment to quit.

Get moving: Being active can curb nicotine cravings and ease withdrawal symptoms. Instead of reaching for a smoke, lace up your walking shoes. Even mild exercise helps.

Eat fruits and veggies: Don't try to diet while you quit. Too much deprivation can backfire. Instead, keep it simple and try to eat more fruits, vegetables, whole grains, and lean protein.

Choose your reward: In addition to all the health benefits, one of the perks of giving up cigarettes is all the money you will save. Reward yourself by spending part of it having fun.

Remember that time is on your side: Only 20 minutes after your last puff, your heart rate goes back to normal. Within a day, your blood's carbon monoxide level falls back into place. In just two to three weeks, you will start to lower your odds of having a heart attack.

COST-SAVINGS EXAMPLE:

The U.S. retail price of cigarettes averages $8 per pack. For a pack-a-day smoker, that's $2,980 per year ... for many, that is multiple paychecks up in smoke.

Smoking-related illness in the U.S. costs more than $300 billion each year, including $170 billion for direct medical care and more than $156 billion in lost productivity, including $5.6 billion in lost productivity due to secondhand smoke. [43]

On a per-person basis, smoking costs more than $1 million in a smoker's lifetime. *The sooner you quit, the sooner you'll start saving ...* [44]

Saving $1 million over 40 years is like getting a $25,000 a year raise!

> ### Did one of these remedies help you?
>
> Share your trusted remedies success with the publisher! We'd love to hear from you. **info@trustedremedies.com**

---

[43] Economic Trends in Tobacco, cdc.gov
[44] Smoking Can Cost You $1 Million to $2 Million in a Lifetime, money.com

4. SUBSTANCE ABUSE

Few health crises are as heartbreaking or as tragic as substance abuse. This disease is deadly, costly, and 100% avoidable (yet often *very* profitable for those who manufacture and distribute these destructive substances – whether legally or illegally – which is why this epidemic keeps getting worse).

If you or a loved one have a substance use problem, seek medical help *today*. If someone is behaving dangerously due to substance abuse, call 9-1-1; it could save a life or be the first step on that person's road to recovery. If there is not currently an emergency, the Substance Abuse and Mental Health Services Administration (**Elinore McCance-Katz, M.D., Ph.D.**, assistant secretary for Mental Health and Substance Use) [45] may be able to help.

SAMHSA is the agency within the U.S. Department of Health and Human Services that leads public health efforts to advance the nation's behavioral health. The agency's mission is to reduce the impact of substance abuse and mental illness on America's communities. As a taxpayer, you help fund SAMHSA – so why not take advantage of it. (See the infographic on the next page.)

SAMHSA Helpline: SAMHSA's National Helpline is **1-800-662-HELP (4357)**. The helpline is a free, confidential, 24/7, 365-day-a-year treatment referral and information service (in English and Spanish) for individuals and families facing mental and/or substance use disorders.

In addition to seeking professional help for substance abuse, the five self-care steps below may aid in recovery according to HelpGuide, the nonprofit organization millions of readers rely on for free, evidence-based resources to understand and navigate mental health challenges (**Neeraj Gandotra, MD**, Chief Medical Officer,[46] SAMHSA).

HelpGuide offers 5 trusted steps to addiction recovery (**Monika White, Ph.D., Board Chair** [47]):

Remind: Remind yourself of the reasons you want to change.

Think: Think about your past attempts at recovery, if any. What worked? What didn't?

Set: Set specific, measurable goals, such as a start date or limits on your drug use.

Remove: Remove reminders of your addiction from your home and workplace.

Tell: Tell friends and family that you're committed to recovery, and ask for their help.[48]

COST-SAVINGS EXAMPLE:

What is the value of a human life, especially your own or a loved one's? *The benefits of avoiding or recovering from substance abuse are PRICELESS!*

---

[45] Dr. Elinore F. McCance-Katz, Urgent And Emerging Issues In Prevention, samhsa.gov
[46] Neeraj Gandotra, M.D., samhsa.gov | Image: Gan Khoon Lay, The Noun Project
[47] Monika White, Ph.D., helpguide.org
[48] HelpGuide, one of the world's leading mental health websites, helpguide.org

SUBSTANCE USE & MENTAL ILLNESS IN U.S. ADULTS (18+)

FROM THE 2014 NATIONAL SURVEY ON DRUG USE AND HEALTH (NSDUH)

Behavioral health (substance use and mental health) issues affect millions in the United States each year.

SUBSTANCE USE IN THE U.S.

Nearly
1 IN 12
adults had a Substance Use Disorder (SUD) in the past year

That's
20.2 MILLION
adults who have SUD

In the past month,
1 IN 4
U.S. adults engaged in binge drinking

That's
59.4 MILLION
adults

In the past month,
1 IN 10
U.S. adults used illicit drugs

That's
24.6 MILLION
adults

MENTAL HEALTH IN THE U.S.

Nearly
1 IN 5
U.S. adults had Any Mental Illness (AMI) in the past year

That's
43.6 MILLION
adults with AMI

Including
9.8 MILLION
adults with Serious Mental Illness (SMI)

Substance Use Disorder (SUD)

7.9 MILLION
adults had both

Any Mental Illness (AMI)

1. **Any Mental Illness (AMI)** is defined as individuals having any mental, behavior, or emotional disorder in the past year that met DSM-IV criteria (excluding developmental and substance use disorders).

2. **Serious Mental Illness (SMI)** is defined as adults with any mental, behavior, or emotional disorder that substantially interfered with or limited one or more major life activities.

3. **Substance Use Disorder (SUD):** Individuals with alcohol or illicit drug dependence or abuse are defined as having SUD. The questions used to measure dependence and abuse are based on criteria in the fourth edition of the Diagnostic and Statistical Manual of Mental Disorders (DSM-IV).

Co-Occurring Behavioral Health Disorders in the U.S.

SOURCE: Substance Abuse and Mental Health Services Administration, Center for Behavioral Health Statistics and Quality, 2014 National Survey on Drug Use and Health.

Substance Abuse and Mental Health Services Administration

✕SAMHSA

www.samhsa.gov

SAMHSA's mission is to reduce the impact of substance abuse and mental illness on America's communities.

5. HIV/AIDS

HIV/AIDS became a national crisis in the 1980s. Unless you know someone currently affected by the HIV virus and the deadly AIDS it causes, you may think this crisis is over. Sadly, the HIV/AIDS crisis is far from over: [49]

Approximately 1.2 million people in the U.S. are living with HIV today. About 14% of them (1 in 7) don't know they have it and need testing.

An estimated 36,400 new HIV infections occurred in the U.S. in 2018. In 2018, there were 15,820 deaths among adults and adolescents with diagnosed HIV in the U.S. (These deaths may be due to any cause.)

The cost of HIV treatment is $14,000 to $20,000 a year, says **Professor Michael Kolber, M.D.**, director of the Comprehensive AIDS Program and Adult HIV Services at the University of Miami Miller School of Medicine in Florida. [50]

If you have HIV/AIDS, you need medical treatment. Still, the home remedies we'll review below may help alleviate some symptoms.

According to America's HIV Epidemic Analysis Dashboard (AHEAD), a program of the U.S. Department of Health and Human Services (**Adm. Brett P. Giroir, M.D.**, **Assistant Secretary For Health**), the human immunodeficiency virus (HIV) attacks cells that help the body fight infection, making a person more vulnerable to other infections and diseases.

The virus is spread by contact with certain bodily fluids of a person with HIV, most commonly during unprotected sex (sex without a condom or HIV medicine to prevent or treat HIV) or through sharing drug-injection equipment. If left untreated, HIV can lead to the disease AIDS (acquired immunodeficiency syndrome). The human body can't get rid of HIV, and no effective HIV cure exists. So, once you have HIV, you have it for life.

Anal sex is the highest-risk sexual behavior. Gay and bisexual men have the largest number of new diagnoses in the U.S. Sharing needles with someone who has HIV also puts you at higher risk. The clear solution to the HIV/AIDS crisis is not to start these behaviors, or to stop them immediately if you already engage in them.

According to Healthline [51] (medically reviewed by **Daniel Murrell, M.D.**), people with HIV or AIDS often use complementary and alternative medicine (CAM) in combination with traditional medical treatments to improve their health and well-being. There is some evidence that CAM treatments can relieve some symptoms of HIV infection or AIDS. Some trusted remedies are:

Body therapies: Yoga and massage therapy may help reduce pain for some people. Yoga can also improve feelings of overall health and cut anxiety and depression. It has been shown to replenish infection-fighting T cells, white blood cells that play an important role in your immune system. Acupuncture may help with nausea and other treatment side effects, says Healthline.

---

[49] U.S. Statistics, People with HIV, Fast Facts, hiv.gov | Image: Shane Willis, The Noun Project
[50] What Is HIV? Symptoms, Causes, Diagnosis, Treatment, and Prevention, everydayhealth.com
[51] Alternative Treatments for HIV and AIDS, healthline.com

Relaxation therapies: Meditation and other forms of relaxation treatment can help reduce anxiety. They may improve the ability to cope with the stress of a chronic illness such as HIV.

Herbal medicine: Herbal remedies should be used with caution. There's not a lot of hard evidence to support the use of herbs for relieving HIV symptoms. However, a brief course of certain herbs may support immunity in people with HIV. Research has shown that milk thistle is one example. Milk thistle is used to improve liver function and does not interact significantly with antivirals. Consult your healthcare provider before any herbal treatments.

Medical marijuana: Marijuana can help reduce pain, control nausea, and, most famously, increase appetite. Medical marijuana is becoming legal in more states. However, smoking marijuana has many of the same health risks as smoking tobacco, so ask your healthcare provider before doing so.

Acupuncture: Medical News Today [52] (**Elaine Hanh Le, M.D., Senior Director of Medical Affairs** [53]) reports that acupuncture therapy may be useful to HIV patients. According to one source, over 70 percent of people with HIV in the United States have tried alternative treatments, and many people use them regularly. Certain health insurance plans may cover some alternative medicines, such as chiropractic and acupuncture therapy.

While alternative treatments do not cure HIV, they may relieve symptoms and can improve a person's quality of life, says Medical News Today. Always talk to a doctor or healthcare provider before trying alternative medicine.

COST-SAVINGS EXAMPLE:

The benefits of avoiding HIV/AIDS – a life-changing and incurable condition – are priceless. Since there is no cure, inexpensive trusted remedies are often the best course of action.

6. MENTAL HEALTH

Anyone can suffer from some form of mental illness at some point in their lives. In fact, one in five Americans is classified as having some form of mental illness.

Many forms of professional help are available for mental health concerns. A very good place to start is by asking your personal physician. If it takes courage to ask for help, realize that the first step to recovery is being honest with yourself. A great second step is being honest with someone you trust and whose only interest is helping you, like your doctor. Simply by asking for help, you've taken the first vital step on your recovery path – which itself should give you hope. Don't put it off, do it today.

---

[52] How can alternative treatments help with HIV? medicalnewstoday.com
[53] Dr. Elaine Hanh Le, doctor.webmd.com | Image: Victoruler, The Noun Project

Many mental health professionals prescribe drugs for the treatment of mental illness. Because mental health drugs often carry a significant risk of side effects, it's wise to seek a second opinion to confirm whether drug treatment is right for you.

Most states and many cities operate mental health hotlines – just ask Alexa, Google, or Siri. Or do a Google search with the name of your city or state and the words *mental health hotline*. Fortunately, there's lots of doctor-trusted self-help available too:

Start with a free test: The site depression.org.nz, a service of the New Zealand Health Promotion Agency (**Dr. Monique Faleafa**, deputy chair), offers *"A self-test can help you decide what to do."* On it, you'll find links to depression and anxiety self-assessments. These tools can help you identify the nature and seriousness of your condition. In about a minute, and without giving any personal information such as your name or email address, you'll get a score along with a link to some simple steps to put yourself in a better place. [54]

Self-assessment tests: Want a second opinion? *Psychology Today* offers self-assessments for depression [55] and anxiety [56] that can be completed in about 15 minutes.

You'll get a summary of results for free and an offer for a detailed report for a small fee. (*Psychology Today* is not a medical publication and does not match our criteria for being doctor-trusted; we offer their information as supporting material that you may find useful.)

Self-help books and programs: Many self-help books are available on Amazon. [57] A popular self-help program is *Attacking Anxiety and Depression* (developed by **Philip Fisher, M.D., Medical Director & co-founder of The Midwest Center for Stress & Anxiety** [58]) offered by StressCenter.com. More than 1.4 million people have benefited from the *Attacking Anxiety and Depression (AA&D)* program.

AA&D is based on the science of cognitive-behavioral modification. Several studies have found the program to be as effective as, and in some cases more effective than, 6+ therapy sessions. The program has been featured on *Oprah, The View, Good Morning America,* and many other shows and magazines. The program has been helping people for over 30 years. [59]

If these trusted remedies are not enough, consider professional help. Life is rarely without its challenges. There are some challenges, however, that can be so overbearing that it seems impossible to move on. Whether it's the death of a loved one or overwhelming feelings of anxiety, it's important you know that help is available for every problem life throws your way.

According to Healthlinc (medically reviewed by **Timothy J. Legg, Ph.D.** [60]), some symptoms or events that a psychologist may help you cope with are: [61]

---

[54] A self-test can help you decide what to do, depression.org.nz
[55] Depression Test, psychologytoday.com
[56] Anxiety Test, psychologytoday.com
[57] Mental health self help books, www.amazon.com
[58] The Midwest Center for Stress & Anxiety
[59] stresscenter.com
[60] Timothy Legg – APA Psychologist Locator, American Psychological Association
[61] When to Consult a Psychologist, healthline.com

- Loss of a loved one – a parent, a child, a spouse, a best friend, even a pet.

- Stress and anxiety, if you fear it's leading to social isolation or depression.

- Depression – when you lose interest in life, experience fatigue, and have trouble managing your emotions.

- Some phobias – fear of heights and spiders – are common but typically transient. However, unusual or unfounded fears can create substantial problems in your life. For example, sitophobia (fear of eating) may lead to serious health problems. A qualified psychologist can help you begin to overcome your fears so that you can live without polyphobia (fear of many things) or phobophobia (fear of fear).

- Family issues – While family and other relationships can be some of the best things in life, they can also be a source of major stress and chronic anxiety, leading to a mental health crisis. A professional can help assess whether the problem person is you (hopefully not), whether your problems can be fixed, or whether your best option is to sever unhealthy relationships.

- Unhealthy habits and addictions – Unhealthy habits such as smoking, drinking, and drug use are often used to escape larger underlying problems or to self-medicate.

A psychologist may be able to help with all of these as well as with sleeping problems, eating disorders, and other behavioral issues that may be taking a toll on your health. Regardless of the individual issue, a psychologist can give you trusted remedies to help improve your thought life and the behaviors that flow from it. Other sources of help may be a clergy member, a community leader, or a trusted and admired friend you can count on for honest and caring advice.

COST-SAVINGS EXAMPLE:

Consider getting a second opinion before filling a prescription for a mental health medication. One drug alone, Abilify, has been called the most profitable drug ever made. Millions take it for depression and anxiety. Abilify is ounce-for-ounce 115 times more costly than gold. A year of refills is priced at $12,557. (A cheaper generic is also available.) [62] **Of course, you should never stop taking any medication before checking with your doctor.**

Attacking Anxiety & Depression Program: A Drug-Free, Self-Help Set is $149.95. [63]

If a self-help program such as this could meet your needs, you could save $12,000 a year!

---

[62] Abilify is $1,046.49 for 150 mg; gold is $60 per gram. Abilify 115 times more expensive than gold.
[63] Attacking Anxiety & Depression Program, A Drug-Free, Self-Help Set, stresscenter.com

7. INJURY AND VIOLENCE

Sadly, injury and violence are not things that happen only to "other people"; they can happen to you too – in a heartbeat and with life-altering consequences.

The best remedy to keep yourself from being a victim of injury and violence is avoidance of people, places, and things that put you at risk.

Some of these avoidance steps are obvious – stay away from swimming in the ocean after a shark report or Man-o-War sighting, don't play golf in a lightning storm, and yes, don't even think about running with scissors.

No one is really looking for remedies to use *after* suffering injury and violence. What you really need are tips to help you avoid being the victim of an accident or assault in the first place. Patient.info has published *"Accidents and Their Prevention"* [64] by **Dr. Hayley Willacy** [65], outlining three levels of accident prevention:

Primary prevention: Remove the circumstances causing injury – e.g., drive slower, fit stair gates for young children, reduce alcohol consumption.

Secondary prevention: Reduce the severity of injury should an accident occur – e.g., use child safety car seats, bicycle helmets, smoke alarms.

Tertiary prevention: Obtain optimal treatment and rehabilitation following injuries – e.g., effective first aid, appropriate hospital care.

The site also offers a useful list of physician-reviewed accident-prevention tips, such as:

- Install smoke detectors on every floor, and renew the batteries regularly.

- Plan a fire escape route for each room of your home.

- Keep portable heaters and candles away from furniture, clothes, and curtains.

- Frying pans are a major fire risk. In case of a frying pan fire, turn off the heat if safe to do so and call 9-1-1. Do not move the pan or pour water on it – this can cause a fireball

- Do not overload electrical circuits, including using multiple adapters in sockets.

- Do not use equipment with cracked plugs or worn cables. Cut off the cords and throw them away.

- Do not touch electrical equipment with wet hands or take it into the bathroom.

- Do not smoke in bed, and keep matches and lighters away from children. You've heard this advice all your life, yet people still die from these preventable fire causes every year.

---

[64] Accidents and their Prevention – patient.info | Image: Headsofbirds, The Noun Project
[65] Dr. Hayley Willacy

- Keep bonfires, burn barrels, and barbecues away from buildings, fences, and trees. Ensure children are supervised around fires. Know and obey local fire ordinances regarding outdoor burning and cooking.

- Be alert to the symptoms of carbon monoxide poisoning (drowsiness and flu symptoms).

- Always ensure cleaners are clearly labeled and out of children's reach.

- Avoid loose rugs and flooring. Clean up spills to avoid slipping.

- Only climb up on something firm and strong.

- When using power tools, use adequate protection including gloves, goggles, sturdy shoes, and a ground fault interrupter.

- Improve lighting in halls and stairways. Consider motion-activated switches or daylight sensors that turn lights on automatically in dim spaces.

- With DIY, always work within your ability, follow instructions, check equipment, and keep tools and chemicals away from children.

The single most dangerous place to be is a highway or public street. The American Medical Association (**Michael D. Maves, M.D., MBA, CEO**) published a "Physician's Guide to Assessing and Counseling Older Drivers." [66] Top tips include:

Always:

- Plan your trips ahead of time. Decide what time to leave and which roads to take. Try to avoid heavy traffic, poor weather, and high-speed areas.

- Wear your safety belt, and wear it correctly (over your shoulder and across your lap).

- Drive at the speed limit. It's less safe to drive too fast or too slow.

- Be alert! Pay attention to traffic at all times. This means not allowing yourself to be distracted by cell phones, audio controls, roadside events, and traveling companions.

- Keep enough distance between you and the car in front of you.

- Be extra careful at intersections. Use your turn signals, and remember to look around you for people and other cars.

- Doublecheck blind spots when changing lanes, backing up, or turning right on red.

- Be extra careful at train tracks. Remember to look both ways for trains every time.

- When you take a new medicine, ask your doctor or pharmacist about side effects. Many medicines may affect your driving even when you feel fine.

---

[66] Physician's Guide to Assessing and Counseling Older Drivers – nhtsa.gov. This is a 252-page pdf. It may be worth your time to review if it helps you keep someone off the road who is no longer safe to drive.

- If your medicine makes you dizzy or drowsy, talk to your doctor to find out ways to take it so it doesn't affect your driving.

Never:

- Drink and drive.

- Drive when you feel angry or tired. If you start to feel tired, stop your car somewhere safe. Take a break until you feel more alert.

- Eat, drink, or use a cell phone while driving. Even in hands-free mode, a cell phone is a distraction.

If:

- You don't see well in the dark, do not drive at night.

- You have trouble making left turns at an intersection, make three right turns instead of one left, or proceed to the next intersection that has a dedicated left-turn arrow.

- Avoid driving in bad weather, such as during rain, sleet, or snow.

Along with highway accidents, relationships with toxic people can rob you of your joy or even your life.

Think of all the times you've heard or read about victims of domestic abuse. If you are in any type of volatile relationship – with a spouse, a family member, even a neighbor – you may want to think about leaving before permanent harm is done. For example, today. Moving may be inconvenient or costly, but it may also save your life.

Dr. Will Cole has written a guide, *The Science Behind How Toxic Relationships Affect Your Health.* In it, he offers the Toxic Relationship Quiz: [67]

When you are with the person, or after you are with the person, do you feel any of the following most of the time (or more than half of the time)?

- Physically or emotionally drained of energy.

- Bad about yourself.

- Like you are always giving without getting anything back, or the other person is always taking without giving back to you.

- Shunned, an outsider, or otherwise not accepted for who you are.

- Isolated from friends, family, or others who are supportive of you, because you don't want you to be around those people.

- Emotionally or physically unsafe or injured.

---

[67] The Science Behind How Toxic Relationships Affect Your Mental Health – drwillcole.com

- Fear.

If you said 'yes' to one or more of these, Dr. Cole suggests you review your options.

Ponder these four choices you have to deal with this negative relationship:

- Accept the relationship as it is and be at peace with it. This can reduce a lot of stress that comes from trying to change someone else.

- Change the relationship by creating boundaries for yourself. Remember that you can't change other people, but you can change how you react and what you will allow into your own life.

- Leave the relationship. Sometimes, sadly, this is the best course if the other person's behavior is intolerable to you.

- Feel miserable. This is the choice that will continue the stress cycle. But it is a choice.

Since every relationship is different, these options will mean different things to each person, but Dr. Coles encourages you not to choose to "feel miserable" anymore. You'll only hurt your health and everyone around you by harboring that negative energy.

COST-SAVINGS EXAMPLE (based on safe driving alone):

The average car accident settlement (provided you are fortunate enough to survive) is about $21,000 for bodily injury. [68]

Safe driver tools offered by many insurers are typically free and could even reduce your insurance premium, in effect paying you to stay safe and healthy! Using a safe driver tool could save you pain, surgery, and painkilling meds, or even your life.

You could also take a safe driver course online for less than the cost of one fill-up at the gas station; for example, the Florida Basic Driver Improvement Course is $7. [69]

Be a safe driver and avoid a $21,000 (or higher) mistake!

---

[68] What Is the Average Car Accident Settlement Worth? tnklaw.com/
[69] Take A Defensive Driving Course Online, drivesafetoday.com/

8. ENVIRONMENTAL QUALITY

According to health insurance provider Cigna Health (**Steven B. Miller, M.D.**, chief clinical officer): [70]

An environmental illness can occur when you are exposed to toxins or substances in the environment that make you sick. These health hazards may be found where you live, work, or play.

Maybe you have headaches that only occur on weekends. Or maybe you began to feel sick and got a rash after moving into a newly built home. These symptoms can be caused by exposure to toxic chemicals. Examples:

- *Those weekend headaches may be caused by a furnace leaking carbon monoxide.*

- *Materials in new buildings may cause nausea and rashes. And the paper that makes up the outside layers of drywall promotes mold growth. Exposure to these molds may cause symptoms and could make you sick.*

- *Materials that cause environmental hazards in your home may include cigarettes, asbestos, smoke or gasses from wood-burning stoves and poorly vented gas ranges, and unsafe drinking water from a public or private water source polluted with pesticides, industrial chemicals, or other poisons, says Cigna.*

Symptoms of an environmental illness may include headache, fever, chills, nausea, cough, muscle aches, or a rash. If you think that exposure to toxic chemicals or other health hazards could be making you sick, talk to your doctor. Cigna recommends these remedies for common household environmental toxins:

- *Improve your air quality by identifying and getting rid of the source of pollution. (A home inspector or HVAC contractor may be able to help.)*

- *Don't allow smoking in your home. If smokers live in or visit your home, ask them to smoke outside.*

- *Increase the amount of fresh air coming into your home. Adjust gas stoves, or replace them with electric ones.*

- *Check to make sure that exhaust fans work. Installing carbon monoxide alarms in your home can also protect you and your family.*

- *Stop the health effects of mold exposure. Keep a dry environment indoors to reduce exposure to mold. If you do find mold, it should be removed. If the moldy area is less than three feet by three feet, you can probably remove the mold yourself. But if the moldy area is bigger, a professional should remove the mold.*

Mold is a special concern when reopening a building that's been closed for a period of time. Lack of heat, humidity control, and air circulation all tend to promote mold growth. These circumstances are especially common in seasonal homes. Mold may also occur in commercial buildings that have been unoccupied for several months, for reasons such as the COVID-19 shutdown.

---

[70] Environmental Illness, cigna.com | Image: Smashicons, Flaticon.com

Mold growth can also be the result of water intrusion from a roof, window, or plumbing leak, or from high humidity as a result of leaving the air conditioning off.

Do-it-yourself mold test kits are sold by Home Depot, Lowes, Ace Hardware, Walmart, and Amazon. For whole-house mold remediation, call a professional. If you're buying a home that may be prone to mold, have it professionally inspected and get a mold disclosure from the seller.

Mold is also a special concern in Florida and other areas with a warm, moist climate. The Florida Department of Health (**Joseph A. Ladapo, M.D., PhD.**, state surgeon general) advises: [71]

> *The adverse health effects associated with poor indoor air quality can be minor or severe, short or long term; sometimes it's not obvious why people are feeling ill.*
>
> *Our recommendation is that you discuss your concerns about your health or the health of your loved ones with the primary healthcare provider first. The provider will seek to provide basic medical diagnostics and a differential diagnosis with the goal of providing effective treatment or management of the illness.*
>
> *In some cases, the primary care provider may be uncertain of the cause of the experienced illness. In those cases, your primary care provider may refer you to an appropriate medical specialist (i.e., allergist/immunologist, pulmonologist, pediatrician, ear/nose/throat specialist, environmental/occupational medicine specialist, medical toxicologist, neurologist, infectious disease specialist, etc.) depending on characteristics of the illness. You may also request a referral from your primary care provider should you feel it is necessary.*
>
> *Although it is not generally recommended by the Department of Health or the medical community, you may decide to seek out a specialist without the recommended input of your primary healthcare provider. You may find that it can be difficult to locate medical specialists in your area. The following provide resources that you may use for locating such specialists:*
>
> - *American Academy of Allergy, Asthma and Immunology*
> - *American Academy of Dermatology*
> - *American Academy of Neurology/Florida Society of Neurology*
> - *American College of Medical Toxicology*
> - *American College of Chest Physicians*
> - *American College of Occupational and Environmental Medicine*
> - *Association of Occupational and Environmental Clinics*
> - *Association of Pulmonary and Critical Care Medicine Directors*
> - *American Academy of Otolaryngology*
> - *American Thoracic Society*
> - *Florida Dept. of Health – Healthcare and Medical License Verification*
> - *Florida Society of Neurology*
> - *Pediatric Environmental Health Specialty Units (PEHSUs)*
> - *Southeast Pediatric Environmental Health Specialty Unit*

---

[71] Locating Specialized Medical Expertise Resources, floridahealth.gov

COST-SAVINGS EXAMPLE #1:

According to Geisinger Hospital [72] (Jonathan Spahr, M.D., director of pediatric pulmonary care [73] ,) looking only at mold, "Those tiny spores could cause a host of health problems, mostly in people with respiratory problems, allergies or a compromised immune system."

The costs could reach tens of thousands of dollars very quickly. People with weakened immune systems are typically treated in the hospital with special antifungal drugs and other measures to support breathing and circulation. (Melissa Conrad Stöppler, M.D., medical author) [74]

On average, homeowners pay about $648 for a professional mold inspection. Depending on your location and the size of your house, the range is $294 to $1,012. You can also get a DIY testing kit for $40 or less, but it does not replace a comprehensive assessment. [75]

Starting for just $40, you could avoid a five-figure hospital bill!

COST-SAVINGS EXAMPLE #2:

"Real estate agents told pollsters that having a regular smoker in a home can reduce its value by 20 percent, on average. About 44 percent of the agents surveyed said smoking will reduce a home's value by some measure." – Chicago Tribune [76]

The U.S. median home price in 2020 was $320,000.

Making your home smoke-free could save you $64,000!

---

[72] Is Mold Making You Sick? geisinger.org
[73] Jonathan Edward Spahr, MD Pediatric Pulmonology, Pediatric Sleep Medicine, geisinger.org
[74] Things To Know About Mold Exposure (Mold Allergy), medicinenet.com
[75] How Much Does A Mold Inspection Cost? homeadvisor.com
[76] Smoking Can Affect A Home's Resale Value, chicagotribune.com

9. IMMUNIZATION

Few health topics attract as much controversy as immunization and vaccines. For straight answers, we looked to the highly regarded physicians of Mayo Clinic (**Gianrico Farrugia, M.D.**, CEO), a 150-year-old, private, nonprofit foundation that is independent of government agencies and vaccine manufacturers.

On its page *"Childhood vaccines: Tough questions, straight answers,"* Mayo Clinic answers common questions including whether vaccines cause autism, if it's OK to skip certain vaccines, and more [77]

Childhood vaccines protect children from a variety of serious or potentially fatal diseases, including diphtheria, measles, mumps, rubella, polio, tetanus, whooping cough (pertussis), and others. If these diseases seem uncommon – or even unheard of – it's usually because these vaccines are doing their job.

Still, you might wonder about the benefits and risks of childhood vaccines. Here are straight answers to common questions about childhood vaccines.

Is natural immunity better than vaccination? A natural infection might provide better immunity than vaccination – but there are serious risks. For example, a natural chickenpox (varicella) infection could lead to pneumonia. A natural polio infection could cause permanent paralysis. A natural mumps infection could lead to deafness. A natural *Haemophilus influenzae* type b (Hib) infection could result in permanent brain damage or even death. Vaccination can help prevent these diseases and their potentially serious complications.

Do vaccines cause autism? Vaccines do not cause autism. [This is a myth created by a quack doctor who thought he could get rich by peddling fake cures. More on this key topic below.]

Are vaccine side effects dangerous? Any vaccine can cause side effects. Usually, these side effects are minor – a low-grade fever, fussiness, and soreness at the injection site. Some vaccines cause temporary headache, fatigue, or loss of appetite. Rarely, a child might have a severe allergic reaction or a neurological side effect, such as a seizure. Although these rare side effects are a concern, the risk of a vaccine causing serious harm or death is extremely small. The benefits of getting a vaccine are much greater than the possible side effects for almost all children. Of course, vaccines aren't given to children who have known allergies to specific vaccine components. Likewise, if your child develops a life-threatening reaction to a particular vaccine, further doses of that vaccine won't be given.

Why are vaccines given so early? The diseases that childhood vaccines are meant to prevent are most likely to occur when a child is very young and the risk of complications is greatest. That makes early vaccination – sometimes beginning shortly after birth – essential. If you postpone vaccines until a child is older, it might be too late.

Is it OK to pick and choose vaccines? In general, skipping vaccines isn't a good idea. This can leave your child vulnerable to potentially serious diseases. And consider this: For some children

---

[77] Childhood vaccines: Tough questions, straight answers, mayoclinic.org | Image: Luis Prado, The Noun Project

– including those who can't receive certain vaccines for medical reasons (such as cancer therapy) – the only protection from vaccine-preventable diseases is the immunity of the people around them. If immunization rates drop, vaccine-preventable diseases might once again become common threats.

If you still have reservations about particular vaccines, discuss your concerns with your child's doctor, says Mayo Clinic. If your child falls behind the standard vaccination schedule, ask your doctor about catch-up immunizations.

"The vaccine-autism myth is one chilling example of fraudulent science."

A common fear cited by vaccine-hesitant parents is that a vaccine may give their child autism. Writing for *TIME* magazine, **Jonathan D. Quick, M.D., MPH**, [78] addresses this persistent – and false – concern. If someone has told you that there is a connection between vaccines and autism, Dr. Quick's commentary is essential reading; children's lives depend on it: [79]

> *As a family physician with four decades of experience fighting preventable disease around the globe and a professor of anthropology and risk and decision science studying global vaccine confidence, I've seen the **deadly harm** that **fraudulent science** and **unfounded claims** can cause. (Emphasis added.)*

> *The vaccine-autism myth is one chilling example of fraudulent science. 2018 marks the 20th anniversary of an infamous article published in the prestigious medical journal, The Lancet, in which Andrew Wakefield, a former British doctor, falsely linked the MMR (measles, mumps, and rubella) vaccine to autism. The paper eventually was retracted by the co-authors and the journal.*

> *Wakefield was de-licensed by medical authorities for his **deceit and "callous disregard"** for children in his care. (Emphasis added.) It took nearly two decades for the UK immunization rates to recover. By the end, UK families had experienced more than 12,000 cases of measles, hundreds of hospitalizations – many with serious complications – and at least three deaths.*

> *Stunningly, the vaccine-autism myth still persists. It was amplified by the British media during its early years, later by celebrity endorsement and more recently by worldwide social media. Wakefield has continued his own relentless personal campaigning, moving well beyond the initial MMR vaccine **scaremongering** to attacking the CDC in his controversial film Vaxxed. (Emphasis added.) The film was pulled before screening at the Tribeca Film Festival but found its way into independent theaters in the U.S. and Europe.*

> *Europe's four-fold increase in measles cases and 35 measles-related deaths in 2017 – due largely to people not getting vaccinated – also reflects how Wakefield's vaccine-autism scare can spark vaccine refusals that lead to **debilitating and fatal cases of measles.** (Emphasis added.)*

---

[78] Jonathan D. Quick, MD, MPH, Duke Global Health Institute, globalhealth.duke.edu
[79] The Vaccine-Autism Myth Started 20 Years Ago. Here's Why It Still Endures Today, time.com

COST-SAVINGS EXAMPLE:

Before widespread use of the measles vaccine, 3 million people got measles each year in the U.S., resulting in 400 to 500 deaths and 48,000 hospitalizations.

Due to parents who refuse to vaccinate their children, the U.S. is suffering the biggest measles outbreak in 25 years. The costs of battling a disease that was "eliminated" in 2000 are adding up to tens of millions, reports *Money* magazine. [80]

A single case of measles now costs health services in the neighborhood of $50,000, reports Nathaniel Smith, M.D., director of the Arkansas Department of Health. [81]

For every $1 spent on childhood vaccinations, our country saves $10.90. The CDC estimates that the vaccination of children born between 1994 and 2018 has saved the U.S. nearly $406 billion in direct medical costs and $1.88 trillion in total society costs. [82]

There are no home remedies that are an alternative to vaccination. Vaccines save lives and money.

Did one of these remedies help you?

Share your trusted remedies success with the publisher! We'd love to hear from you. **info@trustedremedies.com**

---

[80] Here's How Much America's 2019 Measles Outbreak Is Costing Us, money.com/
[81] Same as above
[82] Vaccines Are Cost Saving, vaccinateyourfamily.org

10. ACCESS TO HEALTHCARE

"Lack of insurance contributes to the endangerment of the health of each uninsured American as well as the collective health of the nation."
– *The American College of Physicians-American Society of Internal Medicine* [83]

Access to healthcare has been a major concern in America for decades. The first national attempt to address this issue was the 1993 healthcare reform package proposed by the administration of President Bill Clinton and closely associated with the chair of the task force devising the plan, Hillary Clinton.

This initiative paved the way for the Patient Protection and Affordable Care Act, also known as the Affordable Care Act (ACA) or colloquially as Obamacare. The website HealthyPeople.gov, a service of the U.S. Department of Health and Human Services, offers this guidance for people needing to improve their access to healthcare or help others do the same. As a taxpayer, you've paid for certain resources, so be sure to take advantage of them: [84]

The National Academies of Sciences, Engineering, and Medicine define primary care as "the provision of integrated, accessible healthcare services by clinicians who are accountable for addressing a large majority of personal healthcare needs, developing a sustained partnership with patients, and practicing in the context of family and community."

A primary care provider is usually an internist, family physician, pediatrician, or non-physician provider (family nurse practitioner, physician assistant). Research shows that access to primary care is associated with positive health outcomes.

Primary care providers offer a usual source of care, early detection, treatment of disease, chronic disease management, and preventive care. Patients with a usual source of care are more likely to receive recommended preventive services such as flu shots, blood pressure screenings, and cancer screenings.

However, disparities in access to primary healthcare exist, and many people face barriers that decrease access to services and increase the risk of poor health.

Some of these obstacles include lack of health insurance, language-related barriers, disabilities, inability to take time off work to attend appointments, geographic and transportation-related barriers, and a shortage of primary care providers. These barriers may intersect to further reduce access to primary care.

Lack of health insurance decreases the use of preventive and primary care services and is associated with poor health outcomes. Individuals without health insurance may delay seeking care when they are ill or injured, and they are more likely to be hospitalized for chronic conditions such as diabetes or hypertension.

In addition, children without health insurance are less likely to get vaccinations, a routine

---

[83] No Health Insurance? It's Enough to Make You Sick
[84] Access to Primary Care, healthypeople.gov | Image: VectorsLab, The Noun Project

primary care service. Overall, having health insurance increases the use of health services and improves health outcomes.

Speaking a language other than English at home can negatively impact access to primary care and screening programs. For example, a study found that Hispanic individuals who did not speak English at home were less likely to receive recommended preventive healthcare services for which they were eligible.

Another study examined women of various racial and ethnic groups whose primary language was not English (they spoke Spanish, Cantonese, or Japanese) and found that they were less likely to be screened for breast or cervical cancer. Similarly, older adults with limited English proficiency were less likely to have a usual source of care compared to those who only spoke English.

People may experience reduced access to primary care due to limited provider office hours and availability. Many providers do not offer services during typical off-work hours, posing barriers to workers without sick leave benefits. One study found that even when workers were provided with sick leave, some did not take time off to receive primary care because they still feared they would lose wages.

Factors such as travel distance and the supply of primary care providers can also limit people's ability to get primary care. For example, rural residents may need to travel long distances to get care and thus may be less likely to seek preventive care such as vaccinations. Rural communities also tend to have fewer providers than urban ones, making it harder for rural residents to access primary care.

Primary care is critical for improving public health. Further research is needed to better understand barriers to primary care, offer support to primary care providers, and develop interventions that expand primary care access. This additional evidence will facilitate public health efforts to address access to primary care.

A Google search for "access to healthcare" along with the name of your city or state is likely to yield more resources for you, your family, and those you care about or care for. These resources are designed to be low-cost if not free to the user, so be sure to take advantage of them.

COST-SAVINGS EXAMPLE:

Health insurance can save you money in several ways including discounted rates, cost-sharing, and preventive care coverage, says Credit.com [85]

Lack of health insurance decreases the use of preventive and primary care services and is associated with poor health outcomes (and therefore, higher expenses).

While everyone has a different financial situation with varying constraints, health insurance is a worthwhile investment.

This is the end of Part I: Doctor-Trusted Remedies for the Top 10 Most Common Health Issues. The editors of TrustedRemedies.com suggest setting a reminder to read these 28 pages annually.

---

[85] 4 Ways Health Insurance Can Save you Money, www.credit.com

Part II: A-to-Z Guide to Doctor-Trusted Remedies

*Learn more about any remedy, source, or provider using
the references in the footnotes – 700 footnotes in all.*

ACNE

 **Benzoyl peroxide:** Benzoyl peroxide (BPO) is used to treat acne, either alone or in combination with other treatments. It's on the World Health Organization List of Essential Medicines. In the U.S., BPO is available over the counter. **Allison Arthur, M.D.,** [86] a dermatologist at Sand Lake Dermatology Center in Orlando, FL [87] , explains that benzoyl peroxide unclogs pores, dries out pimples, and kills bacteria. It prevents new acne. BPO is usually sold in gels or lotions.

Dr. Arthur says people sometimes try over-the-counter products just for a couple of weeks; they say it's not working, get frustrated, and stop using the product. In reality, it can take a while to see results. [88] So unless you're having a problem with the medication, like severe irritation or dryness, Dr. Arthur recommends giving it at least 2-3 months before switching to something else.

Chicago dermatologist **Jordan Carqueville, M.D.** [89] also trusts BPO. She tells byrdie.com [90] that benzoyl peroxide removes excess oil on the skin and dead cells that can clog pores.

---

[86] Allison Arthur, M.D., Dermatologist, Sand Lake Dermatology Center, Orlando, FL
[87] Sand Lake Dermatology, Orlando, FL | Image: Llisole, The Noun Project
[88] Selecting the Right Acne Treatment for You, webmd.com
[89] Jordan Carqueville, M.D., General, Surgical and Cosmetic Dermatology, Chicago, carquevillemd.com
[90] Here Are the Best Benzoyl Peroxide Products to Reduce Acne, byrdie.com

Lipo-hydroxy acid: New York City dermatologist **Morgan Rabach, M.D.,** [91] lauds the La Roche-Posay Effaclar Duo, an over-the-counter remedy that pairs BPO with lipo-hydroxy acid to help exfoliate the skin and clear out pores. Find it at Amazon or Ulta, no prescription is needed.

Check your makeup: It's possible your makeup is causing your acne. Here's how to tell, according to the Pueblo County (CO) Medical Society (**Marcel Junqueira, M.D.,** president): [92]

If you have acne cosmetica, you'll likely have many tiny bumps on your face. These bumps usually appear on the cheeks, chin, or forehead. Many women develop whiteheads that rise above their skin slightly. If you have tiny breakouts around your lips, your lipstick or lip balm could be the culprit. Acne cosmetica caused by makeup can take anywhere from a few days to 6 months to appear. The medical society also suggests:

Wash with a mild cleanser: Wash your face twice a day with a mild cleanser, and after any activity that makes you sweat. Dermatologists recommend that you wash your face when you wake up and before you go to bed. In selecting a cleanser, look for the words "oil-free," "won't clog pores," or "non-comedogenic" on the packaging [non-comedogenic simply means no pore-clogging ingredients]. If you don't see any of these terms, look for a cleanser that contains one of these descriptions. Amazon has many such highly rated products starting around $15. [93]

Use fingertip pressure only: Use your fingertips to gently wash and rinse your face. You want to gently apply your cleanser with your fingertips and gently rinse it off with lukewarm water. Don't scrub – even to remove makeup. If you find that you still have makeup on your skin after washing your face, gently remove it with an oil-free makeup remover. After using a makeup remover, rinse it off. Apply makeup gently. Your touch should be feather-light. You want to avoid irritating your skin. Makeup brushes can help you apply everything gently.

Clean and don't share your supplies: Clean makeup brushes every week, and make sure you're the only one who uses them. Acne-causing bacteria, dead skin cells, and oil from other people's skin can stick to your makeup, makeup brushes, and applicators. When you use shared makeup and tools, those acne-causing culprits can spread to your skin. When you share makeup, brushes, or applicators, you can also get contagious diseases, such as pink eye or cold sores.

Prevention magazine [94] (**Joshua Zeichner, M.D.,** Dermatology Medical Review Board [95]) trusts these remedies for acne:

Choose your foundation wisely: The best foundation for acne-prone skin has two crucial qualities: It covers up your pimples without looking cakey, and it doesn't clog pores to create a never-ending cycle of breakouts. Covering marks is important, but you'll make matters worse if you use the wrong products, says Dr. Zeichner. Heavy oils block your pores, leading to an accumulation of bacteria that promote inflammation and cause breakouts.

Besides looking for non-comedogenic products, avoid foundations that contain SD-denatured alcohol, also called isopropyl alcohol, says **Yoram Harth, M.D.,** San Francisco-based

---

[91] Dr. Morgan Rabach, Board Certified Dermatologist, New York, NY. lmmedicalnyc.com

[92] "I have acne! Is it okay to wear makeup?" Pueblo County (CO) Medical Society, pueblocms.org

[93] Amazon.com: Non Comedogenic products

[94] What Causes Adult Acne? 6 Possible Reasons Behind Breakouts, prevention.com

[95] Dr. Joshua Zeichner, New York, NY, zeichnerdermatology.com

dermatologist and co-founder of M.D.acne, an acne-treatment app, and mdacne.com [96].

Look for a liquid foundation with a low concentration of salicylic acid, Dr. Zeichner says. Salicylic acid removes excess oil and exfoliates dead skin cells, working like a pipe cleaner to keep pores clear.

Some dermatologists recommend powder products over liquid foundation for acne-prone skin. Powders are less likely to clog pores since the pigment particles are larger, Dr. Zeichner explains. If you prefer a liquid foundation, avoid products with a dewy finish (this could end up looking greasy by midday), and go for something oil-free and matte instead.[97]

"Doctor, Doctor!"

Alberta Health Services [98] (medically reviewed by **Kathleen Romito M.D** [99]) recommends calling a doctor about your acne if:
- Home treatment is not enough and your acne gets worse.
- You avoid going out or feel embarrassed or depressed because of acne.
- Pimples are large, hard, or filled with fluid. This may be cystic acne, which requires more advanced care.
- One or both of your parents had severe acne and scarring.

COST-SAVINGS EXAMPLE:

Many over-the-counter acne remedies can be purchased for under $40. One good one, Pimple Patches, is only $5, says Intothegloss.com. Professional acne treatments can cost upward of $1,000 per session, and you may need multiple sessions. [100]

Though the cost of professional treatment may be worth it to you, you may be able to heal limited breakouts on your own at a low cost.

ADDICTION – SEE PART I, SUBSTANCE ABUSE

*For guidance on drug addiction, alcohol abuse, or overeating, see **Substance Abuse** in Part I of this directory, **Doctor-Trusted Remedies for the Top 10 Most Common Health Issues**.*

---

[96] Yoram Harth, Dermatologist, San Francisco; An acne treatment crafted just for you, mdacne.com
[97] 15 Best Foundations for Acne-Prone Skin That Conceal Breakouts Without Clogging Pores, Prevention
[98] Acne, Government of Alberta, MyHealth.Alberta.ca
[99] Dr. Kathleen Romito, M.D., Boise, ID, doctor.webmd.com
[100] The Cost Of Acne, intothegloss.com

AGE SPOTS

Age spots are a misnomer; the spots are not caused by age, they are caused by the sun, and it's best to call them what they are – sun spots. The spots are brown, gray, or black and flat on the skin, reports Healthline [101] (medically reviewed by **Cynthia Cobb, Doctor of Nursing Practice** [102]).

Since sun spots are typically harmless, and since lightening them is unlikely to improve your life or have a significant impact on other people's impressions about you or your age, one course of action is to simply ignore them and wear them with pride! Say that you got them the old-fashioned way – you earned them. Remark that you don't need tattoos as your skin is adorned naturally. Say that you're glad you've simply lived long enough to get them. If you still can't manage a positive view of sun spots, you may wish to try various creams and lotions. Remember, though, that these remedies require discipline.

Skin-lightening cream or lotion: To see results, Healthline says you'll have to apply a cream or lotion once or twice a day for weeks or months. You'll find plenty of skin-lightening products that claim to get rid of age spots. Many you can buy without a prescription. Before you buy any product, it's important to know that some contain ingredients that can be harmful to your health. For example, a skin lightener containing mercury can cause serious health problems.

WebMD skin and beauty expert **Laurie Polis, M.D.** [103] says that the most popular at-home treatments are over-the-counter hydroquinone (HQ) preparations. These products inhibit melanin production. But they tend to be more effective for treating melasma or hormonally induced irregular pigmentations than for treating true age spots.

"Doctor, Doctor!"

Sun spots (age spots) can serve as a useful reminder to see a dermatologist to rule out skin cancer and precancerous conditions.

For safety reasons, you may wish to see a board-certified dermatologist before using any skin-lightening product. A dermatologist can recommend a skin lightener that can effectively treat age spots without harming your health. For example, some people have had great results with prescription-strength retinol and HQ creams. These work faster than over-the-counter options. Cleveland Clinic [104] (**Francis Papay, M.D.**, Dermatology and Plastic Surgery Institute [105]) says that seeing a dermatologist can also speed up the fading of your sun spots and save you money on OTC products that may not work for you. If you need a prescription-strength cream, a dermatologist can choose one that meets your needs. Dermatologists also use various medical treatments to lighten sun spots. Some of these procedures require just one treatment; others take two or three sessions. [106]

---

[101] Everything You Need to Know About Age Spots, healthline.com | Image, Magicon, The Noun Project
[102] Cindy Cobb DNP, Allure Enhancement Center, Lafayette, LA, allureenhancement.com
[103] Dr. Laurie J. Polis, Board Certified Dermatologist, New York, NY, mountsinai.org
[104] Age Spots, clevelandclinic.org | Appointments at Cleveland Clinic
[105] Francis Papay, M.D., my.clevelandclinic.org
[106] How to Treat Age Spots, webmd.com

COST-SAVINGS EXAMPLE:

Professional removal of age spots can cost from $150 to $350 per lasering or light therapy session, with multiple sessions recommended – ideally at least three, according to Oprah.com. Cryotherapy typically runs between $50 and $100. [107]

Many self-care products are available for under $100.

Sun spots don't have to cost a penny; wear them with pride! [Just be sure to have a doctor rule out skin cancer, something you should do annually anyway.] Spend your savings on a spa day or a weekend getaway.

ALLERGIES

 Allergy treatment begins with distinguishing seasonal allergies from a cold, says health insurance provider Cigna Health [108] (**Steven B. Miller, M.D., Chief Clinical Officer** [109]). Congestion is a symptom that allergies and colds have in common. While cold-related congestion lessens over time, allergy-related congestion lasts as long as you are exposed to the allergen. Colds develop over a few days and usually clear up within days. Cigna Health trusts these allergy remedies:

Banish bothersome plants: Remove any plants that could be causing your reaction. It's common for people to be allergic to hard-to-see things like pollen. Having plants in your home may also promote the growth of mold. Exposure to molds can lead to symptoms such as stuffy nose, wheezing, and red or itchy eyes, or skin, says the National Center for Environmental Health (**Richard Woychik, Ph.D., Director** [110]).

Pay attention to pollen: Change your daily routine so that you're not around the source of your discomfort. Avoid the outdoors between 5 and 10 a.m. Save outside activities for late afternoon or after a heavy rain, when pollen counts are lower.

Keep pollen out of your home: Change your clothes when you get home to avoid tracking allergens around your living space. Keep windows in your home and car closed to lower exposure to pollen. Instead of opening windows or using window fans, use air conditioners.

Herbal teas: Teas such as ginkgo, milk thistle, red clover, stinging nettle, or yarrow are herbal combinations that can have anti-inflammatory effects, thus effectively reducing allergy symptoms (which are an inflammatory response).

Herbal supplements: Taking herbal capsules containing allium or Euphrasia can help reduce the

---

[107] Everything You Need to Know About Removing Age Spots, oprahmag.com
[108] Environmental Illness, cigna.com | Image, Delwar Hossain, The Noun Project
[109] Steven B. Miller, M.D., Chief Clinical Officer, Cigna Corporation, Medibeacon.com
[110] Richard Woychik, Ph.D., Director, National Institute of Environmental Health Sciences, niehs.nih.gov

allergic response in the body.

Salt water: Gargling with salt water can draw out and wash away impurities such as mold or pollen, and clear your nose and throat of allergens.

How to use a saline rinse

Note the one thing many of these remedies have in common: water, in the form of a salt water rinse, a soothing tea, taking a shower or doing the laundry. As we say throughout this directory, "the solution to pollution is dilution." It's nearly impossible to avoid all allergens all the time. But by diluting them and washing them away, you can minimize their impact on your health

One of the best water-based remedies for allergies and congestion is a saline rinse. **Lara Gross, M.D.** [111] , an allergist and immunologist with Texas Health Presbyterian Dallas explains on Self.com [112] what you'll need to perform a nasal rinse, and how to do it:

Avoid using water straight from the tap. It can contain low levels of bacteria that, while safe to swallow, could cause a potential infection when poured into your nasal passages, per the FDA. [113]

Buy distilled bottled water or boil and cool your tap water to room temperature. Combine three teaspoons of iodide-free salt with one teaspoon of baking soda, and then use one teaspoon of that mixture with eight ounces of water. Tilt your head and pour the solution in the top nostril until it flows out the other nostril, then switch sides. At-home rinses are also available as a squirt bottle or a squeeze bulb. Be sure to thoroughly clean your neti pot or similar device after each use.

San Tan Allergy & Asthma of Gilbert, AZ [114] (**S. Reed Shimamoto, M.D., FAAP**, founder [115]) suggests these trusted remedies, which time has shown to be effective and beneficial:

Local honey: Over time, ingesting a daily spoonful of locally sourced honey can help reduce allergy symptoms. Using local honey is key because it is made from the same flowers and pollen you are allergic to, and over time it can help your body realize it is not a threat.

HEPA filters: Install high-efficiency particulate air filters in your central air system to help filter pollen out of the air inside your home. Additionally, make sure to only use vacuum cleaners with a built-in HEPA filter, to ensure the pollen being vacuumed up from inside your home is not just being released right back out by the vacuum.

Shower: Taking a shower or bath every evening before bed will help wash off any pollen that has clung to your body from your daily activities.

Laundry: Wash your bedding in hot, soapy water at least weekly during allergy season to ensure there is no pollen buildup. [116]

There's an app for that: Multiple smartphone apps are available to help allergy sufferers track

---

[111] Lara Michelle Gross, M.D., Dallas Allergy & Asthma Center, Dallas, TX, texashealth.org
[112] 11 Natural Remedies for Seasonal Allergies at Home, SELF, self.com
[113] Is Rinsing Your Sinuses With Neti Pots Safe? FDA, fda.gov
[114] San Tan Allergy & Asthma, santanallergy.com
[115] Our Providers and Staff, San Tan Allergy & Asthma, Phoenix, AZ
[116] Easy Home Remedies for Allergies You Can Make At Home, santanallergy.com

weather and pollen. According to the website picnic.thirtymadison.com [117] (**Amina H. Abdeldaim, M.D. MPH, Medical Director** [118]), top-rated apps include: My Pollen Forecast; Allergy Alert; WebMD Allergy App; The Weather Channel App; Klarify; Picnic.

"Doctor, Doctor!"

The American College of Allergy, Asthma & Immunology [119] (**David M. Lang, M.D., President** [120]) recommends calling a doctor about your allergies if:

- You have chronic sinus infections or difficulty breathing.
- You experience symptoms several months out of the year, not just during peak allergy season.
- Antihistamines and over-the-counter medications do not control your allergy symptoms, or they create unacceptable side effects, such as drowsiness.
- Your condition interferes with your ability to carry on day-to-day activities.
- Your asthma or allergies decrease the quality of your life
- You are experiencing warning signs of serious asthma, such as:
    - You sometimes have to struggle to catch your breath.
    - You often wheeze or cough, especially at night or after exercise.
    - You are frequently short of breath or feel tightness in your chest.
- You have previously been diagnosed with asthma, and you have frequent asthma attacks even though you are taking asthma medication.

COST-SAVINGS EXAMPLE:

Most of the self-care options given above are inexpensive, such as about $12 for a highly rated neti pot on Amazon, or in the case of closing your windows, free. The ideal self-care for allergies is to live someplace where your allergy triggers are not found; Arizona is a popular choice.

If you don't want to move to the desert, Claritin (30 tablets) costs about $25. One package a month for ten years comes to $3,000. Rather than take medications for a long term, professional treatment to reduce or eliminate your symptoms may be best.

Start with the least expensive options and keep going until you find what works for you. If you've tried everything and your symptoms are still too much to live with, allergy shots may be your best option.

---

[117] The 6 Best Ways to Track Pollen Count Near You, picnic.thirtymadison.com
[118] Dr. Amina Abdeldaim, M.D., MPH, New York, NY, Allergist, zocdoc.com
[119] When To See an Allergist, American College of Allergy, Asthma and Immunology, acaai.org
[120] David M. Lang, M.D., Cleveland Clinic. My.clevelandclinic.org | Appointments at Cleveland Clinic

ANGER

Anger "impairs the function of your arteries, which is linked to future heart attack risk." – Dr. Daichi Shimbo

A Major League Baseball pitcher surrenders a home run pitch in a critical moment of a big game. His manager calls for a relief pitcher, whereupon the angry hurler retreats to the dugout and punches the water cooler with all his might – using the pitching hand that earns him a handsome Big League salary.

Yes, anger is a health issue, and a serious one. Anger can ruin your day, damage your relationships, cut into your income, and trigger serious health problems. Bad things are going to happen to us all, but anger will only make it worse – every single time. Doctors report short- and long-term health consequences linked to unmanaged anger including headache, insomnia, and digestion problems such as abdominal pain; increased anxiety, depression, and skin problems such as eczema; even high blood pressure, heart attack, and stroke. [121]

Let's take just one of these – heart attack. The American Heart Association explains just how quickly anger may contribute to your risk for a heart attack – as fast as eight minutes: [122]

"Anger is bad," says cardiologist Dr. Daichi Shimbo, co-director of the hypertension center at Columbia University Irving Medical Center in New York City. Short bursts of anger may temporarily damage the ability of blood vessels to properly dilate, a function believed to be pivotal in preventing arteries from hardening, new research suggests.

Impairment of the arteries "resulted from just eight minutes of recalling angry feelings, raising questions about the cumulative impact of anger on blood vessel function," says Dr. Shimbo. "If you get angry once, it impairs your ability to dilate," he says. "But what if you get angry 10,000 times over a lifetime? This chronic insult to your arteries may lead to permanent damage."

Do you fume when you're cut off in traffic? Does your blood pressure soar when a loved one says the wrong thing? Anger is a common emotion, says Mayo Clinic, so it's essential to deal with it in a positive way. Start by reviewing these trusted remedies from Mayo Clinic doctors: [123]

Think before you speak: In the heat of the moment, it's easy to say something you'll later regret. Take a few moments to collect your thoughts before saying anything. Also allow others involved in the situation to do the same.

Once you're calm, express your concerns: As soon as you're thinking clearly, express your frustration in an assertive but nonconfrontational way. State your concerns and needs clearly and directly, without hurting others or trying to control them.

Get some exercise: Physical activity can help reduce stress that can cause you to become angry.

---

[121] Department of Health, State Government of Victoria, Australia; Euan Wallace M.D., Secretary | Image: Alice Design, The Noun Project

[122] Anger's role in heart attack risk may start in the arteries, American Heart Association

[123] Anger management: 10 tips to tame your temper, Mayo Clinic News Network

Go for a brisk walk or run. Or spend some time doing other enjoyable physical activities.

Take a timeout: Timeouts aren't just for kids. Give yourself short breaks during times of the day that tend to be stressful. A few moments of quiet time might help you feel better prepared to handle what's ahead without getting irritated or angry.

Identify possible solutions: Shift your focus from being mad to resolving the cause. Does your child's messy room upset you ? Close the door. Is your partner late for dinner often? Have meals later in the evening. Also, accept that you can't control everything. Be realistic about what you can and cannot change. Remember that anger won't fix anything and can only make it worse.

Stick with 'I' statements: Placing blame may only increase tension. Instead, use "I" statements to describe the problem. Be respectful and specific. For example, say, "I'm upset that you left the table without offering to help with the dishes" instead of "You never do any housework."

Don't hold a grudge: Forgiveness is powerful. If you allow anger and negativity to crowd out positive feelings, you may find yourself swallowed up by your own bitterness. Forgiving the other person may help you both learn from the situation and strengthen your relationship. The editors of Trusted Remedies add that this remedy backs up some of the oldest and most repeated advice ever given: *"Forgive us our trespasses, as we forgive those trespass against us."*

Use humor to release tension: Lightening up can help diffuse tension. Use humor to help you face what's making you angry and, possibly, any unrealistic expectations you have for how things should go. Avoid sarcasm, though — it can hurt feelings and make things worse.

Practice relaxation skills: When your temper flares, put relaxation skills to work. Practice deep-breathing exercises, imagine a relaxing scene, or repeat a calming word or phrase, such as "Take it easy." You might also listen to music, write in a journal or do a few yoga poses — whatever it takes to encourage relaxation.

Know when to seek help: Learning to control anger can be a challenge. Seek help if your anger seems out of control, causes you to do things you regret, or hurts those around you.

For more trusted remedies to reduce your risk for a heart attack, turn to the sections in this book on **Tobacco (Part I)**, **High Cholesterol (Part II)**, and **Tachycardia (Part II)**. To prevent a stroke, see our eBook, **WATER CURES: 101 Little-Known Health Remedies Using Only Water.**

"Doctor, Doctor!"

Perhaps you're not keen to talk to your doctor about your anger. But put it off and you may end up talking to a divorce attorney or the cardiologist who's treating you after your heart attack. If anger is a concern in your life, call your doctor. He or she is there to help.

COST-SAVINGS EXAMPLE:

What's the cost of having a heart attack or wrecking a relationship? No one can put a price on these things. The trusted remedies above are inexpensive, if not free. Do yourself and your family a favor ... take these anger management remedies to heart.

ANGINA – SEE CHEST PAIN

ANXIETY

 Anxiety is more than just nervous energy, the butt of a Rodney Dangerfield joke, or the subject of a Mel Brooks comedy. Anxiety can lead to addiction, depression, withdrawal, and other debilitating conditions that can be difficult to recover from. Some anxiety is a normal part of life. But when anxiety turns into a daily struggle, it's time to act. Take control by trying these trusted remedies from Healthline [124] (medically reviewed by **Bethany Juby, PsyD**): [125]

Stay active: Regular exercise is good for your physical and emotional health. Regular exercise works as well as medication to ease anxiety for some people. And it's not just a short-term fix; you may experience anxiety relief for hours after working out.

Don't drink alcohol: Using alcohol to relieve anxiety instead of treating the root cause of the problem may lead to alcohol dependence. For help, see the section on **Substance Abuse** in Part I of this directory, **Doctor-Trusted Remedies for the Top 10 Most Common Health Issues.**

Stop smoking: Smokers often reach for a cigarette during stressful times. Yet, like alcohol, nicotine and other chemicals in cigarette smoke negatively alter pathways in the brain linked to anxiety. For detailed help, see the section on **Tobacco** in Part I of this directory.

Ditch caffeine: Caffeine may cause nervousness and jitters, neither of which is good if you're anxious. In some people, eliminating caffeine may significantly reduce anxiety.

Get some sleep: Insomnia is both a cause and a symptom of anxiety. Make sleep a priority by:

- Only sleeping at night when you're tired
- Not reading or watching television in bed
- Not using your phone, tablet, or computer in bed
- Not tossing and turning in your bed if you can't sleep; get up and go to another room until you feel sleepy
- Avoiding caffeine, large meals, and nicotine before bedtime
- Keeping your room dark and cool
- Writing down your worries before going to bed
- Going to sleep at the same time each night
- In addition, see the remedies listed under **Insomnia** later in this directory

Meditate: Meditation is known for relieving stress and anxiety. Research suggests 30 minutes of daily meditation may alleviate some anxiety symptoms and act as an antidepressant.

Eat a healthy diet: If your anxiety worsens after you eat, check your eating habits. Stay hydrated, eliminate processed foods, and eat a healthy diet rich in complex carbohydrates, fruits and vegetables, and lean proteins.

---

[124] 8 Research-Backed Herbs to Try for Anxiety, healthline.com | Image: Daryl Vandemont, The Noun Project
[125] Dr. Bethany Juby. licensed clinical psychologist, Juby Clinical Services, LLC, healthline.com

Practice deep breathing: Shallow, fast breathing is common with anxiety. Deep-breathing exercises – the deliberate process of taking slow, even, deep breaths – can help restore normal breathing patterns and reduce anxiety.

Try aromatherapy: Aromatherapy uses fragrant essential oils that may be inhaled directly or added to a warm bath or diffuser. Studies have shown that aromatherapy helps you relax, helps you sleep, boosts mood, and reduces heart rate and blood pressure. Some essential oils used in aromatherapy are bergamot, lavender, clary sage, grapefruit, and ylang-ylang.

Drink chamomile tea: A cup of chamomile tea is a common herbal remedy to calm frayed nerves and promote sleep. One study showed the herb may also be a powerful ally against anxiety disorder.

If you're feeling anxious, the trusted remedies above may help calm you down. Remember, these trusted remedies may help ease anxiety, but they don't replace professional help. Increased anxiety may require professional help. Talk to your doctor about your concerns. [126]

Dr. Debra Rose Wilson is a professor, researcher, and holistic healthcare practitioner. She offers several herbal supplements that may be helpful for those experiencing anxiety and depression: [127]

Hops: Hops are a commercially grown herb commonly used in beer. Like chamomile, certain compounds in hops are mildly sedating, making them a useful option for people with anxiety. Studies show that 200 mg of common hops daily can help lower or relieve anxiety over time.

Lemon balm (Melissa officinalis): Lemon balm is another medicinal herb traditionally used to help improve anxiety, depression, and other mood disorders. Research suggests that in addition to providing anti-anxiety benefits, lemon balm may help improve cognition. Studies show that supplements containing 1,000 mg of lemon balm may be helpful for easing symptoms of anxiety.

Valerian: Valerian is another herbal supplement that, along with chamomile, is often found in tea form. Active compounds in the valerian plant have sedative properties, making this herb another popular option for anxiety. Studies show that 100 mg of valerian can help reduce anxiety by changing the brain's chemistry and the way that it connects to anxiety.

"Doctor, Doctor!"

Thomas Jefferson University Hospitals [128] (**Nancy DeAngelis, CRNP,** and **Bruce A. Meyer, M.D., President** [129]) says you should call a doctor about your anxiety if you experience difficulty concentrating, restlessness, irritability, sleep disturbance, or muscle tension. It's important to seek help for these symptoms since they can cause significant distress and affect your life and your relationships at home, in school, and at work.

COST-SAVINGS EXAMPLE:

---

[126] 10 Ways to Naturally Reduce Anxiety, healthline.com
[127] Debra Rose Wilson, Ph.D., healthline.com
[128] 5 Signs You Should Talk To Your Doctor About Anxiety, abingtonhealth.org
[129] Bruce A. Meyer, M.D., MBA, jefferson.edu, Philadelphia, PA

The greatest costs of anxiety come after years of small daily impacts, resulting in such possible outcomes as depression, isolation, or drug and alcohol dependency – conditions that can be costly to treat, in addition to robbing you of your joy.

Standard alcohol and drug rehab costs range from $3,000 to $20,000 for 30 days. Some users recovering from alcohol and opiate addictions require medication at an additional cost. Take your anxiety seriously by trying these inexpensive or free trusted remedies until you find the combination that works best for you.

Control your anxiety today and avoid substance abuse treatment later costing $3,000 to $20,000. [130]

ARTHRITIS

Few conditions have sent more people in search of effective remedies as arthritis, the painful joint condition that affects millions. It's therefore not surprising that arthritis is associated with some of the oldest and best-known medical lore – persistent folk tales that according to science are simply not true:

Gin-soaked raisins? Sorry, this is nothing more than folklore. No evidence supports gin-soaked raisins as an arthritis remedy, says Medical News Today. [131]

Avoid nightshades? Nor is there any evidence that tomatoes or other nightshade vegetables like peppers and eggplant make arthritis worse, reports Medical News Today. [132]

As is often the case, the real harm of unscientific folklore remedies is that they distract people from doing things that are actually known to work – trusted remedies backed by doctors. That said, if you suffer from arthritis pain, you simply need to try to find what works for you. The Global Healthy Living Foundation consulted chronic disease specialist **Susan Blum, M.D., MPH** [133], rheumatologist **Don R. Martin, M.D.** [134], and others. On its aptly named website creakyjoints.org, they share these remedies that doctors generally considered safe and effective: [135]

Chili pepper lotion: Capsaicin, the component that makes chili peppers hot, may help soothe arthritis symptoms, Dr. Martin says. "Rub capsaicin lotion or gel over joints to help ease the pain and reduce swelling," he explains. Decades of scientific evidence show that capsaicin has pain-relieving properties for osteo- and rheumatoid arthritis.

Fermented foods: "One of the most important things you can do to manage arthritis is to have a

[130] How Much Does Rehab Cost? help.org
[131] Do gin-soaked raisins help with arthritis pain? | Image: Gan Khoon Lay, The Noun Project
[132] Nightshade vegetables and inflammation: Do they affect arthritis? Medical News Today
[133] Susan Blum, M.D., MPH, Blum Center for Health, Rye Brook, NY, blumcenterforhealth.com
[134] Don Martin, M.D., Sentara Healthcare, Sentara Healthcare, Harrisonburg, VA, sentara.com
[135] Arthritis Home Remedies that Patients Swear By and Doctors Approve, creakyjoints.org

healthy gut," Dr. Blum says. "You need a gut microbiome that is robust and diverse, which means plenty of good bacteria." Increase your body's supply of good bacteria by eating probiotic, cultured foods, such as yogurt, kefir, sauerkraut, kimchi, sourdough, and kombucha.

Probiotic supplement: Sometimes it's hard to eat enough probiotic-containing foods to balance your gut microbiome (especially if you don't like the taste of fermented foods) so taking a daily high-quality probiotic supplement can fill in this nutritional gap, Dr. Blum says. Pick one with more than one strain of bacteria; the more diverse the better, she says.

Glucosamine/chondroitin supplement: Glucosamine is a natural substance in your body that may slow the deterioration of cartilage, Dr. Martin explains. Glucosamine is commonly used with chondroitin, another substance that occurs naturally in the connective tissues of people and animals. According to a large study, people with mild pain did not see much benefit. Those with more severe pain experienced modest relief with the glucosamine/chondroitin combo.

Turmeric: Turmeric helps reduce swelling and pain from arthritis, Dr. Martin says. A tasty way to enjoy this anti-inflammatory spice is to make "golden milk," a traditional drink made from hot milk, turmeric, ginger, cinnamon, pepper, and a dash of maple syrup. While you can add turmeric to food, you likely need a supplement to consume enough to impact arthritis symptoms.

Fish oil: Fish oils contain anti-inflammatory omega-3 fatty acids, which may help reduce joint pain and stiffness. You can consume omega-3s from your diet – they occur naturally in fish such as salmon, in nuts and seeds, and in certain plant oils such as flaxseed – and are increasingly found in such fortified foods as eggs or yogurt. But supplements can provide much higher doses. If you've tried fish oil in the past and it hasn't helped, the issue may be that you didn't take enough of it, Dr. Blum says. Ask your doctor about the right dose to take for you.

Cannabidiol (CBD): CBD is catching on among people with arthritis and other forms of chronic pain. Derived from hemp or cannabis plants, CBD is not intoxicating like THC, a cannabinoid found in marijuana plants but not in hemp. CBD is available in creams, capsules, oral tinctures, topical lotions, and edibles. **Elyse Rubinstein, M.D.** [136] , a rheumatologist at Providence St. John's Health in Santa Monica, CA says that CBD products appear to have positive effects.

Gluten-free diet: A gluten-free diet may decrease signs and symptoms of inflammatory arthritis even in people who don't have celiac disease, says Anca Askanase, M.D., a rheumatologist and director of rheumatology clinical trials at Columbia University Medical Center. Though more research is needed, gluten may cause underlying inflammation in some people; eliminating it may help reduce pain and stiffness and increase mobility for some people with arthritis.

Reduce sugar: Eating an anti-inflammatory diet is the top natural recommendation of many doctors. One of the most inflammatory foods is sugar – especially when eaten in excess and in processed foods. "The simplest approach to an anti-inflammatory diet is to eat very little refined sugar, which is commonly found in soda, juices, candy, ice cream, and baked goods like cakes, cookies, and white bread," Dr. Blum says. On the other hand, sugar that occurs naturally in healthy whole foods, like fruits and vegetables, is totally fine.

Ergonomic tools: "As a hand surgeon, I deal with thumb and finger arthritis all the time," says

---

[136] Elyse J. Rubenstein, M.D., Providence Saint John's Health Center, Santa Monica, CA, providence.org

A. Lee Osterman, M.D. [137] , a hand and orthopedic surgeon in Philadelphia. This is why it's so important to protect your hands and preserve your joint function by using tools designed to take pressure off hand joints when doing daily tasks, he says. He suggests using devices like mounted jar openers, saw-handle knives, keys mounted in key holders, spring-loaded scissors, and wider pens. Any way you can reduce the pressure on your hand joints is worth the effort, he says.

Hot paraffin soak: Paraffin is a wax that melts at a relatively low temperature. You can dip your hands, forearms, feet, and lower legs into it without getting burned. It sounds odd, but it can truly help reduce pain and swelling from arthritis, Dr. Osterman says. The wax coats your skin and as it dries it holds the heat in longer than a traditional foot soak or warm compress, although those can be very helpful as well. "Therapies that use heat can help reduce stiffness and pain," he says.

Self-massage: Massaging the muscles around inflamed joints can help improve circulation and decrease painful spasms, Dr. Osterman says. While a professional massage is nice, it may not be practical or affordable. Instead, learn some simple self-massage techniques you can do at home. Check out the tutorials at creakyjoints.org [138]for massaging joints with arthritis, including knees, hands and feet, jaw, and neck. You can also talk to a physical therapist who specializes in arthritis to show you some techniques that target the specific joints that are causing you pain.

Gentle exercises: "Motion is lotion" is a popular adage in the arthritis community and with good reason — one of the best things you can do for your joint pain is to keep moving, even when you're in pain, Dr. Askanase says. Exercises that incorporate low-impact cardio — such as walking or cycling — along with gentle stretching are ideal for home workouts, she says. Consider gentle stretches and movements that borrow from yoga, Pilates, or tai chi.

In addition to these trusted remedies, it's important to note that many other lifestyle changes are important in managing arthritis symptoms. These include losing weight if you're overweight, improving sleep, heat therapy and ice therapy, stress relief, water exercises, and more.

"Doctor, Doctor!"

Arthritis tends to get worse with time. Consulting a doctor as soon as you begin having daily joint pain is wise, to help preserve joint function and keep pain in check.

COST-SAVINGS EXAMPLE:

Arthritis drugs cost most patients between $1,500 - $2,000 each year, depending on the medication. Some rheumatoid arthritis drugs run $1,300 - $3,000 per month.

Save up to thousands of dollars per year by managing your arthritis without drugs, or get the most pain relief for your money by combining drug treatment with doctor-approved remedies.

---

[137] A. Lee Osterman, M.D., Philadelphia Hand to Shoulder Center, hand2shouldercenter.com
[138] Creakyjoints.org, Global Healthy Living Foundation

ASTHMA

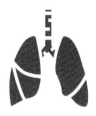

The website molekule.science [139] (**Dr. Y. Goswami, chief scientist** [140]) offers trusted remedies for adults with asthma.

Keep a diary: Keeping an asthma diary can help you learn when and where your asthma symptoms are the most severe. Once you understand your triggers, you can more proactively manage your symptoms. Your asthma journal can also provide key details to your doctor when making decisions about your treatment.

Banish allergens: Clearing your home of known allergy and asthma triggers can reduce symptoms. Clean and vacuum regularly, close windows to keep pollen and air pollution out, and make sure that the air in your home doesn't get too cold or dry. If you think you might stir up dust while cleaning, wear a dust mask or ask someone else to help.

Manage stress: Stress amplifies the immune response to environmental triggers of asthma. Finding ways to mitigate stress may also mitigate stress-related asthma symptoms. You can seek out common science-backed methods to reduce stress such as exercise, yoga, and meditation. See the section devoted to **Stress** later in this directory for a dozen or more doctor-trusted remedies.

Saline rinse: A saline nasal wash can sometimes help with asthma symptoms, say researchers at Birmingham (UK) Regional Severe Asthma Services [141]. Many people with asthma also have allergy symptoms that can exacerbate feelings of breathlessness and chest tightness. Nasal irrigation can help relieve these symptoms. If you decide to do a nasal rinse, make sure to familiarize yourself with the FDA's safety recommendations to avoid infection. [142] Turn back a few pages to the section of this directory about **Allergies** and read **How to use a saline rinse**.

According to **Pat Bass, M.D.**, an internal medicine specialist in Shreveport, Louisiana [143], people with asthma who own a pet may benefit from finding those pets a new home. Animal dander is one of the most common triggers known to worsen asthma symptoms – wheezing, chest tightness, shortness of breath, even a full-blown asthma attack. It may not be an easy decision, but rehoming your furry and feathered friends may be a needed step in controlling asthma. [144]

Richard Firshein, D.O., an integrative medicine and family medicine practitioner located in Manhattan, Upper East Side, NY, offers three natural, drug-free ways to treat asthma: [145]

Breathing exercises: Research suggests that mindful breathing can ward off asthma attacks and decrease asthma symptoms. One approach that the Firshein Center uses is a technique that slows down breathing combined with diaphragmatic exercises. The Firshein method utilizes slow

---

[139] Top Home Remedies for Asthma: Do They Actually Work? molekule.science | Image: dDara, The Noun Project
[140] molekule.com | Though his doctorate is in mechanical engineering, not a health or medical field, Dr. Goswami has used his expertise to develop air purification equipment to improve human health.
[141] Heartlands researchers recommend simple nasal rinse could help relieve some symptoms of asthma, University Hospitals Birmingham (UK) NHS Foundation Trust, hgs.uhb.nhs.uk
[142] Is Rinsing Your Sinuses With Neti Pots Safe? FDA, fda.gov
[143] Pat Bass, M.D., Internal Medicine specialist in Shreveport LA, healthcare4ppl.com
[144] Pet Dander and Asthma, verywellhealth.com
[145] Richard Firshein, D.O., Integrative Medicine & Family Medicine, New York, NY, firsheincenter.com/

breathing with visual imagery and diaphragmatic breathing to enhance respiration. Some research links higher carbon dioxide content in the blood to more dilated airways.

Nutritional counseling: In his books *The Nutraceutical Revolution* and *Reversing Asthma*, Dr. Firshein documents the benefits of using specific nutrients to benefit his patients. Studies show that diets rich in vitamin C, antioxidants, anti-inflammatory foods, and other minerals reduce your risk of asthma.

Foods with anti-inflammatory properties – such as berries, fish, avocados, and herbal teas – may reduce inflammation in your airways, which can minimize symptoms and lower your risk for an asthma attack.Eating a healthy diet also strengthens your immune system, which helps your body fend off allergy attacks and illness, two common triggers of asthma.

Trigger avoidance: Avoiding triggers is critical to avoiding asthma attacks. Common asthma triggers include: smoke, allergen exposure (animal dander, pollen, dust, mold), strong scents (fragrances in soaps, perfumes, and colognes), rapid changes in weather (hot to cold, humid to dry), illness, such as a cold, and exercise. While you don't want to avoid exercise completely, take care to monitor your breathing during exercise. Slow down or back off the intensity if you start struggling to breathe, and only exercise in places where your other triggers aren't present.[146]

"Doctor, Doctor!"

According to the American Lung Association [147] (**Meredith Christine McCormack, M.D.,** [148]), you should call a doctor about your asthma if:

- Call a healthcare provider right away when:
    - You feel faint, dizzy, or weak
    - You have trouble doing a routine activity, such as cooking dinner, cleaning, or taking out the trash
    - You have a cough that won't go away
    - You're wheezing when you breathe in or out, especially if this is different from your usual breathing pattern
    - Your wheezing gets worse even after you have given your medicine time to start working (most quick-relief medicines work within 15 minutes)

- Go to urgent care, go to the emergency room, or call 9-1-1 right away when:
    - Your lips or nails are turning blue
    - Your nostrils are flaring each time you breathe in
    - The skin between your ribs or at the base of your throat appears stretched every time you breathe in
    - You are taking 30 or more breaths per minute
    - Talking or walking at a normal pace is difficult

COST-SAVINGS EXAMPLE:

---

[146] 3 Natural, Drug-Free Ways to Treat Asthma, firsheincenter.com
[147] When To See Your Doctor About Asthma, lung.org
[148] Meredith Christine McCormack, M.D., M.H.S., Associate Professor of Medicine, hopkinsmedicine.org

Asthma costs the U.S. economy more than $80 billion annually in medical expenses, missed work and school days, and deaths. [149] **(Kevin Wilson, M.D., chief, documents & patient education, American Thoracic Society** [150] **)**

More than 25 million Americans have asthma, for approximate costs of $3,200 per patient per year. Avoid these costs by avoiding asthma triggers. [151]

Learn to avoid asthma triggers and save up to $3,200 per year.

ATHLETE'S FOOT

 MedicineNet.com (**Gary W. Cole, M.D.** [152] and **William C. Shiel Jr., M.D.** [153]) offers trusted remedies for treating the fungal infection commonly called athlete's foot. [154] Since there is no single cause of athlete's foot, there is no single treatment, Drs. Cole and Shiel explain. Nevertheless, all causes of this condition benefit by promoting a dry, clean, and friction-free environment for the feet.

Shoes that breathe: Occlusive shoes, such as nurse's shoes and waterproof work shoes and hikers, cause feet to remain moist and provide an excellent area for the fungus to proliferate. Choose shoes that breathe, allowing moisture to escape.

Moisture-wicking socks: Socks that pull water away from your feet may help. People who sweat excessively may benefit by using antiperspirants like those containing 20% aluminum chloride (e.g., Drysol) on their feet.

Foot powders: Powders can also help keep your feet dry. Soaking your feet in a solution of aluminum acetate (Burow's solution or Domeboro solution) and then air drying them with a fan can be very helpful if performed three or four times within thirty minutes. A foot bath of diluted white vinegar, using one part vinegar and about four parts water, followed by evaporation, once or twice a day (as ten-minute soaks) can be helpful.

Over-the-counter medications: Drs. Cole and Shiel say that many effective medications are available for fungus infection. Ask your pharmacist for a recommendation. Many are available without a prescription. If OTC medications are not effective, see your doctor.

Do Not: Topical corticosteroid creams can act as a "fertilizer" for fungus and may worsen fungal infections by suppressing the body's immune defenses. These topical steroid medications have no role in treating fungal foot infections but can be quite effective in treating noninfectious causes of athlete's foot, caution Drs. Cole and Shiel.

---

[149] Asthma Costs the U.S. Economy More than $80 Billion Per Year, thoracic.org
[150] Kevin Wilson, M.D., Professor of Medicine, Boston University Medical Center, bumc.bu.edu
[151] Asthma Facts and Figures, Asthma and Allergy Foundation of America, aafa.org
[152] Dr. Gary William Cole, Dermatology, Huntington Beach, CA | Image: Andrejs Kirma, The Noun Project
[153] William Chapin Shiel Jr, M.D., Rheumatology, Mission Viejo, CA, vitals.com
[154] Athlete's Foot: Best Treatment, Symptoms, and Causes, medicinenet.com

"Doctor, Doctor!"

According to Orthopedic and Sports Medicine Specialists of Anne Arundel Medical Group, Annapolis, MD, (**Robert M. Verklin Jr., M.D.** [155]) call a doctor about your athlete's foot if:

- Your feet have blisters, severe cracking, scaling, or peeling skin.
- You notice signs of bacterial infection, including increased pain, swelling, redness, tenderness, or heat., red streaks extending from the affected area, discharge of pus, fever of 100.4° F (38° C) or higher with no other cause.
- You have diabetes or diseases associated with poor circulation, which increases the risk of a severe bacterial infection of the foot and leg.
- Your symptoms do not improve after 2 weeks of treatment or are not gone after 4 weeks of treatment with a nonprescription antifungal medicine.

For fungus infection, Drs. Cole and Shiel say that many effective medications are available. Ask your doctor or pharmacist for a recommendation. Many are available without a prescription. It is difficult to know which of these drugs is most effective, since they have not been tested against each other. Cost may be the most significant differentiating factor. Treatment for athlete's foot should generally be continued for four weeks or at least one week after all the skin symptoms have cleared.

More advanced or resistant cases of athlete's foot may require a course of an oral (pill) antifungal. Laboratory blood tests to make sure there is no liver disease may be required before you can be prescribed these drugs.

If the fungal infection has spread to the toenails, the nails must also be treated to avoid reinfection of the feet. Often, the nails are initially ignored, only to cause the athlete's foot to keep recurring. Effective nail fungus treatment may be more intensive and require prolonged courses (three to four months) of oral antifungal medications.

COST-SAVINGS EXAMPLE:

Oral antifungal pills used for severe cases of athlete's foot can be expensive, with costs ranging from $8 to $2,632 _per day_, depending on the drug used [156] (George R. Thompson, M.D. [157] and Tom Patterson, M.D. [158]).

Besides the cost of oral antifungal pills themselves, taking them often requires periodic testing for dangerous side effects, costing you both time and money (University of Michigan Medicine, medically reviewed by Patrice Burgess, M.D.). [159]

Use these remedies as soon as signs appear to save up to $2,632 a day.

---

[155] Robert M. Verklin, Jr., M.D., osmc.net | Athlete's Foot Condition Basics, osmc.net
[156] Mycoses Study Group Education and Research, Antifungal therapy cost analysis, drfungus.org
[157] George R. Thompson, M.D., University of California-Davis Medical Center, health.ucdavis.edu
[158] Tom Patterson, M.D., UT Health San Antonio, uthscsa.edu
[159] Athlete's Foot Treatment Overview, uofmhealth.org | Patrice Burgess, M.D., saintalphonsus.org

B

BACKACHE

Back pain is one of the leading reasons people see a doctor or miss days at work, according to a report from the National Institutes of Health [160](**Walter J. Koroshetz, M.D., Director, NIH Neurological Institute** [161]). The condition is a major player in disability and work-related injuries. Back pain is so common, it's considered a public health problem, which explains why the NIH – the top federal agency responsible for health research – is deeply involved.

Back pain can range in intensity from a dull, constant ache to a sudden, sharp, or shooting pain. It can begin suddenly as a result of an accident or lifting a heavy object, or can develop over time as we age. Getting too little exercise followed by a strenuous workout also can cause back pain, says the NIH. There are two types of back pain to know about:

Acute back pain lasts a few days to a few weeks. Most low back pain is acute. It tends to resolve on its own within a few days with self-care, with no residual loss of function. In some cases, a few months are required for the symptoms to disappear.

Chronic back pain is pain that continues for 12 weeks or longer, even after an initial injury or underlying cause of acute low back pain has been treated. About 20% of people affected by acute low back pain develop chronic low back pain with persistent symptoms within one year. Even if pain persists, it does not always mean there is an underlying medical cause that can be easily identified and treated. In some cases, treatment relieves chronic low back pain, but in other cases, pain continues despite medical intervention. Chronic back pain is most often treated with a stepped-care approach, moving from simple low-cost treatments to more aggressive approaches, says the NIH. Specific treatments may depend on the identified cause of the back pain.

The NIH has found these trusted remedies to be most effective:

Heat and cold: Heat and/or ice may help ease pain, reduce inflammation and improve mobility.

Get back to your normal routine: Resuming normal activities as soon as possible may ease pain; bed rest is not recommended.

Back exercises: Exercises that strengthen core or abdominal muscles may help speed recovery from chronic low back pain. Always check with a physician before starting an exercise program and to get a list of helpful exercises.

Over-the-counter medications: Non-steroidal anti-inflammatory drugs, or NSAIDs, can be very

---

[160] Low Back Pain Fact Sheet, ninds.nih.gov | Image: Pham Thanh Loc, The Noun Project
[161] Walter Koroshetz, M.D., National Institute of Neurological Disorders and Stroke, ninds.nih.gov

effective. Follow label directions and do not take more than the recommended dose.

Topical pain relief: Products such as creams, gels, patches, or sprays applied to the skin may provide feelings of warmth or cold to dull the sensation of pain. Common topical medications include capsaicin and lidocaine.

Gentle stretching: Use upon advice by your health care provider.

Acupuncture: Acupuncture may be effective for chronic low back pain. It involves inserting thin needles into precise points throughout the body, and stimulating them (by twisting or passing a low-voltage electric current through them), which may cause the release of naturally occurring painkillers such as endorphins, serotonin, and acetylcholine.

Behavioral approaches: Biofeedback involves attaching electrodes to the skin and using an electromyography machine that allows you to become aware of and better control your breathing, muscle tension, heart rate, and skin temperature, all of which help regulate your response to pain. Cognitive therapy uses relaxation and coping techniques to ease back pain.

TENS: Transcutaneous electrical nerve stimulation involves wearing a battery-powered device that places electrodes on the skin over the painful area to generate electrical impulses designed to block or modify the perception of pain.

Physical therapy: Physical therapy programs to strengthen core muscle groups that support the lower back, improve mobility and flexibility, and promote proper positioning and posture are often used in combination with other interventions.

Chiropractic care: Spinal manipulation and spinal mobilization are approaches in which a chiropractor uses their hands to mobilize, adjust, massage, or stimulate the spine and adjacent tissues. Manipulation uses rapid movement over which the individual has no control; mobilization uses slower movements. The techniques may provide moderate short-term relief for chronic lower back pain, but neither technique is appropriate when a person has an underlying medical cause for the back pain such as osteoporosis, spinal cord compression, or arthritis.

For medical care options, see the page "Low Back Pain Fact Sheet" on the NIH website in the footnote on the previous page.

"Doctor, Doctor!"

The Spine Health Institute at AdventHealth Medical Group [162] (**Chetan Patel, M.D., Medical Director** [163]) recommends calling a doctor about your back pain if:

- Your pain doesn't go away, or you have shooting pain down your arms or legs.
- You have weakness, numbness, or tingling in the arms and legs, or nighttime pain.
- You have a fever along with back pain or weight loss.
- You have problems with balance or controlling your bowels or bladder.

---

[162] 5 Signs It's Time to See a Doctor for Back Pain, Advent Health, adventhealth.com
[163] Chetan K. Patel, M.D., AdventHealth, Zephyrhills, FL, adventhealth.com

COST-SAVINGS EXAMPLE:

Americans spend more on back and neck pain than on any other health issue. [164]

Back pain costs fall into three categories: treatment costs, employer costs, and employee costs due to loss of wages and quality of life. These costs total more than $200 billion per year (American Academy of Orthopaedic Surgeons). [165]

Avoid the potentially crushing financial burden and lifestyle limitations of chronic back pain by controlling your symptoms with these doctor-trusted remedies before they get worse.

BAD BREATH

 How serious is bad breath? Serious enough that people worldwide spend $6.5 billion per year on mouthwash. [166] Also serious enough that we're devoting three pages of this directory to helping you solve this problem. (After **Stress**, it's the second-longest entry in this publication.) The editors of the directory you are now reading used to be part of that lucrative mouthwash market, until we realized that good oral care takes care of bad breath automatically – just take proper care of your teeth and gums. We bought a dentist-recommended electric toothbrush, the top brand of natural toothpaste, and some dental floss and use them all regularly. Mouthwash routine kicked.

Bad breath is often linked with garlic, onions, or other smelly foods. Brushing your teeth or drinking some water can greatly reduce mouth odors. However, chronic bad breath may have an underlying cause that's not going to go away with the swish of some mouthwash. The Maryland Center for Complete Dentistry [167] (reviewed by **Jonathan Silverman, D.D.S.** [168]) explains the common causes of, and most trusted remedies for, bad breath. Let's start with the causes:

Gingivitis: This serious cause of smelly breath occurs due to a buildup of plaque and decay in your teeth. In time, gingivitis can lead to lost teeth and serious infections. If your halitosis is accompanied by dark purple gums, bleeding, inflammation, and painful brushing, you need professional dental care [sooner rather than later] to go along with the trusted remedies below.

Cavities: A cavity will fill with anaerobic bacteria over time. These germs can create a foul mouth odor. This also requires a dentist, as it can turn into a life-threatening infection if ignored.

Dry mouth: Sometimes stinky breath comes from benign causes, like dry mouth. Your mouth can

---

[164] Why Americans Spend More on Back and Neck Pain Than Any Other Health Issue, healthline.com
[165] The Real Costs of Back Pain, Treatment & Prevention, moneycrashers.com
[166] Mouthwash Market Size, Share, Industry Forecast by 2030, emergenresearch.com
[167] How To Stop Bad Breath Remedy, Home Remedies For Bad Breath Halitosis, saveteeth.com
[168] Jonathan Silverman, DDS, Owings Mills, MD, saveteeth.com | Image: Azam Ishaq, The Noun Project

dry out if you snore, breathe with your mouth open, talk a lot, or are in a very dry climate.

Regardless of the cause, you want it to go away fast. These trusted remedies don't replace a dental checkup, but they'll keep your breath fresh until the underlying problem is taken care of.

Water: As we say so often in this directory, "the solution to pollution is dilution." Dr. Silverman appears to agree; if you notice an odor, drink a glass of water. If you're not a fan of plain water, add a splash of Mio or another water flavoring. Eating foods with high water content like celery, watermelon, cucumber, lettuce, and tomatoes will wet your mouth. You should drink about a half-gallon of water each day to avoid dehydration. If you lose count, sip water throughout the day, before you feel thirsty. This should help keep your mouth moist and your breath palatable.

Clean your tongue: Bits of food, dead cells, and bacteria tend to build up on the tongue. This can reek. You'll sometimes see the buildup as a white coating toward the back of the tongue, says Dr. Silverman. Removing it will significantly help with the smell. You can wipe your tongue with a warm washcloth, moistened with a mix of water and lemon juice. Or you can use a simple plastic tongue scraper if you don't have a sensitive gag reflex.

Cut your protein intake: During digestion, the body breaks down proteins with ammonia. The more protein you eat, the more ammonia is used during this process. A high-protein diet may produce too much ammonia. Use these steps and you should notice a difference by the next day"

- Cut down on beef, chicken, fish, pork, and eggs.
- Refrain from protein supplements, protein shakes, and protein bars.
- Balance your diet better by eating more grains and fruits.

Baking soda: Bacteria that cause tooth decay can also make your mouth acidic, which makes it smell. But when the bicarbonate from the baking soda mixes with the bacteria's acid, it reduces both the acid and the odor. Measure a cup of warm water and add 2 teaspoons of baking soda [not to be confused with baking powder]. Swish while you hum the entire "Happy Birthday" song, and then spit. This will stop bad breath until you see your dentist. If you do this regularly, you may also notice a desirable side effect of this remedy: Baking soda whitens teeth!

Herbs: Fresh herbs smell wonderful. So it's no wonder they can help eliminate stinky breath. Ball up a clean sprig and chew on it when your breath starts to smell. Some of the best herbs Dr. Silverman trusts for halitosis are spearmint, peppermint, parsley, basil, thyme, and cilantro. [Thoroughly rinse all fresh herbs before using, just as you would salad ingredients. Your best bet for fresh, whole herbs is to grow your own, though it's still advisable to rinse them before using.]

Spices: Spices also offer naturally pleasant aromatic properties. Spices also trigger the salivary glands to produce more saliva. Not only does this moisten the mouth, but saliva also contains antimicrobial properties that fight bad breath. Better yet, spices may help reduce smelly breath at more than just the surface level.

- The essential oil cinnamic aldehyde helps to get rid of the bacteria that cause halitosis.

- Fennel seeds give off a black licorice taste and scent that'll mask many smells. They also provide antiseptic properties, killing harmful bacteria.

- Cloves will make your breath the perfect mix of spicy and sweet. This spice kills bacteria that can create foul smells when they colonize in the mouth.

De-stress yourself: Stress can actually contribute to dragon breath. People under chronic stress tend to suffer more from gum disease and often eat less, and both of these things lead to halitosis. So de-stress yourself – find creative ways that'll work for you!

- Taking ten minutes to meditate before bed or when you wake up can significantly lower the amount of stress you feel.

- Mindfulness meditation relaxes the body and mind and helps you perceive situations differently so you don't trigger the stress response the way they did before.

- Yoga also helps reduce stress through breathing, meditation, stretching, and movements. Though if yoga isn't your thing, any light exercise [even something as simple as walking] boosts endorphins and lowers cortisol levels in the body.

Also see the trusted remedies in the section on **Stress** later in this directory.

Breathing through your mouth instead of your nose can also be a cause of bad breath, according to Roanoke, VA, dentist **Paul A. Henny, D.D.S.** His solution: taping your mouth shut while you sleep. This remedy is used nightly by the editors of this directory. Dr. Henny advises the following steps to tape your mouth to enhance nose-breathing: [169]

- Purchase some 3M micropore surgical tape, 2" wide, from the drugstore or Amazon. This tape is thin, white, paper-based, and semitransparent. Some prefer 1"-wide tape. Ordinary paper tape from the dollar store may work just as well.

- To facilitate nasal breathing, use nasal irrigation with a mild saline solution made with sterile water to clear your nose. See **"How to use a saline rinse"** in the section on **Allergies** a bit earlier in this directory.

- Tear off 3-4 inches of tape and fold the ends under slightly to create easy "tear-off handles," in case you need to remove the tape to cough, sneeze, burp, or say good-night.

- Put your lips together and puff them out a bit to create a little room for comfortable movement while asleep.

- Gently compress the tape horizontally over your lips and onto the surrounding skin. [170]

"Doctor, Doctor!"

Your dentist can also help you keep fresh breath and a healthy smile, so be sure to keep up with recommended care, says Dr. Silverman. Dentists can also help prevent cancer, heart disease, and of course tooth loss, thus contributing greatly to your overall health.

Barnes-Jewish St. Peters Hospital (**Kenneth Hacker, M.D., Chief of Staff** [171]) says you should call a doctor about your bad breath if you are not satisfied with the results of

---

[169] Dr. Paul Henny, Roanoke, VA, health-centered dentistry, paulhennydds.com
[170] Five Reasons to Consider Taping Your Mouth at Night, dentalsleeppractice.com
[171] Kenneth A. Hacker, M.D., St. Louis, MO, doctors.bjc.org | Bad Breath (Halitosis), bjsph.org

self-care. Dentists diagnose bad breath, based on your health history and mouth odor during the dental exam. The entire mouth is checked to see if a cause can be found, such as an infection.

COST-SAVINGS EXAMPLE:

Scope Mouthwash 33.8 oz is about $10 a bottle. Buy one every three weeks and you'll spend $170 this year on mouthwash. That happens to be nearly the exact price of the 'Cadillac' of electric toothbrushes on Amazon – Philips Sonicare ProtectiveClean 6500 Rechargeable Electric Power Toothbrush with Charging Travel Case and Extra Brush Head, Black, HX6462/08 [$169, 4.7 out of 5 stars, 22,783 reviews.] [172] Choose wisely.

Taking gingivitis (gum disease) alone, treatment costs may be as little as $500, or as much as $10,000, depending on the severity of the disease. [173]

The cost of avoiding gingivitis with regular cleanings is far less than the cost of gum surgery – a few hundred dollars per year at most.

Regular dental visits can help save your teeth, and potentially avoid gum disease treatment costs of up to $10,000.

BEE AND WASP STINGS

According to the *Merck Manual* [174] (**Thomas Arnold, M.D., Emergency Medicine** [175]), a sting usually won't cause more than pain, swelling, and redness right around the sting – what's known as a local reaction. However, a small percentage of people are allergic to insect stings and suffer a much more severe and dangerous reaction, known as a generalized reaction. Stings in these people may cause anaphylaxis and can be fatal.

About 60-70 people in the U.S. die every year as a result of allergic reactions to stings, per estimates from the Centers for Disease Control and Prevention. Tens of thousands more have serious reactions that aren't fatal. Next time you or a child receives a nasty sting, look for signs of a generalized allergic reaction. Anyone who has any of these symptoms should be safely taken to the emergency room immediately; if unsure, call 9-1-1:

- A feeling of uneasiness, tingling sensations, and dizziness
- Generalized itching and hives, swelling of the lips and tongue
- Wheezing and difficulty breathing

[172] Philips Sonicare ProtectiveClean 6500 Rechargeable Electric Power Toothbrush, Amazon.com
[173] W. Peter Nordland, DMD, Nordland Oral Microsurgical Institute, La Jolla, CA, yourdentistryguide.com
[174] Three Steps to Take Immediately After a Bee Sting, merckmanuals.com | Image: Orin zuu, The Noun Project
[175] Thomas Arnold, M.D., Chairman of Emergency Medicine, LSU Health, Shreveport, LA, lsuhs.edu

- Collapse and loss of consciousness – call 9-1-1

If you don't have these symptoms, begin with the trust remedies below. Up to 1 million people go to the emergency department for bee stings every year, yet most of these visits are for local reactions that you can treat at home by the steps below.

People who have had a generalized allergic response in the past will very likely have one again after another sting. However, sometimes people who have never had an allergic reaction to previous stings have a generalized allergic reaction to their next sting. Fortunately, this first reaction is less likely to be one of the fatal ones.

People who know they're allergic should always have access to an epinephrine auto-injector. An auto-injector is a portable device that injects you when you push it against your skin – you don't have to know how to "give a shot." Epinephrine (adrenaline) is a drug that treats allergic reactions and can be lifesaving. Use the auto-injector at the first sign of an allergic reaction.

Note that a more severe local reaction (greater pain or more extreme swelling) is not an indicator of increased risk for a generalized reaction, nor is receiving multiple stings. Use these trusted remedies when the emergency symptoms listed above are not present:

Remove the stinger with a dull-edged object: Bee stings and wasp stings have one major difference. Bees leave a barbed stinger behind and the bee dies. Wasps, on the other hand, have a smooth stinger that can sting multiple times without killing or becoming detached from the insect. Following a bee sting, remove the stinger as quickly as possible. Often, the bee also leaves behind the venom sack, which continues to pump venom as long as it stays intact. So the sooner you can remove it and the stinger, the sooner you can stop the flow of toxins. A blunt object such as a credit card or butter knife gently scraped across the area is the best option. Avoid tweezers or anything that could puncture or squeeze the venom sack and make symptoms worse.

Apply baking soda. Apply a mixture of baking soda and water to reduce the itch. Mix 1 tablespoon of baking soda with just enough water to create a paste. Apply the paste to the bite. After ten minutes, wash off the paste.

Apply a cool compress. Once the stinger is out, a cool compress can help alleviate pain (just don't dunk the whole area in ice). An antihistamine taken orally [Benadryl, or a generic form sold by stores such as Walmart and CVS] or applied as a cream [also made by Benadryl and generically] can help alleviate itching and swelling.

Elevate the area. Depending on the location of the sting, elevating the area can also reduce swelling. The level of swelling caused by a sting can be startling. A sting on the hand can result in the hand swelling up to twice the normal size. This swelling, along with the area feeling warm and tender, can sometimes be confused for infection – also known as cellulitis.

Patients and parents should know it's rare for infection to develop after a sting, especially within the first few days. The swelling caused by a local reaction may decrease within a few hours, but it can take a few days to fully resolve.

The best approach is to avoid being stung in the first place. Here are a few things to keep in mind if you know you or your child will be outside and around bees or wasps.

- Avoid wearing bright colors, scented perfume, and hair spray.
- Remember that bees and wasps are social beings. They only sting to protect their hive. If you don't bother them, they won't bother you.
- Don't panic, just move away. Bees and wasps sting to defend their territory, so get out of it as fast as possible.

COST-SAVINGS EXAMPLE:

Go to an emergency room only if conditions listed above are present – a feeling of uneasiness; tingling sensations; dizziness; generalized itching and hives; swelling of the lips and tongue; wheezing and difficulty breathing, collapse and loss of consciousness. Otherwise, you may incur a large bill for nothing.

If unsure about going to the emergency room, you can call Poison Control for free at 1-800-222-1222 or use the webPOISONCONTROL® online tool at any time for expert guidance if you are stung.

Unnecessary emergency room visits cost at least $47 billion a year. Use the emergency room only for emergencies. [176]

BLACK EYE

The clinical term for a black eye is periorbital hematoma, says All About Vision [177] (**Shane Kannarr, O.D.**, medical editor [178]). Though harder to pronounce, this medical term more accurately describes the condition – it is a collection of blood (hematoma) located in the tissues around, not inside, the eye (periorbital).

A black eye can affect the area under the eye, or it can surround the eye completely. Any blunt force trauma to the eye socket or areas around it can damage small blood vessels under the skin and cause them to leak, leading to a black eye or "shiner." Common causes are sports injuries, walking into something, cosmetic eye surgery, sinus infections, and nasal surgery. Even dental work and tooth infections can cause a black eye.

Another condition often accompanying a black eye is a bright red appearance to the "white" of the eye (sclera). This is called a subconjunctival hemorrhage. Although it looks pretty scary, it usually is not serious and typically resolves without treatment within a couple of weeks.

A black eye will usually disappear within a couple of weeks. During this healing period, it's important to protect the eye from further damage by avoiding any activities that could cause additional injury. You may notice that the color of your black eye will change as the injury heals.

---

[176] Unnecessary ER visits cost $47B a year, Becker's Hospital Review, beckershospitalreview.com
[177] Black eyes: Causes, treatment and prevention, allaboutvision.com | Image: Dan Nemmers, The Noun Project
[178] All About Vision, Shane Kannarr, OD, Pittsburg, Girard and Fort Scott, Kansas, allaboutvision.com

A mild black eye may initially appear red, then darken and get more swollen with time. As a black eye begins to heal, it can turn purple, blue, green, or even yellow.

While there is no magic cure to get rid of a black eye overnight, here are a number of trusted remedies that may help speed up the healing process so your eye can look and feel better faster:

Start with cold: Apply a bag of frozen peas, a chilled spoon, or some other cold object to lower the temperature of the area around the eye as soon as possible after the injury, and frequently thereafter for the first twenty-four hours.

Then switch to warm. After a day or two of applying cold packs, try gently applying warm (not hot) compresses to your black eye. This will increase blood flow to the area to facilitate healing.

Gentle massage: Massage the area surrounding the bruise (not the black eye itself) in the days following the injury. This may help activate the lymphatic system near the bruise and speed the healing process.

Snack on pineapple: This tropical fruit contains a mixture of enzymes that reduce inflammation and speed healing, which may help your black eye go away faster.

Load up on vitamin C. Though vitamin C may do more to reduce how easily you bruise (by strengthening blood vessels, reducing their tendency to leak after blunt trauma), it also may help speed the healing of your black eye.

Try bilberry extract. Bilberry, a relative of the blueberry and cranberry, contains antioxidants that may help reduce or eliminate bruising by strengthening capillaries.

"Doctor, Doctor!"

More serious causes of black eye include cellulitis (an infection) and skull fracture, which tends to result in two shiners, sometimes described as "raccoon eyes." Another serious condition that can accompany a black eye is bleeding inside the eye (between the back side of the cornea and the front of the iris). This is called hyphema (hy-FEE-muh). This is a medical emergency, as it can lead to vision loss from glaucoma if left untreated. Call a doctor immediately or go to the emergency room if you suspect either of these conditions

MedicineNet [179] (**John P. Cunha, D.O.,** medical author, [180] **David Perlstein, M.D., MBA, FAAP**, medical editor [181]) advises calling a doctor about your black eye if:

- You experience changes in vision.
- You have severe pain or swelling that does not go away.
- You have swelling around the eyes that is not related to an injury.
- You have signs of infection (fever, warmth, redness, pus-like drainage).
- You have behavioral changes, forgetfulness, lethargy, nausea, or dizziness.

---

[179] Black eye facts, medicinenet.com
[180] John P. Cunha, D.O., Cross Hospital, Fort Lauderdale, FL, holy-cross.com
[181] David Perlstein, M.D., President and CEO, SBH Health System, Bronx, NY, sbhny.org

COST-SAVINGS EXAMPLE:

A black eye is probably not going to cost you much as long as it's your only injury and you don't need medical attention. However, considering that this is about your vision and your head, seek medical advice if the conditions under "Doctor, Doctor!" are met.

BLISTERS

A blister is a bubble on the skin containing fluid, explains Johns Hopkins Medicine [182] (**Paul B. Rothman, M.D.**, CEO [183]). Blisters are usually circular in shape. The fluid that forms underneath the skin can be bloody or clear. Injury, allergic reactions, or infections can cause blisters. Blisters that are the result of another condition may appear in one area of your body or may be all over your body. Blisters may be painful or itchy. If there is a systemic cause, like an infection, you may also have whole-body symptoms such as fever, pain, or fatigue. Blisters often heal on their own without treatment, says Johns Hopkins. Trusted remedies include:

Wash: Wash the area gently with soap and water, then keep the area clean and dry.

Apply ice: An ice pack wrapped in a clean washcloth may reduce swelling and discomfort.

Do Not: Do not burst or puncture the blister. If the blister bursts, place a bandage or dressing on the area to keep it clean. Watch the area for signs of infection such as warmth, swelling, redness, drainage, pus formation, or pain. If you notice any signs of infection, call your doctor.

"Doctor, Doctor!"

A blister may look like other skin conditions, so Johns Hopkins advises seeing your healthcare provider for a diagnosis if it persists. Foot and Ankle Clinic of the Virginias [184] (**Timothy Donatelli, DPM**, president [185]) says you should call a doctor about your blister if it is infected or shows no signs of healing. Although it may seem that blisters aren't that much trouble, they can lead to much more impacting ailments.

COST-SAVINGS EXAMPLE:

A blister is likely not going to cost you much unless you are a professional musician, baseball pitcher, hand model, or in some other line of work where a blister is going to keep you from working. Avoid future blisters by wearing gloves or taping sensitive areas before engaging in activity that's likely to cause irritation.

---

[182] Blisters, Johns Hopkins Medicine, hopkinsmedicine.org | Image: Alice Design, The Noun Project
[183] Paul Bennett Rothman, M.D. CEO, Johns Hopkins, Baltimore, M.D., hopkinsmedicine.org
[184] When Should You Visit A Foot Doctor For Blisters? Foot and Ankle Clinic of the Virginias, drfootpain.com
[185] Timothy Donatelli, DPM, surgeon specializing in podiatric medicine in Virginia, W. Va., drfootpain.com

BOILS

According to Cleveland Clinic [186] (**Steven M. Gordon, M.D., Chairman, Department of Infectious Disease** [187]), a boil (aka furuncle) is a skin infection most often caused by the bacteria *Staphylococcus aureus*, or staph, though other bacteria or fungi may also be the cause. Unlike ordinary pimples, a boil forms beneath the surface of the skin. A boil may have a pus-filled core, can appear anywhere on the body, and may be painful.

In most boils, says Cleveland Clinic, bacteria also infect hair follicles, which contain hair roots and oil glands. This infection is called folliculitis. A boil can also develop from a cut in the skin.

A carbuncle is a group of boils close together. Carbuncles may have more than one pus-filled cavity. Some people can get boils or carbuncles over and over in one spot of the body. Certain illnesses like diabetes make you more likely to get boils. Another risk factor is having a skin condition such as eczema, or anything that reduces the skin's ability to fight germs.

The bacteria that cause boils can be spread from person to person. On rare occasions, a boil can cause infection of the bloodstream or other body parts or general infection of the body (sepsis). A serious infection with MRSA (methicillin-resistant *Staphylococcus aureus*) can also occur.

A boil may start out as a sore, raised area that is pinkish to red in color. The boil may fill with clear liquid or pus and grow to sizes varying from pea to golf ball. Other symptoms include:

- Swollen, red lump deep in the skin (sometimes a hair will grow from it)
- Painful, especially when touched
- May develop a central, whitish-yellow "head" that may break and release pus
- May "weep" or ooze clear fluid, or develop a crust
- May spread to surrounding skin, creating a carbuncle

HealthLine [188] (medically reviewed by **Debra Rose Wilson, Ph.D.** [189]) offers these trusted remedies to heal a boil:

Apply heat: Heat helps to increase the circulation in an area, bringing more white blood cells and antibodies to the area to fight the infection, so applying heat to a boil is one of the best remedies you can use. Apply a warm compress to the area for 20 minutes at a time. Do this three or four times a day, every day, until the boil is gone.

Tea tree oil: Tea tree essential oil has strong antibacterial and antiseptic properties, which can help treat the bacterial infection causing the boil. Tea tree oil should not be applied directly to the skin, as it can have a burning effect. Mix five drops of tea tree oil with a teaspoon of coconut or olive oil. Put diluted tea tree oil on a cotton swab and apply it to the area two or three times per day. Do this daily until the boil is completely gone.

Turmeric powder: Turmeric powder has both antibacterial and anti-inflammatory properties,

[186] Boils & Carbuncles, clevelandclinic.org | Appointments at Cleveland Clinic
[187] Steven Gordon, M.D., Infectious Disease Specialist, Cleveland Clinic, my.clevelandclinic.org
[188] Home Remedies for Boils, healthline.com | Image: Alina Oleynik, The Noun Project
[189] Debra Rose Wilson, Ph.D., professor, researcher, holistic healthcare practitioner, Walden University

both of which can help heal a boil and get rid of it quickly. It's been used as a natural blood purifier for thousands of years in Eastern medicine for that reason. You can ingest turmeric powder, use it topically to treat boils, or both. To ingest it, boil a teaspoon of turmeric powder in water or milk, and drink it three times daily once cooled. To use it topically, mix turmeric with water and/or ginger to make a paste, and apply it to the boil at least twice a day.

Epsom salt: Epsom salt isn't just relaxing; it has numerous health benefits, including the ability to treat boils. The salt can help dry out the pus, causing the boil to drain. Dissolve Epsom salt in warm water and soak a compress in it. Apply the compress to the area for 20 minutes at a time. Do this at least three times daily until the boil is gone.

Over-the-counter antibiotic ointment: An over-the-counter antibiotic ointment is typically both fast-acting and soothing. Since many people keep a tube of Neosporin in the medicine cabinet, you might not even have to look far to get it. It may also help keep the infection from spreading. Apply at least twice a day until the boil is gone.

Castor oil: Castor oil contains ricinoleic acid, a natural and potent anti-inflammatory. This, combined with its powerful antibacterial properties, makes it a great natural treatment for boils. Apply a small amount of castor oil directly to the boil three times a day until the boil is gone.

Neem oil: Neem oil has antiseptic, antibacterial, and antimicrobial properties that help treat boils fast. Apply the oil three to four times a day. Wash your hands before and after application.

Do Not: A boil or carbuncle should never be squeezed or pricked to release the pus and fluid, says Cleveland Clinic. This can spread the infection to other parts of the skin.

"Doctor, Doctor!"

If left alone, a boil will break and drain on its own over time. See a healthcare provider if the boil persists or comes back, or if it is located on the spine or on your face, says Cleveland Clinic [190]. A doctor may need to cut into the skin to drain the pus. Once the fluid and pus drain from the boil or carbuncle, it will heal. The doctor may also prescribe antibiotics if there is a serious infection. If you have a fever or other serious symptoms with the boil, see your doctor. Patients who have diabetes or who have a condition that affects the immune system should see a doctor for the treatment of the boil.

COST-SAVINGS EXAMPLE:

In most cases, a common boil is likely not going to cost you much beyond some discomfort. You may be able to save the cost of a doctor's visit if these home remedies work for you. But pay attention to the "Doctor, Doctor!" tips above for more difficult cases, and don't put off getting professional treatment if needed.

---

[190] Can I treat a boil at home? Clevelandclinic.com | Appointments at Cleveland Clinic

BRONCHITIS

 Bronchitis is a contagious viral infection that causes inflammation and swelling of the bronchial tubes, the airways that carry air into your lungs, says the American Academy of Family Physicians (AAFP) [191] (**Ada D. Stewart, M.D., President** [192]). Mucus forms, narrowing the airways and making it harder to breathe.

An acute case typically resolves in a few days, though the cough can last for several weeks while the bronchial tubes heal. Chronic bronchitis is long-lasting and can reoccur. It is usually caused by constant irritation, such as from smoking, or may signal another issue, such as asthma or pneumonia.

Symptoms of bronchitis include chest congestion or tightness, cough that brings up clear, yellow, or green mucus, shortness of breath or wheezing, sore throat, fever, chills, and body aches.

The same viruses that cause colds can cause acute bronchitis by migrating from your nose, sinuses, and throat into the bronchial tubes, says the academy. You are at higher risk of catching the virus if you have had close contact with someone who has a cold or acute bronchitis. You can help prevent acute bronchitis by staying healthy and avoiding germs. Wash your hands with soap often to kill any contagious viruses.

If you smoke, the best defense against acute bronchitis is to quit (look under **Tobacco** in Part I of this directory, **Doctor-Trusted Remedies for the Top 10 Most Common Health Issues**).

Smoking damages your bronchial tubes, puts you at risk for infection, and slows healing.

Since most cases of acute bronchitis are caused by a virus, antibiotics usually won't help. The infection needs to run its course and almost always goes away on its own. Several trusted remedies can help ease the symptoms:

Drink fluids: Throughout this directory, you'll find the advice, "the solution to pollution is dilution." To get rid of sticky secretions, you need to thin them out by drinking plenty of weather. But avoid caffeine and alcohol while your body is fighting off an infection.

Get lots of rest. Your body is fighting an infection while simultaneously experiencing weakness in key organs, your lungs. Take a break from normal activities until recovery is well underway.

Use a humidifier: Increase the humidity in your home or use a humidifier. This is another way to get moisture into your lungs and bronchial passages to thin out mucus.

OTC pain relief: Take over-the-counter pain relievers to reduce inflammation, pain, and fever. These could include acetaminophen (such as Tylenol) or ibuprofen (Advil).

OTC cough medicine: Some over-the-counter cough medicines can help break up or loosen mucus. Look for the word "guaifenesin" on the label, or ask your pharmacist for a suggestion.

---

[191] Acute Bronchitis, familydoctor.org | Image: Ian Rahmadi Kurniawan, The Noun Project
[192] Ada D. Stewart, M.D., Columbia, SC, Board Chair, American Academy of Family Physicians, aafp.org

Do Not: Never give aspirin to a child. It has been linked to Reye syndrome, which can harm the liver and brain, says the academy.

Do Not: Do not hold in a cough that brings up mucus. This type of cough helps clear mucus from your bronchial tubes. If you smoke, quit. It will help your bronchial tubes heal faster.

"Doctor, Doctor!"

Some people who have acute bronchitis need inhaled medicine. You might need this if you are wheezing. It can help open your bronchial tubes and clear out mucus. You usually take it with an inhaler. Your doctor will decide if this treatment is right for you. If your doctor thinks bacteria have caused your bronchitis, he or she may give you antibiotics.

According to CareNow Urgent Care, a division of Medical City Healthcare [193] (**Joseph Parra, M.D., Chief Medical Officer** [194]), call a doctor about your bronchitis if you have any of these symptoms: cough with bloody mucus, trouble breathing, fever higher than 100° F, inability to sleep, or prolonged cough. Also, young children, the elderly, people who have asthma, people who have other health issues (such as cancer or diabetes), and people who haven't gotten vaccines for flu, pneumonia, or whooping cough.

COST-SAVINGS EXAMPLE:

Chronic bronchitis is a serious and costly condition. Acute worsening of the clinical symptoms of the disease has a major effect on healthcare costs. [195]

Some popular combination drugs, which combine a bronchodilator with a corticosteroid, typically cost between $300 and $400 per prescription.

For these reasons, you do not want acute bronchitis progressing to chronic bronchitis. Mind the *"Doctor, Doctor!"* signs above, and don't put off needed treatment.

BURNS

Burns range from minor annoyances that heal quickly to life-altering, life-threatening emergencies. The American Academy of Dermatology Association (AADA)[196] (**Joseph Parra, M.D., Chief Medical Officer** [197]), with more than 20,000 physician members worldwide, says that first-degree burns are common and frequently occur after one accidentally touches a hot stove,

---

[193] Bronchitis, CareNow Urgent Care, carenow.com
[194] Joseph Parra, M.D., Chief Medical Officer, Medical City Healthcare, medicalcityhealthcare.com
[195] Healthcare Costs Generated By Patients With Chronic Bronchitis, Environmental Litigation Group P.C., Birmingham, AL and Washington, DC, elglaw.com
[196] How To Treat A First-Degree, Minor Burn, aad.org | Image: kiddo, The Noun Project
[197] Joseph Parra, M.D., Hospitalist, Medical City Healthcare, Dallas, TX, medicalcityhealthcare.com

curling iron, or hair straightener. Sunburn can also be a first-degree burn.

Although first-degree burns involve only the top layer of the skin, they can still leave a scar if not properly treated. If you have a first-degree burn, your skin may be red and painful, and you may experience mild swelling. First-degree burns usually heal on their own without treatment from a doctor. To treat a first-degree burn, dermatologists trust these remedies:

Cool the burn immediately: Immerse the burn in cool tap water or apply cold, wet compresses. Do this for about ten minutes, or until the pain subsides.

Petroleum jelly: Apply petroleum jelly two to three times daily. Do not apply ointments, toothpaste, or butter to the burn; as mentioned elsewhere, folklore remedies like these can make matters worse, possibly leading to an infection.

Bandage: Cover the burn with a nonstick, sterile bandage. If blisters form, let them heal on their own while keeping the area covered. Do not pop the blisters.

OTC pain relief: Consider taking over-the-counter pain medication. Acetaminophen or ibuprofen can help relieve the pain and reduce inflammation.

Do Not: Do not apply topical antibiotics such as bacitracin or Neosporin.

Once the burn heals, protect the area from the sun by seeking shade, wearing protective clothing, or applying a broad-spectrum, water-resistant sunscreen of SPF 30 or higher, says AADA.

"Doctor, Doctor!"

AADA says to call 9-1-1 or take the victim to an emergency room if a burn is very large, the victim is an infant or elderly person, or you think the burn is more severe (second- or third-degree). Second- or third-degree burns affect multiple skin layers and even the tissue beneath. They require immediate medical attention; when in doubt, call a doctor.

COST-SAVINGS EXAMPLE:

These trusted remedies are inexpensive, but get medical care for anything except minor first-degree burns to reduce chances of scarring or permanent tissue damage.

BURSITIS

Bursitis is a painful swelling of a small sac of fluid called a bursa, says Stanford Healthcare (**Niraj Sehgal, M.D., M.P.H.,** chief medical officer).[198] Bursae (plural of bursa) cushion and lubricate areas where tendons, ligaments, skin, muscles, or bones meet. Repeating the same movement over and over or putting continued pressure on a joint in your job, sports, or daily activities leads to a greater chance of getting bursitis. These trusted remedies can often reduce pain and let the bursa heal.

---

[198] Niraj Sehgal, M.D., Stanford Health Care, stanfordhealthcare.org | Image: Brand Mania, The Noun Project

Rest the affected area: Avoid any activity or direct pressure that may cause pain.

Apply ice or cold packs: Cool the area as soon as you notice pain in your muscles or near a joint. Apply ice 10 to 15 minutes at a time, as often as twice an hour, for 3 days (72 hours). Cover the ice pack with a clean cloth to avoid direct skin contact. You can try heat, or alternating heat and ice, after the first 72 hours.

OTCs: Use over-the-counter non-steroidal anti-inflammatory pain relievers (NSAIDs), such as ibuprofen or naproxen, to reduce pain and inflammation. NSAIDs come in pills and also in a cream that you rub over the sore area. Acetaminophen (such as Tylenol) can also help with pain.

Range-of-motion exercises: Do range-of-motion exercises daily. If your bursitis is in or near a joint, gently move the joint through its full range of motion, even during the time that you are resting the joint area. This will prevent stiffness. As the pain goes away, add other exercises to strengthen the muscles around your joint. You can find doctor-approved resources online, such as *Shoulder Range Of Motion Exercises,* Johns Hopkins Division of Shoulder Surgery [199].

Do Not: Don't rely on medicine to relieve pain so that you can keep overusing the joint.

"Doctor, Doctor!"

Intermountain Healthcare (**J.P. Valin, M.D., Chief Clinical Officer** [200]) advises calling a doctor about your bursitis if your joint pain is sharp, keeps you from daily activities, worsens with time, or doesn't get better with self-care remedies. Your doctor may suggest physical therapy to strengthen the muscles around your joints. [201]

COST-SAVINGS EXAMPLE:

To you: insurance deductibles and out-of-pocket costs, plus the costs of reduced quality of life, lost productivity due to time away from work, and potential disability.

To employers: direct costs of $10,000-$20,000 per case plus the costs of lost productivity, absenteeism, and turnover.

To the U.S. economy: direct care costs over $20 billion every year, plus the costs of lost productivity and disability. [202]

In medical costs and lost wages and productivity, bursitis is a multi-billion dollar problem. Minimize your costs by faithfully using these trusted remedies; however, the cost of medical care may be well worth it to protect your income and maintain your mobility.

---

[199] Shoulder Range Of Motion Exercises (pdf), Johns Hopkins Division of Shoulder Surgery
[200] JP Valin, M.D., Intermountain Healthcare
[201] Bursitis, intermountainhealthcare.org
[202] Bursitis: Symptoms, Causes, and Treatment, biofunctionalhealth.com

C

CALLUSES AND CORNS

 To treat corns and calluses, members of the American Academy of Dermatology Association [203] (**Mark D. Kaufmann, M.D., President** [204]) trust these remedies:

Warm water soak: Soak the corn or callus in warm water for 5-10 minutes, or until the skin softens.

Pumice stone: File the corn or callus with a pumice stone. Dip the stone in warm water, then gently file the area. Use circular or sideways motions to remove dead skin. Be careful not to take off too much skin, which could cause bleeding and infection.

Moisturize: Apply moisturizing lotion or cream to the area daily. Look for a moisturizing lotion or cream with salicylic acid, ammonium lactate, or urea. These ingredients will help gradually soften hard corns and calluses.

Moleskin: To guard against further irritation, cut a piece of moleskin into two half-moon shapes and place around the callus. Moleskin is a densely woven cotton fabric with a brushed surface that looks like suede or the fur of a mole (but is not made with animal skin!)

Protective pads: To prevent a corn from making contact with your shoe, surround with donut-shaped adhesive pads. These products are available online and at drugstores.

Better fitting shoes: A common cause of corns is a shoe that isn't the right size and shape for your foot. To get the right fit, shop for shoes at the end of the day, when your feet may be slightly swollen. Ask a clerk to measure your foot, and choose shoes that aren't too loose or tight.

Trim your toenails. Long nails can force the toes to push up against your shoe, causing a corn to form over time. To remove this pressure, keep your toenails trimmed.

"Doctor, Doctor!"

Most corns and calluses gradually go away when the friction or pressure causing them stops. However, if you're unsure what's causing your corn or callus, if the area is painful, and especially if you have diabetes, see a dermatologist. It's also a good topic to raise at your annual physical or at your next skin check with your dermatologist.

---

[203] How to treat corns and calluses, American Academy of Dermatology Association, aad.org
[204] Mark Kaufmann, M.D., Mount Sinai, New York, mountsinai.org | Image: ProSymbols, The Noun Project

COST-SAVINGS EXAMPLE:

The best overall corn, callus, and wart remover is Curad Mediplast, $30 at Amazon, per a review by Verywellhealth [205] (medically reviewed by Leah Ansell, M.D. [206]) At $5, Amazon's best budget option is Dr. Sholl's Salicylic Acid Callus Remover Cushion.

If a home remedy resolves your problem (probably because you took action sooner rather than later), you'll save the cost of a podiatrist, typically $195 for your first visit and $110 for subsequent visits, or $305 total for two visits.

Successful treatment with Curad Mediplast saves you $275 compared with the cost of a visit and a follow-up with a podiatrist.

CANCER

Home remedies – *for cancer?* Yes, many DIY health treatments are completely appropriate and very helpful for people with cancer. Of course, this does not mean that home remedies will *cure* cancer, or that they *replace* necessary medical care which may include surgery or chemotherapy. In fact, if you see a home remedy claiming to "cure" cancer, that should set off red flags; as mentioned nearby, *"Folklore remedies only put you at greater risk for dangerous diseases,"* per Good Housekeeping. [207]

Always consult a doctor if a cancer screening comes back positive. Do not stop any treatment without consulting your doctor. Discuss all alternative treatments and self-care remedies with your doctor to assure they are appropriate for your personal treatment case. That said, what self-care remedies do doctors recommend for cancer patients? Mayo Clinic trusts several remedies that are generally safe [208] (**Edward T. Creagan, M.D., Oncologist** [209]):

Acupuncture: Acupuncture may be helpful in relieving nausea caused by chemotherapy. It may also help relieve certain types of pain in people with cancer. Ask your doctor for names of trusted practitioners. Acupuncture isn't safe if you're taking blood thinners or if you have low blood counts, so check with your provider first. A related technique is acupressure, in which mild pressure is applied to certain areas, such as the wrist, to help relieve nausea.

Aromatherapy: Aromatherapy oils provide a calming sensation that may help relieve nausea, pain, and stress, says Mayo. Oils infused with scents such as lavender can be applied to your skin during a massage or added to bath water. Fragrant oils can also be gently heated to release their scents into the air. Aromatherapy is safe, though oils applied to your skin can cause allergic reactions. People with cancer that is estrogen sensitive, such as some breast cancers, should

[205] The 7 Best Callus Removers of 2022, verywellhealth.com
[206] Leah Ansell, M.D., Treiber Dermatology Associates, Rye, NY, treiberderm.com
[207] GoodHousekeeping.com | Image: Shrikantha Urala C K
[208] Alternative Cancer Treatments: 11 Options To Consider, Mayo Clinic
[209] Edward T. Creagan, M.D., Mayo Clinic | Appointments at Mayo Clinic

avoid applying large amounts of lavender oil and tea tree oil to the skin. Amazon offers a wide selection of aromatherapy products. Trusted Remedies Publishing, the publisher of this directory, cautions against purchasing any health-related products shipped from outside the United States; foreign shippers may evade U.S. health and safety requirements and know you have little recourse if problems arise.

Cognitive behavioral therapy: Cognitive behavioral therapy (CBT) is a common type of talk therapy. During a CBT session, a mental health counselor works with you to view challenging situations more clearly and respond in a more effective way, Mayo explains. For people with cancer, CBT may help with sleep problems. The counselor might help you identify and replace thoughts and behaviors that cause or worsen sleep problems with habits that promote sound sleep. Ask your doctor for a referral to a specialist if you're interested in trying CBT.

Exercise: Many studies show that an exercise program may help people with cancer live longer and improve their overall quality of life. Exercise may help you manage symptoms during and after treatment. Gentle exercise may help relieve fatigue and stress and help you sleep better. Check with your provider before beginning an exercise program. Start slowly, adding more exercise as you go. Aim to work your way up to 30 minutes of exercise most days of the week.

Hypnosis: Hypnosis is simply a deep state of concentration. During a hypnotherapy session, a therapist may hypnotize you by talking in a gentle voice and helping you relax. The therapist will then help you focus on goals, such as controlling your pain and reducing your stress. Hypnosis may be helpful for patients who are experiencing anxiety, pain, and stress. When performed by a certified therapist, hypnosis is safe. But tell your therapist if you have a history of mental illness.

Massage: Massage is so effective in treating the symptoms of cancer patients that many cancer centers have massage therapists on staff. During a massage, your practitioner kneads your skin, muscles, and tendons in an effort to relieve muscle tension and stress and promote relaxation. Massage can be light and gentle, or it can be deep with more pressure. Mayo reports that massage can be helpful in relieving pain in people with cancer. It may also help relieve anxiety, fatigue, and stress. Ask your provider to refer a massage therapist who regularly works with people who have cancer. Don't have a massage if your blood counts are very low. Ask the therapist to avoid surgical scars, radiation treatment areas, and tumors. If you have cancer in your bones or other bone diseases, ask the therapist to use light pressure, rather than deep massage.

Meditation: Meditation helps people with cancer by relieving anxiety and stress and improving mood, says Mayo. Meditation is a state of deep concentration when you focus your mind on one image, sound, or idea, such as a positive thought. When meditating, you might also do deep breathing or relaxation exercises. You can meditate on your own for a few minutes once or twice a day or you can take a class with an instructor. Online courses and apps are also available.

Music therapy: Music therapy is another Mayo-trusted remedy that produces real results – relieving pain, controlling nausea and vomiting, and dealing with anxiety and stress. That's why many medical centers have certified music therapists on staff. In music therapy sessions, you listen to music, play instruments, sing songs, or write lyrics. A therapist may lead you through activities designed to meet your specific needs, or you may participate in a group setting.

Relaxation: Relaxation techniques may be helpful in relieving anxiety and fatigue. Techniques focus your attention on calming your mind and relaxing your muscles. Techniques include visualization exercises and progressive muscle relaxation. They may also help people with cancer sleep better. Relaxation techniques are safe. Typically, a therapist leads you through these exercises and eventually, you may be able to do them on your own or with the help of guided relaxation recordings. All see the trusted remedies in the section on **Stress** later in this directory.

Tai chi: This form of exercise combines gentle movements and deep breathing to relieve stress. Tai chi can be led by an instructor, or learn on your own using books or videos. The slow movements of tai chi don't require great physical strength, and they can be easily adapted to your abilities. Still, talk to your doctor before beginning, and don't do any moves that cause pain.

Yoga: Yoga provides stress relief for people with cancer while improving sleep and reducing fatigue. Ask your doctor to recommend an instructor who works with people with health concerns. Avoid poses that cause pain; a good instructor can give you safe alternatives.

Many people try supplements to prevent or treat cancer. Mayo's affiliate, ThedaCare (**Matthias Weiss M.D., Medical Director, Cancer Center** [210]), says that supplements should be chosen based on individual need and cancer type. Ask your doctor to help guide your choices. [211]

Turmeric: A supplement that has the backing of one of America's foremost cancer treatment centers is turmeric. Turmeric reduces inflammation, which is at the root of many diseases, including cancer, according to Memorial Sloan Kettering Cancer Center. You can go ahead and add turmeric to your favorite foods, says MSK pharmacist **Dr. Jason Hou** [212] . But before you stock up on turmeric capsules or vitamins, he advises talking to your healthcare provider. [213]

Do Not: Some supplements can do more harm than good, so base your decision on expert clinical advice. For example, antioxidant supplements reduce the efficacy of radiation therapy and some chemotherapy drugs, and fish oil may reduce how well platinum-based chemotherapy works. The same goes for using supplements for prevention. Supplemental beta-carotene, for example, may actually increase the risk of developing lung cancer in smokers. Talk to your provider before you add any supplements to your diet. [214]

"Doctor, Doctor!"

Cancer screening saves lives and should be a regular part of your life, says the American Cancer Society [215] (**William L. Dahut, M.D.**, Chief Scientific Officer [216]). Screening tests are used before a person has symptoms to help find cancer early, when it may be easier to treat. Follow American Cancer Society screening recommendations based on your age. See the footnote below, "Cancer Screening Recommendations."

---

[210] Matthias Weiss, MD, Oncology Physician Leader, ThedaCare, thedacare.org
[211] Myth vs. Reality: Natural Cancer Cures, ThedaCare, thedacare.org
[212] Yen-Nien (Jason) Hou, Herb Information Center Coordinator, MSK Cancer Center, New York, NY
[213] What Are the Benefits of Turmeric? Memorial Sloan Kettering Cancer Center, mskcc.org
[214] Cancer & Blood Disorder Treatments, ThedaCare, thedacare.org
[215] Cancer Screening Recommendations, American Cancer Society, www.cancer.org
[216] William Dahut, M.D., American Cancer Society

COST-SAVINGS EXAMPLE:

In 2018, U.S. patients paid $5.6 billion out-of-pocket for cancer care. The remedies above are inexpensive next to that. It's impossible to say whether these remedies will save you money; most are intended to be used in addition to medical treatment, not in place of it. But if they are part of an overall strategy to improve your life and maybe save it, they are worth your time and attention. [217]

Give your cancer treatment the best chance of success by adding these trusted remedies to your treatment plan.

CANKER SORES

 Canker sores are tiny, painful ulcers that spring up in the mouth, says **Dr. William H. Stiles** of Stiles Dental Care, Medford, NJ. [218] Canker sores can form on the tongue, the inner lining of the cheeks, inner lip, gums, or back of the mouth, on the soft palate at the roof of the mouth. Remedies Dr. Stiles suggests to try at home for treatment and relief of canker sores include:

B-Complex vitamins: If you know your diet is low in B vitamins, consider taking a B-complex supplement. B-12, as well as other B vitamins, have been shown to help the healing process and even lessen pain associated with canker sores.

Baking Soda Rinse: Combine ½ cup of water with 1 teaspoon of baking soda. Let it dissolve, then swish it in your mouth for up to 30 seconds before spitting it out. Repeat every few hours.

Coconut oil: With its antimicrobial and anti-inflammatory properties, coconut oil can reduce pain and redness and prevent spreading. Apply generous amounts of the oil onto the canker sore. Reapply as needed throughout the day.

Echinacea: With its immune-boosting and wound-healing abilities, Echinacea is ideal for treating canker sores. Combine a teaspoon each of warm water and liquid Echinacea. Swish inside your mouth for at least two minutes. Swallow or spit out.

Honey: Honey is nature's elixir. Apply unpasteurized, unfiltered honey directly on the canker sore up to four times per day for relief and increased healing.

Hydrogen peroxide and water rinse: To reduce mouth bacteria and thoroughly clean your canker sore, combine equal parts hydrogen peroxide (3 percent solution) and water. Use a cotton swab to apply rinse to the canker sore up to two times a day. You can also rinse your mouth out daily with diluted hydrogen peroxide.

---

[217] Cancer Costs and Options for Care in the U.S., Assn. for Accessible Medicines, accessiblemeds.org
[218] Dr. William H. Stiles, Stiles Dental Care, Medford, NJ, medfordsmiles.com | Image: Llisole, The Noun Project

Saltwater rinse: Although salt may aggravate the pain, a saltwater rinse can help speed up the healing process by drying out the sores. Combine ½ cup of warm water with a teaspoon of salt. Let the salt dissolve completely. Swish around inside your mouth for up to 30 seconds, then spit out. Repeat as needed every few hours.

Yogurt: Eat one cup or more of yogurt per day. Canker sores are potentially caused by bacteria or a condition in the gut, and the probiotic cultures in yogurt may help.

Zinc lozenges: Zinc is known to boost the immune system and fight off bacteria, including that which causes canker sores. Pop a zinc lozenge in your mouth and let it slowly dissolve.

Along with these remedies, avoid acidic foods, brush your teeth with soft bristles, and avoid toothpaste containing sodium lauryl sulfate, which means all versions of Crest toothpaste. [219]

"Doctor, Doctor!"

If any of these accompany a canker sore, see your dentist right away, says Dr. Stiles:

- Sore remains for three weeks or longer
- Pain continues although you've taken pain medication
- Canker sore grows larger or spreads to other areas
- You experience difficulty drinking fluids or eating.
- A fever develops

COST-SAVINGS EXAMPLE:

A basic dental exam will cost you $50-$200. Regular dentist visits should actually save you money because the costs of tooth decay, gum disease, and delayed treatment for them can be substantial. However, if one of the self-care remedies given here saves you an extra trip to the dentist, that's up to $200 saved.

CARPAL TUNNEL SYNDROME

Carpal tunnel syndrome (CTS) is a painful condition that is caused when inflammation puts pressure on the median nerve, explains **Michael Cunningham, M.D.** [220] of Hackensack Meridian Health in Edison, N.J. [221]

Located on the same side of your hand as your palm, the median nerve delivers sensation to the fingers as well as impulses to the muscle leading to the thumb. When the wrist swells from overuse, it can compress the nerve.

In addition to pain, it can cause tingling, weakness, or numbness near the thumb. The condition

---

[219] What to Know About Canker Sores and 14 Ways to Treat Them, Stiles Dental Care, Medford, NJ
[220] Michael J. Cunningham, M.D., Orthopedic Surgery, hackensackmeridianhealth.org
[221] 8 Ways to Get Carpal Tunnel Relief, Hackensack Meridian Health | Image: nauraicon, The NounProject

may be caused by repetitive tasks or an underlying medical condition. For these reasons, it is important to see a doctor. Permanent relief for severe pain usually requires surgery, but until you reach that point, these remedies may help:

Wear a splint: A splint can hold your wrist in a way that relieves pressure on the median nerve. Sleeping in the splint is a good way to hold the wrist in a proper position for a substantial amount of time, and it means you do not have to wear the splint during the day.

Add warmth: Fingerless gloves or warm water can be another way to relieve carpal tunnel pain, as light warmth can help during regular activities.

Ice it: Putting your hand in an ice bath or applying an ice pack to the area of pain can offer temporary relief, as it can lower inflammation.

Give your wrists a workout: While you should minimize flexion to reduce carpal tunnel pain, moving the hand and wrist can help. One carpal tunnel exercise that works is to make a fist and then slide your fingers until they are open. When you repeat the movement five to 10 times, it can alleviate pressure on your wrist.

Raise the wrist: CTS that is caused by a fracture, pregnancy or other issues related to fluid retention can be alleviated by raising hands. You may be able to elevate your hands and wrists more comfortably at home.

"Doctor, Doctor!"

Severe cases of carpal tunnel, or those that are less responsive to the aforementioned treatments, may be best off treated by surgery. Surgery involves cutting the ligament pressing on the median nerve. If you're experiencing significant carpal tunnel syndrome, it might be time to see an orthopedic surgeon.

COST-SAVINGS EXAMPLE:

The typical cost for carpal tunnel surgery in 2020 was $6,928 per hand without insurance. With insurance, the co-payment (including aftercare, therapy, and rehab) was about $1,000 – a small investment in restoring the use of your hand. Still, if the remedies given here help you avoid or delay the need for surgery, you'll save.

Avoid carpal tunnel surgery costs of about $7,000 per hand by trying trusted remedies to protect your wrists and reduce pain.

Remember that throughout this directory you can find further information by using the sources at the bottom of every page and in the resources listing beginning on page 259.

CAT BITES

Verywellhealth.com offers useful guidance on how to treat cat bites and scratches (reviewed by **Michael Menna, D.O.**). Follow these steps: [222]

Stay safe and act fast: Secure the cat, the patient, or both. Move one away from the other. Cats may bite or scratch if frightened or if their kittens are threatened, so leave them alone. Start treatment as soon as you're confident the cat won't attack again. If you are not the patient, practice universal precautions and wear personal protective equipment if available.

Pressure and elevation: Control any bleeding by using direct pressure and elevation. Avoid using a tourniquet unless there is severe bleeding that cannot be controlled any other way. That's unlikely with a cat (unless the cat is a mountain lion). If direct pressure cannot be maintained for an extended period of time, it can be achieved using a pressure dressing.

Wash: Once the bleeding is controlled, clean the wound with soap and warm water. Clean inside the wound, being sure to rinse away all the soap so it won't cause irritation later. Any regular soap will do. There's no reason to use any antibacterial or antiseptic soap.

Bandage: Cover the wound with a clean, dry dressing. If available, put an antibiotic ointment on the bite before covering it, but that is not necessary.

Medline Plus, a service of the U.S. National Library of Medicine (**Dr. Patricia Flatley Brennan, RN, Ph.D., Director** [223]), advises that cat scratch disease (CSD) is an illness caused by the bacterium *Bartonella henselae*. [224] Almost half of all cats carry the infection at some point. The infection does not make cats sick. However, the scratch or bite can cause symptoms in people, including swollen lymph nodes, fever, headache, fatigue, and poor appetite. For people with weak immune systems, CSD may cause more serious problems.

The best way to avoid CSD is to avoid rough play with cats that could lead to scratches or bites. If you do get a scratch or bite, start by washing the area well with soap and water, says Medical News Today [225] (medically reviewed by **Dr. Debra Sullivan, Ph.D., MSN, R.N.** [226])

"Doctor, Doctor!"

Regardless of how severe you think the bite is, always consult a physician right away, says Dr. Sullivan. Since they are often deep, cat bites and scratches are of particular concern for infection. The wound may need stitches. A doctor should evaluate injuries on the face or hands because of the likelihood of scarring and potential loss of function.

Also see a doctor if a cat scratch or bite is not healing, if a red area around the injury continues to get bigger, or for a fever. Watch for signs of infection – redness, swelling, heat, oozing pus. Any unidentified cat runs the risk of carrying rabies. If the cat cannot be

---

[222] Michael Menna, DO, White Plains Hospital, White Plains, New York , verywellhealth.com

[223] Dr. Patricia Flatley Brennan, RN, PhD, Director, MedlinePlus | Image: Denis Sazhin, The Noun Project

[224] Cat Scratch Disease: MedlinePlus, medlineplus.gov

[225] Cat Bite: Safety, First Aid, And Seeking Help, Medical News Today, medicalnewstoday.com

[226] Debra Sullivan, Ph.D., MSN, R.N., Walden University College of Nursing, medicalnewstoday.com

identified or the owner cannot show proof of rabies vaccination, the patient must seek medical attention. Rabies is always fatal to humans if not treated.

COST-SAVINGS EXAMPLE:

This is _not_ a condition that warrants an attempt to avoid the cost of medical care. Even if the bite doesn't look that deep, cat bites have a high risk of infection.

Because cat teeth are sharper than dog teeth, they can penetrate very deeply, which can seed bacteria under your skin. In rare cases, these infections can be fatal. Once you've performed first aid, _visit your doctor or an urgent care center quickly_. [227]

CHAPPED LIPS

 Cold, dry weather, sun damage, and licking your lips are some reasons your lips may be dry and chapped, says the American Academy of Dermatology Association [228] (**Joseph Parra, M.D., Chief Medical Officer** [229]). To prevent and treat chapped lips at home, follow these tips from board-certified dermatologists. You should see improvement in 2-3 weeks, and often a lot less.

Lip balm: Use non-irritating lip balm, lipstick, and other products that you apply to your lips. Many people mistake discomfort, such as burning, stinging, or tingling, as a sign that the active ingredients in a product are working. That's not what's happening. You're actually irritating your lips, so you want to stop using any product that irritates your lips. Apply a non-irritating lip balm (or lip moisturizer) several times a day and before bed. If your lips are very dry and cracked, try a thick ointment, such as white petroleum jelly.

Sunscreen: Slather on a non-irritating lip balm with SPF 30 or higher before going outdoors. Even in the winter, it's important to protect your lips from the sun. The sun can burn dry, chapped lips more easily, which could trigger cold sores.

Water: Drink plenty of water. Chapped lips are dry lips, so you want to stay hydrated.

Humidify: Plug in a humidifier at home. A humidifier in your bedroom can be especially helpful, especially if you breathe through your mouth at night.

Do Not: Do not lick, bite, or pick at your lips. Moistening your lips with saliva worsens the problem. As saliva evaporates, your lips become drier. Avoid touching metal to your lips. Paperclips, jewelry, and other metallic objects can irritate your already sensitive lips.

---

[227] How Serious Are Cat Bites? AFC Urgent Care, afcurgentcarefarraguttn.com
[228] How To Prevent And Treat Dry, Chapped Lips, Tips From Board-Certified Dermatologists, AAD Assn.
[229] Joseph Parra, M.D., Hospitalist, Medical City Healthcare, Dallas, TX, medicalcityhealthcare.com |
Image: Llisole from NounProject.com

"Doctor, Doctor!"

These self-care tips usually heal dry, chapped lips in 2 to 3 weeks. If not, see a board-certified dermatologist. Your chapped lips could be caused by an allergic reaction, yeast infection, or something more serious like actinic cheilitis, a precancerous condition.

Signs and symptoms of lip cancer include: a flat or slightly raised whitish discoloration of the lip; a sore on your lip that won't heal; tingling, pain, or numbness of the lips or the skin around the mouth. Make an appointment with your doctor if you have any of these or other persistent signs or symptoms that worry you.

COST-SAVINGS EXAMPLE:

Many of these trusted remedies are inexpensive – as low as $5 or less. Chapped lips are not typically a cause for medical care except in the cases mentioned above. However, an annual skin check by a dermatologist is wise as it can detect skin cancer in its earliest and most treatable stages.

CHEST PAIN

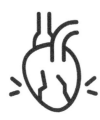

Chest pain takes many forms and has many causes. One of the most common is angina, a condition marked by severe pain in the chest, often spreading to the shoulders, arms, and neck, caused by an inadequate blood supply to the heart. According to medical experts at verywellhealth.com [230] (medically reviewed by **Richard N. Fogoros, M.D.** [231]), angina is often a symptom of coronary heart disease or other heart condition. Physicians stand behind these trusted remedies:

Hawthorn: Often used by herbalists for high blood pressure, hawthorn has been found in some studies to aid cardiac function in people with heart disease. Many types of hawthorn supplements are available on Amazon. The highest rated options cost about $20-25 for a month's supply.

L-carnitine: Derived from the amino acid lysine, L-carnitine occurs naturally in the body and is also sold as a dietary supplement. L-carnitine may help decrease the swelling that causes arteries to narrow. A 50-day supply of Amazon's highest rated supplement goes for about $17.

Yoga: In a study of people with angina or risk factors for coronary artery disease, researchers found that a 14-week yoga program helped improve heart health. Other relaxation techniques such as meditation and tai chi may help manage angina by lowering your stress.

St. Luke's Heart & Vascular Institute of St. Louis [232] (**Ronald Leidenfrost, M.D.**, chairman [233]) advises preventing angina by modifying as many risk factors for heart disease as possible. These

---

[230] Natural Treatment of Angina, verywellhealth.com | Image: Vectors Point, The Noun Project
[231] Richard N. Fogoros, M.D., Cardiologist (Retired), Consultant, verywellhealth.com
[232] Complementary and Alternative Medicine, stlukes-stl.com
[233] Ronald Leidenfrost, M.D., Chairman, Heart and Vascular Institute, stlukes-stl.com

include the following, many of which are covered in Part I of this directory, **Doctor-Trusted Remedies for the Top 10 Most Common Health Issues**.

Stop smoking: The health benefits of quitting begin immediately. Quitting is hard, but many have done it. See the section on **Tobacco** in Part I of this directory.

Maintain a proper weight: Excess weight puts a strain on your heart. That angina pain could literally be a wake-up call to finally shed some excess pounds. See Part I for trusted remedies.

Control blood pressure, diabetes, and cholesterol: Each of these issues has a profound impact on your overall health, and on your heart health. Part I offers many trusted remedies.

Eat a diet low in saturated fats and high in whole grains, fiber, fruits, and veggies: See Physical Activity and Nutrition in Part I for trusted remedies from more than a dozen physicians.

Exercise at least 30 minutes a day, five days a week: You've heard this a thousand times. The reason is that it works. Turn your exercise into fun by choosing a favorite activity – swimming, cycling, walking, and golf without a cart all qualify. Get started with trusted remedies in Part I under **Physical Activity and Nutrition**.

Reduce stress: It happens in real life just as it does in the movies – people experience sudden, extreme stress and drop dead of a heart attack. But it's not just sudden and extreme stress that's bad for your heart, and sudden death is not the only risk. In fact, more people probably suffer gradual heart damage from chronic, unmanaged daily stress than from a sudden event like being chased by a bear. Recognize that stress is something you are doing to yourself, which means it's voluntary and can be reversed. See the trusted remedies in Part I under Mental Health.

"Doctor, Doctor!"

If you're considering any form of alternative medicine, speak with your primary care provider first. Self-treating a heart condition and avoiding or delaying standard care may have real consequences. Since an increase in the severity of angina symptoms can indicate worsening heart health or the threat of a heart attack, it's important to closely monitor your condition and notify your doctor of any changes. You should seek immediate medical attention if your chest pain lasts longer than a few minutes and doesn't subside after you take angina medication.

Given the serious nature of angina, it's crucial to work with a physician to manage the condition. Traditional medical treatments based on an individual's unique needs and conditions have been shown to reduce mortality when applied appropriately. Use trusted remedies to manage or reduce your symptoms, but WebMD (reviewed by **James Beckerman, M.D., FACC** [234]) says you should also call a doctor about your angina if:

- Call 9-1-1 if it gets worse, lasts for more than 5 minutes, or doesn't improve after you've taken nitroglycerin. Doctors call that "unstable" angina," and it's an emergency that could be related to a heart attack that is about to happen.

- If you have "stable" angina – the most common kind – your symptoms usually

---

[234] James Beckerman, M.D., FACC, Cardiologist, St. Vincent Medical Center, Portland, OR, webmd.com

happen after a trigger (like a strong emotion, physical activity, extreme hot and cold temperatures, or even a heavy meal). The symptoms go away if you rest or take the nitroglycerin that your doctor has prescribed. If not, call 9-1-1.

COST-SAVINGS EXAMPLE:

Patients with angina are significantly more likely to be hospitalized, visit the emergency department, have office visits, and have certain procedures. They have higher inpatient costs and higher pharmacy costs than those without angina.

Total average medical and pharmacy costs for patients with angina were two to three times higher than for those without angina, adding as much as $14,000 over a two-year period (the study period was 2004-2006 – costs are much higher now).

Self-care to avoid or eliminate angina may help you avoid costly procedures and medications. However, it is not an alternative to medical care if the conditions given above under "Doctor, Doctor!" are present.

COLD SORES

Cold sores are small, fluid-filled blisters or sores that appear on the lips, mouth, or nose, says emedicinehealth.com [235] (**Melissa C. Stöppler, M.D., Medical Editor** [236]). Caused by the HSV-1 virus, sores can be painful and usually last a few days. Unlike most viral infections, HSV-1 is not completely eliminated by body defenses, so sores often recur.

Wash your hands: People with cold sores should wash their hands often, especially after touching the face. Cups and eating utensils should not be shared with another person.

Cold compresses: Applying a cold compress may relieve pain temporarily. Wrap an ice cube or bag of frozen vegetables in a cloth to avoid damaging your skin and lips with direct contact.

Do Not: Do not place much faith in lysine, vitamin E oil, vitamin supplements, or changes in diet to fight the HSV-1 virus. These folk remedies lack evidence, says emedicinehealth.

"Doctor, Doctor!"

The first time someone gets a cold sore, symptoms can be severe, says emedicinehealth. The first attack may be associated with fever, swollen glands, bleeding gums, and many painful sores around the mouth and nose. These symptoms may last several days to weeks. If the attack is severe, call a doctor. The doctor may prescribe medications that

---

[235] How to Get Rid of Cold Sores: Home Remedies, Causes, Symptoms, emedicinehealth.com
[236] Melissa Conrad Stöppler, M.D., MedicineNet | Image: Olena Panasovska, The Noun Project

can shorten the attack, preferably at the onset of symptoms. Difficulty in eating and drinking may lead to dehydration, which may also require medical attention.

COST-SAVINGS EXAMPLE:

To help prevent cold sores, wear sunscreen and lip balm with sun protection, which usually cost less than $10, says costhelper.com.

Preventing a cold sore can lead to significant savings. Per-outbreak prescription drug costs could be $33 to $200 or more. [237]

Self-care to avoid a cold sore may help you avoid medications costing $200 or more per outbreak.

COMMON COLD

There is still no cure for the common cold and no antiviral medications that can fight the viruses that cause it, according to the makers of Vicks VapoRub, a remedy that's been relieving coughs and other symptoms for over 125 years. Here are some of the best ways to get rid of cold symptoms courtesy of Vicks, Mayo Clinic, Penn State, the National Institutes of Health, and others: [238]

Drink lots of fluids: Staying hydrated with plenty of fluids can thin your mucus and make it easier for you to drain it from your nose and sinuses.

Drink warm liquids: Warm drinks soothe you and make you comfortable when you have a cold.

Sleep it off: When you're sleeping, your body makes proteins called cytokines, which are important for fighting infection and inflammation. Do your best to adjust your sleep schedule to get that extra rest that will help your body fight off the cold virus.

Meditate or pray: Keep stress at bay so your body can focus on keeping your immune system in check. Mayo Clinic [239], the nation's highest-rated hospital whose founders and first caregivers included nuns, specifically endorses the healing power of prayer. Daily meditation or prayer can ease stress and help you stay calm: Just close your eyes and remain peaceful for a few minutes.

Use saline nasal drops and sprays: Non-medicated nasal saline sprays can help to relieve congestion from a cold. A saline nasal spray helps to keep nasal passages open by washing out any thick or dried mucus, resulting in a more fluid mucus that can drain faster.

Use a neti pot to flush out mucus: To use it, make a mild solution of saltwater; test the solution

---

[237] How Much Does Cold Sore Treatment Cost? Costhelper.com
[238] 15 Tips & Home Remedies to Get Rid of Cold Symptoms, Vicks; Sources: NIH, Mayo Clinic, Penn State Hershey Medical Center, more, vicks.com | Image: Webtechchops LLC, The Noun Project
[239] Building your spiritual life during changes brought about by COVID-19, Mayo Clinic Health System

on your wrist to make sure it's not too hot or too cold. Bend your head sideways over the sink, place the spout of the neti pot in the upper nostril, and then pour the solution into your upper nostril and let the water drain down the lower nose. You can also try devices such as a squeeze bottle or bulb – easy to use in the shower, and helpful even at times when you don't have a cold.

Gargle saltwater: Gargle with water containing salt to get relief for a sore throat from a cold. The typical measurement is ¼ to ½ teaspoon of salt dissolved in an 8-ounce glass of warm water.

Add moisture to the air: Dry air may cause irritation inside the nose and throat. Use a humidifier or cool mist vaporizer in your bedroom to add moisture into the air while you sleep.

Breathe in some steamy air. Try sitting in the bathroom with a warm shower running. You can also breathe in steam from a bowl of hot water. Inhaling warm (not hot) water vapor can make the mucus thinner, which will help it drain better.

Soothe your cough. "Put Vicks on it" is a common refrain in many households. Apply Vicks VapoRub on your throat and chest and breathe in the medicated vapors with the familiar scents of eucalyptus, menthol, and camphor to help relieve your cough from a cold.

Adjust your sleeping position. When you lie horizontally, mucus collects instead of draining, resulting in congestion and cough. When you go to bed, try propping your head up with pillows to help gravity work better for you. Sleeping at a sloped angle allows the fluid in your sinuses to keep flowing to avoid congestion and other cold symptoms. A wedge-shaped pillow may help.

Keep things clean. It's just as important to keep the virus from spreading to friends and family. Make sure to clean and disinfect frequently touched surfaces at home and work. Be especially mindful to do so during cold and flu season, or whenever someone around you is sick. Better yet? Stay home from work, school, or stores to avoid spreading the cold virus to others.

Eat foods that support your immune system. Foods with vitamin C can help to maintain your immune system and get you back to normal quicker. Foods that have vitamin C include oranges, lemons, strawberries, red peppers, mangoes, broccoli, and many more fruits and vegetables.

Eat plenty of vegetables, herbs, and spices. Foods that support your immune system are bell peppers, broccoli, curry, and garlic – all known for treating inflammation and speeding relief.

Use the right over-the-counter (OTC) meds. Non-prescription medicine can help ease your cold symptoms. NyQuil Cold & Flu and DayQuil Cold & Flu contain both a pain reliever/fever reducer and a cough suppressant. Versions marked 'SEVERE' add ingredients such as a nasal decongestant or expectorant; check labels for the product best suited for your symptoms. Similar formulas may be available in generic brands, such as Equate sold at Walmart.

"Doctor, Doctor!"

For adults – generally, you don't need medical attention for a common cold, says Mayo Clinic (**Sandhya Pruthi, M.D.**, Chief medical editor [240]). But call a doctor if you have:

- Symptoms that worsen or fail to improve

---

[240] Sandhya Pruthi, M.D., Mayo Clinic Faculty Profiles | Appointments at Mayo Clinic

- Fever greater than 101.3° F (38.5° C) lasting more than three days
- Fever returning after a fever-free period
- Shortness of breath, wheezing, severe sore throat, headache or sinus pain

For children — seek medical attention right away if your child has any of the following:

- Fever of 100.4° F (38° C) in newborns up to 12 weeks
- Rising fever or fever lasting more than two days in a child of any age
- Severe symptoms, such as headache, throat pain or cough
- Difficulty breathing or wheezing
- Ear pain, extreme fussiness, unusual drowsiness, lack of appetite [241]

COST-SAVINGS EXAMPLE:

The cost of these self-care home remedies is small. Use them at the first sign of a cold and you may be able to reduce the number of days you miss at work.

The annual national cost of the common cold is in the billions of dollars, primarily in the form of millions of lost work days.

Improper use of antibiotics to treat common cold and influenza-like symptoms has contributed to the development of antibiotic resistance, an area of growing public health concern and a substantial driver of rising medical costs. [242]

Common-sense prevention can save you money. "The absolute cheapest thing you can buy is water" to stay hydrated and boost your immunity, says Ken Majkowski, Doctor of Pharmacy. [243] Wash your hands and change toothbrushes often. [244]

Use trusted remedies to shorten the duration and reduce the symptoms of a cold and you could save a day or more of lost wages and reduced productivity.

Remember that throughout this directory you can find further information by using the sources at the bottom of every page and in the resources listing beginning on page 259.

---

[241] Common Cold, Symptoms And Causes, Mayo Clinic, mayoclinic.org
[242] The Societal Costs Of A Common Cold, chr-hansen.com
[243] Ken Majkowski, Doctor of Pharmacy, KEM Consulting, LinkedIn
[244] 7 Ways To Meet The Costs Of Cold And Flu Season, USA TODAY, usatoday.com

CONJUNCTIVITIS

People often call conjunctivitis "pink eye" because it can cause the white of the eye to take on a pink or red color. [245] The most common causes are viruses, bacteria, and allergens. It can be difficult to tell the exact cause of the condition, as some symptoms may be the same no matter the cause. Viral conjunctivitis can be caused by a number of different viruses and is very contagious. Large outbreaks can result, depending on the exact virus.

Regardless of the cause, NYU Langone ophthalmologists [246] (**Kathryn A. Colby, M.D., Ph.D., Chair, Department of Ophthalmology** [247]) offer several trusted remedies to alleviate discomfort and prevent a recurrence of conjunctivitis:

Avoid contact lenses: If you've been diagnosed with viral or bacterial conjunctivitis, your doctor may recommend removing contact lenses and wearing glasses instead for 10 to 12 days, or until the condition has gone away, says NYU Langone. Rarely, previously worn contact lenses may be a source of reinfection. For this reason, your doctor may ask you to carefully disinfect or discard those lenses and even their cases. For some people, eye makeup may be a source of contamination and reinfection, so your doctor may recommend that you discard certain products.

Avoid triggers: If you know your triggers, try to avoid them. If you are prone to allergic conjunctivitis, limit the time you spend outside when pollen levels are high, or take allergy medications to reduce symptoms. Keep windows and doors closed during times of high pollen counts to reduce allergens in your home. Try not to let dust gather at home, and treat any mold.

Compresses: To relieve the discomfort of viral, bacterial, or allergic conjunctivitis, doctors often recommend applying a compress – a moist washcloth or hand towel – to your closed eyelids several times a day. Warm compresses help reduce the buildup of discharge on the eyelids or crust that forms on your eyelashes, while cold compresses help relieve itching and inflammation,

Rinse your eye: When you're exposed to allergens, your body releases a chemical called histamine, causing redness, tears, and itching in the eye. For conjunctivitis caused by a mild irritant, like shampoo or perfume spray, sometimes rinsing the eye with cold or lukewarm water for at least five minutes can help relieve the discomfort.

<u>Do Not</u>: If you have allergic conjunctivitis, it's important to avoid rubbing the eye, since this can worsen your symptoms. If you only have conjunctivitis in one eye, avoid touching both eyes with the same cloth to reduce the risk of spreading the condition from one eye to the other.

"Doctor, Doctor!"

Call your doctor if you have conjunctivitis along with any of the following:

- Pain or intense redness in the eyes, sensitivity to light, or blurred vision that does not improve when discharge is wiped from the eye

---

[245] Pink Eye (Conjunctivitis), National Center for Immunization and Respiratory Diseases, CDC, cdc.gov
[246] Home Treatments for Conjunctivitis, NYU Langone Health, New York, NY, nyulangone.org
[247] Kathryn A. Colby, M.D., PhD, NYU Langone Health, nyulangone.org | Image: Eucalypt, The Noun Project

- Symptoms that get worse or don't improve, including pink eye thought to be caused by bacteria which does not improve after 24 hours of antibiotic use

- A weakened immune system, for example from HIV infection, cancer treatment, or other medical conditions or treatments, or the patient is a newborn. [248]

Due to the risk of spreading the condition to others, the editors recommend calling the doctor for *all* suspected cases of conjunctivitis.

COST-SAVINGS EXAMPLE:

Conjunctivitis is associated with a heavy economic burden in terms of direct medical costs plus medically related absenteeism. Family health care costs increase with transmission time and with each family member infected with conjunctivitis, and decrease with prompt treatment of the initial patient. [249]

CONSTIPATION

The remedy for constipation may be as close as your kitchen. At most, these cures are no further away than your favorite supermarket. Try these trusted cures from The Healthy for quick relief [250] (medically reviewed, **Tia Jackson-Bey, M.D.** [251]).

Castor oil: Take 1-2 teaspoons on an empty stomach; expect results in about eight hours. A component in the oil converts into a substance that moves your bowels.

Coffee: Coffee can stimulate your colon. Coffee is also a diuretic, however, so make sure to keep drinking water or your constipation could become worse.

Exercise: In this case, move it *and* lose it! Exercise increases muscle activity in your intestines. Even a daily 15-minute walk can help move food through your bowel more quickly.

Fiber: Fiber acts like a pipe cleaner, scrubbing food and waste particles from your digestive tract and soaking up water. Mayo Clinic suggests aiming for 20 to 35 grams of fiber a day to stay regular. Foods particularly high in fiber include bran cereals, beans, lentils, oatmeal, almonds, barley, many vegetables, and fresh and dried fruits. Just be sure to drink more water than usual.

Healthy fats: Olive oil, nuts, and avocados contain healthy fats, which can help lubricate your intestines and ease constipation. Good options: a salad with fiber-rich leafy greens and a simple olive oil dressing, a small handful of nuts, or a tablespoon of natural nut butter on fruit or toast.

Mint or ginger tea: Peppermint contains menthol to relax the digestive tract. Ginger is a warming herb that causes the body to generate more heat; herbalists say this can help speed up

---

[248] Treating Pink Eye (Conjunctivitis), CDC, cdc.gov
[249] Direct and Indirect Costs of Infectious Conjunctivitis, PubMed Central, National Library of Medicine
[250] 11 Surprising Home Remedies for Constipation Relief, The Healthy, thehealthy.com
[251] Tia Jackson-Bey, M.D., RMA of New York, rmany.com | Image: Muhammad Ridho, The NounProject

digestion. In tea, the hot water will also stimulate digestion and provide constipation relief.

Lemon water: The citric acid in lemon juice acts as a stimulant to your digestive system and can help flush toxins from your body, providing constipation relief. Squeeze fresh lemon juice into a glass of water every morning, or add lemon to tea.

Molasses: One tablespoon of blackstrap molasses before bed should help ease your constipation by morning. Blackstrap molasses is boiled and concentrated three times, so it has significant vitamins and minerals; magnesium, in particular, will help you achieve constipation relief.

Prunes: Three prunes have 3 grams of fiber, and contain a phenolic compound that triggers the intestinal contraction that makes you want to go. Another great dried fruit choice is figs.

Raisins: High in fiber, raisins contain tartaric acid, which has a laxative effect. Cherries and apricots are also rich in fiber and can help kick your constipation. Eat these fruits with a bowl of yogurt for the added benefits of gut-soothing probiotics.

Sesame seeds: Their oily composition works to moisturize the intestines, which can help if dry stools are a problem. Add the seeds to cereals or salads for crunch, or pulverize them in a coffee grinder and sprinkle them on food like a seasoning.

"Doctor, Doctor!"

If someone has constipation along with severe abdominal pain, this could be a sign of a more serious health condition, says **Dr. Christopher Almario** [252], a gastroenterologist at Cedars-Sinai [253]. Blood in the stool, unintended weight loss, an unexpected new onset of constipation – all of these are signs to seek medical attention. "For someone who has had regular bowel movements all their life, then all of a sudden develops chronic constipation, this can be a red flag as well," Dr. Almario says.

COST-SAVINGS EXAMPLE:

Since 2017, the FDA has approved five new prescription drugs to treat constipation. Without insurance, they cost about $500 a month. None are available yet as a low-cost generic. So even with insurance, you may be hit with a sizable co-pay – ample reason to take care of this matter with trusted self-care remedies if at all possible. [254]

Replace some of the foods in your current diet with those listed above as constipation remedies and you may be able to get your system moving again without the substantial cost of medical intervention.

These trusted remedies for constipation could save you $500 a month.

[252] Christopher V. Almario, M.D., MSHPM, Cedars-Sinai, cedars-sinai.org
[253] When to See a Doctor for Constipation, Cedars-Sinai, cedars-sinai.org
[254] Best Drugs for Constipation, Consumer Reports, consumerreports.org

COUGH

Coughing is the body's natural reflex when something irritates your throat or airways, says Insider Health [255] (medically reviewed by **Dipesh Navsaria, M.D.** [256]). Occasional coughs are normal and even healthy, as they help the body flush out built-up mucus and debris, but they can still be uncomfortable. Here are some doctor-trusted remedies to soothe your cough naturally:

Honey: Honey works like a cough drop, coating the lining of the throat, alleviating soreness or scratchiness. Commonly available clover honey is fine, but if available, dark honey, such as dark buckwheat honey, may be better. Honey also has anti-inflammatory, antioxidant, and antibacterial properties. Children under the age of one shouldn't take honey because it can contain bacteria that cause infant botulism, a rare but life-threatening illness.

Saltwater: Gargling salt water can help kill bacteria, loosen mucus, and clear your sinuses. A saltwater gargle can also help reduce swelling and irritation caused by coughing. Most people prefer to gargle warm salt water, but cold water may bring the same relief, says **Jason McKnight, M.D.** [257] Just add about ½ half a teaspoon of salt to an eight-ounce glass of water.

Ginger: Like honey, ginger has antioxidant, antimicrobial, and anti-inflammatory properties. The spicy taste stimulates saliva production and can help improve a dry mouth or throat. Dr. McKnight says reactions to spices, herbs, and spicy foods vary between people, so start with a small amount. For some, it may be helpful; for others, it can cause further irritation and worsen your hacking. People consume ginger via fresh or dry ginger root or as a supplement in either a capsule or tincture formulation. For added relief, try adding ginger and honey to your tea.

Moist air: Breathing in warm, moist air helps loosen nasal congestion. This will make blowing your nose easier and, if you're experiencing post-nasal drip, release built-up mucus in the throat. Moisturizing a sore throat may also provide pain relief. For temporary relief, take a hot shower and breathe in the steam.

Air purifier: Air purifiers help remove allergens from your home that trigger sneezing, coughing, and a runny nose. They work by moving the air in your home through a series of filters that clear mold, bacteria, or dust – producing fresh, clean air. Dr. McKnight says that air purifiers may be especially helpful for people who suffer from seasonal allergies. It's also important to regularly clean purifiers to ensure the filters work properly.

Marshmallow root: This herbal supplement is thought to soothe irritated membranes in the throat and mouth. Marshmallow roots and leaves contain mucilage, a thick substance that takes on a gel-like texture when mixed with water. The gel can coat the throat, much like honey. Relief begins within 10 minutes. The herb is available in dried leaf form, teas, tinctures, or capsules.

Thyme: This herb is thought to soothe smooth muscle spasms, including those caused by coughing. To relieve coughing, thyme can be consumed as a tincture, herbal tea, or in pill form.

---

[255] 8 Of The Best Home Remedies To Soothe A Cough Naturally, According To Doctors, Insider.com
[256] Dipesh Navsaria, M.D., American Family Children's Hospital, Madison WI, uwhealth.org
[257] Dr. Jason McKnight, M.D., Texas A&M Health Family Care, stjoseph.stlukeshealth.org | Image: Fiki Ahmadi, The Noun Project

Water: One of the easiest and safest ways to improve your cough is to stay hydrated. Drinking water helps thin mucus, allowing it to leave the body through your mouth or nose. It can also help those who are sick replace lost fluids from sweating or having a runny nose. Remember, the solution to pollution is dilution … water will dilute and help eliminate many causes of illness.

The most concerning form of cough is chronic cough – lasting longer than eight weeks in an adult and four weeks in a child. To relieve the symptoms of chronic cough, use the trusted remedies above, along with:

Elevate your head while sleeping: Use extra pillows at night to prop up your head and upper body. This promotes drainage and reduces the accumulation of fluids in your throat.

Try cough drops: herbal or non-medicated versions may be as effective as the medicated kind.

OTC meds: Try over-the-counter cough medicines containing guaifenesin or dextromethorphan.

To prevent chronic cough, Cleveland Clinic advises: [258]

- Quit smoking, the leading cause of chronic cough. Look under **Tobacco** in Part I of this directory, **Doctor-Trusted Remedies for the Top 10 Most Common Health Issues**.
- Avoid contact with anyone who may have bronchitis or pneumonia.
- Eat fruit and foods that contain fiber. Research suggests that a combination of fiber and flavonoids found in fruit may prevent chronic cough.

"Doctor, Doctor!"

While self-care can calm a cough, these remedies won't cure an underlying illness or infection, says **Susan Roberman, M.D.** [259] , St. Joseph and Texas A&M Health Network, Bryan, TX. Call a doctor if you have trouble catching your breath, are coughing up blood or discolored mucus, have fever or a headache, or your cough persists for several weeks.

COST-SAVINGS EXAMPLE:

About $3,266 per patient is spent on annual medical costs for treating a chronic cough (for prescriptions, office visits, and hospitalizations). Nationally, costs for OTC cough medicine, which suppress symptoms temporarily, are up to $3 billion. [260]

Most trusted remedies given above are very inexpensive, the most costly being an air purifier (Amazon's most popular model sells for $239.99). Try these self-care steps at the first sign of a cough; anything you can do to avoid developing a chronic cough will not only save you a lot of money, but improve your quality of life.

Avoid $3,266 in annual medical costs by preventing chronic cough.

---

[258] Chronic Cough: Causes, Diagnosis & Treatment, Cleveland Clinic | Appointments at Cleveland Clinic
[259] Dr. Susan Roberman, M.D., Primary Care, Bryan, TX, stjoseph.stlukeshealth.org
[260] Preparing for a new era in chronic cough management, American Journal of Managed Care, ajmc.com

COVID-19 (Novel Coronavirus, SARS-CoV-2)

 COVID-19 has peaked, but the risk from novel viruses is far from over; the original SARS-CoV-2 has taken the path of viruses before it, morphing from pandemic to endemic, from one variant to the next. While the trusted remedies below may ease some COVID symptoms, prevention is the better option; COVID effects can be long-lasting and significantly reduce your quality of life.

Mild cases of COVID-19 (which is most of them) can be managed at home, but continue to monitor your symptoms in case they worsen. To self-treat COVID-19, use these doctor-trusted remedies for viral illnesses from Houston Methodist, the Texas hospital ranked among the nation's best by U.S. News & World Report [261] (**Marc L. Boom, M.D., President and CEO** [262]):

Get plenty of rest: While fighting any new virus, expect your body to be busy. Give yourself plenty of time to rest; you'll help provide your body with the energy it needs to get the job done.

Drink plenty of water: As noted throughout this directory, the solution to pollution is dilution; water helps flush away all sorts of contaminants and unwanted conditions. Staying well-hydrated aids your immune system as it fights off any virus, says Houston Methodist. Fevers are usually accompanied by increased perspiration. Drinking more water can help replenish the water you're losing. If you have a dry cough, a teaspoon of honey in hot water can help soothe your throat. For congestion, a warm, non-caffeinated beverage or warm shower can help loosen mucus.

Use over-the-counter medications when necessary: If you have a high fever, a fever reducer such as acetaminophen can help bring it down. If you have body aches, a sore throat, or a cough, a pain reliever can help lessen the discomfort these symptoms can bring. You may also consider taking a nasal decongestant for a stuffy nose and an expectorant for chest congestion. Just be sure to follow the dosage recommendations on the bottles and don't take any medications that may conflict with any other medications you're taking or any health conditions you may have.

What options might be useful for preventing COVID-19?

Supplements: According to **Robert H. Shmerling, M.D., Senior Faculty Editor,** [263] Harvard Health Publishing [264] – "Based on the science, there is reason to be hopeful that supplements such as vitamin C or D, zinc, or melatonin might help in the fight against COVID-19. While there's no proof yet that they do, additional research could show a benefit in certain situations, or with a different dose or formulation of the supplement. So it's worth keeping an open mind."

Making a non-political vaccine decision: Most people have made their decision and either became vaccinated or plan to remain unvaccinated. We'd like to help you remain healthy no matter which camp you fall into; we can't expect anyone to change their mind about COVID vaccines based on what they read here. But the fallout of the vaccine debate weighs on both sides; *vaccines have become highly politicized, which benefits no one but the politicians.*

Politicians' priorities are to get on the 6 o'clock news and to get re-elected; this includes both

---

[261] How to Treat Mild COVID-19 Symptoms at Home, Houston Methodist, houstonmethodist.org
[262] Marc L. Boom, M.D., Houston Methodist, houstonmethodist.org | Image: Mas Dhimas, The Noun Project
[263] Robert H. Shmerling, M.D., Harvard Health, health.harvard.edu
[264] Do vitamin D, zinc, and other supplements help prevent COVID-19 or hasten healing? Harvard Health

pro- and anti-vax politicians, even politicians who are also doctors. Take medical advice from politicians at your own peril. Better idea: *take your medical advice from your personal doctor.*

With notable exceptions, the majority of doctors agree that the best way to prevent the worst effects of the novel coronavirus is to get vaccinated. This is also true of many politicians; vaccinated politicians include Presidents Joe Biden and Donald Trump, Vice Presidents Kamala Harris and Mike Pence, and Governors Gavin Newsom (D) and Ron DeSantis (R).

A notable politician who is not vaccinated is Congressman Rand Paul, M.D. (R-Ky.), who wrote:

> *"It's time for us to stand up to Washington bureaucrats who think you're not smart enough to make your own decisions."* [265]

Making your own informed decisions for your healthy future is what this directory is all about. Making an informed decision about COVID vaccines is extraordinarily challenging because both pro- and anti-vaccination forces are frequently guilty of misinformation. We can't tell you what the right answer is for you; we suggest looking for non-vested interests as sources of information – admittedly not easy to find, as political influence, financial gain, and confirmation bias all figure prominently in the vaccine debate.

For those over age 65 or with comorbidities, most doctors say that the risks of contracting SARS-CoV-2 are significantly greater than the risks from COVID vaccines. [266] It's unfortunate that some vaccine opponents have floated baseless claims to bolster their positions, such as claiming that vaccines cause "injuries" in a high percentage of people who receive them. Such claims are based on counting normal vaccine reactions as injuries, which they are not. Pain at the injection site and minor flu-like symptoms are fleeting, predictable, and harmless reactions to many vaccines, not just the COVID vaccine. They show that the vaccine is active; they are *not* "injuries." [267]

Other people say they have not been vaccinated because of concerns that the vaccines are too new, that the longterm effects are unknown, or they wanted to wait for more information. However it's also true that the SARS-CoV-2 virus is relatively new and that its longterm effects are unknown. Similarly, while it's true that COVID vaccines may increase the risk for myocarditis, an inflammation of the heart muscle, getting the virus increases the risk much more. [268]

While these are all legitimate concerns to discuss, *The Lancet* (which published in the UK and is neither a politically controlled government agency nor a profit-motivated vaccine maker) reports the following conclusions based on the billions of COVID vaccine doses that have been given: [269]

- "COVID-19 vaccines show excellent efficacy in clinical trials and effectiveness in real-world data."

- "Vaccination (compared with no vaccination) was associated with reduced odds of hospitalization or having more than five symptoms."

---

[265] Op-Ed: Rand Paul: "The science proves people with natural immunity should skip COVID vaccines"
[266] Risk factors and disease profile of post-vaccination SARS-CoV-2 infection … The Lancet
[267] COVID-19 vaccine myths debunked - Mayo Clinic Health System
[268] COVID-19 infection poses higher risk for myocarditis than vaccines | American Heart Association
[269] Risk Factors And Disease Profile Of Post-Vaccination SARS-CoV-2, The Lancet, thelancet.com

- "Almost all symptoms were reported less frequently in infected vaccinated individuals than in infected unvaccinated individuals."

- "Vaccinated participants were more likely to be completely asymptomatic, especially if they were 60 years or older."

- "Nonetheless, some people still contract COVID-19 after vaccination, and further virus variants could evolve with increased transmissibility."

For the concern that the vaccines are associated with increased risk for myocarditis, we now have a large amount of data on this as well. The American Heart Association reports:

- "Individuals with COVID-19 infection were at least 11 times more at risk for developing myocarditis in the 1-28 days after testing positive if COVID-19 infection occurred before COVID-19 vaccination."

- "The risk of developing myocarditis was substantially lower in the 1-28 days after COVID-19 vaccination than after COVID-19 infection, except for after a second dose of the Moderna vaccine."

- "Among nearly 43 million people ages 13 and older who received 1-3 doses of a COVID-19 vaccine, fewer than 3,000 were hospitalized or died with myocarditis."

- "Only 617 of the nearly 3,000 cases of myocarditis occurred during days 1-28 after receiving a COVID-19 vaccination," suggesting many of these cases would have occurred anyway without the vaccine.

It's just as important to acknowledge that vaccine advocates have also used false statements and have pursued policies based on politics, not science, to advance their side:

- President Joe Biden flatly stated: "You're not going to get COVID if you have these vaccinations." Snopes analyzed Biden's statement and concluded: "Biden's statements above clearly contradict the conclusions of medical authorities such as the CDC." It is a safe assumption that most politicians shoot from the lip.

- Government mandates raise the concern that the benefits of the vaccines do not sufficiently outweigh the risks for most people to take it voluntarily. Mandates cast a shadow of mistrust over official health guidance, including guidance that is accurate.

"Doctor, Doctor!"

Harvard Pilgrim Health Care says that if you or a loved one are experiencing any of the following, call 9-1-1 or go to your closest emergency room: difficulty breathing, persistent pain or pressure in the chest, new confusion or inability to arouse, bluish lips or face.

For non-emergency symptoms of COVID-19, first call your doctor for their expert opinion. Your doctor may offer telemedicine allowing you to have a virtual consultation via your computer, tablet, or smartphone. [270]

---

[270] Should you go to urgent care, your doctor, or the ER? Harvard Pilgrim Health Care, harvardpilgrim.org

COST-SAVINGS EXAMPLE:

Long COVID has affected as many as 23 million Americans through 2022. Estimated annual medical costs associated with long COVID average $9,000 per patient. [271]

Unvaccinated people are 7 times more likely to be hospitalized than vaccinated people, and 14 times more likely to be in intensive care, according to a private university study. [272]

Hospital care for COVID-19 costs between $51,000 to $78,000, based on age. [273] Unvaccinated patients are at greater risk for longterm, expensive hospitalization. [274]

If you are over 65 or have comorbidities for COVID-19, most evidence points to the benefit of getting vaccinated. Regardless of your age or health status, make a vaccine decision free of political considerations.

CUTS AND SCRAPES

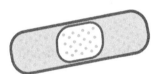

From a playground boo-boo to a big-girl bike crash, you're likely at some point to be dealing with an abrasion that has broken the skin.

Tom's of Maine (**Dr. Amy Shah, double board-certified M.D. and Tom's of Maine wellness expert** [275]) produces a variety of natural body care products, including the only brand of toothpaste used by the editors of this directory. Tom's says some of the best natural remedies for wounds can be found in your kitchen pantry. Minor scratches, bug bites, cuts, and scrapes will all feel better with healthy, simple self-care.

Before anything else, says Tom's, assess and clean the wound. If there is bleeding, apply compression. If the bleeding continues more than a few minutes, visit the nearest urgent care center as soon as possible.

For scrapes with redness or tiny specks of blood, wash the skin to clear away dirt and bacteria. Cool, clear water and a soft cloth should do the job. If you have antibacterial soap, use that too. Then apply one of these soothing, natural remedies for wounds.

Pure raw honey: Use of honey as a salve dates back as far as 2100 BC. This natural healer is a fabulous antibacterial that works to potentially control inflammation and prevent infection when

[271] Long COVID may be 'the next public health disaster' — with a $3.7 trillion economic impact, cnbc.com
[272] Hospitalization rates confirm COVID vaccines' benefits, McGill University, mcgill.ca
[273] Average cost of hospital care for COVID-19, Healthcare Finance News, healthcarefinancenews.com
[274] Unvaccinated COVID patients cost the US health system billions, Kaiser Family Foundation, kff.org
[275] Dr. Amy Shah, AmyMDWellness.com, Scottsdale, AZ | CC0 image

used topically to a clean wound. Apply a thin layer of raw honey, and then bandage the scrape.

Flowering yarrow: If this common ground cover flower is growing nearby, pick some. Rinse off any contaminants, then rub the blooms and leaves together into a mash-up that can be applied directly to a wound. The secret to this medicinal flower is that it can possibly reduce inflammation and soothe your cut for some natural wound healing.

Chamomile: Moisten a chamomile tea bag, and press it onto the sore spot. The natural plant oils can speed the rate of healing by helping your skin regenerate fresh tissue. If you can moisten the tea bag with cold water, it can help numb the area temporarily to provide additional relief.

Aloe Vera: A dab of pure aloe from a fresh clipping of this common houseplant can be a great remedy for mild sunburns or for minor road rash from a spill off your bike. The thick liquid helps collagen form, which in turn can heal the skin and keep infections at bay.

Whether you're away from home or are trying to green your routine, choosing natural remedies for wounds makes sense. Enjoy these natural ingredients while reducing your exposure to unnecessary drugs and chemicals. [276]

"Doctor, Doctor!"

According to Physicians Premier [277] (**Dr. David Kenyon, M.D.**, Managing Partner [278]), you should go to your local emergency room or call 9-1-1 right away if:

- Blood is spurting out
- The cut is jagged or gapping and is deeper than ¼ inch
- There is severe bleeding
- The cut is made by a rusty object
- The cut is over a joint and opens every time you move
- The bleeding won't stop even after ten minutes of applying steady pressure
- Muscle, fat or bone can be seen through the wound.

Absent the above, a cut, scratch, or scrape is probably no big deal, unless it gets infected, says Nemours Children's Health [279] (medically reviewed by **Melanie Pitone, M.D.** [280]).

A skin infection happens when germs get into the skin.If you notice any of these signs of infection, call your doctor right away: redness around the cut; red streaking spreading from the cut; increased swelling or pain around the cut white, yellow, or green liquid coming from the cut; fever.

The doctor will prescribe antibiotics to help fight off the infection. Luckily, most small cuts, scratches, and abrasions will go away on their own, thanks to your body's amazing ability to heal itself. If a cut looks serious or infected, though, call your doctor.

---

[276] 4 Natural Remedies for Wounds and Scrapes, tomsofmaine.com
[277] Scrapes & Cuts: Should I Go to the Emergency Room or an Urgent Care? Physicians Premier ER
[278] Texas Freestanding Emergency Rooms, Physicians Premier ER, mdpremier.com
[279] Cuts, Scratches, and Scrapes (for Teens), Nemours KidsHealth, locations in DE, FL, NJ, and PA
[280] Dr. Melanie L. Pitone, M.D. | Wilmington, DE | Pediatric Emergency Medicine Physician

COST-SAVINGS EXAMPLE:

Emergency room treatment can cost thousands of dollars and require hours of waiting time. Most cuts and scrapes can be handled at home. Moderate cases including those that may require stitches can be handled quickly and for a reasonable price at an urgent care center.

A standard first aid kit is $10 to $75 at any drug store or online retailer. Have one on hand and know how to use it.

Self-care for minor cuts and scrapes can save hundreds or even thousands of dollars, and be completed faster and with less stress than a visit to a medical facility.

———

Folklore remedies only put you at greater risk for dangerous diseases.

– *Good Housekeeping, May 3, 2022*

Use physician-trusted remedies instead!

D

DANDRUFF

 Nearly all people have dandruff at some point, says emedicinehealth.com [281] (**Nili N. Alai, M.D.,** medical author [282]). It affects not just the scalp but also the ears, eyebrows, sides of the nose, beard, or other areas with hair. Dandruff is seen in all ethnicities and all ages. In other words, it's normal. Still, you probably want to wash it away before it lands on your collar.

Dandruff shampoo: The best choices are those containing zinc pyrithione, selenium sulfide, and tar-based shampoos. According to bestreviews.com, top-rated brands are Nizoral, Head and Shoulders, and Neutrogena. Walmart's Equate Everyday Clean is comparable to Head and Shoulders, costs less, and is the personal choice of the editors of Trusted Remedies.

Baking soda: It's also possible to control dandruff with homemade, all-natural treatments, says byrdie.com [283] (**Jenny Liu, M.D.,** Board-Certified Dermatologist [284]). Baking soda's gritty texture removes dirt and excess oil from your hair, as well as loose skin cells from your scalp. Unlike commercial products, this will not strip your scalp of much-needed natural oils. Over time, this may lead to a healthier scalp and hair. Combine one tablespoon of baking soda for each cup of water and mix well. Pour over your hair, massage it into your scalp, then rinse thoroughly. While not really a shampoo, use this trick once a week or every four to five shampoos. It should not be done very often and instead done only for an occasional extra deep cleanse.

"Doctor, Doctor!"

If dandruff is worsening despite proper skin care and hair hygiene, call a dermatologist. As with any other condition, if someone is so uncomfortable with their dandruff that their social, sleep, work, or other daily activities are disrupted, see a healthcare practitioner.

COST-SAVINGS EXAMPLE:

Prescription shampoos such as ketoconazole are no better than over-the-counter brands, says emedicinehealth.com, despite their high average retail cost of $113. [285]

Save $100+ with OTC dandruff shampoos or a baking soda/water mix.

[281] How to Get Rid of Dandruff: Shampoo, Home Remedies, Causes, Treatment, emedicinehealth.com
[282] Nili Alai, M.D., Skin Center at Laguna, CA, emedicinehealth.com | Image: corpus delicti, The Noun Project
[283] How to Make Homemade Dandruff Shampoo and Rinse, byrdie.com
[284] Jenny Liu, M.D. FAAD, Skincare expert (@derm.talk), Instagram
[285] Ketoconazole Generic Extina and Nizoral, GoodRx, goodrx.com

DENTURE DISCOMFORT

 If you are experiencing pain during your initial denture break-in period or if you feel like your dentures don't fit the way that they used to, call your dentist, says **Dr. David Koepsel** of Wichita, KS [286] . The dentist will examine your dentures and can make adjustments as needed or order new ones if necessary. While you are waiting for your appointment, Dr. Koepsel advises these trusted remedies to relieve your denture pain: [287]

Soft foods: Only eat soft foods in the first few weeks after you get your new dentures; soft foods are gentler on the gums and easier to chew as you get used to the dentures

Topical oral pain relievers: Use topical gels or creams that are intended specifically to relieve oral pain on any sore spots on your gums. Amazon has many highly rated options for under $10.

Salt water rinse: Rinse your mouth with warm salt water with your dentures removed for 15 to 30 seconds.

Gum massage: Regularly massage your gums to increase circulation and minimize swelling

Denture adhesive: Use a denture adhesive after the dentist has given the go-ahead; you may need to wait a few weeks after you get your dentures to start using an adhesive

Aloe vera: Apply aloe vera gel to your dentures one to two times per day to soothe your gums

OTC pain relievers: Take over-the-counter pain relievers such as acetaminophen or ibuprofen

No dentures at night: Remove your dentures while you sleep to give your gums a break

Dr. Koepsel also highly recommends that patients consider implant-supported dentures. The implants in these dentures provide a sturdy support system for the denture that greatly reduces the rubbing, slipping, and soreness that traditional dentures can cause, making the overall denture experience more comfortable. With implant-supported dentures, you can forget that you're even wearing dentures and focus on what matters most to you in life.

"Doctor, Doctor!"

While your dentures may never feel as comfortable as your natural teeth, they shouldn't cause any discomfort, says Silverado Family Dental [288] (**Dr. R. Garth Harris** [289]). If you notice jaw soreness, uneven pressure, or other discomfort, talk to your dentist. If you have pain on or near your canine teeth, especially when you bite down, this may indicate bone reabsorption. Address this issue with your oral health advisor as soon as possible.

COST-SAVINGS EXAMPLE:

---

[286] Dr. David Koepsel, East Wichita Dentist, eastwichitadentist.com | Image: Nico Strobl, The Noun Project
[287] Dentist in Wichita, KS Explains Remedies For Pain From Wearing Dentures, East Wichita Dentist
[288] 11 Signs Your Dentures Need Adjustment or Repairs, Silverado Family Dental, Las Vegas, NV
[289] Dr. R. Garth Harris, Silverado Family Dental, Las Vegas, NV, silveradofamilydental.com

While you may be tempted to procrastinate and avoid dealing with your oral health, the costs of delay are high, says Ormond Beach Periodontics and Implant Dentistry [290] **(Dr. Raymond A. Kenzik). The sooner you call your dentist, the lower your treatment cost is likely to be, and the sooner you'll experience relief.**

DEPRESSION

Being depressed is painful and debilitating, says Intrepid Mental Wellness of Denver, CO [291] . About 10 percent of adults in the United States suffer from symptoms of depression each year, resulting in family strife, loss of productivity, and misery for the person affected by the condition and those around them.

Depression is a disease and should be diagnosed and treated by a mental health professional. The path to recovery can begin with a simple discussion with your own doctor. However, self-care is an essential element of treatment and recovery. Depression is closely linked with anxiety; see the trusted remedies listed earlier in this directory under **Anxiety**. (You may also find help in Part I, **Mental Health**). Here are remedies mental health professionals trust for mild to moderate depression (**Chelsey Lahr, Psychiatric-Mental Health Nurse Practitioner** [292] ; **Debra Fulghum Bruce, Ph.D.** [293] ; and **Jennifer Casarella, M.D.** [294]).

Get some exercise: Exercise has multiple benefits beyond helping with depression, such as improved heart health, weight loss, and reduced risk for many chronic diseases. Exercise helps with the symptoms of depression because it increases brain chemicals called endorphins. Even a few minutes a day of mild exercise can improve mood by elevating endorphin levels.

Challenge negative thoughts: When you're depressed, your self-talk includes "I'm a failure," "No one likes me," or "I'll always feel this way." These thoughts become a habit, reinforcing your depression. A simple solution is challenging negative thoughts with positive ones. For example, challenge a negative idea with "How do I know that?" or by thinking of a time when you felt differently about life. We often accept our thoughts as real without challenging them. There is much wisdom in the saying, "Don't believe everything you think."

Regularly eat wholesome foods: Sugary, salty, and high-fat junk food can bring a temporary feeling of comfort, but ultimately these foods cause spikes in blood sugar, weight, and bad moods. The solution is finding wholesome foods you like, making sure you have plenty on hand, and eating these foods every day. Fresh fruit, salads, lean meats, oily fish such as salmon, and whole-grain bread are all good options. Adopting a healthy diet also gives you a reason to give yourself a pat on the back, itself a good antidote for depression.

Get adequate sleep: Sleep is vital for your brain and body to regenerate, repair, and renew. Getting a good night's sleep each night improves overall health and energy levels, reducing

---

[290] Full Service Dental and Periodontal Care in a Boutique Environment, Ormond Beach Periodontics, FL
[291] 9 Self-Help Solutions for Reducing Symptoms of Depression, Intrepid Mental Wellness, Denver, CO
[292] Chelsey Lahr, PMHNP-BC, Intrepid Mental Wellness, Denver, CO | Image: Public Domain
[293] Debra Fulghum Bruce, Ph.D., amazon.com
[294] Jennifer Casarella, M.D., webmd.com

symptoms of depression. Making changes in your routine may help with getting a more restful sleep throughout the night. For example, go to bed at the same time every day, don't watch TV or use a computer in the bedroom, and do not eat for at least one hour before going to bed.

Drink plenty of water: Water is essential for all bodily functions. Drinking adequate water daily assists in removing toxins and enhances clear thinking. Many people do not drink enough water and instead fill up on soft drinks, caffeinated beverages, and alcoholic drinks, all of which cause the body to lose water, leading to dehydration. If drinking plain water is a challenge, consider these: flavored sparkling water, iced or hot herbal teas (mint, chamomile, ginger, hibiscus, or jasmine), or adding a tablespoon or two of fruit juice to water to improve the taste. For optimal health, adults need two to three quarts of water a day beyond what they get from food.

Make a change in routine: When you're depressed, you may fall into a routine that reinforces the symptoms of depression. For example, you may get up, go to work, come home, watch the same shows on TV each night, and then binge on unhealthy foods before bedtime. A schedule like this can keep you feeling bad about yourself. Making a change in routine does not need to be complicated. For example, instead of heading straight for the TV after getting home from work, take a short walk first. Changing routines can help rewire the pathways in the brain, a key step in restoring feelings of happiness. The changes do not need to be large to have a positive effect.

***Get* a routine:** For other people, the problem is not having enough structure to their day. In this case, establishing a more structured routine can be of benefit. It can start as simply as getting up and getting dressed in the morning, rather than lounging around in pajamas. Other ideas are calling friends each day, taking a short walk, writing in a journal, or spending half an hour listening to pleasurable music. Establishing new habits and routines also increases dopamine levels, which can reduce feelings of depression.

Laughter: Laughing is another effective way to increase dopamine in the brain. Watching comedy shows or movies instead of dramas, laughing with others, or merely thinking about amusing things that result in laughter can boost dopamine levels and reduce depression.

Help someone else: There is a strong tendency when we are depressed to become self-absorbed. Our problems loom large in our minds, adding to the feeling of being overwhelmed. A simple solution is to do something helpful for another person or a pet. Calling a friend to ask how they are doing, volunteering at a charity, helping a neighbor, or adopting a pet are a few examples. When we help others, it raises our self-esteem and gets our minds off our troubles. Any reprieve from depressed feelings can assist in improving positive thinking and elevating mood.

Starting these self-help actions may seem challenging at first for a depressed person. However, making even a small change each day can quickly build momentum and increase energy as symptoms of depression begin to subside. Taking small, daily steps toward a healthier life can have a significant effect on the reduction of mild to moderate symptoms of depression.

"Doctor, Doctor!"

If you're already wondering whether professional mental health help is right for you or someone you care about, the answer could well be 'yes,' and the first step is easy. Call your doctor. Remember, depression affects an estimated one in ten people, making it more common than nearly any other disease. You are not alone, and help is available from the doctor you already know, and many other professionals. The American Psychological Association offers a page full of resources. [295] USNews.com has a directory of over one thousand Psychiatric Nurse Practitioners, searchable by location. [296] Or simply search for the letters PMHNP followed by your zip code.

COST-SAVINGS EXAMPLE:

Untreated depression can cost you everything you have. It can ruin relationships, cost you your job and your livelihood, and make it more difficult to overcome other illnesses, says Dr. Bruce. Untreated depression also increases the chance of self-destructive choices such as drug or alcohol abuse. [297]

Many of the trusted remedies above are inexpensive, if not free. Many professional resources are available – some at no cost, others covered by insurance. The greatest cost by far is inaction ... take at least one step right now toward climbing out of your depression and back to the happy and content person you were meant to be.

DERMATITIS AND ECZEMA

Eczema occurs when the skin's protective barrier is abnormally weak, explains Greatist.com [298] . Without a strong barrier, moisture escapes, and bacteria and viruses get in. That can cause patches that are dry, red, and itchy. It's thought that people with eczema have overactive immune systems that cause their skin to become inflamed. The trusted remedies below are backed by doctors (medically reviewed by **Debra Sullivan, Ph.D.** [299]) and get stellar reviews from people living with eczema:

Use a gentle body wash: It's essential to use the right cleanser. A mild, soap-free product is less likely to strip your skin of its natural barrier. Look for one that's free of dyes and perfumes, which can trigger irritation. Top brands include CeraVe, Cetaphil, Dove, Eucerin, and Vanicream – all rated 4.5 (or higher) out of 5 on Amazon with thousands of positive reviews each.

Moisturize: Hydrating with an ointment or cream eases or prevents dryness and acts as a barrier to block out irritants. Go with a dense moisturizer or petroleum jelly; avoid perfumes and dyes. Apply within a minute or two after bathing and reapply often. For serious rejuvenation for hands and feet, apply before bedtime, put on cotton socks or gloves, and wake up to refreshed skin.

Take cooler showers: Bathe in water as close to body temperature as you're comfortable with.

[295] Crisis hotlines and resources, American Psychological Association, apa.org
[296] Find a Psychiatric Nurse Practitioner, US News Doctors, health.usnews.com
[297] Side Effects of Untreated Depression, WebMD
[298] 13 Natural Remedies for Eczema Treatment and Prevention, Greatist.com
[299] Debra Sullivan, Ph.D., Nurse Educator, healthline.com | Image: Marie Van den Broeck, The Noun Project

A shower hot enough to steam up your bathroom also steams protective oils out of your skin.

Don't scratch: Scratching takes dry, irritated skin from bad to worse. Try an over-the-counter spray like TriCalm Extra Strength Spray. It's recommended by the National Eczema Association and doesn't require touching (and therefore aggravating) your itchy skin. To reduce scratching yourself while you're dozing, wear cotton gloves to bed.

Walk, don't run: Heat and sweat cause itch, so avoid activities that elevate body temperature. Wear loose, breathable clothing to reduce perspiration and maintain a normal body temperature.

Take a very dilute bleach bath: Mix a maximum of 1/4 to 1/2 cup of bleach in a full bathtub of warm water. "Full" means your tub is filled to the overflow drainage hole. Be sure to avoid splashing bleach on your skin or eyes; if you do so accidentally, flush immediately with plenty of water. Soak for 10 minutes, then rinse your skin with plain warm water before gently patting it dry. Don't take a bleach bath more than 2 to 3 times a week.

Soak in colloidal oatmeal: Colloidal oatmeal contains natural emollients that calm red, inflamed skin and ease uncomfortable irritation. It's available as a finely ground powder that's easy to sprinkle into a warm bath.

Use a humidifier: Dry indoor air can make skin even more parched, especially in the winter. But a humidifier can add moisture to the air and help you feel more comfortable. Keep one in any room where you spend a lot of time, like your bedroom, office, or living room.

Get real about relaxation: Unchecked tension causes your body to produce too much of the stress hormone cortisol. This can suppress your immune system and cause skin inflammation.

"Doctor, Doctor!"

Even if you're proactive about caring for your skin, it's normal to experience periods of dryness or mild discomfort with eczema, says Greatist.com. But if things seem worse than usual, you should see your healthcare provider if your itching or discomfort is so bad it interrupts your daily activities or sleep; if you develop new symptoms related to your eczema; you notice you're getting flare-ups more often; if your eczema seems to be getting worse or spreading to new parts of your body; or if you have a dry patch that seems like it might be infected.

COST-SAVINGS EXAMPLE:

Out-of-pocket costs for people with atopic dermatitis, the most common type of eczema, run about $600 a year. 42% spend $1,000 or more annually on the condition, and 8.5% spend $5,000 and up.

Reduce or eliminate these costs – and avoid drug side effects and extra medical appointments – by using home remedies whenever possible.

Save $600 - $5,000 a year if you can use these remedies effectively.

DIABETES

Type 2 diabetes (diabetes mellitus) requires medical diagnosis and lifelong medical care. Trusted remedies can improve your condition significantly, but can never replace the need for regular medical care. Poorly controlled diabetes kills people, so do not neglect medical appointments or your doctor's instructions.

That said, people with type 2 diabetes often look to physician-trusted remedies in addition to conventional medicine for help in treating their disease. Natural remedies are an effective way to complement your diabetes treatment, says **Danielle E. Greenman, M.D.** [300] However, if done without the correct knowledge or guidance, the mixing of herbs, supplements, and medicines can lead to an unsafe drop in blood sugar, she warns. Before starting any new remedies, consult your doctor. Here are some of Dr. Greenman's most trusted remedies for type 2 diabetes.

Aloe Vera: Support is growing for use of aloe vera gel, the slippery stuff inside aloe vera leaves. Taking two tablespoons of aloe vera juice per day can cause blood sugar levels to fall in people with type 2 diabetes, according to a study reported by Healthline [301] (medically reviewed by **Owen Kramer, M.D.** [302]) Be sure that any product you buy is free of the sap components aloin and anthraquinones, as the sap (which is different from the gel) is known for its laxative effect.

Apple Cider Vinegar: Acetic acid is the essential ingredient believed to be responsible for ACV's many health benefits. Take 2 tablespoons before bed to reduce morning fasting sugar levels. Even better, 1-2 tablespoons with meals can decrease the glycemic load of a carbohydrate rich meal. ACV can be taken alone or mixed into salad dressings or other foods and beverages. At a minimum, have a glass of water to cleanse your mouth, throat, and esophagus of acid.

Berberine: This botanical compound is found in goldenseal, barberry, Oregon grape root, and other plants. Current evidence supports its use for decreasing blood sugar and A1C. This herb can interfere with the metabolism of traditional pharmaceuticals, so check with your doctor before taking it. Berberine should never be taken while pregnant.

Chromium: Mainly found in brewer's yeast, deficiency in chromium impairs the metabolism of glucose. Evidence supports chromium for lower blood sugar and A1C levels. Be careful with this supplement if you have kidney disease, cautions Dr. Greenman.

Cinnamon: This medically beneficial indulgence helps lower blood sugar and cholesterol levels.

Fenugreek seed: This ancient spice is well known for its ability to lower cholesterol and A1C.

Fiber and barley: Fiber decreases blood sugar and insulin concentrations. Most people get only 6-8 grams, well below the daily recommendation of 30 grams. The best way is to eat your veggies. Barley is a high-fiber, high-protein grain known for its value in improving blood sugar, insulin, cholesterol, and general inflammation. Barley does not require soaking and can be cooked in 15 minutes on the stovetop with just some water and salt. Other high-fiber foods include beans, broccoli, berries, avocados, popcorn, whole wheat, apples, dried fruits, and nuts.

---

[300] Danielle Greenman, M.D., Functional Medicine, Blum Center for Health, blumcenterforhealth.com
[301] Aloe Vera for Diabetes: Research, Pros, Cons, and More, Healthline
[302] Owen Kramer, M.D., Pinnacle Dermatology, Elmhurst, IL, pinnacleskin.com

Nopal: You may have seen nopales in a Mexican grocery or on the menu at a Mexican restaurant. Nopales are the pads of the prickly pear cactus and when cooked right are delicious. Over 100 species of nopal grow in Mexico, where it is a common ingredient in numerous dishes. Give them a try and know you've chosen a food that helps lower your blood sugar. Caution: nopals are called prickly for a reason, handle with care; check YouTube for preparation tips.

Zinc: People with diabetes are often zinc deficient. Studies show taking zinc can reduce blood sugar and A1C, have an antioxidant effect, lower blood sugar, and help with diabetes complications. Large doses can cause problems, so ask for guidance for appropriate dosing.

In addition, EverydayHealth.com offers 10 tips to lower blood sugar naturally [303] (medically reviewed by **Kacy Church, M.D.** [304]). Experts agree that individuals with type 2 diabetes can improve their symptoms with a few simple lifestyle tweaks (you may notice some overlap with Dr. Greenman's remedies above; this is simply reinforcement that these remedies really work):

- Keep an eye on your carb intake
- Avoid eating large meals
- Fill up on fiber
- Get more quality shuteye
- Lose a little weigh
- Get a handle on stress
- Never skip eating breakfast
- Drink more water
- Add more resistant starch to your plate
- Ramp up your movement each day

According to Dr. Church and the authors, these lifestyle changes can sometimes eliminate the need for medication. While that is not the same as saying that your diabetes is cured, it may be the best possible news any diabetes patient could receive.

"Doctor, Doctor!"

Remember, these remedies are not medical advice. Diabetes is all about body chemistry, which varies from one person to the next. People with diabetes should use home remedies only as advised by their doctor. This is true of *any* diabetes remedy you hear of or read about. Diabetes is a chronic, life-threatening disease. Insufficient diabetes care can lead to blindness, organ failure, amputation, and death. Once you've been diagnosed, keeping up with your medical care and treatment is essential. Also, ask your doctor what diabetes self-care steps she recommends. Mayo Clinic, WebMD, Good Rx, and the Joslin Diabetes Center all agree – *there is no known cure for diabetes*, therefore you are strongly advised to get an opinion from a doctor before using anything touted as a diabetes "cure."

COST-SAVINGS EXAMPLE:

The cost of diabetes medications and insulin has risen sharply in recent years. If you are finding it hard to pay for your medications, talk to your doctor. Never cut back or stop taking your medication. Discuss with your doctor the possibility that trusted remedies and self-care can reduce your need to take insulin and other drugs. [305]

---

[303] 10 Tips to Lower Blood Sugar Naturally, everydayhealth.com
[304] Dr. Kacy A. Church M.D., Endocrinologist in Burlingame, CA, Sutter Health, sutterhealth.org
[305] Living Well with Diabetes, Minnesota Department of Health, health.state.mn.us

Self-care can make costly diabetes treatment more effective and may delay the onset of common complications, which are also costly. But besides the money you might save, the biggest benefit is quality of life.

DIAPER RASH

Try these soothing solutions for diaper rash, including guidance from **Dr. Sally S. Robinson**, a pediatrician and medical professor at the University of Texas [306], and **Dr. Catherine Gritchen**, pediatrician at MemorialCare Medical Group in Long Beach, CA [307] , and **Dr. S. Daniel Ganjian**, a pediatrician at Providence Saint John's Health Center in Santa Monica, CA. [308]

Boil cloth diapers after laundering: For starters, it bears noting that cloth diapers can harbor a host of unwanted germs if not washed properly, according to Dr. Robinson. "If using cloth diapers and washing them yourself, use very hot water and rinse several times to make sure all the detergent is removed," she says. "Boil them for 15 minutes after washing to make sure that all the germs are killed, and all soap is removed."

Here are trusted remedies for diaper rash from diarrhea, yeast infection and other common triggers, courtesy of Care.com [309] , which offers dozens of practical home care articles for children, seniors, pets, and more:

Make your own diaper rash cream: Make your own natural diaper cream, such as the protective barrier balm found on the Mommypotamus blog. The balm combines olive oil, shea butter, coconut oil (an antifungal that can tackle yeast diaper rash) and zinc oxide. In between diaper changes, store your homemade diaper rash cream in the refrigerator. Before applying the cream to your baby, warm it up by rubbing it between your hands first.

Use breast milk: Breastfeeding moms might already know that liquid gold does more than just nourish their little one's tummy. "I will sometimes tell parents to use a bit of breast milk on a diaper rash," shares Dr. Gritchen. "Though there is no clear evidence that this would always be helpful, there is certainly no harm in this practice. Breast milk has many amazing biodynamic properties, as well as natural anti-infective properties, and is full of antibodies."

Use apple cider vinegar: Laura of Clean Chef, Messy Mom recommends adding a cup of apple cider vinegar to your baby's bath water to get rid of a yeast-caused diaper rash quickly. "Not only will the apple cider vinegar kill bacteria that could worsen the rash, it will also kill off yeast that is prone to cause a rash," she writes. "You can also dilute a tablespoon of apple cider vinegar in a cup of water and wash your baby's bottom with it each time you do a diaper change."

Reach for olive oil: Dr. Ganjian recommends parents use a mild cleanser, such as Cetaphil, after

[306] Sally Robinson, M.D., The University of Texas Medical Branch at Galveston | Image: Flaticon.com
[307] Catherine D Gritchen, M.D. MemorialCare Medical Group, Los Altos, CA, memorialcare.org
[308] Daniel S. Ganjian, M.D., The Doctors of Saint John's, Santa Monica, CA, providence.org
[309] 7 Home Remedies For Diaper Rash, Care.com

their baby's bowel movements and plain water and cotton balls after wet diapers. But a soothing alternative can be olive oil, which possesses anti-inflammatory and antimicrobial properties. Ganjian recommends this soothing protocol for irritant dermatitis diaper rash, as well as rash caused by allergic contact dermatitis.

Apply cornstarch: Dr. Ganjian recommends using cornstarch to dry your baby's bottom instead of talcum powder. Keep a container of cornstarch near your diaper changing area and apply it after using homemade diaper rash cream. Just be sure to keep cornstarch (or any powder) away from little lungs.

Consider coconut oil: I usually recommend a greasy or emollient-type product," Dr. Gritchen says. "These are hydrating and soothing, in addition to providing a moderate amount of barrier protection." One of the most natural products to fit into this category is one you may already have at home: coconut oil. This remedy may be especially helpful for diaper rash caused by yeast, as multiple published studies confirm coconut oil is a powerful antifungal.

"Doctor, Doctor!"

Dr. Gritchen says, "If the rash is not resolving, I always recommend that parents bring the baby in to see the doctor to be evaluated, and make sure there's not an infectious component. Often, a rash that begins as a simple irritant rash can become secondarily infected with bacteria or fungus because the broken skin is more vulnerable to infection. Your doctor can then determine if they need a prescription-strength treatment, such as prescription-strength steroid, bacterial ointment, an antifungal cream, or oral antibiotics."

COST-SAVINGS EXAMPLE:

Diaper rash is inexpensive to treat. It's wise to keep a supply of diaper rash ointment on hand for cases when the above remedies do not provide immediate relief.

DIARRHEA

In many parts of the world, diarrhea is a leading cause of death, especially in infants and children. While diarrhea may seem like a short-term annoyance, it's best to take it seriously – because obviously, you'd like to be done with it ASAP. You also want to be aware that it may be a sign of an underlying condition. Here are the 10 best natural remedies for diarrhea, according to Livestrong.com [310] (medically reviewed by **Jennifer Logan, M.D., MPH** [311]):

Eat foods with soluble fiber: While the BRAT diet (bread, rice, applesauce, toast) used to be the gold standard for diarrhea, research shows it doesn't help much, says Livestrong. Instead, choose foods with soluble fiber, which move more slowly through the digestive system. Per Mayo Clinic, foods high in soluble fiber include: oats, peas, beans, apples, citrus, carrots, and barley.

---

[310] The 10 Best Natural Remedies for Diarrhea, Livestrong, livestrong.com
[311] Jennifer L. Logan, M.D., Logan Medical Writing, loganmedicalwriting.com | Image: Flaticon.com

Stick to plain and smaller meals: Eating 5-6 smaller meals during the day may be easier on your system than three larger ones. Eating bland, easy-to-digest foods helps stop diarrhea fast. That means skip heavy seasonings and sauces; choose lean proteins like chicken, fish and eggs, dd mashed potatoes, noodles, and rice; go with smooth peanut butter and well-cooked vegetables

Try probiotic foods: Probiotics may help stop diarrhea, **Randy Meisner, M.D.** [312] told Livestrong. Though Dr. Meisner says some patients benefit from probiotics – microorganisms that live in the GI tract and also occur in some foods – in cases of diarrhea caused by an acute infection. Probiotic-rich foods include yogurt, kefir, sauerkraut, kimchi, miso, and tempeh

Stay well hydrated: Pure clean water is best. Hydrating alone won't get rid of diarrhea, but it's essential to help avoid dehydration, a potentially serious consequence of diarrhea, Dr. Meisner explains. Symptoms of dehydration include dizziness, feeling lightheaded or weak, concentrated urine and decreased urination, confusion and thirst, says Mayo Clinic.[313] An electrolyte solution such as Gatorade, Pedialyte, or Amazon's Basic Care Electrolyte Solution may help.

Nix artificial sweeteners: Some foods can cause diarrhea or make it worse, Dr. Meisner says, and artificial sweeteners are high on that list. Sugar substitutes – aspartame or Splenda – are often culprits behind diarrhea, Dr. Meisner says, because they can pull water into your gut.

Dial back on dairy: Lactose, the sugar found in dairy products, can cause diarrhea for some people, Dr. Meisner says. Having diarrhea after eating or drinking dairy foods is a common sign of lactose intolerance. An estimated 30 to 50 million people in the U.S. have lactose intolerance, so it's something to consider if your diarrhea is occurring after eating or drinking dairy.

Ginger root: Ginger can help alleviate nausea and vomiting, symptoms that often accompany diarrhea, according to Cleveland Clinic. [314]

Forgo fatty or fried foods: Eliminating some fatty foods may also help stop liquid diarrhea. High-fat foods like fried chicken or potato chips can be tough for some people to digest, says Harvard Health Publishing. When these foods aren't broken down well, they go to the colon, where the fat is turned into fatty acids, causing the colon to secrete fluid — and voilà, diarrhea.[315]

According to the USDA, high-fat foods to avoid include: Fast foods (McDonald's, Taco Bell, etc); fried foods like fried chicken; whipped cream; fatty meats, such as beef short ribs; fatty snack foods, such as potato and corn chips; processed meats, such as pepperoni, bacon and sausage; desserts, such as dulce de leche and chocolate cake; high-fat salad dressings. [316]

Skip spicy foods: Holding off on spicy foods like chili that can irritate your GI tract. Other food intolerances could be causing your diarrhea. Other symptoms of food intolerance include stomach pain or cramping, gas, and bloating, per the Cleveland Clinic. Keeping a food journal can help you identify possible trigger foods and limit or avoid them going forward. [317]

---

[312] Randall Meisner, M.D., Gastroenterology, Grand Rapids, MI, findadoctor.spectrumhealth.org

[313] Dehydration, Symptoms and Causes, Mayo Clinic | Appointments at Mayo Clinic

[314] Ginger Ale and Saltine Crackers? 5 Ways to Ease Stomach Pain and Nausea, Cleveland Clinic

[315] Is something in your diet causing diarrhea? Harvard Health, health.harvard.edu

[316] Top 10 High Fat Foods to Avoid, MyFoodData.com

[317] Food Intolerance: Symptoms, Causes and Treatment Options | Appointments at Cleveland Clinic

Cut out caffeine: Caffeine speeds up digestion, according to Harvard Health Publishing. When waste gets pushed through too quickly, your digestive system doesn't have a chance to absorb enough of the liquid, causing loose stools. To treat watery diarrhea, cut back on foods and drinks that contain caffeine, such as coffee, tea, soda, energy drinks, and chocolate.

Avoid alcohol: It's best to say no to alcohol when you're trying to treat watery diarrhea. Drinking too much alcohol may cause diarrhea the next day, especially when it comes to beer and wine, according to the International Foundation for Gastrointestinal Disorders [318] (by **W. Grant Thompson, M.D.**, University of Ottawa, Ontario, Canada [319]).

Make sure it's actually diarrhea: Dr. Meisner notes that if you're having chronic or recurring diarrhea, it's important to assess whether it could be fecal incontinence instead. Diarrhea is defined as an increased amount of stool, but fecal incontinence is when you are unable to control your bowel movements.

This often results in accidents or soiling of undergarments, and not necessarily an increased quantity of stool. The difference is important, Dr. Meisner says, and a doctor will need to assess the two conditions differently, so don't be afraid to speak with your doctor if you are actually experiencing incidents of incontinence and not just diarrhea. [320]

"Doctor, Doctor!"

Chronic, recurring diarrhea can be indicative of a more severe illness, Dr. Meisner warns. If your diarrhea has gone on for more than a few days, it's time to call your doctor. Mayo Clinic also notes you should see a doctor for diarrhea accompanied by symptoms such as fever, severe pain or stools that appear bloody or black.

COST-SAVINGS EXAMPLE:

In the United States, diarrhea is inexpensive to treat. It's wise to keep a bottle of diarrhea medication on hand for cases when the above remedies do not provide immediate relief.

DIVERTICULOSIS/DIVERTICULITIS

Throughout this section, pay close attention to the terms <u>diverticulosis</u> and <u>diverticulitis</u> – they are not the same. Whether you use self-care or medical care, it is vital to understand the difference between these related conditions.

A diverticulum is a pouch-like structure that can form through points of weakness in the muscular wall of the colon (i.e., at points where blood vessels pass through the wall), **John H. Pemberton, M.D.,**[321] Professor of Surgery at Mayo Medical

[318] Common Causes of Chronic Diarrhea, International Foundation for Gastrointestinal Disorders, iffgd.org
[319] W. Grant Thompson, M.D., Rome Foundation, theromefoundation.org
[320] The 10 Best Natural Remedies for Diarrhea, Livestrong, livestrong.com
[321] Dr. John H. Pemberton, Doctors Gallery, doctorsgallery.org | Image: Flaticon.com

School, writes for the patient education site uptodate.com. [322]

Diverticulosis merely refers to the presence of diverticula, he explains. The condition is often found during a test done for other reasons, such as a colonoscopy. Most people with diverticulosis have no symptoms and will remain symptom-free for the rest of their lives.

Inflammation of a diverticulum (diverticulitis) occurs when there is thinning and breakdown of the diverticular wall. This may be caused by increased pressure within the colon or by hardened particles of stool, which can become lodged within the diverticulum. A person with diverticulosis may also have diverticulitis, or diverticular bleeding.

The most common symptom of diverticulitis is pain in the left lower abdomen. Other symptoms can include nausea and vomiting, constipation, diarrhea, and urinary symptoms such as pain or burning when urinating or the frequent need to urinate.

People with diverticulosis who do not have symptoms do not require treatment. However, most clinicians recommend increasing fiber in the diet, which can help to bulk the stools and may prevent worsening of the condition. Two dietary remedies are commonly followed, but it turns out that only one has a confirmed medical basis:

Increase fiber: Fruits and vegetables are a good source of fiber. The fiber content of packaged foods can be calculated by reading the nutrition label.

Seeds and nuts: Patients with diverticular disease have historically been advised to avoid whole pieces of fiber (such as seeds, corn, and nuts) because of concern that these foods could cause an episode of diverticulitis. However, this belief is completely unproven. We do not suggest that patients with diverticulosis avoid seeds, corn, or nuts, says Dr. Pemberton.

"Doctor, Doctor!"

> If you develop one or more of the following signs or symptoms, seek immediate medical attention, says Dr. Pemberton: temperature >100.1° F (38° C); worsening or severe abdominal pain; or inability to tolerate fluids. In addition, it is *not* normal to see blood in a bowel movement; this can be a sign of several conditions, most of which are not serious (e.g., hemorrhoids) but some of which require immediate treatment. Anyone who sees blood after a bowel movement should consult their healthcare provider.

COST-SAVINGS EXAMPLE:

> **The cost of treating diverticulitis can be high, as it may include hospitalization and surgery. Each year, Mayo Clinic alone diagnoses and treats approximately 20,000 people with diverticulitis.**
>
> **You want to avoid this disease if at all possible. The surgical mortality rate for diverticulitis is 18%.**

---

[322] Patient education: Diverticular disease (Beyond the Basics), UpToDate, uptodate.com

The most trusted remedy for diverticulosis is simply to replace more of the foods in your diet with high-fiber foods; this may not only save you money, but also your life.

The cost of eating more high-fiber foods for diverticulosis is low. The cost of medical care for diverticulitis is high and may cost you your life. Congratulate yourself right now for prioritizing these trusted remedies!

DIZZINESS

Dizziness is the feeling of being unbalanced or lightheaded, says Healthline.com [323] (medically reviewed by **Nancy Hammond, M.D.** [324]). You may feel you're about to faint or your surroundings are moving or spinning around you.

Both feelings can occur along with nausea or vomiting, Healthline explains. Dizziness is not a medical condition on its own, but a symptom of an underlying cause. Consult a doctor for recurring or unexplained episodes of dizziness. Fortunately, several foods and nutrients may help relieve symptoms of dizziness.

Water: One of the best is water. Dehydration is a common cause of dizziness as well as more serious health conditions. When you're dizzy, your body may be telling you to drink water and stay hydrated.

Ginger: Ginger is known to help relieve motion sickness, nausea, and dizziness. Ginger is available in many forms. Add fresh or ground ginger to your food, drink ginger tea, or take ginger supplements. However, Dr. Hammond reminds people to consult their doctor before taking any kind of supplement, even if it's natural. Some supplements can interfere with other medical conditions you have or medications you take.

Vitamins: Other key nutrients for ending dizziness are vitamins C and E, says Dr. Hammond.

"Doctor, Doctor!"

About 20 to 30 percent of people experience dizziness, says Houston-based Prime Urgent Care [325] (**Dr. Niharika Mehra, D.O., CEO** [326]). So a bout of dizziness isn't necessarily something to worry about. However, if you're a normally healthy person with an unusual bout of dizziness, it makes sense to go to urgent care to call a medical professional.

Visiting an urgent care facility is especially important when your dizziness has a sudden onset or feels especially aggressive (accompanied by nausea or difficulty walking), says

---

[323] How to Get Rid of Dizziness, Healthline.com | Image: Chanut is Industries, The Noun Project
[324] Nancy Hammond, M.D., Neurology, University of Kansas Medical Center, kumc.edu
[325] When Should I See a Doctor for Dizziness? Urgent Care Clinic, Pearland, TX, primeuc.com
[326] Dr. Niharika Mehra, DO, Family Medicine Specialist in Pearland, TX, Healthgrades, healthgrades.com

Prime Urgent Care. You should see a doctor or visit the ER without delay if your dizziness is accompanied by other unusual symptoms like blurred vision, slurred speech, pain/numbness (especially in your arms), nausea, headache, chest pain or shortness of breath, these can be signs of a serious health issue that you should address immediately.

As you age, feeling dizzy or losing balance can be a more common sign of a serious health issue like a stroke, where blood flow to the brain is reduced. So if dizziness does not resolve quickly and you are over the age of 60, you should visit an emergency room as quickly as possible.

COST-SAVINGS EXAMPLE:

If drinking water resolves your dizziness, you've spent nothing and possibly learned a valuable lesson, the need to stay well hydrated. A well-hydrated person has pale or nearly clear urine, and ample opportunities to check. [327]

If indeed your dizziness is a sign of dehydration, remember that you should drink at least five glasses of water per day, and this will reduce your risk of stroke by 53%, according to a recent study by Loma Linda University. [328]

The average cost of a hospital stay for a stroke patient ranges from $20,396 to $43,652. Worse, stroke patients often lose their income from employment. [329]

Dizziness is a risk factor for stroke. Stay hydrated, avoid dizziness and stroke, and you could save tens if not hundreds of thousands of dollars compared with people who suffer strokes.

DOG BITES

In addition to this information below on treating dog bites, see general guidance elsewhere in this directory under S – Scratches, Bites, and Stings.

Dog bites pose a serious health risk to our communities, says the American Veterinary Medical Foundation. [330] More than 4.5 million people are bitten by dogs each year in the United States, and more than 800,000 receive medical attention for dog bites. At least half bite victims are children.

Infection is the biggest danger with dog bites, according to Cleveland Clinic [331] (**Stephen Sayles**

[327] Urine Color: What It Says About Your Health, Cleveland Clinic, health.clevelandclinic.org
[328] What Can Help Prevent a Stroke? Lone Star Neurology, health.clevelandclinic.org
[329] Covering the cost of stroke, Washington National Insurance Company, washingtonnational.com
[330] Dog bite prevention, American Veterinary Medical Foundation (AVMF), avma.org
[331] If a Dog Bites You, Do These 7 Things Now, Cleveland Clinic, health.clevelandclinic.org

III, M.D., emergency medicine physician [332]). Roughly 50% of dog bites introduce bacteria, including *staphylococcus, streptococcus,* and *Pasteurella,* as well as *capnocytophaga.* Unvaccinated and feral dogs can also carry – and transfer – rabies, so your doctor will want to know details about the dog that bit you.

Avoid situations where you may come into contact with unfamiliar dogs. For example, while waiting for an elevator, stand well back from the door, as you do not know whether someone may be getting off the elevator with a dog. Know the dog laws in your area; if your city has a leash law and you see an unleashed dog, report it to police immediately. If you see a dog attack in progress, call 9-1-1. If a dog bites someone, take these steps right away, says Cleveland Clinic:

Wash: Wash the wound with mild soap.

Flush: Run warm tap water over it for five to ten minutes.

Control bleeding: Slow the bleeding with a clean cloth.

Antibiotic cream: Apply over-the-counter antibiotic cream such as Neosporin if you have it.

Bandage: Wrap the wound in a sterile bandage. Keep the wound bandaged and see your doctor. Change bandages several times daily.

Observe: Watch for signs of infection: redness, swelling, increased pain, and fever.

Your doctor will want to know more about the dog that bit you and how it happened, Cleveland Clinic explains. He or she will also likely clean the wound again, apply antibiotic ointment, and prescribe oral antibiotics, such as Augmentin, if there's an infection concern.

After any bite, you should make sure you know when your last tetanus shot was – and that you're up to date. While a tetanus immunization is good for ten years, Dr. Sayles notes, your doctor may recommend a booster if the wound is dirty and it's been more than five years since your last shot. Depending on the wound, your doctor may also recommend stitches. Generally, though, dog wounds are left open to heal unless they are on the face or if they could leave particularly severe scars if left unsutured. Ultimately, Dr. Sayles says, caring for a dog bite is about keeping bacteria from causing an infection.

The website dogbites.org [333] offers another seven-step checklist (the site was founded by a dog bite victim, not a doctor; use this supporting information in addition to the physician-approved remedies above):

Identify the dog and its owner: Immediately identify the owner of the dog or the person who had custody of the dog when it attacked you. Obtain the names and addresses and request proof of rabies vaccination. If this information cannot be obtained, you may be forced to undergo a series of rabies shots, which are expensive (exceed $3,000).

Seek medical care: Depending on the severity of the dog bite, contact first responders (9-1-1) for immediate medical attention, or have someone drive you to emergency care. Always seek professional medical treatment after being bitten or attacked by a dog. The risk of infection from

---

[332] Stephen Sayles, III, M.D., Cleveland Clinic, my.clevelandclinic.org
[333] Steps To Take After A Dog Bite, Dog Bite Victim Guide, Dogsbite.Org

a dog bite is far too great to ignore.

File a dog bite report: After you've been medically treated – even if the injury was minor – file a dog bite report with local authorities, as required by law in many jurisdictions. This documents your case and provides help to the next victim who may be bitten or attacked by the same dog. Without a paper trail, authorities cannot enforce effectively.

Gather more information: After identifying the dog and its owner, find out more about the dog. Obtain the dog license information and any records pertaining to its history. Had the dog bitten or attacked a person or animal prior to biting you? Has the dog been legally designated "potentially dangerous" or "dangerous" by authorities?

Photograph your injuries: Take photos of your injuries, even if you need to unwrap gauze. Confer with a doctor or nurse as needed. They will tell you a safe manner in which to do so. Photograph all of your wounds, including bruises, as well as all torn, bloody clothing and the location of the attack.

Contact an attorney: Contact a dog bite attorney right away. The legal issues surrounding dog bites are complex and difficult to navigate. Your dog bite lawyer (or personal injury lawyer) is the only person besides the medical doctor who treats your injuries and will look after your best interests from this point forward.

Begin a journal: If you seek compensation for your injury, start a journal as soon as you can. Spend a little time each day recording your thoughts for the few first weeks after the attack. Dog bite claims often take several years to complete. Anticipate keeping this journal on a weekly basis throughout this time.

"Doctor, Doctor!"

Always call a doctor about a dog bite. Untreated animal bites can lead to sepsis. Sepsis is a severe reaction to infection, and it can be life-threatening. In addition, call Animal Control; this is important to reduce risk to potential future victims.

<u>COST-SAVINGS EXAMPLE:</u>

Costs of treating a dog bite can exceed $30,000. Insurance settlements for dog bites total over $530 million per year. If you are bitten by a dog, you may be eligible for compensation for medical bills, lost wages, pain and suffering, and other damages.

Avoiding a dog bite can save you $30,000 or more in medical costs, in addition to the psychological damage, lost wages, and risk of death.

DRY EYES

Dry eye disease occurs when you lack tear quantity or quality, says Advanced Eye Care Center [334] of Saskatchewan, Canada (**Dr. Myles Bokinac** and **Dr. Rhea Anderson** [335]). Dealing with the discomfort of dry eyes can be a daily battle, and the condition can affect your vision. The condition includes various symptoms, such as dry eyes, redness, watery eyes, blurred vision, light sensitivity, and irritated or scratchy eyes.

There are many causes of dry eyes, from allergies to medical conditions to computer use. Knowing the cause can be helpful, particularly if it's a treatable condition or a removable environmental factor. However, if you're not a master detective, sometimes focusing on managing symptoms can be the difference between another lousy day or a day without dry eyes. So here are 10 home remedies trusted by Drs. Bokinac and Anderson for dry eye relief.

Eye drops: If you're not producing enough tears, you can try over-the-counter lubricating eye drops to protect the surface of your eye. Many eye drops contain preservatives that stop harmful bacteria from forming after opening the product. Unfortunately, although rare, some eyes can react to the preservatives, resulting in inflammation. If your eye drops seem to cause discomfort, talk to your optometrist about eye drops without preservatives. These are often sold in single-use applicators, eliminating the need for preservatives.

Limit screen time and take breaks: A common symptom of digital eye strain is dry eyes. The average person blinks 12 times a minute, but only 5 times per minute when using a computer. As a result, our wide-open eyes are more prone to dryness, leading to eye strain, headaches, and feeling irritated. Taking frequent screen breaks gives our eyes time to relax. For more, see the section on **Eyestrain (Computer Vision Syndrome)** elsewhere in this directory.

Warm compress: Using a warm compress can help treat symptoms of many eye conditions. Heat can soothe irritation or inflammation caused by dry eyes. Additionally, it may also stimulate the gland that produces tears. It's also a chance to close your eyes and allow them some rest.

Eye massage: A gentle eye massage can alleviate tension, improve blood flow, and relax muscles. Massaging feels very relaxing and should never be painful. According to **Dr. Marc Grossman** [336], you can perform acupressure massage on yourself to alleviate tension in your eyes and improve overall eye health. Each massage point in this image can be gently massaged. Move around the eye's orbit, beginning with B-1. Gently massage each point in succession for about 5-10 seconds, moving upward and toward the outer edge of the eye. You can do one eye at a time, or both eyes simultaneously. And you can massage your eyes as often as you wish. Some points will be more tender than others, indicating some tension there.

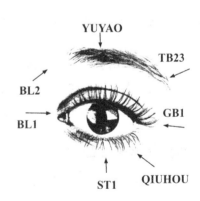

---

[334] Advance Eye Care Center, Saskatchewan, advanceeyecarecenter.com | Image, CC0

[335] Dr. Myles Bokinac and Dr. Rhea Anderson, Advance Eye Care Center, Saskatchewan

[336] Natural Eye Care, New Paltz, NY, Dr. Marc Grossman, Optometrist, Acupuncturist, naturaleyecare.com

Clean eyes: Keeping your eyelids, lashes, and ocular area clean is essential in protecting eye health. It can prevent the buildup of bacteria which can cause conditions such as blepharitis. Blepharitis is an inflammation of your eyelids caused by clogged oil glands located behind your eyelashes. Although blepharitis is preventable, the condition is irreversible. It can cause eye irritation, redness, dryness, or burning. If you suspect you have blepharitis, see your optometrist.

Better sleep: Sleep is crucial for resting your mind and body. It's the only time when your eyes stay closed for an extended time, giving them protection and rest. Healthy sleep benefits multiple functions of our body, including stress repair, memory, heart health, metabolism, energy levels, cognitive skills, and immune system (inflammation). Sleep is especially crucial if your dry eyes result from an immune disorder, as sleep regulates inflammation.

How much sleep you need will change with age and wellness. For example, you might need more rest to fight a cold. Generally, adults range between 7–9 hours. Seniors need less sleep as they age. On the other end, children and teens need more rest.

Drink water: Although water isn't the only ingredient in tears, it is the most significant. Water comprises 98% of a tear, with 2% oils, salt, and over 1,500 proteins. So if you're not drinking enough water, you're drying out your tear production. You might have heard adults should drink 6–8 glasses of water per day. It's a helpful guideline, but it isn't a perfect recommendation for everyone. How much water you need depends on your activity level, health, and environment. If you're unsure how much water is best for you, start with the guideline of 6–8 glasses.

Humidifier: If the room is dry, it might be affecting your eyes. A humidifier adds moisture into the air and can ease symptoms caused by dryness. Humidifiers can also improve other health issues related to dryness – dry skin, dry cough, dry throat, nose irritation and more.

Omega-3 fatty acid: You can reduce your risk of dry eye by 17% if you add fish oil to your diet. In addition, omega-3, commonly found in fish oil, can benefit your eye health by soothing symptoms and improving your tear quality. Although eating fish is an option for a natural dose of omega-3 fatty acids, you can also take supplements.

Eyewear: Using eyewear, from sunglasses to sports goggles, is a wise practice for eye safety. It can keep irritants or particles from aggravating your dry eyes. Sunglasses protect your eyes from UV damage. Sunglasses also reduce brightness. If your eyes are sensitive to light (photophobia), you can experience dry eyes. Eyewear provides a shield between your eyes and irritating environmental factors, like dust, wind, and chemical irritants (perfumes, cleaning products, etc.).

"Doctor, Doctor!"

Knowing these trusted remedies can be helpful when symptoms of dry eye flare up. But if your symptoms are increasing or you're ready for alternative treatment, an optometrist such as Advanced Eye Care Center [337] can help you find more options. Dry eyes can be uncomfortable, but they can also indicate developing eye conditions. Since your eyesight is invaluable and irreplaceable, an annual eye exam is wise. To learn about your eye health and how to get dry eye relief, schedule an eye exam with an optometrist near you.

---

[337] Advance Eye Care Center, Saskatchewan, advanceeyecarecenter.com

COST-SAVINGS EXAMPLE:

These trusted remedies are free (eye massage) or inexpensive (eye drops). Insufficient treatment for dry eyes may lead to the need for eyelid surgery, which can cost about $200 for blepharitis treatment (which may need to be repeated annually) to $1,500 or more for one-time blepharoplasty. [338]

Avoid hundreds or thousands of dollars in treatment costs by taking care of your eyes with low-cost trusted home remedies.

DRY MOUTH

Most of us have experienced a dry mouth at some point, says **Alan S. Berger, M.D.,** [339] double board-certified rhinoplasty surgeon and founder of the BergerHenry ENT Specialty Group, a provider of ear, nose, and throat care in the Philadelphia, PA area. [340]

It may have been after a long workout, before a big job interview, or while trekking through the desert after severely underestimating how much water you should have brought, to name a few. While these are normal responses to temporary situations, some people suffer from a chronically dry mouth, known in the medical world as xerostomia.

Saliva plays a key role. Healthy saliva production contributes to cleansing the mouth, digestion of food, speech, chewing, and swallowing, and keeping bacteria and fungi at bay. Chronic dry mouth as a result of inadequate saliva can have a significant impact on your quality of life. Women and the elderly are especially at risk.

Apart from a dry mouth itself, other symptoms can include sore throat, constant thirst, hoarse voice, headaches, dry eyes, nasal passages, and/or skin, cracked, dry lips, burning sensation in the mouth, difficulties chewing or swallowing, or needing to sip fluids in order to eat dry foods comfortably, changes to taste sensation, and bad breath. People who suffer from dry mouth may also find themselves more prone to dental problems, such as tooth decay and gingivitis. Here are several easy self-care remedies Dr. Berger trusts to help alleviate a dry mouth. [341]

Water: Obvious perhaps, but people forget to drink enough water. Another option is to suck on ice cubes (but don't crunch them, you could break a tooth).

Cut back on caffeine, alcohol, and tobacco: All three have a drying effect.

Nasal breathing: Breathe through your nose, not your mouth. To get in the habit of being a nasal breather, try taping your mouth shut while you sleep with ordinary paper tape. "Nasal breathing

---

[338] How Much Does A Blepharoplasty Cost? Stein Plastic Surgery, Raleigh, NC, facialdoc.com
[339] Alan S. Berger, M.D., Berger Henry ENT, Philadelphia | Image: Petai Jantrapoon, The Noun Project
[340] Berger Henry ENT Specialty Group, Willow Grove and other southeastern Pennsylvania locations
[341] Home Remedies for Dry Mouth (Xerostomia) by Alan S. Berger, M.D., bergerhenryent.com

increases nitric oxide production in the sinuses, which has been linked to reduced inflammation, improved sleep, improved memory, and an overall increase in immune system function," explains **Mark Burhenne, DDS** [342] of Sunnyvale, CA. [343] "When you breathe mainly through the nose, you wake up feeling more rested, without a dry mouth or a sore throat." The editors of Trusted Remedies, publisher of this directory, use this remedy and agree that it works very well.

Humidify: Use a humidifier in the room, particularly at night during sleep. Find a highly rated room humidifier on Amazon, starting at about $50.

"Doctor, Doctor!"

Make an appointment to see your family physician or dentist if you experience more than minor daily discomfort due to dry mouth symptoms, says WebMD [344] (medically reviewed by **Dan Brennan, M.D.** [345]). Also see your ENT doctor if you suffer difficulties with nose breathing, as this can be a symptom of another issue such as a deviated septum or nasal polyps. A healthcare professional can make a firm diagnosis of dry mouth and determine the best course of treatment for you.

COST-SAVINGS EXAMPLE:

Trusted home remedies for dry mouth are inexpensive and may provide relief without the need for a costly office visit.

DRY SKIN AND WINTER ITCH

Dry skin is a common problem and often worse during the winter when humidity is low (i.e., "winter itch"), explains dermatologist **Mary S. Stone, M.D.** [346] of University of Iowa Hospitals & Clinics [347] . She suggests these trusted remedies:

Shorter showers: Take short baths or showers (no more than 10 minutes) only once in a 24-hour period. Bathing should be in warm rather than hot water, which literally steams the oils out of your skin. Use soap minimally and where/when needed (for example, under the arms, the groin and genitals, the feet, and the face). Mild soaps should be used (unscented, those designed for sensitive skin).

Dry off gently: After showering, quickly and gently pat the skin partially dry with a towel (do not rub!). Within three minutes of getting out, apply a moisturizer, cream, or ointment to seal the

---

[342] Ask the Dentist, the website of Mark Burhenne, DDS, functional dentist, askthedentist.com
[343] Mouth Taping: The Cheapest Life Hack for Better Sleep, Everyday Health, everydayhealth.com
[344] Remedies for Dry Mouth, WebMD
[345] Dr. Dan Brennan, SantaBarbaraPediatrics.com
[346] Mary S. Stone, Dermatologist, University of Iowa, uihc.org
[347] Winter dry skin, University of Iowa Hospitals & Clinics | Image: Created byProSymbols, The Noun Project

water in the skin before it evaporates.

Moisturize: Moisturizers should be reapplied liberally during the day and evening when possible, especially to those areas prone to dryness. If dry skin affects your hands, reapply moisturizer after handwashing.

Use skin creams: Treat any red patches with a topical cortisone (steroid) cream or ointment for a 5- to 15-day course. When using both a cortisone product and a moisturizer, always use the cortisone first and the moisturizer second. Be careful about using other over-the-counter anti-inflammatory and itch-suppressing creams or lotions. Many of these products contain chemicals that can irritate or cause allergic reactions in dry skin.

Humidify: Increasing the humidity level in the air of your home and workplace would be advisable. Consider adding a humidifier to the central heating system of your home. If you use a portable humidifier, make sure it is used in your bedroom at night. Find a highly rated room humidifier on Amazon, starting at about $50.

Get set for winter: Dry skin is usually a long-term problem that often recurs, especially in winter. When you notice your skin beginning to get dry, resume your moisturizing routine and harsh soaps. If the itchy, dry, skin rash returns, use both the moisturizers and a steroid cream.

Another effective natural remedy to improved skin health is offered by Healthline [348] (medically reviewed by **Dr. Cynthia Cobb**):

Grapeseed oil: Grapeseed oil improves the skin's moisture and softness. Grapeseed oil helps the vitamin E and vitamin C in your skin to be more efficient and effective at preserving your skin.

"Doctor, Doctor!"

> Over-the-counter cortisone creams and ointments can occasionally be helpful, but prescription-strength products are often required to calm down this type of dermatitis. Make sure you understand where the cortisone cream or ointment is to be applied (only on the red patches unless instructed otherwise) and how often (no more than twice daily). The appearance of yellow crusts or pus in these areas indicates a bacterial infection; consult your doctor. Also, if your skin is very dry, or if you have an associated red dermatitis, it is a good idea to seek the advice of your dermatologist or family physician.

COST-SAVINGS EXAMPLE:

These treatments from a dermatologist may cost between $80 and $275 per visit.

Effective self-care for your skin may save you hundreds of dollars per year. It's no wonder such a wide variety of affordable skin care products are available in stores and online.

---

[348] Grapeseed Oil for Skin, Dr. Cynthia Cobb, DNP, Founder of Allure Enhancement Center, Lafayette, LA

EARACHE AND EAR INFECTION

 If you've ever had an ear infection, you know how uncomfortable they can be. Symptoms include inner ear pain, fever, hearing loss, trouble sleeping, difficulty balancing, fluid draining from the ear, and sore throat. SingleCare Team [349] – a provider of free-to-consumers prescription drug savings cards – offers several trusted remedies for ear infections (medically reviewed by **Anis Rehman, M.D.** [350]):

Cold or warm compresses: Hold either a hot pad or cold washcloth against the ear for 10-15 minutes, or alternate between hot and cold for an easy ear infection remedy, especially for kids.

Neck exercises: Exercises that rotate the neck can help relieve pressure in the ear canal:
- Sit or stand up straight. Rotate your neck to the right, so it's parallel with your right shoulder. Hold for five to 10 seconds. Repeat this exercise on the left side.
- Raise your shoulders high, like you're trying to reach your earlobes with them. Hold for five to 10 seconds. Repeat these exercises throughout the day.

Mullein: Oil made from the mullein flowers is an effective pain reliever for ear infections. Find mullein at health food stores as a stand-alone tincture or as an ingredient in herbal ear drops.

Vitamin D: Vitamin D boosts the immune system, and a healthier immune system is less prone to ear infections. A study showed that the risk of ear infections might be reduced by increasing serum levels of vitamin D through food consumption, supplements, and direct sunlight.

Garlic oil: With antimicrobial, antiviral, and antifungal properties, garlic oil ear drops can be applied to the ear canal to help kill bacteria or viruses that might be causing an ear infection. You can also soak crushed garlic cloves in warm olive oil to make your own garlic oil ear drops.

Hydrogen peroxide: This remedy can help keep ears clean and prevent dirt and bacteria from entering the middle ear. It's especially helpful for swimmer's ear. Apply a few drops onto the ear canal, but be careful that too much doesn't get into the ear itself. Tilt your head to allow the liquid to drain out. Dry with a tissue, not a q-tip.

Ginger: Well known for its anti-inflammatory properties, ginger in the form of juice or infused oil can be applied to the outer ear canal, but it should never be put directly into the ear.

Changing sleeping positions: If you're a side sleeper, try sleeping with your affected ear facing up instead of down into the pillow. The pressure of sleeping with your affected ear on a pillow could aggravate your ear even more.

---

[349] 13 home remedies for ear infections, SingleCare | Image: Leszek Pietrzak, The Noun Project
[350] Anis Rehman, M.D., District Endocrine, Woodbridge, VA, districtendocrine.com

Apple cider vinegar: Apple cider vinegar contains acetic acid, which is antibacterial. Mix equal parts warm water and apple cider vinegar, then apply a few drops to the affected ear. Tilt your head to let the liquid to drain; dry with a tissue, *not* a q-tip.

NSAIDs: If these remedies aren't enough, over-the-counter pain relievers may help. Non-steroidal anti-inflammatory drugs can help relieve pain and fevers that are caused by ear infections. The three of the most common NSAIDs are ibuprofen, aspirin, and naproxen; do not give aspirin to children, as it can cause the condition known as Reye syndrome.

"Doctor, Doctor!"

Most ear infections will clear up on their own in a few days, says Getwell Urgent Care.[351] But you should contact your doctor immediately if:

- The symptoms do not improve within 3 days or the pain becomes severe
- Body temperature rises above 100.4 degrees
- Ear infections are being experienced regularly, which could lead to hearing loss
- The symptoms are present in a child younger than 6 months
- There is a discharge of fluid, pus, or bloody fluid from the ear
- Vomiting, headaches, a stiff neck, drowsiness, and a loss of balance occur.

COST-SAVINGS EXAMPLE:

Most ear infections are inexpensive to treat. A course of antibiotics might cost about $110, while over the counter ear drops cost $20 or less. Just be sure to take prompt action to treat an ear infection before it can get worse.

EARWAX

 Earwax cleans, lubricates and protects your ear canal by trapping dirt and slowing the growth of bacteria, says Mayo Clinic [352] (**Colin L. Driscoll, M.D., Chair, Otolaryngology** [353]). Blockages occur when you try to clean your ears with things like cotton swabs. But this just pushes wax in deeper, which can damage your ear canal or eardrum. In frustration, some people have tried to dig out hardened wax with items such as a paper clip or a hairpin, but this can cause injury or push the wax in even further. According to Mayo, symptoms of earwax blockage may include earache, dizziness, or coughing; feeling of fullness in the affected ear; or ringing or noises or decreased hearing in the affected ear. These self-care measures may help you remove excess earwax that's blocking your ear canal (caution: do not use if your eardrum has a hole in it or a drainage tube has not been placed in it):

Soften the wax: Use an eyedropper to apply a few drops of baby oil, mineral oil, glycerin or

---

351 When Should You Go to the Doctor for an Ear Infection? Southaven, MS, urgentcaresouthaven.com
352 Effective Earwax Removal, Mayo Clinic News Network | Image: Aaron K. Kim The Noun Project
353 Colin L. Driscoll, M.D., Mayo Clinic, mayoclinic.org | Appointments at Mayo Clinic

hydrogen peroxide in your ear canal.

Use warm water: In a day or two when the wax is softened, use a bulb syringe (about $5 on Amazon) to gently squirt warm water into your ear. Tilt your head and pull your ear up and back to straighten the canal. Tip your head to the side to let the water run out. When finished, gently dry your outer ear with a towel or hand-held dryer on the lowest heat setting. *Never put a hair dryer in a bed or a child's crib; never leave a small child unattended with a hair dryer.*

You may need to repeat this wax-softening and irrigation procedure a few times. However, the process may only loosen the outer layer of wax and cause it to lodge deeper in the canal or against the eardrum; in that case, you'll need to see a doctor.

<u>**Do Not:**</u> One remedy to avoid is earwax candling. As mentioned in the preface of this directory, "Folklore remedies only put you at greater risk for dangerous diseases." [354] The practice of ear candling is a prime example. The American Academy of Otolaryngology [355] (**Troy D. Woodard, M.D., Chair** [356]) warns, "Ear candling or ear coning is NOT a safe option for earwax removal."

"Doctor, Doctor!"

If symptoms don't improve after a few treatments, see a health care provider. Having an earache or decreased hearing doesn't necessarily mean you have wax buildup, so it's important to have a doctor rule out other medical conditions involving your ears.

<u>COST-SAVINGS EXAMPLE:</u>

Earwax self-care is inexpensive. Clinics such as CVS Minute Clinic charge around $100 for earwax removal – well worth it if it ends discomfort and restores your hearing. [357]

EMPHYSEMA

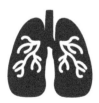 Emphysema is a life-threatening condition and requires medical care. According to the National Emphysema Foundation [358] (**Laurence G. Nair, M.D., President** [359]), people with lung-related illnesses should be cautious when using supplements to treat or manage their condition. Here are several supplements that have been said to remedy lung-related symptoms, as well as comments from experts on their effectiveness – or lack thereof – to help you decide what's right for you.

Bromelain: A supplement created from the enzymes found in a pineapple's stem and juice, bromelain is said to reduce lung inflammation. However, according to the National Institutes of

---

[354] GoodHousekeeping.com | Image: Shrikantha Urala C K
[355] Why Ear Candling Isn't Safe, American Academy of Otolaryngology via Healthline, healthline.com
[356] Troy Woodard, M.D., Department of Otolaryngology, Cleveland Clinic, my.clevelandclinic.org
[357] Ear Wax Removal Cost, health.costhelper.com
[358] National Emphysema Foundation, Can natural remedies help treat COPD? emphysemafoundation.org
[359] Laurence Gopal Nair, M.D., MidState Medical Center, Meriden, CT | Image: Vector Point, The Noun Project

Health, scientific evidence to support this claim is lacking.

Coenzyme Q10: This antioxidant, which is naturally produced by the body, has been said to increase cell activity and ease inflammation in people with lung disease. However, studies have not proven that taking the supplement improves conditions.

L-Carnitine: Typically produced by the body, L-carnitine helps burn fat and boost energy. In some patients, this supplement appears to help strengthen muscles and improve endurance when exercising. Further, research has proven that those people who take L-carnitine supplements do significantly better during walking exercise programs.

N-acetylcysteine: An antioxidant available as an over-the-counter dietary supplement, N-acetylcysteine has been researched for its role in breaking down the mucus that can clog the lungs of people living with COPD. To date, research has shown mixed results on the supplement's effectiveness.

Antioxidant vitamins: With properties of antioxidants, vitamins A, C and E have been said to improve the lung function. Studies show that people living with lung conditions may have low levels of these vitamins, resulting in decreased pulmonary function. Further, studies have proven that patients whose diets are rich in fruits and vegetables – a good source of these vitamins – saw improved lung function.

"Doctor, Doctor!"

Note that natural remedies cannot serve as the sole source of treatment, says the National Emphysema Foundation. Consult your pulmonologist or other physician before using these supplements to ensure they do not interfere with current treatment methods.

COST-SAVINGS EXAMPLE:

Emphysema home remedies do not replace medical care, however they may be an economical way to make your care more effective.

ERECTILE DYSFUNCTION

Few conditions receive as much attention in the quest for effective remedies as. Ideally, attraction to his partner is all a man needs to "get ready." And at some time in the past, you and your partner may have enjoyed such a perfect world. But stress, medical issues, and age take a toll. It's common for this toll to show up in the bedroom, and always at the most inopportune moment.

If there were indeed a simple, safe, effective home remedy for ED that worked for nearly all men nearly every time, we wouldn't be bombarded with advertising for "blue pills" and various medical interventions most men would rather skip.

But that's certainly not going to keep a guy from trying, is it? Ginseng is a long-reputed natural treatment for ED. James Bond thought oysters would do the trick. What works? What doesn't? What might be worth a try? Here's what doctors have to say on this ever fascinating topic (by SingleCare Team [360] ; medically reviewed by **Michael L. Davis, M.D.** [361]), starting with vitamins and minerals:

Arginine: Also known as L-arginine, arginine is a naturally present amino acid which helps to increase the body's production of nitric oxide, which in turn helps blood vessels dilate, thereby increasing blood flow to the penis and facilitating erections.

DHEA: Dehydroepiandrosterone is an over-the-counter hormone supplement that converts into estrogen and testosterone, potentially helping alleviate erectile dysfunction.

Ginseng: This herb used for centuries to aid male sexual function. As with many herbs, researchers say that more studies with larger sample sizes must be conducted for conclusive evidence. However, current research in panax ginseng (red ginseng) is promising.

Horny goat weed: Used for years to treat sexual dysfunction, as the name more or less suggests. Some research indicates that the main component, icariin, acts similarly to Viagra by allowing blood to fill the arteries of the penis, thereby facilitating erections. Horny goat weed is available over-the-counter as a tea, capsule, powder, and tablet.

Yohimbe: Extracted from the bark of an African tree, yohimbe was often recommended by doctors to men with erectile dysfunction before Viagra was available. Though some small studies show yohimbe to have positive effects on erection issues, it's not widely recommended by medical professionals, says SingleCare Team.

Other reputed male potency herbal supplements: These include ginkgo biloba, rhodiola rosea, maca, and ashwagandha. However, there is little research to support their claims, which is not uncommon with herbal remedies – they just don't have the sales potential of registered drugs.

Vascular health, circulation, and excess weight are often significant contributors to impotence, says SingleCare. If you are overweight, losing weight can greatly help. It's no surprise, then, that many men first make changes to their diet as a means to achieve consistent erections. But what foods help erectile dysfunction? Try adding more of these foods and beverages to your diet:

Apple cider vinegar: ACV can reduce the impact of some conditions that cause erectile dysfunction, including obesity, high cholesterol, and heart disease. For best results, mix no more than two tablespoons of ACV in a glass of water and drink prior to eating once a day.

Caffeine: According to one study, people who drink the equivalent of two to three cups of coffee per day had reduced likelihood of having erectile dysfunction when compared to other participants. It's believed to work by improving circulation.

Dark chocolate: The antioxidants it contains, called flavonoids, may also help lower blood pressure and cholesterol, two factors known to contribute to erectile dysfunction.

---

[360] Natural Cures And Treatments For Erectile Dysfunction, SingleCare | Carrot illustration: freesvg
[361] Michael L. Davis, M.D., Florida Hospital Physicians Group, Riverview, FL, adventhealth.com

Eggs: A clinical study [362] by **Dr. Alessandra Barassi** [363] of the University of Milan and others links a lack of vitamin D to greater risk for ED. Sunshine is a solution for a vitamin D deficiency, but that's not always possible in seasons or places with limited daylight hours. Fortunately, you can boost your vitamin D intake through foods such as eggs, fortified milk, and cheese.

Pistachios: Thought to aid with ED due to the amino acid arginine, which is known to relax blood vessels for increased circulation to the penis. In a study, men who ate a nut-heavy diet for several weeks saw significant improvement in sexual health. If you are going to try this, go for the unsalted variety. In addition to pistachios, consider almonds, walnuts, and cashews. (Peanuts don't qualify, as they are legumes, not actual nuts.)

Pomegranate juice: This antioxidant-rich beverage could reduce the risk of heart disease and high blood pressure. It's not uncommon for doctors to recommend pomegranate juice – it could help with ED. But even if it doesn't, it may come with other health benefits.

Oysters and shellfish: Claimed by common lore (and Agent 007) to be natural aphrodisiacs. This reputation could be due to their high levels of zinc, which plays a key role in the production of the testosterone – essential to male sexual health. Be cautious of raw oysters, which may contain the deadly bacteria vibrio; cooking does not reduce the mineral content of oysters.

Spinach, celery, and beets: These veggies may help alleviate ED by increasing circulation, thanks to their high concentration of nitrates and antioxidants. Beet juice in particular is known to be high in nitrates, the compounds Cialis and other ED drugs are based on.

Tomatoes and pink grapefruit: These two colorful salad ingredients are full of the phytonutrient lycopene, which is great for circulation.

Watermelon: This melon is full of phytonutrients known to relax the blood vessels involved in erections. Studies support the connection between watermelon and improved sexual function, including research cited by **Bhimu Patil, Ph.D.** [364] of Texas A&M University. [365]

"Doctor, Doctor!"

Always speak with a doctor before taking any new supplements, says SingleCare. For example, yohimbe can cause jitteriness and headaches, and may interact with medications you're taking, while apple cider vinegar has a reputation for worsening esophageal reflux.

In addition, Urology Clinics of North Texas [366] (**Gregory Robert Thoreson, M.D., Urologist** [367]) advises that ED can be an important symptom of other medical concerns. If your ED is happening more than the occasional fluke, it is time to talk to your doctor to rule out any underlying health concerns. If your ED is caused by an unknown health issue, resolving it can not only lead to a healthier life, it can also help remedy the ED.

---

[362] Vitamin D and erectile dysfunction, The Journal of Sexual Medicine, pubmed.ncbi.nlm.nih.gov
[363] Alessandra Barassi, Associate Professor, University of Milan, Italy, clinhypertensionjournal.com
[364] Bhimu Patil, Ph.D., Texas A&M University, hortsciences.tamu.edu
[365] Watermelon May Have Viagra-Like Effect, Texas A&M Today, today.tamu.edu
[366] 5 Reasons You Should See the Doctor About Your Erectile Dysfunction, Urology Clinics of North Texas
[367] Gregory Robert Thoreson, M.D., Urology Clinics of North Texas, urologyclinics.com

Some of the common causes of ED are:

- Heart disease – Blood flow to create an erection needs good circulation. Blocked arteries and high blood pressure can result in ED.
- Diabetes – Uncontrolled blood glucose levels damage blood vessels and impact the ability to transport blood to the penis.
- Obesity – Increases your risk of heart disease and diabetes.
- Changes in hormones – Hormonal disorders such as an overactive or underactive thyroid, low testosterone, and steroid use, can all cause ED.
- Medications – Drugs used to treat other issues can have ED as a side effect.

Recurrent ED can cause other issues beyond sexual performance. Having ED can lead to depression, anxiety, and strained relationships. All good reasons to call a doctor.

COST-SAVINGS EXAMPLE:

Some men pay up to $80 a pill for Viagra. However, generic Viagra is now as cheap as $6 a tablet, so the cost savings are not as dramatic as they used to be. But self-care remedies that work by helping you lose weight ... by increasing your blood flow on an ongoing basis ... or by boosting your heart health have far greater overall benefits.

If you can postpone or reduce the need to treat heart disease, diabetes, or obesity, then your cost savings can be significant. So if ED is a concern, you have plenty of reason to find two or three trusted remedies that work for you.

EYESTRAIN (Computer Vision Syndrome)

Digital eye strain can include eyes that itch and tear up, and are dry and red, says The StayWell Company [368] and Cedars-Sinai Medical Center [369] (medically reviewed by **Christopher L. Haupert M.D., Ophthalmologist** [370]). The problems Your eyes may feel tired or uncomfortable. You may not be able to focus normally. These problems are caused by lots of computer or digital device use, says StayWell and Cedars-Sinai.

Most computer or digital device users have at least some symptoms. Reading text on a screen or digital device is often harder for the eyes than reading printed text. This is why working on a computer for a few hours may cause symptoms of digital eye strain, but reading a book may not.

Several factors cause digital eye strain, such as glare, poor lighting, poor posture while using a

---

[368] Computer Vision Syndrome, The StayWell Company | Image: Circlon Tech, The Noun Project
[369] Cedars-Sinai, Los Angeles, Rated #1 in California and #2 in the nation by US News & World Report
[370] Christopher L. Haupert, M.D., Ophthalmologist, Iowa Retina Consultants, Des Moines, iowaretina.com

computer, viewing a computer at the wrong distance and angle, and uncorrected vision problems.

Another issue is you may blink less when using a computer than when reading printed text, causing dry eye and contributing to digital eye strain. Some conditions make dry eye more likely. If you use antihistamines or have thyroid disease or certain autoimmune diseases, you are at greater risk of having dry eye. Most of these symptoms are short-term, but may get worse if you don't resolve the problem. Remedies revolve around creating a better work environment.

Rest your eyes: Take a 15-minute break after each 2 hours of screen time.

Follow the 20-20-20 rule: Every 20 minutes, look into the distance at least 20 feet away from your device. Do this for at least 20 seconds.

Zoom in: Enlarge the text on your computer screen or digital device.

Reduce glare: Light sources in your environment may be reflecting off your screen. Consider using a screen glare filter.

Correct your eye angle: Place your screen so that the center is about 4 to 5 inches below eye level. This allows your neck and your eyes to be in neutral positions, reducing strain.

Not too close or too far: Place your screen 20 to 28 inches from your eye, about arm's length.

Remember to blink often: This helps lubricate your eyes and avoid dry eyes. If you have an underlying dry eye problem, see the section on Dry Eyes earlier in this manual.

Check your posture: Adjust your chair height so your feet rest easily on the floor. Don't slump over the screen.

"Doctor, Doctor!"

The page you are now reading was written by an editor wearing prescription eyeglasses made specially for computer use. Schedule an eye exam and tell your provider you want a prescription for computer glasses. Measure the distance to your screen in advance of your visit, or use the arms' length rule suggested above (20-28"). Glasses with the correct focal distance for screen use will transform your screen experience. Your eye care provider will also need to treat any hidden health problems or underlying eye conditions that may be adding to your digital eye strain. Call Cedars-Sinai [371] or a provider near you.

COST-SAVINGS EXAMPLE:

These trusted remedies cost next to nothing. A full eye exam costs about $200. You can buy top quality monofocal glasses online for about $50 from highly rated sellers such as Zenni Optical [372] and others. Prescriptions are good for two years, so set a reminder to check your glasses after about 23 months in case you want a new pair.

---

[371] Find A Doctor - Eye Exams (Contacts and Glasses), Cedars-Sinai, cedars-sinai.org
[372] Zenni Optical, zennioptical.com

F

FATIGUE

General weakness fatigue, or lethargy, refers to a loss of physical strength that may or may not be due to physical exertion, says eMediHealth [373] (reviewed by **Mark Travis, M.D., Internist** [374]). These remedies have helped others and may help:

Almonds: Almonds are packed with vitamin E that can help you stay energetic.

Bananas: Bananas are a great source of natural sugars namely; sucrose, fructose, and glucose. These sugars can effectively give you a quick and substantial energy boost. Bananas also contain potassium, a mineral your body requires to convert sugar into energy. If you suffer from heart or kidney disease, discuss with your doctor how much potassium is safe for you to consume.

Coffee: The caffeine in coffee perks up the brain and gives you an instant energy boost. In addition to making you feel energetic, it can help increase endurance, improve focus, reduce pain, and improve your metabolism rate.

Eggs: Eggs are loaded with nutrients such as protein, iron, biotin, vitamin A, folic acid, riboflavin, and pantothenic acid.

Ginseng tea: For centuries, ginseng has been known as a powerful antioxidant. It can give you energy whenever you feel weak. Owing to its calming and soothing nature, this herb also has a soothing effect on your nerves. Note: Ginseng is not suitable for those who have high blood pressure or any type of heart disease.

Gooseberry: Also known as amla, Indian gooseberry is a highly nutritious fruit that can help boost your energy level. It is a good source of vitamin C, calcium, protein, iron, carbohydrates, and phosphorus. Note: Again, because of the phosphorus content, discuss the use of Indian gooseberry with your physician if you have kidney disease or you are on dialysis.

Milk: Milk is considered one of the best sources of calcium and vitamin D, which are shown to support healthy muscles and bones.

Strawberries: This low-calorie addition to a healthy diet can help you stay energetic throughout the day. Strawberries are packed with vitamin C, an antioxidant that helps in tissue repair, boosts immunity, and wards off free radical damage.

According to the Centers for Disease Control and Prevention, patients suffering from CFS often have symptoms including muscle pain and impaired memory. Just what triggers CFS is unclear, and there is neither a cure nor a prescription drug designed specifically to treat the condition.

---

[373] 8 Home Remedies to Cure Weakness & Fatigue, eMediHealth, emedihealth.com
[374] Mark S. Travis, M.D., Internist in Chicago, IL, md.com | Image: Webtechops LLP, The Noun Project

Still, certain therapies and lifestyle changes may help relieve symptoms. These can include over-the-counter sleep products and pain-relievers. Some people with ME/CFS might benefit from trying techniques like deep breathing and muscle relaxation, massage, and movement therapies (such as stretching, yoga, and tai chi). These can reduce stress and anxiety, and promote a sense of well-being. [375]

"Doctor, Doctor!"

If you still feel tired most of the time even after trying these remedies, make an appointment to see your doctor, says eMediHealth. You may have Chronic Fatigue Syndrome (CFS), a debilitating disorder in which extreme fatigue isn't alleviated by bed rest and persists in the absence of underlying medical conditions.

COST-SAVINGS EXAMPLE:

The trusted remedies above cost nothing or next to nothing. A full eye exam should cost about $100 to $200. You can buy top quality monofocal glasses online for about $50. Prescriptions are generally good for two years, so set a reminder to check your glasses after about 23 months to decide if you want a new pair.

FEVER

Here are some physician-approved remedies to make yourself or your child more comfortable during a fever, courtesy of Mayo Clinic [376] (**Gianrico Farrugia, M.D., CEO and President**):

Drink plenty of fluids. Fever can cause dehydration, so drink water, juices or broth. For a child under age one, use an oral rehydration solution such as Pedialyte. These solutions contain water and salts proportioned to replenish fluids and electrolytes. Pedialyte ice pops are also available.

Rest: You need rest to recover, and activity can raise your body temperature.

Stay cool: Dress in light clothing, keep the room temperature cool, and sleep with a light cover.

OTC meds: In the case of a high fever, your doctor may recommend an over-the-counter drug, such as:

- Acetaminophen (Tylenol, others) or ibuprofen (Advil, Motrin IB, others). Use these according to the label instructions or as recommended by your doctor. Be careful to avoid taking too much. High doses or long-term use of acetaminophen may cause liver or kidney damage, and acute overdoses can be fatal. If your child's fever remains high after

---

[375] Myalgic Encephalomyelitis/Chronic Fatigue Syndrome (ME/CFS), CDC, cdc.gov
[376] Home Remedies: Fighting a fever, Mayo Clinic News Network | Image: Forma, The Noun Project

a dose, don't give more medication; call your doctor instead. For temperatures below 102° F (38.9° C), don't use fever-lowering drugs unless advised by your doctor.

- Aspirin, for adults only. Don't give aspirin to children; it may trigger a rare, but potentially fatal, disorder known as Reye's syndrome.

You have a fever when your temperature rises above its normal range. What's normal for you may be a little higher or lower than the average normal temperature of 98.6° F (37° C).

"Doctor, Doctor!"

For babies: An unexplained fever is greater cause for concern in infants and in children than in adults. A newborn has a lower than normal temperature – less than 97° F (36.1° C). Very young babies may not regulate body temperature well when they're ill and may become cold rather than hot. Call your baby's doctor if your child is:

- Younger than age 3 months and has a temperature of 100.4° F (38° C) or higher.
- Between ages 3 to 6 months and has a temperature up to 102° F (38.9° C) and seems unusually irritable, lethargic or uncomfortable or has a temperature higher than 102° F (38.9 C).
- Between ages 6 to 24 months and has a temperature above 102° F (38.9 C) that lasts more than one day but shows no other symptoms. If your child also has other symptoms, such as a cold, cough or diarrhea, you might call your child's doctor sooner based on severity.
- When in doubt, call the doctor.

For children:

There's likely no cause for alarm as long as your child is responsive – making eye contact, responding to your facial expressions and your voice – and is drinking fluids and playing. Call your child's doctor if your child:

- Is listless or irritable, vomits repeatedly, has a severe headache or stomach ache, or has any other symptoms causing significant discomfort.
- Has a fever after being left in a hot car. Seek medical care immediately.
- Has a fever that lasts longer than three days (in children age 2 and older).
- Appears listless and has poor eye contact with you.

Ask your child's doctor for guidance in special circumstances, such as a child with immune system problems or with a pre-existing illness. Your child's doctor may also recommend precautions if your child has just started taking a new prescription medicine.

For adults:

Call your doctor if your temperature is 103° F (39.4° C) or higher, or if you've had a fever for more than three days. In addition, seek immediate medical attention if any of these signs or symptoms accompanies a fever:

- Severe headache
- Severe throat swelling
- Mental confusion
- Persistent vomiting

- Seizure
- Difficulty breathing or chest pain
- Extreme listlessness or irritability
- Abdominal pain or pain when urinating
- Unusual sensitivity to bright light

- Unusual skin rash, especially if it's rapid
- Stiffness or pain when bending your head forward
- Muscle weakness or sensory changes
- Any other unexplained signs or symptom

You can also learn more by looking up your symptoms at Mayo Clinic's Symptom Checker. [377]

COST-SAVINGS EXAMPLE:

The trusted remedies above cost nothing or very little, and should help resolve most cases of fever. However, a fever can also be a sign of something more serious. It costs nothing to call a doctor and discuss your symptoms, so do make that call if any of the circumstances given above are present.

FIRE ANT STINGS

 The fire ant bites the flesh to grab hold, and this is done so quickly and sharply that there is little initial pain, says the Medical University of South Carolina [378] (**James Lemon, D.M.D, Chair**). [379]

The burn is inflicted by venom injected by a stinger, MUSC explains. The venom is water-insoluble, nonproteinaceous, and contains hemolytic factors that release histamine and other vasoactive amines. In lay terms, none of this is good, and it all hurts.

The venom produces immediate itching and redness, followed by a pustule site after several hours. The venom also contains several allergenic proteins that can cause anaphylaxis [which is life-threatening] in patients who are allergic to the proteins. Antigenic similarity exists between these proteins and bee and wasp venoms. First aid for fire ant stings calls for acting fast:

Escape: Move rapidly away from the nest.

Eliminate: Quickly remove or kill ants on skin and clothing to prevent further stings.

Wash: Gently use soap and water to rid the skin of any venom on it.

Disinfect: Disinfect the bite(s) with alcohol.

Cool: Place a cool cloth or ice cloth on sites for fifteen minutes to reduce pain and inflammation.

OTC medications: Consider applying hydrocortisone cream such as Cortizone or taking a systemic oral antihistamine such as Benadryl.

[377] Symptom Checker - Mayo Clinic, mayoclinic.org
[378] Treatment for a Hot Time - Fire Ant Therapy, Medical University of South Carolina, muschealth.org
[379] James Lemon, DMD, Midlands Oral & Maxillofacial Surgery, Columbia, SC | Image: Ben Davis, The Noun Project

Other options: Try dabbing the site with one of the following: Kleen 'Em Away Naturally, calamine lotion, enzyme cleaner, or meat tenderizer.

Do Not: Do not scratch the pustule, this can lead to infection.

The natural course is for the site to burn for several hours, then over twenty-four hours a pustule develops with itching, and over several days – *if not scratched* – the lesion will slowly disappear. Scratching can introduce infection, which is why it's so important to use the trusted remedies above to minimize the itch and irritation. Scratches should be cleaned with alcohol.

The bottom line: Be careful to avoid fire ants – when out, scan the ground for mounds or other evidence of these vicious pests. The sting is painful, and the pustule persists for about a week. These ants can do more than ruin a picnic, so be prepared in case you do encounter them.

"Doctor, Doctor!"

Rarely, patients will have an allergic response immediately or over the first few hours. A severe allergic reaction can be life-threatening, says WebMD (medically reviewed by **Stephanie S. Gardner, M.D.** [380]). Symptoms include hives, cramping with nausea or diarrhea, chest tightness, trouble breathing, dizziness, and swelling of your tongue or throat. Call 9-1-1 right away. If you have an EpiPen, use it, and repeat after 5 to 15 minutes if symptoms don't improve. You'll still need medical care, even if symptoms seem to stop, in order to prevent a delayed reaction. If the sting is very large and painful, WebMD recommends seeing a doctor for a prescription of antihistamines or steroids. [381]

COST-SAVINGS EXAMPLE:

The physician-trusted remedies above cost nothing or next to nothing, while the cost of prescription of antihistamines or steroids is typically low. If self-care is not enough to make the pain bearable, medical care should be very affordable. Get the help you need to relieve your pain and find another way to cut costs.

FLATULENCE

"Fart proudly." – Ben Franklin
"Pull my finger!" – Steve in sixth grade
"Did someone step on a duck?" – Al Czervik, *Caddyshack*

Bloating, burping and passing gas may be the topic of many wisecracks, but if they're making you uncomfortable, you're in the right place to find doctor-approved remedies. Gas is usually caused by swallowed air or the breakdown of food through digestion, says Mayo Clinic. To reduce bloating, it may help to avoid or reduce the amount of gas-producing foods you eat. [382]

---

[380] Dr. Stephanie Gardner, M.D., Dermatologist - Johns Creek, GA | Sharecare, sharecare.com
[381] What Should I Do If I Get Stung By A Fire Ant? webmd.com
[382] Home Remedies: Gas, belching and bloating, Mayo Clinic | Image: Hans Gerhard Meier, The Noun Project

Many foods cause gas, including beans, broccoli, Brussels sprouts, cabbage, carbonated drinks, cauliflower, chewing gum, fruit – apples, peaches and pears – hard candy, lettuce, dairy products, onions, sugar alcohols found in sugar-free foods (sorbitol, mannitol and xylitol), whole-grain food. So if you're looking for an excuse not to eat broccoli, you're welcome.

Belching or burping is your body's way of expelling excess air swallowed from your stomach, says Mayo. You may swallow excess air if you eat or drink too fast, talk while you eat, chew gum or suck on hard candies, drink carbonated beverages, or smoke.

Acid reflux or gastroesophageal reflux disease (GERD) can have the same effect. If stomach acid backs up into your esophagus, you may swallow repeatedly to clear the material. This can lead to swallowing more air and further belching.

Some people swallow air as a nervous habit — even when they're not eating or drinking. In other cases, chronic belching may be related to inflammation of the stomach lining (gastritis) or to an infection with Helicobacter pylori, the bacteria responsible for some stomach ulcers.

Bloating, belching, gas and gas pains can be embarrassing and uncomfortable. Here's what causes these signs and symptoms — and how you can prevent them.

Try smaller portions: Many of the foods that can cause gas are part of a healthy diet. So, try eating smaller portions to see if your body can handle it without creating excess gas.

Eat slowly: Chew your food thoroughly and don't gulp. If you have a hard time slowing down, put down your fork between each bite.

Avoid chewing gum: Sucking on hard candies and drinking through a straw also cause you to swallow air, so avoid them.

Check your dentures: Loose dentures can cause you to swallow excess air when you eat.

Don't smoke: Cigarette smoking can increase the amount of air you swallow.

Exercise: Physical activity may help move gas through the digestive tract.

If the odor from passing gas concerns you, limiting foods high in sulfur-containing compounds may reduce distinctive odors. These foods include such as broccoli, Brussels sprouts or other cruciferous vegetables, beer, and foods high in protein.

"Doctor, Doctor!"

When gas and gas pains interfere with your daily activities, there may be something wrong. If the remedies above don't resolve the issue, you may need to see your doctor.

COST-SAVINGS EXAMPLE:

Flatulence is not a disease. In most cases, no medical care is needed. Try the inexpensive home remedies above; if they do the trick, you can save the time and expense of a doctor's visit for something more serious.

FLU (Influenza)

Do natural cold and flu remedies really work? Some do, and Barbara Austin, RN, a nurse and case manager at Piedmont Sixty Plus [383] (**Patrick Battey, M.D., CEO, Piedmont Atlanta** [384]), suggests these best natural cold and flu remedies.

Hydration: Austin's number one recommendation for recovering quickly from a cold or flu virus is staying hydrated. "When you're hydrated, your body has a natural ability to flush germs out of your system," she says. She recommends 64 ounces (four pints) of fluid a day, but talk to your doctor about your specific needs. Some people, such as those with congestive heart failure, should drink less water.

Vitamin C: While vitamin C hasn't been proven to prevent cold symptoms, some studies have indicated it can shorten the lifespan of a cold. Plus, it boosts your overall health, including your immune system. Austin recommends getting the vitamin through your diet. The fresher the food, the better. Think oranges, rather than orange juice or supplements. Overdoing it on vitamin C supplements (not dietary vitamin C) can lead to upset stomach and kidney stones.

Sleep: "It's so important to get plenty of rest during cold and flu season," says Austin. Sleep helps your immune system function at its best to ward off nasty viruses and bacteria.

Honey and tea: "I'm a honey fanatic," she says. "It has natural antiviral and antimicrobial properties." Add the natural sweetener (opt for a local variety when possible) to a cup of ginger or cinnamon tea to relieve a scratchy throat and stay hydrated.

Chicken soup: Sometimes mom really does know best! Hot liquids, such as soup, help reduce mucus buildup and keep you hydrated. A University of Nebraska Medical Center study found chicken soup has anti-inflammatory properties, which help cut a cold's unpleasant side effects.

Aromatherapy: Break up mucus by rubbing a bit of camphor or menthol salve around – not in! – your nose. You can also reduce congestion by breathing in aromatherapy oils, such as peppermint and eucalyptus.

A steamy shower. A steamy shower or sauna is a great decongestant, says Austin. One caveat: If you are dizzy or weak from the flu, sit in a chair in your bathroom while you run a hot shower.

Gargling warm salt water. Dissolve 1/2 a teaspoon of salt in a cup of warm water, then gargle to relieve a sore throat.

Sleep with an extra pillow. To help your sinuses drain, sleep with an extra pillow under your head, or switch to a wedge-shaped pillow.

Natural cold remedies to use with caution

Nasal irrigation: "Nasal irrigation can be helpful in hydrating nasal passages so they aren't dry and cracked, which can break the skin's protective barrier against viruses and bacteria," she says.

---

[383] Nine Of The Best Natural Cold And Flu Remedies | Piedmont Healthcare, 1,400 Locations in Georgia
[384] Dr. Patrick Mell Battey, M.D., Vascular Surgery, Atlanta, GA | Image: Skylar Small, The Noun Project

"However, it's important to do it safely. Talk to your doctor before starting nasal irrigation."

Never use tap water for nasal irrigation – you honestly don't know what's in it. Use boiled and cooled tap water, sterile or distilled water, or saline solution instead.

Herbal supplements and vitamins: Some people swear by echinacea or zinc, but research on their benefits is inconclusive. "If you're considering any alternative medicine, talk to your healthcare provider," says Austin. "Vitamins and supplements are not FDA-approved and there often isn't good research on their effectiveness. It's trial and error to find what works best."

Flu shots are available at urgent care locations, primary care offices, and at pharmacies nationwide. [385]

"Doctor, Doctor!"

If you are at special risk of complications, call your doctor as soon as symptoms begin, says University of California San Francisco [386] (**Joshua Adler, M.D., Chief Clinical Officer** [387]). Those at increased risk for serious complications include persons who:

- Are 50 years of age or older
- Are a resident of a long-term care facility and have chronic medical conditions
- Have chronic heart or lung conditions, including asthma
- Have metabolic diseases including diabetes, kidney disease, anemia or other blood disorders
- Have a weakened immune system due to HIV/AIDS, cancer treatment, or steroid therapy
- Are between 6 months and 18 years of age and receive long-term aspirin therapy
- Will be in the second or third trimester of pregnancy during flu season
- Are 6 months to 2 years of age

If you are otherwise healthy and not at increased risk of complications, seek medical advice if your flu symptoms are unusually severe, such as:

- Trouble breathing
- A severe sore throat
- A cough that produces a lot of green or yellow mucus
- Feeling faint

Also, see your doctor immediately if you think you might have signs or symptoms of pneumonia, which may include a severe cough that brings up phlegm, a high fever and a sharp pain when you breathe deeply.

For Children

Parents, do not hesitate to contact your child's doctor if you have concerns about the flu, questions about your child's symptoms or if you think your child should receive the flu

---

[385] Piedmont Healthcare, Book Appointment Online, doctors.piedmont.org
[386] When to Call Your Doctor About the Flu, University of California San Francisco Health, ucsfhealth.org
[387] Joshua Adler, M.D., University of California San Francisco, UCSF Health, ucsfhealth.org

vaccine. The doctor will be able to answer your questions and go over information specific to your child's age, as well as any pre-existing conditions he or she may have.

Take your child to the pediatrician or to the emergency department if he or she displays any of the following symptoms:

- Rapid or labored breathing
- Bluish skin color
- Not drinking enough to maintain hydration
- Not waking up or interacting
- Irritability to the point that he or she doesn't want to be held

Also consult a doctor if your child's flu symptoms improve but then return and include a fever and worse cough.

COST-SAVINGS EXAMPLE:

Influenza is very common and in most cases, no medical care is needed. Try the inexpensive, trusted remedies above; if they do the trick, you can save the time and expense of a doctor's visit for something more serious.

Even so, the flu is so widespread that many people do die from it, especially the elderly. If any of the situations described above exist, call your doctor and save money elsewhere.

FOOD POISONING

An estimated 1 in 6 Americans gets sick with food poisoning every year, says New York-based K-Health, an online medical and health services company [388] (**Neil Brown, M.D., Chief Medical Officer** [389]).

Symptoms of food poisoning can include diarrhea, vomiting, upset stomach, fever and chills, headache, and nausea. These symptoms can appear within a few hours of eating food contaminated with bacteria, parasites, viruses, or toxins.

Staphylococcus and E. coli are the most common causes of food poisoning. Food can get contaminated with these bacteria and other germs through unclean food preparation, not storing foods at the proper temperature, undercooking meat or eggs, and other means of contamination.

Generally, people who get food poisoning recover in a couple of days. During this time, several at-home remedies can help you to feel better, according to K Health:

---

[388] 10 Home Remedies for Food Poisoning: How to Feel Better Fast, K-Health, khealth.com
[389] Dr. Neil Brown, Emergency Medicine, K-Health, khealth.com

Rest your body: Resting your body can help your body to recover when you feel unwell from food poisoning. If you can, taking time off from school or work can help you to feel better faster.

Drink electrolytes: Two of the most common symptoms of food poisoning, diarrhea, and vomiting, can lead to a loss of fluids and electrolytes in the body. Replacing lost fluids and electrolytes can help to prevent dehydration and make you feel better.

Ways to replace fluids and electrolytes lost as a result of diarrhea and/or vomiting include drinking water, fruit juices, sports drinks, and clear broths. Eating saltine crackers can also help. Alternatively, you can buy an over-the-counter (OTC) oral rehydration powder that can help to replace lost fluids and minerals.

Eat foods with soluble fiber: While the BRAT diet (bread, rice, applesauce, toast) used to be the gold standard for diarrhea, research shows it doesn't help much, says Livestrong. Instead, choose foods with soluble fiber, which move more slowly through the digestive system. Per Mayo Clinic, foods high in soluble fiber include: oats, peas, beans, apples, citrus, carrots, and barley.

As symptoms improve even further and you feel ready to eat, it's a good idea to stick to a bland diet and eat small amounts of gentle foods that are easy to digest. If your stomach feels worse after eating, take a break until your symptoms improve.

Try a probiotic supplement: Probiotic supplements help to reintroduce beneficial bacteria into your stomach and digestive system. Though researchers are still studying the use of probiotics to treat food poisoning, some evidence suggests that certain probiotic supplements may help to reduce the duration of some food poisoning symptoms, like diarrhea.

However, it's important to speak with your provider before taking probiotics for food poisoning.

Take OTC medications: Some over-the-counter (OTC) medications can help to treat diarrhea caused by food poisoning. These OTC medications include loperamide (Imodium) and bismuth subsalicylate (Pepto-Bismol). Keep in mind that these medications are not intended for use in children. Bismuth subsalicylate (Pepto-Bismol) can cause your stools to appear black.

Ginger ale: The ginger plant has been shown to have a soothing effect on the stomach and digestive system. Though there's no evidence that ginger ale can help to treat food poisoning, it can be soothing to drink and easy on the stomach when you feel unwell.

Use Peppermints: Sucking on a peppermint candy or drinking peppermint tea may help to soothe an upset stomach caused by food poisoning. In fact, one review found that peppermint oil (one of the main ingredients in both peppermint candy and peppermint teas) may help to relax the smooth muscle found in the gastrointestinal tract

"Doctor, Doctor!"

In most cases, symptoms of food poisoning will resolve on their own within 24-72 hours, says K-Health [390]. But if your symptoms are not improving or if you experience any of the following severe symptoms, reach out to a medical professional for urgent care:

---

[390] Contact Us & Frequently Asked Questions, K-Health, khealth.com

- Diarrhea and a fever above 102° F
- Diarrhea for more than three days
- Bloody diarrhea
- Weakness
- Frequent and consistent vomiting
- Inability to keep liquids down
- Dehydration (dry mouth and throat, feeling dizzy when standing up, not urinating as frequently)

COST-SAVINGS EXAMPLE:

Self-care remedies for food poisoning are inexpensive and generally sufficient.

However, if any of the conditions above are present, call your doctor (free to call) or visit an urgent care clinic, where you might spend about $150 – probably well worth it if you saves you from a day of discomfort, saves you from losing a day's pay, or reveals an underlying medical condition that requires further care.

FOOT ODOR

When you get home from the gym, a run, or from playing sports, you can expect to smell sweaty feet. But if your feet smell all the time, several foot care remedies may help, says the Foot and Ankle Center of the Rockies [391] (**Dr. Daniel J. Hatch, Fellow of the American College of Foot and Ankle Surgery** [392]):

Antibiotic ointment: Bacteria, not sweat, causes foot odor. Try adding antibiotic ointment to your routine. Many options are available on Amazon for under $10. Simply apply the ointment to your feet, toes, and toenails before bed. Put on clean socks and the ointment will work to kill off the odor-causing bacteria while you sleep.

Lavender oil: Lavender helps kill the bacteria leading to your smelly feet. Place a few drops of lavender oil on your feet and rub it in well. Also, be sure to rub the oil between your toes. Put clean socks on your feet before bed to enhance the potency of your foot rub.

Vinegar foot soak: Neutralize foot odor with a warm water soak. Simply fill a foot basin with water (any temperature that's comfortable), add 1/3 cup of apple cider vinegar or white vinegar and soak your feet for 15 minutes. You can do this foot soak 2-3 times per day if you wish.

Epsom salt foot bath: Epsom salt is one of the best things you can add to a foot bath to control the bacteria causing foot odor. Follow the same instructions as above for the vinegar soak.

Try moisture-wicking socks: Do you wear socks? If not, now is a good time to start. Consider making the switch to socks that are specially designed to wick moisture away, keeping your feet

---

[391] 6 Must-Know Home Remedies for Smelly Feet, Foot and Ankle Center of the Rockies, facrockies.com
[392] Dr. Daniel J. Hatch, Foot and Ankle Center of the Rockies | Denver, Longmont, and Greely, Colorado

dry and sweat-free. Synthetic materials tend to work best for moisture-wicking.

Try a deodorant: Take a look at your deodorant to see if it can be used on your feet. Many antiperspirants can be applied to your feet to remove that stinky odor you're dealing with.

New shoes: Finally, if your shoes smell, consider treating yourself to a new pair. Smelly shoes are only going to reinfect your feet with the same bacteria over and over again.

"Doctor, Doctor!"

There are many good reasons to see a foot specialist – arch pain, fractures, bunions, gout – but foot odor is probably not one of them. However, if new shoes, moisture-wicking socks, and foot ointments and soaks aren't solving your problem, go ahead and call a podiatrist. You should also see a doctor if any part of your foot is discolored, oozing, or won't heal. If you have diabetes, you should be seeing a foot specialist on a regular basis.

COST-SAVINGS EXAMPLE:

Self-care remedies for foot odor are inexpensive. The most costly might be replacing your smelly old shoes with a new pair.

If these remedies work for you, you could save anywhere from $50 and $300 per visit for podiatrist care. So start with home remedies, but don't be afraid to seek professional care if needed.

Save $50 - 300 on podiatrist care with trusted remedies for foot odor.

FOOT PAIN

Sore feet affect nearly all of us at one point or another, says Leigh Brain & Spine of Chapel Hill, North Carolina [393] (**Drs. Cosmas and Trish Leigh** [394]). Sometimes the condition is temporary due to things like overextending the tendons during exercise. Standing for long periods while wearing shoes that don't offer appropriate foot support can also cause pain. Other times, foot pain is chronic, due to rheumatoid arthritis or plantar fasciitis. Fortunately, several effective self-care remedies are available for foot pain relief, say the Drs. Leigh:

Epsom salt soak for soothing foot pain relief: Epsom salt (magnesium sulfate) is commonly used to ease sore, aching muscles and loosen stiff joints. Add a half of a cup to a pan of warm water and soak your feet for 15 minutes. You can also add a cup to bath water for full-body

---

[393] Get Foot Pain Relief with These 4 Home Remedies | Image: iconsmind.com, The Noun Project
[394] Best Chiropractic Services Chapel Hill, NC, Leigh Brain & Spine, leighbrainandspine.com

relaxation. For added relief, add lavender essential oil – these remedies can work wonders.

At-home massage for sore feet: It's no surprise that long hours of standing for work, jogging, and pregnancy puts a strain on your feet. And causes aching, a bruised sensation, and swelling. For mild pain and swelling, massaging the area can provide relief for foot pain.

DIY foot massage technique: Press your thumbs into the bottom of your foot and rub in circular motions from the heel to the ball of the foot. Pay extra attention to any tense or tender areas. Gently massage the pads of each toe with your thumb. Use the heel of your hands to gently rub circles below the ankle at the tops of the feet. To revive tired feet and ease muscle pain, add a few drops of peppermint, wintergreen, or camphor essential oil to an unscented massage oil.

Ice packs bring quick foot pain relief: If inflammation is causing your pain, ice is an effective way to reduce swelling, soothe inflammation, and provide relief. Rolling a frozen water bottle along the arch of your foot can soothe the fascia, the ligament that connects your toes and heel. Or try soaking your foot in a pan of ice and water. It's important to note that ice is better to use when you're relaxing. Stretching out or exercising on cold tendons and muscles can cause injury.

Wear appropriate foot support: While it may not bring immediate relief, making sure your feet are well-supported can often prevent sore feet. Whether you spend hours at a time on your feet, you exercise regularly, or even if you live a more sedentary lifestyle, supporting your feet is crucial to avoiding pain. If you have workout shoes or athletic shoes and the tread is worn, that probably means the support inside is also broken down, and it's time to replace them. For dress shoes and more casual shoes, well-cushioned insoles can prevent pain.

"Doctor, Doctor!"

While at-home remedies can be an excellent solution for occasional foot pain, if you're experiencing pain on a more frequent basis, you may benefit from professional treatment. Leigh Brain & Spine and other providers specialize in providing foot pain relief to people with foot pain caused by all types of issues. [395]

COST-SAVINGS EXAMPLE:

If these inexpensive remedies work for you, you'll save $50 to $300 per visit for podiatrist care; costs for chiropractic care are similar. Multiple visits can reach $1,000 per year. So start with self-care remedies, but don't hesitate to get professional care if needed because chronic foot pain may limit your future mobility.

---

[395] Leigh Brain & Spine, Chapel Hill, NC, leighbrainandspine.com

FROSTBITE

Frostbite occurs when the skin – and sometimes the tissue beneath it – freezes due to exposure to cold, says the American Academy of Dermatology Association [396] (**Mark D. Kaufmann, M.D., President** [397]). This can lead to severe or permanent damage. First signs of frostbite are redness, stinging, burning, throbbing, or prickling sensations, then numbness. If this occurs, use these two remedies right away:

Head indoors. The longer you are exposed, the longer it will take to warm frozen skin.

Gradually bring feeling back to the body. Using warm water or a warm washcloth. Never rub frostbitten skin or place hands or feet directly into hot water.

"Doctor, Doctor!"

Always call a doctor about frostbite. If you do not feel sensation returning to your body, or if the skin begins to turn gray, go to an emergency room immediately.

COST-SAVINGS EXAMPLE:

Frostbite is a potential medical emergency that can lead to tissue death, gangrene, and amputation. Do not delay treatment due to cost or any other reason.

Remember that throughout this directory you can find further information by using the sources at the bottom of every page and in the resources listing beginning on page 259.

> **Did one of these remedies help you?**
>
> Share your trusted remedies success with the publisher! We'd love to hear from you. **info@trustedremedies.com**

---

[396] How to prevent and treat frostbite, American Academy of Dermatology Association, aad.org
[397] Mark Kaufmann, M.D., Advanced Dermatology, Ft. Lauderdale, FL | Image: Publicdomainvectors.org

G-H

GINGIVITIS

If you've noticed that your gums are swollen and red, you may have the beginning stages of gum (periodontal) disease, which is called gingivitis, says Williamsburg Dental [398] (**Michael Kotopka, D.D.S.** [399]).

Although more serious issues definitely require treatment from a dentist, you may be able to take care of mild gingivitis on your own. These trusted remedies may help.

Salt water rinse: Salt is a natural disinfectant. As a result, rinsing with a diluted salt solution may help curb harmful bacteria. It can also relieve discomfort from sensitive, bleeding gums and help with bad breath. Mix about ½ teaspoon of salt in a glass of water, swish it in your mouth for about 30 seconds, and spit it out. Repeat two or three times per day for a few days. However, this treatment is a temporary option, as repeated exposure to its acidity can erode tooth enamel.

Clove: Clove has long been known for its natural healing properties and may help reduce gum inflammation. Finely mince one teaspoon of clove. Using a damp cotton ball, dab the minced clove, so it sticks to the cotton ball. Gently rub the clove onto the inflamed gums and wait about a minute. Rinse your mouth with water, making sure to catch all bits of clove, and spit it all out.

Brush and floss: For maintenance, says Williamsburg Dental, you need to brush twice and floss once daily Visit your dentist twice every year for checkups and cleanings to keep bacteria and plaque under control. On top of these, you can also implement the following into your lifestyle:

- Use a soft bristle toothbrush and replace it every three months.
- Eat or drink less sugar.
- Do not use tobacco products in any form.
- Drink plenty of water each day.

Ultimately, you play the leading role in keeping your smile healthy, but you don't have to do it alone. By taking these steps at home and working with a dentist you trust, you can reverse the infection in your gums and have a strong smile for whatever the future brings.

"Doctor, Doctor!"

If your gums are bleeding or painful, and you've not seen a dentist in six months, call and make an appointment. Don't be embarrassed about missed check-ups, it's very common in the post-pandemic era. Caring for gums now can save your teeth later – don't put it off.

---

[398] 3 Easy Home Remedies for Getting Rid of Gingivitis, Williamsburg Dental, williamsburgdentalllc.com
[399] Michael Kotopka, DDS, Williamsburg Dental, Lincoln, NE | Image: Studio 365, The Noun Project

COST-SAVINGS EXAMPLE:

The cost of untreated gum disease is high, including tooth loss, oral surgery, and dentures. Costs can run in the tens of thousands of dollars, and your function will never return to what it was when you had a full set of natural teeth.

Oral self-care in the form of brushing, flossing, and rinsing can save $50,000 or more in the future cost of gum surgery, implants and dentures. Take care of your oral health today and save a small fortune.

GOUT

While prescription medications remain the mainstay for treating gout, there are some legitimate self-care remedies for gout, says CreakyJoints.org, the website of the Global Healthy Living Foundation [400] (**Daniel Hernandez, M.D.,** Director of Medical Affairs and Hispanic Outreach [401]).

Anyone who's experienced a gout attack knows it can be excruciating, causing red, hot, painful, and swollen joints, says CreakyJoints.org. Gout, a form of arthritis, typically affects joints in the feet, ankles, or knees; around half the time it strikes in the big toe, which can make it impossible to wear shoes. Even a light sock can be aggravating.

"The joint becomes a battlefield," says **Theodore Fields, M.D.,** professor of clinical medicine at Weill Cornell Medical College and a rheumatologist at New York's Hospital for Special Surgery.[402]

Because the pain from an attack can be so bad, people with gout will often try anything to get relief, leading to a boom in so-called gout home remedies. But there are a few effective remedies for a gout attack, according to doctors. These include:

Resting the joint: Combine with the use of ice packs to reduce swelling.

Drinking cherry juice: Cherry juice is high in vitamin C, which makes uric acid come out in the urine. Cherry juice can also increase the risk of kidney stones and shouldn't be used in anyone who is predisposed to them.

Lose weight if you need to: Being overweight can increase uric acid levels as well as put pressure on the joints.

Follow a low-purine diet: Another effective way to reduce uric acid levels is to follow a low-purine diet. Purines are organic compounds that break down into uric acid. Following a

---

[400] Gout Home Remedies: What Works and What Doesn't, creakyjoints.org | Image: Flow Icon, The Noun Project
[401] Daniel Hernandez, M.D., Director of Medical Affairs and Hispanic Outreach, ghlf.org
[402] Theodore R. Fields, M.D., FACP, Rheumatology, Hospital for Special Surgery, New York, hss.edu

low-purine diet means avoiding "the big four" — alcohol, shellfish, red meat, and high fructose corn syrup. Limiting these foods is also beneficial for heart health — and people with gout are at higher risk for heart disease.

As for the many supplements and other purported home remedies available for gout, including turmeric and bromelain, there is no significant evidence backing them up as of now, and there's no adequate evidence showing that they have any effect even comparable to that of medicines.

"Doctor, Doctor!"

> Don't go overboard with dietary changes to relieve gout, advises Dr. Fields. "You can find lists of thousands of different foods you're not supposed to have if you have gout. Those recommendations are impossible to follow and can make you crazy." He also cautions against relying solely on home remedies to relieve gout instead of taking medicine because the longer you wait, the longer it will take for your gout to get better.

> "From my point of view," says Dr. Fields, "the home remedy concept to gout is often harmful because it keeps patients from taking medications that we know are effective." So if you think you have gout, see a doctor.

COST-SAVINGS EXAMPLE:

> **Gout remedies such as increasing vitamin C and losing weight don't cost much and may have other far-reaching health benefits. Still, historical figures known to have gout – King Henry VIII of England, Benjamin Franklin, Sir Isaac Newton – probably would have been thrilled to have today's medical options available to them. So if you have gout, the effort and the cost to seek medical care is probably worthwhile.**

HAIR LOSS

Brett King, M.D. [403], a dermatologist at Yale School of Medicine, recently told *The New York Times* science reporter Gina Kolata, "there is an endless array of useless hair growth remedies, often at significant cost." Yet because people are desperate, such hair growth remedies continue to abound. [404]

Experts at Mayo Clinic appear to concur with Dr. King's outlook. The clinic regularly shares scientifically sound remedies with readers, yet here is everything Mayo has to say on the topic of trusted remedies for hair loss:

"You might want to try various hair care methods to find one that makes you feel better about how you look. For example, use styling products that add volume, color your hair, choose a hairstyle that makes a widening part less noticeable. Use wigs or extensions, or

[403] Brett King, M.D., Associate Professor of Dermatology, Yale School of Medicine, medicine.yale.edu
[404] An Old Medicine Grows New Hair for Pennies a Day, Doctors Say, The New York Times, nytimes.com

shave your head. Talk with a hair stylist for ideas. These approaches can be used to address permanent or temporary hair loss. If your hair loss is due to a medical condition, the cost of a wig might be covered by insurance."

Dr. Cynthia Cobb, DNP [405] is a doctor nurse practitioner specializing in aesthetics, cosmetics, and skin care. In a post on Medical News Today [406], she suggests exploring the following self-care remedies to encourage hair growth. What's more, her recommendations are safe, inexpensive, and likely very good for your overall health anyway:

Eat more protein: Eating high-protein foods can help the body grow new hair. It takes protein to grow new hair. Hair loss can arise due to a protein deficiency. Examples of healthful dietary protein sources include beans, eggs, fish, nuts, lean meats, and seeds. Daily protein needs vary based on how physically active you are and how much muscle mass you have.

Increase iron intake: Iron is another nutrient the body requires to grow healthy hair. Dietary iron sources include clams, lentils, oysters, pumpkin seeds, spinach, white beans, lean beef, and turkey. Many manufacturers fortify their foods with iron, which means that they have added iron to them. People who do not eat meat have nearly double the iron requirements as those who don't because the body does not absorb non-animal sources of iron as effectively.

Aromatherapy and essential oils: Herbs suggested to promote hair growth include cedarwood, lavender, rosemary, thyme, and tulsi. When using essential oils on the scalp, mix only a few drops into a carrier oil, such as grapeseed oil, which is well absorbed. More research is needed before we can say how effective essential oils are for hair loss. Allergic reactions are possible with essential oils, so try a small test patch 24 hours before applying oil to the whole head.

Massage the scalp: Massage stimulates blood flow, which could promote hair growth. Again, it feels good and probably can't hurt in moderation. A study found that men who massage their scalps for 4 minutes a day with a scalp massager had thicker hair after 6 months. Devices to massage the scalp are available in drug stores and online, or just use your fingertips.

Pumpkin seed oil: Researchers looked at whether pumpkin seed oil could help hair growth. They discovered that men taking 400 mg of pumpkin seed oil for 6 months experienced a 40 percent increase in average hair count, whereas those taking a placebo only experienced a 10 percent increase. The men all had a history of male pattern baldness. They were not currently taking other supplements for hair loss and were between 20 and 65 years old.

Saw palmetto: Saw palmetto supplements may increase hair growth in men with male pattern baldness. Men took 320 mg a day for the duration of the study. After 2 years, they experienced hair growth on the top and back of the scalp, this most common site for bald spots in men.

"Doctor, Doctor!"

If you've assessed your lifestyle, considered your goals, and found home remedies for hair loss to be insufficient, by all means call a doctor about medical solutions. Remember that hair loss may be considered a normal part of aging and not a disease, so insurance

---

[405] Dr. Cynthia Cobb, Allure Enhancement Center, allureenhancement.com
[406] The best home remedies for hair growth, Medical News Today | Image: iconcheese, The Noun Project

coverage may be limited. However, medical treatments for hair loss – both surgical and pharmaceutical – are more plentiful, more effective, and less costly than ever.

COST-SAVINGS EXAMPLE:

WebMD says that the price of a hair transplant will depend largely on the amount of hair you're moving, but it generally ranges from $4,000 to $15,000 – and most insurance plans don't cover it. This can make self-care remedies seem suddenly more attractive. If these remedies provide adequate results, you may be satisfied. [407]

Also consider that Dwayne "The Rock" Johnson is viewed as one of the sexiest men alive, in spite of his shaved head. We know a bald gentleman who jokes he has to pay extra for a haircut due all the time it takes for the barber to find his hair. Adopting a bald-is-beautiful mentality can keep life simple and save you a lot of money.

Save as much as $15,000 on hair replacement procedures by choosing either trusted self-care remedies or the Dwayne Johnson look.

HANGOVER

Hangovers seem to be the body's way of reminding us about the hazards of overindulgence, says Harvard Medical School. The fatigue, headache, nausea, and shaking combine to make you miserable. Your blood pressure can go up, the heart beats faster, and sweat glands overproduce. You may even become sensitive to light or sound or suffer a spinning sensation, says Harvard. [408] **Robert Swift, M.D.** [409] coauthored one of the most frequently cited papers on the topic of hangover remedies. Here's his view of leading morning-after fixes:

"Hair of the dog": The thought is that hangovers are a form of alcohol withdrawal, so a drink or two will ease the withdrawal. However, Dr. Swift does not buy into this popular theory. "The hair of the dog just perpetuates a cycle," he says. "It doesn't allow you to recover."

Drink fluids: Alcohol promotes excess urination. If your hangover includes diarrhea, sweating, or vomiting, you may be even more dehydrated. Although nausea can make it difficult to get anything down, even just a few sips of water might help your hangover, says Harvard.

Eat carbohydrates: Drinking may lower blood sugar levels, so some of the fatigue and headaches of a hangover may be from a brain working without enough of its main fuel. Moreover, many people forget to eat when they drink, further lowering their blood sugar. Toast and juice is

---

[407] Hair Transplant Procedures: Average Cost, What to Expect, and More | WebMD Care
[408] 7 steps to cure your hangover, Harvard Health, health.harvard.edu | Image: Luis Prado, The Noun Project
[409] Robert Swift, M.D., Providence Veterans Affairs Medical Center in Rhode Island, vivo.brown.edu

an easy meal to gently nudge carb levels back toward normal.

Avoid darker-colored alcoholic beverages: Trials have shown that "white" liquors, such as vodka and gin, are less likely to cause hangovers than dark ones, like whiskey, red wine, and tequila. Keep that in mind for future occasions where you might be having more than one or two.

Take a pain reliever, but not Tylenol: Aspirin, ibuprofen (Motrin, other brands), and other non-steroidal anti-inflammatory drugs (NSAIDs) may help with the headache and the overall achy feelings. NSAIDs, though, may irritate a stomach already irritated by alcohol. Don't take acetaminophen (Tylenol); it may compound the toxic effects your liver is already dealing with. Goody's Hangover and Alka-Seltzer are two classic over-the-counter hangover remedies.

Drink coffee or tea: Caffeine may not have any special anti-hangover powers, but as a stimulant, it could help with the grogginess – one more step in the right direction.

B vitamins and zinc: A study in The Journal of Clinical Medicine [410] (**Dr. J.C. Verster** [411] et al.) evaluated the diets for 24 hours before and after excessive drinking. People who consumed food and beverages with greater amounts of zinc and B vitamins had less severe hangovers.

PRO TIP: Besides hangovers, other common after effects of over-consumption are the urgent need to urinate and driving under the influence. Make it a definite habit to use the restroom before leaving any place where you've consumed alcohol. Additionally, do not drink and drive, not even "just once." Calling a cab or a rideshare will cost you a few dollars that you'll soon forget about; driving under the influence can cost you everything, and you'll never forget it.

"Doctor, Doctor!"

One hangover is no reason to call for medical attention unless you've also sustained an injury such as a possible concussion. However, if you are experiencing frequent hangovers, you may wish to consider a professional consultation for possible alcohol dependence. Long term alcohol abuse harms your brain, your liver, your mental health, and your relationships. Recovery can open the door to new experiences and greater achievements. Former President George W. Bush, actor Mel Gibson, and performer Tim McGraw are all individuals who experienced greater success after giving up alcohol.

COST-SAVINGS EXAMPLE:

The best hangover remedies are water and time, and they're both free. A first-offense DWI can cost $6,000-10,000, while felony DWI can send you to jail. So as you recover from your hangover, consider whether it's a possible warning sign of trouble ahead.

Frequent hangovers can serve as a wake-up call that you may be drinking too much. Cutting back, or quitting altogether, could save you many thousands of dollars ... as well as your life.

---

[410] Dietary Nutrient Intake, Alcohol Metabolism, and Hangover Severity, NIH PubMed Central, nih.gov
[411] Dr. J.C. (Joris) Verster, Utrecht University, The Netherlands, uu.nl

HEADACHE

Headaches can wreak havoc on your day says SelectHealth [412], a not-for-profit health plan serving more than 1,000,000 members in Utah, Idaho, and Nevada (**Stephen L. Barlow, M.D.**, Medical Director [413]) . Whether your pain is mild or more intense, you just want it to go away – without meds, if possible. These natural, at-home remedies are known to ease the pain of occasional headaches:

Drink more water: Dehydration may be the cause of your headache. Drinking more water may help to alleviate a headache as well as prevent other ones in the future. Most people will find relief from a dehydration headache within 30 minutes to three hours of drinking water.

Try essential oils: Peppermint and lavender oils seem to be helpful for headache relief. Both have relaxing properties. SelectHealth suggests applying a small amount of peppermint oil to the temples (be sure not to get it in your eyes). Aromatherapy with lavender oil can also be effective to ease the pain of migraines. Consider diffusing it in an essential oil diffuser or apply a tiny amount into your palms, rub your hands together, and then inhale the scent.

Use a cold compress: Applying a cold compress to your forehead helps reduce inflammation. Use either a cold, wet, clean washcloth or fill a small bag with ice and wrap it in a soft towel.

Massage pressure points: Apply gentle pressure to your temples and rub in a circular motion. Rubbing the spot in between your thumb and index finger for four to five seconds is thought to ease stress, headaches, and other types of pain.

"Doctor, Doctor!"

These tips and tricks to cure a headache may be the first step to try at home. But if you're experiencing frequent headaches and home remedies aren't helping, SelectHealth advises talking to a healthcare provider, as it may be a symptom of an underlying condition. [414]

COST-SAVINGS EXAMPLE:

Headache remedies are inexpensive. However, since it is your head we're talking about here, you don't want to cut corners; recurring headaches should be discussed with a doctor to rule out larger concerns. Head pain can be a warning sign of a serious condition; the sooner it's diagnosed, the more successfully it can be treated.

HEARING LOSS ... SEE EARACHE AND EAR INFECTION, EARWAX

---

[412] 4 Natural Remedies to Get Rid of a Headache, selecthealth.org | Image: Sasha Sash, The Noun Project
[413] Dr. Stephen L. Barlow, M.D., Internist, Murray, UT, US News Doctors, health.usnews.com
[414] SelectHealth serving Utah, Idaho and Nevada, selecthealth.org

HEART DISEASE – SEE PART I, PHYSICAL ACTIVITY AND NUTRITION, OVERWEIGHT AND OBESITY; PART II, CHEST PAIN, HIGH BLOOD PRESSURE, HIGH CHOLESTEROL

HEARTBURN

 If you're trying to avoid acid reflux or relieve heartburn fast, here are ten ways to get it done, as provided by Houston Methodist, a leading academic medical center serving the Greater Houston area [415] (**Marc L. Boom, M.D., President, CEO** [416]):

Eat a ripe banana: The high potassium content of a banana makes it a fairly alkaline food, which may help counteract the stomach acid irritating your esophagus. Other alkaline foods are melons, cauliflower, fennel, and nuts.

Chew sugar-free gum: Chewing gum increases saliva production. According to one study, this helps reduce heartburn since saliva can promote swallowing – helping keep acid down and neutralizing the acid that's refluxed into your esophagus from your stomach.

Keep a food journal and avoid trigger foods: You can identify the specific foods most likely to give you issues by keeping a food and symptom log, says Houston Methodist. Once you do identify them, avoid these foods and drinks whenever possible.

Resist the urge to overeat or eat quickly: Having too much food in your stomach may put pressure on the valve that keeps stomach acid out of your esophagus, making heartburn more likely. If you're prone to heartburn, watch your portion sizes; consider eating smaller meals more frequently. Eating quickly can also trigger heartburn, so slow down and take time.

Avoid late meals, snacking before bed and eating before exercising: Laying down with a full stomach can trigger acid reflux and make heartburn worse. Don't eat within 3 hours of bedtime, so your stomach has time to empty. You may also want to wait for 2 hours before exercising.

Wear loose-fitting clothing: If you're prone to heartburn, tight-fitting belts and clothing that squeeze your belly may be contributing to your symptoms.

Adjust your sleep position: Elevating your head and chest higher than your feet as you sleep can help prevent and ease acid reflux and heartburn. You can do this using a foam wedge placed under the mattress or by raising bedposts using wood blocks. Beware of piling pillows, as this usually isn't effective and may even make your symptoms worse. Additionally, sleeping on your left side is thought to aid digestion and may work to limit stomach acid reflux.

Take steps to lose weight if you are overweight: Excess weight puts extra pressure on your stomach, increasing your risk of acid reflux and heartburn. Eating a well-balanced diet and getting

---

[415] Home Remedies for Heartburn: 10 Ways to Get Rid of Acid Reflux | Houston Methodist On Health
[416] Marc L. Boom, M.D., President and CEO, Houston Methodist | Image: Gan Khoon Lay, The Noun Project

150 minutes of physical activity per week are the first two steps to maintaining a healthy weight and losing excess weight, says Houston Methodist.

Stop smoking if you smoke: Smoking reduces the amount of saliva produced and impacts the effectiveness of the valve that keeps stomach acid from entering the esophagus, both of which make heartburn more likely. Quitting smoking can reduce the frequency and severity of acid reflux and, in some cases, even eliminate it.

What to do if heartburn is severe or frequent: For mild, occasional heartburn, over-the-counter medications such as antacids and histamine blockers can help relieve symptoms. Always read the product label before taking an antacid or histamine blocker, and never take a larger dose or take doses more frequently than directed.

Reduce stress: Chronic stress takes a toll on your body, including slowing digestion and making you more sensitive to pain. The longer food sits in your stomach, the more likely stomach acid is to reflux. Additionally, having an increased sensitivity to pain can make you feel the burning pain of heartburn more intensely. Reducing stress may help prevent or ease the effects of acid reflux and heartburn. See the trusted remedies in the section on **Stress** later in this directory.

"Doctor, Doctor!"

If you're experiencing heartburn frequently, consult your doctor before taking heartburn medications, since these can interfere with many other medications and affect underlying health conditions you may have.If you have severe heartburn, as well as if it persists or worsens after taking steps to relieve it, consult your doctor, says Houston Methodist. In some cases, heartburn can be a sign of an underlying condition, such as gastroesophageal reflux disease (GERD), or possibly a side effect of a medication you're taking.

COST-SAVINGS EXAMPLE:

Occasional reflux isn't usually serious. However, when reflux occurs often and is left untreated, it can lead to more serious conditions that are uncomfortable, expensive to treat, and even life-threatening.

The most recent report on the national cost of treatment for GERD was $15 - 20 billion, in 2009. About 50 million people have the condition for an average treatment cost of $400 per year – but much higher for those needing surgery, which may cost between $7,000 and $22,000.

Use heartburn self-care remedies on a regular basis to reduce or delay GERD. Savings to you and your insurer start at around $400 per year and go up to $22,000 or much more over your lifetime.

HEAT EXHAUSTION/HEAT STROKE

 Heat exhaustion happens when your body gets too hot, says the American Academy of Family Physicians [417] (**Beth Oller, M.D.,** medical review panel [418]). If you don't treat heat exhaustion, it can lead to heatstroke, says AAFP. This occurs when your internal temperature reaches at least 104° F. Heatstroke is much more serious than heat exhaustion. It can cause shock, organ failure, or brain damage. In extreme cases, heatstroke can kill you; for this reason, the remedies below are very important, but prevention is key.

Heat exhaustion: Symptoms of heat exhaustion are muscle cramps, heavy sweating, pale or cold skin, weakness and/or confusion, dizziness, headache, nausea or vomiting, fast heartbeat, dark-colored urine, which indicates dehydration.

Heat stroke: In addition to these symptoms, warning signs of heatstroke include fever of 104° F or higher, flushed or red skin, lack of sweating, trouble breathing, fainting, seizures

Hot weather and exercise are the main causes of heat exhaustion and heatstroke, says AAFP. Be mindful of the temperature outside. The heat index is not the same as the temperature. It measures the air temperature plus the effects of humidity. A heat index of 90° F or higher calls for extreme caution. Babies, children, and the elderly are more sensitive to heat and require extra attention. You also are at greater risk if you are ill or obese, or have heart disease. People who work outside or in a hot setting also are at risk of heat exhaustion and heatstroke.

Don't go outside when the temperature and heat index are high. If possible, stay indoors in air-conditioned areas. If you must go outside, wear lightweight, light-colored, loose-fitting clothing, wearing a hat or using an umbrella, and apply sunscreen.

Drink plenty of water throughout the day. Dehydration and lack of salt contribute to heat-related illnesses. Some sports drinks can help replenish the salt in your body lost through sweating. Dark-colored urine is a sign that you're dehydrated.

Certain medicines can also put you in danger of heatstroke. They affect the way your body reacts to heat. Talk to your doctor if you take any of these or have an ongoing health problem.

If someone else has heat exhaustion, treat symptoms with these home remedies, says AAFP:

- **Get out of the heat quickly and into a cool place, or at least shade.**
- **Lie down and elevate your legs to get blood flowing to your heart.**
- **Take off any tight or extra clothing.**
- **Apply cool towels to your skin or take a cool bath.**
- **Drink water or a sports drink.** Do not guzzle, but take sips. Avoid caffeine and alcohol.

After you've had heat exhaustion or heatstroke, you will be sensitive to heat. This can last for about a week. It's important to rest and let your body recover. Avoid hot weather and exercise. Ask your doctor when it's safe to return to your normal activities.

---

[417] Heat Exhaustion and Heat Stroke, Symptoms, familydoctor.org | Image: Luis Prado, The Noun Project
[418] Beth Oller, M.D., Post Rock Family Medicine, Plainville, KS, postrock.us

"Doctor, Doctor!"

If a person is displaying known heat illness symptoms, take their temperature. You should call 9-1-1 and get medical care right away if:

- The person has a temperature of 104° F or more, meaning they probably have heatstroke, which can cause life-changing, irreversible organ damage, or death
- Symptoms don't improve or they still have a fever of 102° F after 30 minutes of treatment
- The person goes into shock, faints, or has seizures
- The person is not breathing. Begin CPR right away to try and revive them.

COST-SAVINGS EXAMPLE:

Water and sunscreen are cheap; use them regularly. Know the signs of heat exhaustion and respond accordingly. Heat stroke commonly leads to a very expensive ambulance ride followed by a very expensive emergency room visit.

Prevent heat exhaustion, or treat it immediately if it occurs. The typical cost for an ambulance trip is $1,277. An emergency room visit costs $2,200 on average for a total of $3,477 – possibly much higher, and possibly not entirely covered by insurance.

HEMORRHOIDS

Hemorrhoids are nearly as common as the body part they are found in – everybody has one. **Jeremy Lipman, M.D.,** [419] colorectal surgeon at Cleveland Clinic, explains: "First, realize that hemorrhoids are a normal part of our anatomy. Usually, they do not cause pain." [420]

But because bleeding is a common sign of both normal hemorrhoids and more serious conditions, Dr. Lipman recommends seeing a doctor before self-treating. It's after you're properly diagnosed that he recommends you start exploring these trusted remedies:

Sitz baths: Experts recommend people with painful hemorrhoids sit in warm water for 15 minutes, several times a day – especially after a bowel movement. A sitz bath is a small bowl that fits right over your toilet and offers a convenient way to soak and soothe the area, and is generally available at any pharmacy. You can also just sit in a bathtub filled with warm water.

Psyllium husk: Psyllium husk is a supplement that helps increase your fiber intake and softens stools to make them easier to pass and making your hemorrhoids are more likely to resolve. Be

[419] Jeremy Lipman, M.D., Cleveland Clinic | Appointments at Cleveland Clinic
[420] 5 Best and Worst Home Remedies for Your Hemorrhoids, Cleveland Clinic

Image: Amethyst Studio
The Noun Project

careful not to increase fiber too much, too quickly, as it may also cause gas or stomach cramping. Also be sure to drink plenty of water if you take this supplement.

Aloe vera: The anti-inflammatory properties of aloe vera may help soothe inflammation of hemorrhoids. Although research isn't available for its use on hemorrhoid relief specifically, it has shown some benefits for other inflammatory skin conditions. Dr. Lipman says this is safe to try only if it's pure aloe (and not in a cream with other ingredients).

You may have also heard of these two folklore remedies for getting rid of hemorrhoids fast. Dr. Lipman wants you to avoid these for hemorrhoid pain relief if you can.

Don't use apple cider vinegar: Some patients say that apple cider vinegar can bring instant relief to hemorrhoids, reducing itching and pain. "I don't recommend using this remedy as it may burn the skin with overuse and exacerbate problems," says Dr. Lipman.

Don't use tea tree oil: Some people say the antiseptic and anti-inflammatory properties of tea tree oil may reduce swelling and itching caused by hemorrhoids. Some early research found that a gel made with tea tree oil decreased symptoms, but studies are lacking. Dr. Lipman recommends not trying this remedy as it isn't well studied.

Always ask your doctor before trying a self-care remedy and if issues arise with any treatment, stop your attempt at an at-home hemorrhoids cure immediately.

Remember, to help treat and prevent hemorrhoids it's important to eat enough fiber (25 grams a day for women, 38 grams a day for men) and to drink at least eight glasses of water a day. These dietary changes can make stool easier to pass and keep the problem from recurring.

"Doctor, Doctor!"

Any change you notice around your anus should prompt an exam by your doctor to make sure nothing more serious is going on, says Dr. Lipman, especially if you see blood.

COST-SAVINGS EXAMPLE:

Self-care remedies for hemorrhoids are inexpensive. Use them to help keep the problem from becoming more serious, possibly avoiding the need for surgery.

HERPES

There is no known cure for genital herpes, which becomes dormant in the body after the first outbreak, advises men's health clinic Craft Medical [421] (**Robert Mitchell, M.D., Medical Advisor** [422]). When a new outbreak occurs, you may wonder how to treat it at home. Here are some doctor-trusted remedies:

---

[421] How to Treat Genital Herpes at Home, Craft Medical, craftmedical.com | Image: Sandra, The Noun Project
[422] Craft Medical: A Low T Men's Health Clinic, Tulsa, Oklahoma, craftmedical.com

Warm or cool compress: As soon as you feel a sore forming, apply heat to help minimize the pain. If you cannot do a warm compress, try a cold compress to help to reduce swelling. Place an ice pack wrapped in a clean cloth on the affected area and repeat every 4 hours. Avoid placing ice directly on your skin. You can also wash the affected area gently with saltwater.

Petroleum jelly: Apply to the affected area to reduce discomfort, especially from urinating. You can find gels specifically for herpes online or from pharmacies near you. Wash your hands before and after applying any gel to prevent spreading the virus to other parts of your body.

Aloe vera: The plant's gel has anti-inflammatory and antiviral properties and is safe to apply directly on sores. The plant also has a cooling effect that can help with the pain and speed up the healing process. Wash your hands before and after applying.

Supplements: Some nutritional supplements can help prevent outbreaks, so keep them on hand:

- **Vitamin D** helps to protect your body against infections by boosting your immune system and reducing the chance that the herpes infection will reactivate.

- **Vitamin E** has antioxidative properties to lower the stress herpes infections put on your immune system. Vitamin E also helps to repair and regenerate damaged skin cells.

- **Lysine** is an amino acid that you can get from food or supplements. Studies show that people who take one gram of lysine three times a day have fewer occurrences, reduced severity, and faster healing time of herpes flare-ups.

Cornstarch Paste Or Baking Soda Paste: Cornstarch can help dry out the sores of an outbreak. Dip a Q-tip in cornstarch and apply on and around the affected area. Baking soda works, too.

Warm Bath: Taking a warm bath can help relieve the pain, keep sores clean, and help you relax. Add Epsom salt to your bath to promote healing and speed recovery. Make sure to dry the affected area carefully after your warm bath because excess moisture can prolong the sores.

Rest: An outbreak signifies that the dormant virus is attacking again. Find time to rest and allow your immune system to do its job. Also avoid stress, which suppresses your immune system.

Pain Relievers: Using over-the-counter pain relievers such as ibuprofen, aspirin, or acetaminophen can also help reduce the pain associated with herpes symptoms.

Wear loose-fitting cotton underwear: Avoid any nylon or synthetic underwear or tight-fitting clothing. Cotton is breathable and absorbs moisture better than synthetic fabric.

Things NOT To Do At Home: Now that you know what to do at home, here are a few things you should avoid when you have a herpes outbreak, according to Craft Medical:

Do Not: Do not bandage the sores; exposure to air speeds up the healing process.

Do Not: Do not pick at the sores; they could get infected, and this slows the healing process.

Do Not: Do not touch or scratch lesions caused by herpes; this can cause the infection to spread.

"Doctor, Doctor!"

If it's your first outbreak of herpes, it's wise to consult a doctor to properly diagnose you through tests and go through the best antiviral options to consider. A doctor can assist not only with your herpes, but any other sexual health complication. In some cases, you don't even have to leave your house; you can quite literally treat your herpes right at home. [423]

COST-SAVINGS EXAMPLE:

Once you have herpes, it's with you for life. Keeping your immune system in peak condition will reduce the frequency and severity of outbreaks, thereby reducing your medical expenses. However, the lifetime direct medical costs of genital herpes is only about $972 (in 2019 dollars) per treated case, for the simple reason that there are not a lot of medical treatments for the condition.

The clinical visit at which genital herpes is first diagnosed accounts for about 25% of lifetime costs. Medications related to treatment account for 60% of lifetime costs, and subsequent clinical visits account for the remaining 15%. [424]

Make full use of these doctor-trusted remedies to keep your medical costs below the typical lifetime total of about $1,000 per patient.

HICCUPS

Hiccups seem like no big deal, until you have them and they won't stop. Here are ten doctor-trusted cures from Medical News Today [425] (medically reviewed by **Debra Sullivan, Ph.D.** [426]) – you only need to find one that works for you.

Hold your breath: Take a deep breath. Hold it for 10 seconds. While still holding your breath, inhale another sip of air and hold 5 seconds. Take one more sip and hold 5 more seconds. Then exhale. The idea is to relax your diaphragm, briefly increase carbon dioxide levels, and create positive airway pressure. Do not exceed these intervals; if it doesn't work in one try, go to the next cure.

Stick your fingers in your ears for 30 seconds: You can also press your fingers in the soft area right behind your earlobes at the base of your skull. Touching your ears this way signals your vagus nerve to relax, which will relax your diaphragm spasm and hopefully stop your hiccups.

Stretch your diaphragm: This stretch is easy to do. Take a very deep breath so that your belly and lungs feel completely full of air. It should feel like you can't inhale any more air. Hold the air

---

[423] Craft Medical, online men's health clinic, craftmedical.com

[424] Lifetime Medical Costs of Genital Herpes in the U.S., American STD Assn., pubmed.ncbi.nlm.nih.gov

[425] Hiccups: Causes, treatments, and complications, medicalnewstoday.com

[426] Debra Sullivan, PhD, Sleepingocean.com | Image: Webtechops LLP, The Noun Project

in for as long as you can. When you need to breathe, exhale slowly. Are your hiccups gone? If not, try this diaphragm stretch one or two more times.

Suck on sugar: Drop dry sugar directly onto your tongue from a spoon, packet, or your fingers. Then close your mouth and suck on the sugar until it dissolves. This action disrupts the nerve impulses to the vagus nerve that cause the spasms that lead to hiccups. It also changes your breathing pattern, which can stop the spasms.

Drink water in a weird way: Drink from the sink faucet or from the opposite side of a glass with your head upside down. This sounds silly, but it confuses your nervous system enough to stop the diaphragm spasms that cause hiccups.

Use your hands: Cup your hands over your mouth and nose and take normal breaths until your hiccups stop. Another hands-on technique is to firmly press into the palm of one hand with the thumb of the other hand. The discomfort provides a distraction for your nervous system.

Ice your hiccups: Tell your hiccups to cool it by holding an ice pack over your diaphragm in the area between your rib cage and your navel. Be sure to wrap the ice pack with a towel to protect your skin. Hold it there until your hiccups go away. The theory is that cooling the diaphragm stops the spasms. It may also be a mental distraction for your nervous system.

Put paper behind your ear: This clever mental distraction is also easy. Simply tear off a piece of paper and twist it, so you can hang it behind your ear. Your brain gets so busy wondering "why does this person have a piece of paper behind their ear?" that it forgets to hiccup. Grandmothers swear by this remedy, so it's definitely worth a try.

Sip dill pickle juice: Here's one for the list of "it's so crazy, it might work" remedies. It must be dill and not sweet pickles. Sour flavors are often recommended in hiccup remedies and you can try taking a sip of vinegar as an alternative.

Hit the hot sauce: Shake a few drops of hot sauce into your mouth. This discomfort shifts your body's focus to what's happening in your head and it'll forget all about hiccuping.

"Doctor, Doctor!"

If hiccups last longer than 48 hours, contact a doctor, says Medical News Today [427] . This tends to be more common in men and could signify a more serious medical condition.

COST-SAVINGS EXAMPLE:

According to Mayo Clinic, medical treatment for hiccups may require extensive testing, all possibly resulting in a very large bill. It's in your best interest to try the above remedies as soon as your hiccups begin to find one that works. [428]

---

[427] Hiccups: Causes, Treatments, And Complications, Medical News Today, medicalnewstoday.com
[428] Hiccups Diagnosis and treatment, Mayo Clinic, mayoclinic.org | Appointments at Mayo Clinic

HIGH BLOOD PRESSURE

You've heard this before, but stop for a moment and let it sink in ... *high blood pressure is the silent killer.* There are no obvious symptoms to indicate that something is wrong, says the American Heart Association [429] (**Mariell Jessup, M.D., Chief Science and Medical Officer** [430]).

Yet even though you can't see it, hear it, or feel it, high blood pressure, also called hypertension, can send you to an early grave. Untreated high blood pressure can lead to heart attack, stroke and other deadly threats, says the AHA. Several physician-trusted remedies are highly effective in reversing or preventing hypertension:

Eat a well-balanced diet that's low in salt: Aim to eat a diet that's rich in fruits, vegetables, whole grains, low-fat dairy, skinless poultry and fish, nuts and legumes, and non-tropical vegetable oils. Limit saturated and trans fats, sodium, red meat, and sugar.

Limit alcohol: Too much alcohol can raise your blood pressure. If you have been diagnosed with high blood pressure, your doctor may advise you to cut back on alcohol consumption.

Enjoy regular physical activity: Physical activity not only helps control hypertension, it also helps you manage your weight, strengthen your heart and lower your stress level. Even moderate activity, such as brisk walking, is beneficial when done regularly.

Manage stress: Stress is known to contribute to risk factors like a poor diet and excessive alcohol consumption. Learn to fight stress by making choices like talking with family and friends and making time for physical activity. These habits not only improve your health – they also rejuvenate your general well-being.

Maintain a healthy weight: Weight loss reduces the strain on your heart. Being overweight puts extra strain on your heart, increasing the risk for developing high blood pressure and damage to your blood vessels that can lead to serious health threats. Even a small weight loss can help manage or prevent high blood pressure in many people.

Quit smoking: Smoking is the leading preventable cause of early death in the U.S.. Decide today that the tobacco industry is not going to control your life. For help, see **Tobacco** in Part I of this directory, **Doctor-Trusted Remedies for the Top 10 Most Common Health Issues**.

"Doctor, Doctor!"

Since hypertension has no outward symptoms, there are no flags to look for that would trigger to see your doctor about possible blood pressure. Instead, make sure you get your pressure checked once a year during routine exams or at free clinics offered in most communities. Your local pharmacy may take your blood pressure for free.

COST-SAVINGS EXAMPLE:

---

[429] Why High Blood Pressure is a "Silent Killer", heart.org | Image: Eucalyp, The Noun Project
[430] Dr. Mariell L. Jessup, M.D., Cardiologist, Philadelphia, PA, US News Doctors, health.usnews.com

The cost of high blood pressure can be your life; don't take it lightly. With or without insurance, the cost of prescription medications can be high. Research shows that the price for 30 doses of a typical blood pressure medication averages $329, and once you're on it, you may be on it for life. The cost may vary depending on the type of medication you are prescribed and whether it is brand-name. [431]

HIGH CHOLESTEROL

It's normal to feel a bit anxious after learning you have high cholesterol, says GoodRx [432] (written by **Karla Robinson, M.D.**, reviewed by **Patricia Pinto-Garcia, M.D.** [433]). Common concerns include the health risks of high cholesterol, medication costs, and side effects. And with so many classes of medications for cholesterol to choose from, it's hard to know where to start.

But there may be some easy changes in the foods you eat and choices you make that can help. Natural ways to lower your cholesterol might help to decrease how much medication you need to take. Lowering your cholesterol naturally may feel like a daunting task. But there are small steps you can take to make it more manageable. Here are 10 natural ways that can help you start to lower your cholesterol today.

Increase your fiber intake: Dietary fiber comes in both soluble and insoluble forms, and is an important part of a healthy diet. Adding over 10 grams of soluble fiber to your diet can help to decrease your LDL (low-density lipoprotein) cholesterol levels. LDL is often called "bad cholesterol" because it increases your risk of heart disease. Common sources of soluble fiber include oats, beans, lentils, fruits (apple, pears, oranges), peas and psyllium. Fiber also decreases your risk of heart disease. This is true with both soluble and insoluble forms of fiber.

Adopt a plant-based diet: Plant-based foods are high in unsaturated fats, fiber, and plant proteins. These help to support lower cholesterol levels. A plant-based diet will usually include vegetable oils, nut butters, seeds, quinoa, hummus, legumes, and leafy vegetables.

Exercise: Exercise is a natural way to raise your HDL. Get 150 minutes of moderate-intensity aerobic activity per week. One study found that moderate aerobic exercise 3 times a week for 40 minutes increased HDL cholesterol by over 10%. Forms of aerobic exercise include walking, biking, jogging, swimming, and playing tennis. Experts also recommend moderate- to high-intensity resistance training at least twice per week. This includes strength training by lifting weights, body weight exercises, or resistance bands.

Increase omega-3 intake: Omega-3 fatty acids have the greatest impact on triglycerides, a type of fat in the blood that can also raise your risk of heart disease. At doses of 4 grams per day, omega-3 fatty acids can decrease triglycerides by up to 30%. Omega-3 can come in the form of supplements, prescription, or from your diet. Omega-3 rich foods include fatty fish, nuts, seeds,

[431] How Much Does Blood Pressure Medication Cost Without Insurance in 2022? Mira, talktomira.com
[432] 10 Natural Ways to Lower Your Cholesterol, GoodRx.com | Image: supalerk laipawat, The Noun Project
[433] Karla Robinson, M.D., GoodRx.com | Patricia Pinto-Garcia, M.D., MPH, GoodRx.com

and plant oils. The American Heart Association recommends eating fatty fish at least twice per week. Examples are salmon, tuna, mackerel, anchovies, black cod, and herring.

Weight management: Being overweight raises your risk for high cholesterol. But that risk is reversible. Even modest weight loss can have a huge effect on LDL cholesterol and triglycerides. See the section **Overweight and Obesity** in Part I of this publication, **Doctor-Trusted Remedies for the Top 10 Most Common Health Issues**.

Limit alcohol: With moderate intake, alcohol is sometimes thought to be protective against heart disease. But drinking more than moderate levels of alcohol can increase triglycerides. Experts recommend that women have no more than 1 drink per day and men have no more than 2. See the section **Substance Abuse** in Part I of this publication.

Stop smoking: Along with other health effects, smoking is bad for your cholesterol. Smoking lowers HDL and also raises LDL. Once you stop smoking, this effect is highly reversible; HDL levels can rise in as little as 3 weeks after quitting smoking. Breaking a smoking habit can be tough. See the section **Tobacco** in Part I of this directory for tools to help you quit.

Decrease stress: There's evidence that stress increases both LDL and triglycerides. The rise in cholesterol isn't just a response to long-term stress; rapid changes in cholesterol are also due to short-term stress. Some easy and helpful ways to decrease stress are staying active, practicing mindfulness, eating a balanced diet, using relaxation techniques, and getting enough sleep. See the section **Mental Health** in Part I of this publication.

Take supplements: Some dietary supplements can boost the cholesterol-lowering effect of a healthy diet and exercise. Supplements that may help lower your cholesterol include chia, flaxseed, whey, stanol and sterol, and garlic. In some cases, supplements can have similar effects as medication. This is especially true for red yeast rice. This supplement can have the same active ingredient as lovastatin. It can also have the same side effects.

Drink green tea: Green tea may decrease both LDL and total cholesterol. This may be because it contains flavonoids, compounds that reduce the amount of cholesterol your body makes. Research shows that 375 mg of green tea per day may lower LDL cholesterol by over 15%. Consume green tea as a drink or a dietary supplement. Drink no more than 6 to 8 cups per day.

"Doctor, Doctor!"

> Discuss any herbs and supplements you plan to take with your healthcare provider to be sure it's safe for you to do so. High cholesterol is often a silent condition, meaning it produces no obvious symptoms and can go easily unnoticed (and untreated) for decades, says Wellmark Blue Cross and Blue Shield [434] (**Timothy R. Gutshall, M.D., Chief Medical Officer** [435]). That's why a cholesterol test should be part of your regular physical. Ask your doctor if you're up-to-date on cholesterol monitoring.

COST-SAVINGS EXAMPLE:

---

[434] Cost of high cholesterol in the workplace, Wellmark, wellmark.com
[435] Timothy R. Gutshall, M.D., Emergency Medicine Specialist, Des Moines, IA, md.com

According to WebMD, high cholesterol levels are linked to a higher risk of cardiovascular disease. Heart disease is the leading cause of death in the U.S., and costs around $207 billion annually in lost productivity and medical expenses. [436]

You don't want to be part of these statistics. Keep your cholesterol in check by following a heart-healthy diet and getting your cholesterol checked at intervals recommended by your doctor.

HIV/AIDS – SEE PART I

HIVES

Hives are itchy welts on the skin, says the American Academy of Dermatology Association [437] (**Mark D. Kaufmann, M.D., President** [438]). Also called wheals, these welts may be red, pink, white, or skin-colored. They can be caused by an allergic reaction; by a physical trigger, such as cold, water, or pressure; or by a medical condition, such as an infection or autoimmune disease.

Hives come in many shapes, sizes, and patterns, but tend to clear within hours. You may have a flare-up and never get hives again. Or may have many flare-ups, a condition called chronic urticaria. The best treatment for chronic hives often depends on the cause and your medical history. The AADA offers these home remedies for chronic hives:

Avoid overheating. Wear loose-fitting, cotton clothes.

Apply a cold compress, such as ice cubes wrapped in a washcloth, to the itchy skin several times a day—unless cold triggers your hives.

Use anti-itch medication that you can buy without a prescription, such as an antihistamine or calamine lotion.

Prevent dry skin by using a fragrance-free moisturizer several times a day.

Avoid pressure points. The pressure of a purse strap can cause chronic hives where the strap rests on your body.

Stay calm. Stress can trigger hives. If you often feel stressed, healthy ways to reduce your stress include exercising every day, meditating, and practicing mindfulness.

Keep track of your flare-ups: Notating your symptoms and flare-ups may help you determine what triggers your hives. Common triggers include foods, food additives, medications, cold, heat, UV light, adrenalin, pressure on your skin, or touching a plant, animal, or chemical. In rare cases, vibration or touching water can cause hives. In some cases, the cause is never determined.

---

[436] Cost of high cholesterol in the workplace | Wellmark.com | WebMD Care, doctor.webmd.com
[437] 10 Ways To Get Relief From Chronic Hives, American Academy of Dermatology Association, aad.org
[438] Mark Kaufmann, M.D., Ft. Lauderdale, FL, advancedderm.com | Image: Luis Prado, The Noun Project

Take photos of your hives: These will be useful when you decide it's time to see a doctor. Pics can help your doctor make sure you really have hives; other skin conditions can look like hives.

In addition, verywellheath.com [439] (by **Daniel More, M.D.** [440]) suggests complementary and alternative medicines for hives:

Colloidal Oatmeal: If the itching and swelling are driving you mad, the fastest form of relief may be a cooling bath. It helps reduce swelling and tempers hyperactive nerve signals that trigger itchiness. One additive that may help further relieve symptoms is colloidal oatmeal.

Some smaller studies have suggested that colloidal oatmeal—a finely milled oatmeal suspended in liquid, gel, or cream—can reduce the intensity of itching while softening inflamed skin.

Mind-Body Therapies: Stress does not cause urticaria, but can aggravate it. Mind-body therapies may help relieve stress and the health problems it can cause. These practices include meditation, deep breathing, guided imagery, progressive muscle relaxation, and biofeedback.

"Doctor, Doctor!"

> If you choose to use a natural remedy for your hives (urticaria), speak with your doctor first to ensure that it doesn't interact with any medications you may be taking. When you have flare-ups for six weeks or longer, make an appointment to see a board-certified dermatologist, allergist, or primary care doctor. Most people who have hives are otherwise healthy, but it's still helpful to see a doctor.
>
> A thorough medical exam can help rule out possible causes, such as an infection or medication, which could be causing your hives. It's also possible for a disease, such as a thyroid condition, rheumatoid arthritis, or diabetes to cause hives. If signs indicate that this may be the cause, medical testing can find or rule out these causes.
>
> While medications and medical conditions can cause hives, there are many other causes, including foods, insect bites, and pressure on the skin. Sometimes, it's not possible to find the cause. If that happens, your dermatologist can still recommend lifestyle changes and prescribe medication that can help reduce your flare-ups.

<u>COST-SAVINGS EXAMPLE:</u>

> **While urticaria-related hospitalizations are uncommon, the mean total healthcare cost for patients with chronic urticaria was over $9,000 per year, according to a 2015 study published by the American Journal of Clinical Dermatology [441] (Michael S. Broder, M.D. [442]). With medical inflation, that's about $10,926 in 2022. Try to avoid some of these costs by treating your hives with self-care remedies.**

---

[439] How Urticaria (Hives) Is Treated, verywellhealth.com
[440] Daniel R. More, M.D., Allergy Partners of the California Central Coast, allergypartners.com
[441] Resource Use and Costs in an Insured Population of Patients with Chronic Idiopathic/Spontaneous Urticaria, NIH PubMed Central, ncbi.nlm.nih.gov
[442] Michael S. Broder, M.D., Partnership for Health Analytic Research, pharllc.com

Save some or all of the $10,926 annual medical costs of patients with chronic hives by trying these doctor-approved remedies.

HOT FLASHES

The North American Menopause Society [443] (**Chrisandra L Shufelt, M.D., President**) [444] offers these doctor-reviewed self-care remedies for hot flashes:

Black cohosh: Results of studies of this herb's effectiveness in reducing hot flashes are mixed. However, says NAMS, some women report that the herb has helped. Black cohosh has had a good safety record over a number of years.

Red clover: No consistent or conclusive evidence has been found that red clover leaf extract reduces hot flashes. As with black cohosh, however, some women claim that red clover has helped. Studies report few side effects and no serious health problems with use.

Dong Quai: This remedy has been used in Traditional Chinese Medicine to treat gynecologic conditions for more than 1,200 years. Outside of that, the herb has not been well studied. Dong quai should never be used by women with fibroids or blood-clotting problems, or those taking drugs that affect clotting such as warfarin (Coumadin) as bleeding complications can result.

Ginseng: Research has shown that ginseng may help with some menopausal symptoms, such as mood symptoms and sleep disturbances, and with one's overall sense of well-being, all of which are very important. However, it has not been found to be helpful for hot flashes *per se*.

Use with caution: Of course, as with all therapies, there are some risks. People usually take herbal therapies as supplement pills, not as a preparation made directly from the herb by a trained herbalist. The women's health experts at NAMS remind us that herbal supplements are not as closely regulated as prescription drugs. The concentration, quality, safety, and purity may vary between brands or even between batches of the same brand.

Herbal remedies may interact with prescription drugs, dramatically changing the effect of the herb, the drug, or both. Tell your provider all herbs you are considering, says NAMS, and stop all herbal treatments at least 2 weeks before planned surgery. Learn more about herbal products at HerbMed and the NIH National Center for Complementary and Alternative Medicine.

Lifestyle modifications: In addition, lifestyle modifications such as avoiding caffeine, alcohol, and spicy foods, and dressing in layers can help relieve hot flashes, says Penn Medicine Lancaster General Health [445] (**John J. Eichenlaub, M.D., Chair, Department of Obstetrics and Gynecology** [446]).

Deep breathing: Practice slow, deep breathing if you feel a hot flash coming on, says Penn

---

[443] Natural Remedies for Hot Flashes, North American Menopause Society, pharllc.com
[444] Chrisandra L. Shufelt, M.D., MS, NCMP, FACP, 2021-2022 NAMS President, pharllc.com
[445] 4 Ways to Stop Hot Flashes, Penn Medicine Lancaster General Health, pharllc.com
[446] John J. Eichenlaub, M.D., PennMedicine.org, Lancaster, PA | Image: Lorie Shaull, The Noun Project

Medicine. Some women find relief through meditation and other stress-reducing techniques. And finally, be conscious of anything that triggers your hot flashes and avoid them.

Exercise: Exercise can also help during your transition through menopause, Penn Medicine adds. It helps prevent weight gain, relieves stress, improves your mood, and benefits your cardiovascular fitness. Remember, heart disease is the No. 1 cause of death in women.

"Doctor, Doctor!"

If you have any concerns, see your doctor, says Penn Medicine. Just as each woman experiences menopause differently, there is no one-size-fits-all approach to treating menopausal symptoms.

COST-SAVINGS EXAMPLE:

Oral HRT: Monthly prescription costs run $130 to $240 per month, for an annual fee of $1,560 to $2.,440. But, because most insurance companies pay for HRT pills, most people only see their prescription co-pay costs, which typically average $30 per month or $360 per year, says Hormone Therapy Center of America (HTCA) [447].

Creams, gels, & patches: The prices are about the same, $120 to $1,020, but you have much more work to do on your own, says HTCA. On the plus side, you may also have fewer side effects using creams, gels, and patches.

Injectable hormone therapy primarily relates to men, although some women do prefer this method, reports HTCA. It's one of the more expensive options, running as high as several thousand dollars per year and requiring frequent doctor visits.

The Fountain of Youth has proven elusive, but that hasn't stopped women or men from searching for it, or spending on it. However, if you can obtain results satisfactory to you using home remedies, you could easily save tens of thousands of dollars over the years.

Remember that throughout this directory you can find further information by using the sources at the bottom of every page and in the resources listing beginning on page 259.

---

[447] How much does hormone replacement therapy cost? Hormone Therapy Center of America, ht-ca.com

I

INCONTINENCE

 Urinary incontinence is a common problem, says Mayo Clinic [448] (**Bradley C. Leibovich, M.D., Chair, Urology** [449]). The severity ranges from occasional leaks when you cough or sneeze to having an urge to go that's so sudden and strong, you don't get to a toilet in time. Though it occurs more often as people age, incontinence isn't inevitable, says Mayo. For many people, simple lifestyle changes can ease discomfort and stop urinary incontinence and the embarrassment that often comes with it.

Bladder training: This involves learning to delay urination every time you get the urge to go. Start by trying to hold off for 10 minutes. The goal is to lengthen the time between toilet trips until you're going every two to four hours. Bladder training may also involve double voiding – urinating, then waiting a few minutes and trying again to empty your bladder more completely.

Schedule toilet trips: The idea is timed urination – going to the toilet according to the clock, rather than waiting for the need to go. Try to go every two to four hours.

Fluid and diet management: You may be able to simply modify your daily dietary habits to regain bladder control. You may need to cut back on or avoid alcohol, caffeine or acidic foods.

Pelvic floor muscle exercises: These exercises, called Kegels, strengthen the abdominal muscles that control urination. Imagine you're trying to stop the flow of urine. If you're using the right muscles, you'll feel a pulling sensation. Pull in your pelvic muscles and hold for a count of three. Relax for a count of three. Work up to 10 to 15 repetitions each time you exercise. Do Kegels at least three times a day. Within 12 weeks, you may notice an improvement in bladder control.

Prevent skin irritation: Problems with leakage may require taking extra care to prevent skin irritation, says Mayo:

- **Use a washcloth to clean yourself.**

- **Allow your skin to air-dry:** Avoid frequent washing and douching because these can overwhelm your body's natural defenses against bladder infections.

- **Consider using a barrier cream,** like petroleum jelly or cocoa butter.

Improve toilet access: If you have urge incontinence or nighttime incontinence, make the toilet more convenient by moving any rugs or furniture you might trip over or collide with on the way

---

[448] Home Remedies: Urinary incontinence can be embarrassing, Mayo Clinic, newsnetwork.mayoclinic.org
[449] Bradley C. Leibovich, M.D., Urology, Mayo Clinic, mayoclinic.org | Image: Gan Khoon Lay, The Noun Project

to the toilet. Use a night light to illuminate your path and reduce your risk of falling. If you have functional incontinence, you might keep a bedside commode in your bedroom, install an elevated toilet seat, or widen an existing bathroom doorway.

"Doctor, Doctor!"

If urinary incontinence affects your daily activities, don't hesitate to see your healthcare provider. If you feel uncomfortable discussing incontinence with your doctor, remember that he or she has heard it all before and is only there to help.

If incontinence is frequent or is affecting your quality of life, it's important to seek medical advice because: urinary incontinence may indicate a more serious underlying condition; it may cause you to restrict your activities and limit your social interactions; or it may increase the risk of falls in older adults as they rush to the toilet. Ask your doctor about special cleansers made to remove urine that may be less drying than other products.

COST-SAVINGS EXAMPLE:

Incontinence is very expensive, says idiaper.com. Expect to pay $80 - $160 a month for adult diapers. [450] **Try to avoid the need for long term incontinence products by using the trusted remedies given here as soon as incontinence becomes a concern.**

Save up to $1,920 per year by putting these trusted remedies to use before incontinence becomes difficult to reverse.

INGROWN HAIR

 Whether they're springing up as bumps on your legs or wreaking havoc on your bikini line, ingrown hairs are an unwelcome guest that can lead to serious discomfort, inflammation, and even scarring, says beauty and self-care site byrdie.com [451] (medically reviewed by **Lucy Chen, M.D., Board-Certified Dermatologist** [452]). A few doctor-trusted remedies can make everything right:

Aspirin-Honey Treatment: This recipe does double duty. Not only does aspirin contain salicylic acid, but honey also has antibacterial properties, which can help reduce the possibility of inflammation and infection, says Shaurya. Together, aspirin and honey will help ward off infection and reduce swelling when applied to your skin. Here's how to make the treatment.

Ingredients:

- 3 uncoated aspirin tablets

---

[450] How Much Should I Budget For Adult Diapers? iDiaper.com
[451] 8 home remedies for soothing and preventing ingrown hairs, Byrdie.com | Image: Laymik, The Noun Project
[452] Lucy Chen, M.D., Riverchase Dermatology, Miami, FL, riverchasedermatology.com

- 1 tsp. honey
- 1/2 to 1 tsp. water or oil

Directions:

- Add warm water or oil to a bowl.
- Add honey.
- Crush aspirin tablets.
- Mix together.
- Leave the mask on for 10 minutes.
- Wipe off entirely with warm water.

Coconut Oil-Sugar Scrub: You can use an exfoliant or another mild granular ingredient (like sea salt or granulated sugar), mix it with a carrier (like avocado or coconut oil—something that won't immediately dissolve the granules), and make any DIY scrub. This combination of ingredients keeps follicles clear of any blockages and gently massages ingrown hairs out before they become inflamed or infected. Use this scrub daily until you see an improvement, and then you can switch to two or three times a week. Just be careful that the scrub isn't too abrasive.

Ingredients:

- 1 cup of raw sugar
- 1/2 cup of coconut oil
- 10 drops of tea tree oil or your preferred essential oil

Directions:

- Combine sugar and coconut oil in a bowl.
- Add in essential oil.
- Mix together.
- Apply, and then rinse using warm water.
- Dry with a clean towel.

Baking Soda-Oatmeal Treatment: Baking soda, an amazing exfoliator, helps reduce and prevent ingrown hairs. Soothing oatmeal reduces redness and irritation caused by exfoliation (**Blair Murphy-Rose, M.D.** [453]).

Ingredients:

- 1 tbsp. baking soda
- 1 cup of water
- 1 tbsp. ground oatmeal

Directions:

- Mix baking soda and oatmeal together.
- Add water to the bowl; stir until it has a paste-like texture.
- Using a cotton pad, scoop up the mixture.

---

[453] Dr. Blair Murphy-Rose, Laser & Skin Surgery Center Of New York, laserskinsurgery.com

- Apply to the affected area, let it sit for 10 minutes. Then rinse with warm water.

These aren't the only ways to treat an ingrown hair; see more in the post *8 Home Remedies for Soothing and Preventing Ingrown Hairs* at brydie.com.

"Doctor, Doctor!"

If ingrown hairs become infected, you may need medical treatment to prevent complications, such as scarring or hair loss, says Healthgrades [454]. Contact your doctor right away if these symptoms occur or don't improve with home care: pus draining from the area of the ingrown hair; pain, warmth, or tenderness in the area; fever or chills.

You also want to contact a doctor if you keep getting ingrown hairs or are unsure what the problem is. People often mistake flat warts or the fungus ringworm for ingrown hairs. Your doctor can offer guidance on what causes ingrown hairs and how to prevent them.

COST-SAVINGS EXAMPLE:

Ingrown hairs are inexpensive to treat with self-care remedies. But if they don't clear up on their own, the cost of medical care should not be too great.

Save yourself a trip to the dermatologist by trying these trusted remedies for an ingrown hair before calling a doctor.

INGROWN TOENAIL

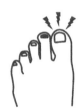 Ingrown toenails can be painful, irritating, and can make it hard to wear shoes or even walk normally, says Phoenix-area clinic Advanced Ankle and Foot [455] (**Dr. Jessica Prebish, DPM** [456]). An ingrown toenail occurs when the nail grows into the surrounding skin and flesh, making it inaccessible to toenail clippers. These trusted remedies may ease the pain and irritation:

Soak in warm, soapy water: A soak in warm, soapy water will soften the nail and the surrounding skin, relieving the pressure and offering some relief. Also, the soap works to keep the area clean, preventing infection from starting before you can see us. Doing this regularly is a good option for home care for your ingrown toenails.

Soak in apple cider vinegar: Apple cider vinegar is a natural disinfectant that can also help with the inflammation surrounding the ingrown toenail. A ratio of one-quarter cup of apple cider vinegar to a basin of warm water is a good measurement to start with.

Soak in Epsom salt solution: Epsom salts are great for "drawing" things out, and while they won't remove the toenail from your surrounding skin, they can help relieve the pain and pressure

---

[454] Ingrown Hair: Causes, Symptoms, and Treatments, healthgrades.com
[455] Home Remedies for Ingrown Toenails, Advanced Ankle & Foot, Gilbert, AZ, advancedanklefoot.com
[456] Dr. Jessica Prebish, Podiatrist, Advanced Ankle & Foot | Image: Aenne Brielmann, The Noun Project

that the ingrown toenail causes. Adding a couple of tablespoons to a basin filled with warm water and soak for 10-20 minutes will help to provide some much-needed relief.

Hydrogen peroxide cleanse: Hydrogen peroxide is another potent disinfectant to keep your toes clean and free from infection. Adding a small amount to a basin of warm water will help to keep the area clean; however, it works best on fresh wounds and shouldn't be the only remedy used.

Wear comfortable, correct-fitting shoes: Since ill-fitting footwear is a cause of ingrown toenails, it only makes sense that comfortable, well-fitted shoes help relieve the irritation. Doing this as a general rule may even help to prevent the condition in some cases. Ensure that your shoes have plenty of room for your toes and that they don't pinch, squeeze, or rub your feet.

Apply antibiotic ointments: Antibiotic ointments are helpful in the prevention of harmful bacteria, but they also help some wounds to heal faster as well as help with pain and irritation. Starting them when the ingrown toenail first occurs is best, and subsequently afterward.

Do Not: Do not perform "bathroom surgery," warns Advanced Ankle and Foot. In a small number of cases, ingrown toenails require surgery, but this should be done by a doctor. Still, some people try this at home in a desperate attempt to find relief – a bad idea. While it may be tempting, don't do it. The risks of DIY surgery are high, and you could hurt yourself badly.

Do Not: Do not self-medicate. Taking the wrong medicine or applying prescription antibiotics without the approval of a doctor can do more harm than good.

"Doctor, Doctor!"

If none of these remedies are helping, the area is infected, or you are in pain, seeing a podiatrist is the best choice. They'll know how to best treat your toenail, so you can get the relief you need and return to your normal activities. If you're unsure about anything related to your ingrown toenail, a doctor can advise which remedies might work for you.

COST-SAVINGS EXAMPLE:

These self-care remedies – while very affordable – are meant to ease discomfort and reduce infection. In most cases, seeing a podiatrist is the only way to correct the ingrown condition. Treatment can be done in the office for about $350 to $1,000. [457]

Trusted remedies may let you put off seeing a podiatrist for an ingrown toenail, but they may not prevent it. If the condition does not improve quickly, out-of-pocket medical costs may be needed and worthwhile.

Remember that throughout this directory you can find further information by using the sources at the bottom of every page and in the resources listing beginning on page 259.

---

[457] Ingrown Toenail Surgery Cost, The Pricer

INSOMNIA

More than 60 million Americans suffer from poor sleep, report experts at Johns Hopkins Medicine. [458] Sleep loss is more than an inconvenience that leaves you dragging the next day, they explain: it affects your emotional and physical health, too. It can even harm your memory, concentration and mood, and boosts your risk for depression, obesity, diabetes, heart disease and hypertension.

Charlene Gamaldo, M.D. [459], medical director of Johns Hopkins Center for Sleep at Howard County General Hospital, offers easy, natural fixes that can improve your sleep:

Drink up: No, not alcohol – it can interfere with sleep. Gamaldo recommends warm milk, chamomile tea, and tart cherry juice for people who want treatment without drug side effects.

Exercise: Physical activity during the day can improve sleep. Moderate aerobic exercise boosts the amount of nourishing slow wave (deep) sleep you get. But you have to time it right: avoid working out within two hours of bedtime.

Use melatonin supplements: "Melatonin is a hormone that is naturally released in the brain four hours before we feel a sense of sleepiness," Gamaldo explains. It's your body's response to reduced light exposure, which should naturally happen at night. However, exposure to artificial light prevents melatonin release, which can make it hard to fall asleep. Melatonin is available as an over-the-counter supplement online or at your local pharmacy. Find a brand that works for you and stick to it. "Because melatonin supplements are unregulated, dosages and ingredients may differ. Stick with one brand, and don't buy it from an unknown source," Gamaldo cautions.

Keep cool. "The ideal temperature for your thermostat is between 65 and 72 degrees," Gamaldo says. Women who are going through menopause and experiencing hot flashes should keep the room as cool as possible and wear cotton or breathable fabrics to bed.

Go dark. It's known that the light from a smartphone interferes with sleep. But what about your bathroom light? If you have the urge to go at night, don't flick on the lights. "The latest recommendation is to use a flashlight if you need to get up at night," Gamaldo says, because it offers less visual disruption. And remember: If you do wake up for a bathroom break, it might take up to 30 minutes to drift back off. This is completely normal, she says.

Medicinenet [460] also offers a number of doctor-approved remedies for insomnia (medically reviewed by **Shaziya Allarakha, M.D.** [461]) . These include:

Stick to a sleep schedule: Practice good sleep hygiene by sticking to a regular sleep schedule every day. Set a regular bedtime and a regular wake-up time so that your body gets into the habit of sleeping during those hours. Avoid napping throughout the day, as napping can make it difficult to fall asleep and stay asleep at night.

Minimize stress: Stress can make you even more tired than you normally would be. This can

---

[458] Home Remedies to Help You Sleep, hopkinsmedicine.org | Image: Draftphic, The Noun Project
[459] Dr. Charlene Gamaldo, M.D., Neurology Specialist in Columbia, MD | Healthgrades
[460] What Is the Best Home Remedy for Sleep? 11 Insomnia Remedies, MedicineNet.com
[461] Shaziya Allarakha, M.D., medicinenet.com

create a vicious circle—when you are wiped out during the day from not getting enough sleep, you tend to feel even more stressed, which in turn affects your sleep.

Make your bedroom comfortable: Make sure that your room is dark, as this makes it easier to fall and stay asleep. Use thick curtains or blinds to block out light that can wake you up, or try sleeping with an eye mask. Keep your room at a comfortable temperature.

Avoid electronic devices before bed: Avoid watching TV or using your devices before going to bed. Electronic gadgets emit blue light that has a stimulating effect, making it harder to sleep.

Follow a bedtime routine: Make sure to complete the most demanding tasks earlier in the day so that you can relax before bed. Follow a bedtime routine that helps you unwind, such as taking a bath, getting into your pajamas, and reading or listening to music.

Practice prayer, meditation or yoga: Positive effects include reducing stress, improving mood, and even enhancing immunity. Practice 15 minutes of simple yoga poses such as neck rolls, shoulder rolls, and arm and back stretches to help your muscles relax before hitting the sheets.

Progressive muscle relaxation: PMR is a technique that can help your whole body relax and promote feelings of sleepiness. It focuses on tightening and relaxing one muscle at a time. The American Academy of Sleep Medicine recommends relaxation techniques such as PMR as effective treatments for chronic insomnia.

Lavender oil: This essential oil acts as a natural remedy to improve sleep and promote calm and relaxation. It can be used as a pillow spray or as a patch, massage oil, or aromatherapy diffuser.

Valerian root: This herbal extract is a natural supplement used for managing both anxiety and insomnia. It may reduce the time needed to fall asleep and improve sleep quality. Valerian is taken in the form of a tea, tincture, capsule, or tablet.

Kava: Kava is a herbal remedy that is used to relieve stress and anxiety and may also help with insomnia. Although research findings of its sedative properties are conflicting, some experts believe it may induce relaxation without hindering memory or motor function.

Magnesium: This mineral helps relax muscles, reduce stress, and encourage a healthy sleep-wake cycle. A daily magnesium supplement can help you sleep better and for longer.

St. John's wort: This yellow, weed-like flower is commonly used to ease depression symptoms such as anxiety and insomnia.

Passionflower: This is a tropical flower that acts as a mild sedative. Dip a teaspoon of passionflower in boiling water for 10 minutes before drinking.

"Doctor, Doctor!"

Insomnia is such a widespread problem, it's no wonder that sleep clinics and sleep medicine experts are available nearly everywhere – but start with your primary care physician, says Mana Medical Associates [462] (**Michael A. Eckles, M.D., Pulmonary**

---

[462] When Should You See a Doctor for Sleep Problems, Medical Associates of Northwest Arkansas

Medicine and **Christie M. Hancock, APRN, Sleep Medicine** [463]). The more your primary doctor knows about what's going on in your life, the better care he or she can provide.

COST-SAVINGS EXAMPLE:

The cost of insomnia treatment ranges from about $200 a year for a generic sleeping pill to up to $1,200 for behavioral therapy, according to James K. Walsh, Ph.D. [464] **, President of the National Sleep Foundation.** [465]

Take care of your sleep loss with trusted remedies before your insomnia reaches the point of needing professional treatment and save $1,200.

IRRITABLE BOWEL SYNDROME

(IBS) is a chronic disorder of the digestive system, explains PrimeHealth Denver [466] , a functional medicine practice that offers a personalized, evidence-based approach for reversing IBS . Symptoms of IBS include cramping, abdominal pain, stool irregularities, bloating, flatulence, and diarrhea or constipation. Living with IBS can be frustrating – the effects on your daily life are significant. PrimeHealth Denver (**Soyona Rafatjah, M.D.**, board-certified family physician [467]) lists these natural remedies as best for IBS.

Follow a specialized diet: The first step to naturally treating IBS is to avoid foods that trigger your symptoms, says PrimeHealth Denver. There are 7 diets that may help: low FODMAP diet, gluten-free diet, lactose-free diet, high fiber diet, low-fiber diet, elimination diet, elemental diet.

A low-FODMAP [468] diet is the best natural remedy for IBS. Avoid these foods: artichoke, kidney beans, fermented cabbage, cauliflower, asparagus, pickled vegetables, scallions, soybeans, cherries, cranberry, blackcurrant, figs, guava, peaches, watermelon, mango, honey, malt syrup.

Instead, fill your plate with low-FODMAP foods: bean sprouts, chives, broccoli, kale, cucumber, carrots, eggplant, zucchini, fennel, pumpkin, spinach, turnip, spring onions, dragon fruit, orange, mandarin, papaya, strawberry, raspberry, feta cheese, dark chocolate. Remember that quantity matters; even a lower-FODMAP food can trigger symptoms if you eat too much of it.

Try intermittent fasting: Intermittent fasting is based on timed fasting periods. It involves caloric restriction for several days a week (or every day), typically for 14-20 hours at a time.

---

[463] Find a Doctor, Medical Associates of Northwest Arkansas, mana.md
[464] James K. Walsh, Ph.D., Sleep and Health Journal, Chicago, sleepandhealth.com
[465] Insomnia costing U.S. $63.2 billion a year in lost productivity, American Academy of Sleep Medicine
[466] 11 Natural Remedies for IBS [Backed by Science], PrimeHealth Denver.com, Lakewood, CO
[467] Soyona Rafatjah, M.D., Family Physician, PrimeHealth Denver | Image, Symbolon, The Noun Project
[468] FODMAP stands for fermentable oligosaccharides, disaccharides, monosaccharides and polyols. These are carbohydrates (sugars) that the small intestine absorbs poorly, leading to digestive distress.

Caloric restriction leads to improved blood pressure and insulin sensitivity. One clinical study found that fasting individuals had significant improvements in 7 out of 8 IBS symptoms, including abdominal pain, abdominal distention, diarrhea, decreased appetite, nausea, anxiety, and quality of life. Talk to your provider about what fasting method is right for you.

Exercise: Regular physical activity increases strength and cardiovascular fitness, leading to improvements in overall health. One of the best physical activities you can do for IBS is yoga. Yoga is a mind-body exercise, and many postures in yoga are a form of body weight training that uses your body weight for resistance. One hour of yoga every day for 4 weeks significantly improves IBS symptoms, according to a 2018 systematic review of available evidence.

Reduce stress in your life: Chronic stress increases the hormone cortisol and can impact our digestive system. IBS is a stress-sensitive disorder, so treatment of IBS must focus on managing stress and stress-induced responses. Ways to reduce IBS-related stress include mindfulness meditation, proven to be the strongest predictor of gastrointestinal symptoms and quality of life improvement. Yoga, as mentioned above, is also a great exercise to reduce your stress.

Try biofeedback: Biofeedback is a mind-body therapy that retrains the body to control specific responses. During biofeedback, individuals are connected to sensors that help monitor physiological processes like breathing, heart rate, skin sensations, muscle contractions, temperature. Studies suggest that 55% to 82% of patients who undergo biofeedback therapy maintain symptom improvement, including more regular bowel movements.

Get acupuncture: Acupuncture involves swiftly inserting hair-thin needles through a person's skin at strategic points (nerve-rich areas) on the body to various depths. One study compared abdominal acupuncture to traditional Western medication. The result was that acupuncture was more effective as an IBS treatment, reducing diarrhea, bloating, and stool abnormality.

Take probiotics: Probiotics are live microorganisms (bacteria) beneficial to your digestive system, says PrimeHealth Denver. A healthy balance of gut bacteria is associated with health benefits, such as improved digestion, boosted immune function, prevention of bowel diseases, alleviation of postmenopausal disorders, reduced traveler's diarrhea, probiotics may also help with anxiety, depression, blood cholesterol, and skin health. Fermented foods, like yogurt and buttermilk, contain a variety of beneficial microorganisms. Fermented drinks such as kombucha and kefir are also good dietary sources of probiotics. Besides food, you can add probiotics to your diet through dietary supplements. Consult your doctor before starting a new supplement.

Try CBD: Cannabidiol (CBD) is a compound found in the Cannabis sativa plant. Ingesting CBD may help with digestive symptoms, including IBS. When searching for a quality CBD product, always check the CBD source for a detailed certificate of analysis (COA) from a reputable third-party lab. Pay attention to the potency, which varies quite a bit and can impact the benefits you can expect. Check with your doctor before trying this remedy.

Increase your prebiotics/fiber intake: Prebiotics are the dietary fiber that feeds the good bacteria in your gut. This allows your gut bacteria to produce nutrients for your colon cells, contributing to a better digestive system. You can find prebiotics in many fruits, vegetables, and whole grains such as banana, barley, onions, cocoa, flaxseed, chicory root, apples, konjac root.

Another effective way to control IBS comes from the intake of different fiber types, including via fiber supplements. Many physicians recommend that people with IBS increase their dietary fiber intake to 20-35 grams daily to regulate stools and lessen abdominal pain. These foods are rich in soluble fiber: Blueberries, Brussels sprouts, Eggplant, Sweet potatoes,

Get plenty of vitamin D: Vitamin D is essential to digestive health. In one study, more than half of patients with IBS had vitamin D deficiency. To consume more vitamin D, spend 15-30 minutes in the sun each day and eat vitamin D-rich foods. You may also consider vitamin D3 supplements, especially if you live in an area that is frequently overcast. Try these foods, which are naturally among the richest in vitamin D: salmon, canned tuna, shiitake mushrooms, egg yolk, sardines. The recommended daily amount of supplemental vitamin D3 is: 400 international units (IU) for children up to 12 months; 600 IU for people ages 1–70; 800 IU for people over 70.

However, according to PrimeHealth Denver, the above recommendations are not enough for many adolescents and adults to reach optimal vitamin D levels. It often takes closer to 5,000 IU of vitamin D_3 daily in order to reach those levels. It's important to have your vitamin D levels checked via a blood test by your healthcare provider, so you can learn exactly how much vitamin D you require to stay in that optimal range. A few reported interactions with vitamin D may impact digestive disorders, so check with your doctor before taking it.

Consider other herbal remedies & IBS supplements: If you are searching for herbal remedies, lifestyle changes, and over-the-counter treatments to naturally ease the symptoms of irritable bowel syndrome, remember that they aren't one-size-fits-all. You'll need to talk to your healthcare provider about what makes sense for your individual IBS triggers. These natural remedies for IBS are supported by scientific evidence: peppermint oil for constipation; aloe vera for IBS-D; psyllium fumaria, chamomile, artichoke leaf extract (to regulate bowel movements; glutathione for detox; ginger for nausea relief; triphala to restore the lining of gi tract and relieve constipation; and several more. [469]

"Doctor, Doctor!"

While all of these trusted remedies are considered beneficial, IBS should also be treated by a physician. Call your doctor if you have symptoms of IBS.

COST-SAVINGS EXAMPLE:

IBS drugs cost between $4,319 and $16,844 per year, says a study by the journal Digestive Diseases and Sciences (Eric D. Shah, M.D. [470]). Self-care remedies used with your doctor's supervision may reduce or even eliminate your need for these drugs.

Reduce or eliminate the need for drugs costing $4,319 per year or more by using these doctor-approved self-care remedies for your IBS. [471]

---

[469] 11 Natural Remedies for IBS [Backed by Science], PrimeHealth Denver.com, Lakewood, CO
[470] Eric D. Shah, M.D., MBA, Gastroenterology and Hepatology, Dartmouth Hitchcock Medical Center
[471] Price Is Right: Exploring Prescription Drug Coverage Barriers for Irritable Bowel Syndrome Using Threshold Pricing Analysis, Digestive Diseases and Sciences, sites.duke.edu

J-K-L

JELLYFISH STINGS

If you live in Denver, you'll probably never have to give a thought to jellyfish stings until you take a coastal vacation. Honolulu, on the other hand, gets over a thousand 9-1-1 calls for jellyfish encounters *per month*.

Stings can occur while wading, swimming, or diving in salt water, says Seattle Children's Hospital [472] (**Jeff Sperring, M.D., CEO** [473]). Even beached or dying jellies can sting. Pieces of tentacles can release venom for up to two weeks. When a stinger makes contact with your skin, it pierces it and injects venom, causing symptoms. Local reactions are most common. Symptoms are raised, red lines that cross each other with pain or burning at the site. Hives in the sting area occur. Severe pain lasts up to two hours. The itch may last for a week. Seattle Children's offers these self-care remedies for jellyfish stings:

Look before you leap: Scan the water before you jump in. Check with lifeguards, surf shops, or local health authorities for reported jellyfish activity in the area. Do not go in the water where jellies are seen or reported.

Use vinegar to stop the venom in stingers: Consider carrying a small bottle (such as a repurposed hotel shampoo bottle or a small spray bottle) of vinegar in your beach bag. If you don't have vinegar, move on to scraping off the stingers. DO NOT USE ammonia, urine, rubbing alcohol, fresh water, or ice; they all can trigger the release of more venom.

Call the Poison Help Hotline: Get fast, free help by calling **1-800-222-1222** from anywhere in the United States. The toll-free national Poison Help Hotline will let you talk to experts in poisoning. They will give you further instructions. This is a free and confidential service. It does NOT need to be an emergency. You can call for any reason, 24 hours a day, 7 days a week. [474]

"Doctor, Doctor!"

Most jellyfish stings get better with self-care, says Doctor's Urgent Care, a group of urgent care clinics in the Tampa, FL area (**David B. Dean, M.D.,** medical director [475]). Severe reactions require emergency medical care:

---

[472] Jellyfish Sting, Seattle Children's Hospital, seattlechildrens.org | Image: Richard Cordero, The Noun Project

[473] Jeff Sperring, M.D., Chief Executive Officer, Seattle Children's, seattlechildrens.org

[474] Jellyfish Stings, University of Florida Health; Jacob L. Heller, M.D., Emergency Medicine, Seattle, WA.

[475] David Dean, M.D., Doctors Urgent Care, Citrus Park, Tampa, FL area, yourdoctorsurgentcare.com

General reactions can occur if there are many stings. More stings means a higher dose of venom. Blisters can occur, and red or purple lines can last for weeks. Symptoms of large envenomation are vomiting, dizziness, weakness, and headache. All of these are reasons to visit urgent care or call a doctor.

Life-threatening reactions (anaphylaxis) are possible but very rare with jellyfish stings, most often caused by box jellyfish in the South Pacific and Australia. Symptoms are trouble breathing, trouble swallowing, and hives. It starts rapidly, most often within 20 minutes of the sting. If you see these symptoms, call emergency services immediately.

Also call 9-1-1 if the affected person:
- Has previously had a severe allergic reaction to jellyfish stings.
- Has trouble breathing or swallowing, or is drooling.
- Is wheezing, hoarse, or has a cough or tightness in the throat or chest.
- Is slurring their speech or acts or talks in a confused manner.
- Has passed out (fainted) or is too weak to stand.
- Seems to be having a life-threatening emergency.

Call a doctor or seek care right away if:
- The sting is inside the mouth or on the eye.
- The sting covers a large area (more than one arm or leg).
- The person has stomach pain or is vomiting.
- The person has a fever and the site looks infected (spreading redness).
- Severe pain has not improved after two hours using care advice.
- The person looks or acts very sick.

Contact the doctor within twenty-four hours if:
- Blisters appear.
- More than 48 hours have passed since the sting, redness is getting larger.

Contact the doctor during office hours if:
- Severe itching is not better after twenty-four hours of using steroid cream.
- The redness or rash lasts more than forty-eight hours.
- The last tetanus shot was more than ten years ago. [476]

COST-SAVINGS EXAMPLE:

Severe jellyfish injuries are often treated in emergency rooms, where astronomical bills are becoming the norm. Or skip the long wait, exposure to serious illnesses, and big bill of the ER by going to urgent care. You can ask your smartphone for "urgent care near me", but be aware that the results may include hospital ERs. [477]

---

[476] Jellyfish Sting, Seattle Children's Hospital, seattlechildrens.org
[477] UrgentCare247.com; Locations in Arizona, Florida, Georgia, North Carolina, Ohio, and Texas

JET LAG

You've flown halfway across the world – or just from L.A. to New York – and now you're "trudging through your dream destination like a zombie," note the travel experts at Condé Nast Traveler (CNT) [478] . Jet lag can get in the way of the experiences you've worked so hard (and spent so much) to implement. Here are doctor-approved remedies CNT and others suggest to beat the fatigue of jet lag.

Adapt to your new time zone before you depart: "For every time zone change, it takes on average one day to adapt," says **Dr. Steven Brass, M.D.** [479] , a neurologist specializing in sleep medicine tells CNT. "Consider adapting your schedule to the destination several days before departure. If you know you'll be three hours ahead, start three days before." That means shifting the time you go to bed, the time you wake up, and meal time, if possible, says Dr. Brass.

Stay hydrated: Airplane cabins have very low humidity levels, causing water loss through your skin and breath. Even mild dehydration can cause problems with blood pressure, heart rate, and body temperature, says the University of Rochester Medical Center [480] (reviewed by **Eric Perez M.D.** [481]). More severe dehydration leads to weakness or confusion. Take a reusable water bottle with you and sip, sip, sip; water bottle filling stations are located in most airport concourses.

Use different strategies when you travel east versus west: It's generally easier to travel west than to travel east, largely because it's easier to go to bed when you're tired than it is to force yourself to go to bed early, explains CNT. Dr. Brass says:

> *"It has to do with what causes jet lag in the first place. There's a mismatch in your brain's clock and what's going on around you. If you're going east across fewer than six time zones, expose yourself to morning light at the destination. Or if you arrive at night, don't expose yourself to bright light in the evening. When going west across fewer than six zones, you want afternoon light – which means being outside as much as possible."*

Eat less: While many of us plan travel around once-in-a-lifetime meals, sleep researcher **Dr. Rebecca Robbins** [482] tells CNT that a bit of planning will enable better sleep. "It's tempting to indulge in heavy dinners, but attempt to have a hearty breakfast and lunch, and make dinner a lighter meal. That will aid in digesting, allowing you to slip into the covers and not toss and turn while your body is digesting." And if you absolutely can't hold back on that tasting menu in the evening? Try to eat on the earlier side or factor in time to go for a walk before crawling into bed.

Avoid – or reduce – alcohol intake: "It's a good idea to avoid alcohol" while traveling, says Dr. Brass. "Alcohol interrupts sleep in general." And even if you don't want to completely forego wine in France or that special beer in Germany, consider cutting back on the number of drinks.

Take melatonin: "There are no jet lag diets or supplements other than melatonin that have

[478] Jet Lag Remedies That Actually Work | Condé Nast Traveler | Image: BomSymbols, The Noun Project
[479] Dr. Steven D. Brass, M.D., Neurologist, UC Davis Medical Center, Verdi, health.usnews.com
[480] Dehydration, Health Encyclopedia, University of Rochester Medical Center, urmc.rochester.edu
[481] Dr. Eric Perez, M.D., Emergency Medicine, Pompton, NJ, US News Doctors, health.usnews.com
[482] Rebecca Robbins, rebecca-robbins.com, Instructor in Medicine at Harvard Medical School

enough scientific evidence to recommend them," says **Michael Breus, PhD** [483], a fellow at the American Academy of Sleep Medicine. He tells CNT that 0.5 milligrams of melatonin at bedtime can help; travelers can also take 1-3 mg. for the first three nights in a new destination.

There's an app for that: Dr. Breus suggests downloading the TimeShifter app [484], which was developed with help from scientists at NASA and Harvard. The app nudges you when it's time to get outside, take a nap, and take melatonin. Dr. Breus, who serves on the application's advisory board, calls TimeShifter "the number one fix … a behavioral and supplement-based program."

"Doctor, Doctor!"

Jet lag probably does not need medical attention unless accompanied by other symptoms such as fever, nausea or vomiting, cough, sore throat, other flu or coronavirus symptoms. Also call your healthcare provider if jet lag symptoms don't go away or get worse more than one week after traveling.

COST-SAVINGS EXAMPLE:

The costly aspect of jet lag isn't so much the treatment as it is losing out on the adventures you expected on your vacation, or having a less than optimal business trip. Avoid these costs by planning ahead and using our "away-from-home remedies" as needed.

KNEE PAIN

When you can't use or bend your knee without pain, it can cause a lot of problems in your day-to-day life, says Babylon Health, a coast-to-coast network of healthcare professionals. [485] Here are some self-care remedies Babylon Health trusts to manage knee pain without heading into the doctor's office. [486]

Lifestyle Changes: If you're at risk for knee pain due to obesity, weight loss is a good way to reduce your risk. If you're experiencing knee pain from tight muscles, a combination of daily stretching, massage therapy, and exercise from a physical therapy program to strengthen surrounding joint structures can help you maintain a healthier gait. People with osteoarthritis may find that low-impact exercise like cycling or tai chi helps improve range of motion and manage pain.

Over-the-Counter Pain Relievers and Supplements: Many people are able to manage their pain with products like ibuprofen or aspirin, says Babylon Health. Both are called NSAIDs and have anti-inflammatory properties that help with various causes of knee pain. In addition,

---

[483] Dr. Michael J. Breus, Fellow of the American Academy of Sleep Medicine, thesleepdoctor.com

[484] Timeshifter, The Jet Lag App®, timeshifter.com

[485] Babylon Health, 24/7 access to care plus tools and advice to stay healthy, babylonhealth.com

[486] Home Remedies for Knee Pain, Babylon Health, babylonhealth.com [sourced from Mayo Clinic, Cleveland Clinic, Cedars-Sinai, Arthritis Foundation, more]

over-the-counter supplements have helped some people with joint pain. Chondroitin may help prevent cartilage breakdown. It's often combined with glucosamine, which also supports cartilage to cushion the joint. Curcumin, the active ingredient of turmeric, is also available as a supplement. It's an antioxidant, which means it can help reduce pain from inflammation.

At-home Solutions: Homemade topical ointments can provide as much relief as some OTC methods. Cinnamon, ginger, mastic, and sesame oil are other homemade ingredients that have been tried on joint pain. Antioxidants can also be added into your diet, says Babylon Health, in everything from ginger tea to spinach.

RICE for Knee Pain: RICE stands for Rest, Ice, Compression, and Elevation. It's commonly used as an at-home treatment for strains and sprains. First, rest and get off your feet. Put a cold compress, ice, or a bag of frozen vegetables (wrapped in a towel) on the affected area. Wrap your knee in a compression bandage, being careful to allow blood flow. Elevate your knee with a pillow or some other stable surface.

"Doctor, Doctor!"

If your knee pain is severe, or prevents you from living your life, Babylon Health recommends checking in with a healthcare professional. A qualified healthcare provider can point you in the right direction or help create a treatment plan for you. Schedule an appointment if you have any of the following: [487]

- severe pain or swelling, severe bruising or a deformed knee
- you can't support your weight on your knee, or it feels weak or ready to give out
- you can't fully bend or unbend your knee, or your knee pain started with an injury
- you have a fever or other signs of infection

You can also speak to your provider about the risks versus benefits of trying supplements.

COST-SAVINGS EXAMPLE:

For just one cause of knee pain – osteoarthritis – total national treatment cost was estimated at $5.7 billion or more in 2017. [488] Avoid or postpone the costs of medical treatment for knee pain by using the doctor-approved remedies above. But if medical treatment improves your mobility and preserves your independence, it's probably very worthwhile (which explains why so much money is spent on it.)

Avoid or postpone the need for costly surgery and prescription drugs by trying physician-approved self-care for your knee pain.

---

[487] Our services, Babylon Health, babylonhealth.com
[488] Real-World Health Care Resource Utilization and Costs Among US Patients with Knee Osteoarthritis Compared with Controls, Angela V Bedenbaugh, PharmD, dovepress.com

LACTOSE INTOLERANCE

When you have lactose intolerance, your body is unable to digest significant amounts of lactose, says Verywell Health [489] (medically reviewed by **Jay N. Yepuri, M.D.** [490]) .

Lactose is the major sugar found in milk and milk products. Lactose intolerance is caused in part by a shortage of lactase, an enzyme produced in the small intestine. Lactase breaks lactose down into simpler forms of sugar, like glucose, so they can be absorbed and used by the body.

Infants have the highest levels of lactase, helping them digest their mother's milk, explains Verywell Health. In about 70% of the world's population, a genetic trait causes lactase levels to decline after babies are weaned. This drop is irreversible and in time, most lactase activity is lost.

Even though most people experience this drop, they won't all have symptoms after eating or drinking normal amounts of lactose. But among those who do have symptoms, the result is usually gas, bloating, and diarrhea.

The best way to manage these symptoms is to prevent them, says Verywell Health, by avoiding foods that cause them. If you do eat or drink something that has lactose, you can take steps to reduce the symptoms. Over-the-counter treatments include:

- For gas and bloating, try a product like Gas-X (simethicone).
- For diarrhea, take a medication like Imodium AD (loperamide).
- For diarrhea along with gas and bloating, you can try Imodium capsules (which contain both loperamide and simethicone) or Pepto Bismol (bismuth subsalicylate).

Many people try dietary supplements to prevent the discomfort of lactose intolerance, despite the lack of specific scientific support for claims that these treatments work. Popular options include:

Acidophilus and Other Probiotics: Lactic acid bacteria in the intestines break lactose down into simpler sugars that can be absorbed by the colon. Supplements may help with this process. They are available in capsule, tablet, or powder form. You can find them in health food stores, grocery stores, drugstores, and online.

Yogurt: In alternative medicine, yogurt containing live active bacteria is believed to help people to digest lactose.2 When yogurt is consumed, bile acids disrupt the cell walls of the bacteria in yogurt. This releases a key enzyme into the intestines that can boost lactose digestion.

Acidophilus Milk: Acidophilus milks are made by adding Lactobacillus acidophilus to cold milk. Studies have not proven that this helps, but many users believe it does; try it and see.

Lactase Supplements: Tablets containing lactase can be taken before eating foods with lactose.2 For many people, lactase supplements are only needed when they eat or drink large amounts of lactose. If one form of supplement doesn't work, it may be worthwhile to try others. Some people

---

[489] How to Stop Lactose Intolerance Pain, Verywell Health | Image: Douglas Machado, The Noun Project
[490] Jay N. Yepuri, M.D., Gastroenterologist, Fort Worth, TX, dfwgidoctor.com,

find the tablet form works better than the chewable form.

Diet: It's quite common for people to avoid lactose-containing foods completely; however, this usually isn't necessary and may even cause your calcium levels to become too low. Instead of giving up dairy completely, you can try making changes to your diet such as:

- Drink less than one cup of milk at a time.

- Eat milk and milk products with meals rather than alone.

- Try reduced-lactose milk and yogurt instead of milk.

"Doctor, Doctor!"

When to Get Emergency Treatment: Seek immediate medical help if you have any of these symptoms: sudden or severe stomach pain, vomiting up blood or dark flecks, black or bloody stools. severe or persistent constipation, or inability to keep anything down.

For routine care, speak with your healthcare provider before trying supplements or other self-care remedies, says Verywell Health. Self care may reduce but should completely replace professional medical care. If you have new symptoms that could point to lactose intolerance, talk with your healthcare provider. Those symptoms include:

- A change in your bowel habits

- Constipation, diarrhea, or gas that gets worse

- Heartburn that keeps you from sleeping

- Other symptoms that are causing concern

Lactose intolerance can also be caused by medications, or by other health conditions that damage the lining of the intestines – all of which should be discussed with a doctor. [491]

COST-SAVINGS EXAMPLE:

A Quora user posted the question, 'On average, how much does being lactose intolerant increase one's cost of living?' Typical answers included 'Very little, if at all' and 'It does not increase my cost of living by one cent.'

Most lactase supplements are inexpensive. Amazon's price for a year's supply of Best Naturals Fast Acting Lactase Enzyme Tablet is only about $25, based on taking one tablet per day.

Remember that throughout this directory you can find further information by using the sources at the bottom of every page and in the resources listing beginning on page 259.

---

[491] How to Stop Lactose Intolerance Pain, Verywell Health, verywellhealth.com

LARYNGITIS

Laryngitis is an inflammation of the larynx (voice box) that often results in a lost voice, explains CENTA Medical Group of South Carolina [492] (**William Giles, M.D.**, otolaryngologist [493]). Laryngitis usually clears up after a few days, but in the meantime, can leave you feeling pretty miserable. Fortunately, self-care can help speed up the healing process.

Laryngitis is most often associated with overuse or misuse of the voice box, irritation or infection, says CENTA. Causes include viral or bacterial infections; vocal strain; acid reflux; chronic sinusitis; environmental irritants; smoking and alcohol. In rare cases, a more serious condition such as cancer, vocal cord paralysis or bowing of the vocal cords due to age is responsible. CENTA doctors recommend these trusted remedies for treating laryngitis:

Resting the voice: The best thing you can do to promote healing of your voice is to not use it! Giving your voice a rest helps reduce swelling and irritation of the vocal cords, enabling them to heal more quickly. Some people think it's okay to whisper, but doing so actually places more strain on the vocal cords than speaking quietly.

Gargle with saltwater: Saltwater helps kill harmful bacteria and soothes throat pain. Mix half a teaspoon of salt in an eight ounce glass of warm water, stirring until it dissolves. Gargle in the back of the throat and then spit it out, being careful not to swallow the water. Repeat several times a day for a minimum of 24 hours.

Use a humidifier: A humidifier adds moisture to the air, which can help soothe a dry or inflamed throat. Try adding cooling essential oils, such as menthol or eucalyptus, for an added boost—but if you have pets, it's best to skip this step.

Eat foods with antibacterial properties: Garlic, ginger root and honey all have proven antibacterial properties that have been demonstrated to ease cold and flu symptoms and help you recover from an infection more quickly. It's easy to incorporate garlic into many different foods; ginger and honey can both be mixed into hot water or tea, which will also help with throat discomfort. Honey also works as a cough suppressant.

Drink plenty of fluids: Staying hydrated is important when you're suffering from a sore throat or laryngitis. Both warm and cool liquids will help soothe vocal cords and moisten a dry throat; stay away from soda, very hot beverages, and milk, all of which can worsen symptoms.

Manage acid reflux: If you experience frequent heartburn, try over-the-counter antacids; avoid large meals; wait at least three hours after eating to go to bed; and avoid foods that can trigger acid reflux symptoms, says CENTA. Common triggers include caffeine, chocolate, spicy foods, fatty foods, and peppermint.

Avoid smoking and alcohol: Cigarettes and alcohol can both contribute to inflammation, so it's best to stay away from these substances when you're experiencing laryngitis.

Use OTC pain relievers: Over-the-counter medications can help relieve swelling and throat

---

[492] At-Home Laryngitis Remedies, centamedical.com | Image: Amethyst Studio, The Noun Project
[493] William Giles, M.D., CENTA Medical Group, Lexington and Columbia, SC, centamedical.com

discomfort, making you more comfortable while your illness runs its course. Generic pain relievers such as ibuprofen and acetaminophen work well, too. Aspirin might help, but do not give it to children; it has the potential to cause a life-threatening illness called Reye's syndrome.

"Doctor, Doctor!"

If throat pain and laryngitis do not resolve within two weeks and you have tried these self-care remedies, make an appointment with your doctor or an ear, nose and throat specialist in order to rule out anything serious.

COST-SAVINGS EXAMPLE:

Treatment of vocal cord paralysis depends on the cause, severity, and time from the onset of symptoms, says Mayo Clinic. Treatment may include voice therapy, injections, or surgery, all of which can be costly. However, your doctor may want to delay advanced treatment for up to a year from the beginning of your vocal cord paralysis, as the condition will sometimes clear on its own in that time. [494]

Most of these trusted remedies are inexpensive or free. They may increase your comfort and decrease your symptoms while you give your condition a chance to clear.

LEG PAIN

Are aching legs affecting your mobility and limiting your independence? ZendyHealth, a service of the Zendy Provider network [495] (**Vish Banthia, M.D., FACS,** Founder & Chief Medical Officer [496]), offers a few trusted remedies to ease the pain and help you move around with ease again.

Turmeric: An abundance of antioxidants, combined with anti-inflammatory properties, makes turmeric an effective remedy for pain and inflammation. Add half a teaspoon of turmeric powder in a glass of milk and drink it daily.

Heat/Cold Packs: If your leg pain is caused by stiff muscles, heat packs can help eliminate the pain. The heat helps to relax the muscles and provide comfort, ZendyHealth explains. Severe pain can also result when the sciatic nerve is compressed. By applying the heat pack, you can release the pressure on the nerve, bringing the pain to an end. Cold packs can be effective in dealing with leg pain that you might experience after strenuous physical activity. It can reduce the pain by numbing the area and controlling any inflammation.

Epsom Salt Soak: Magnesium is a key component of Epsom salt and thus it is an effective way

---

[494] Vocal Cord Paralysis, Diagnosis And Treatment, mayoclinic.org | Appointments at Mayo Clinic
[495] Home Remedies for Aching Legs and Leg Pain, ZendyHealth.com
[496] Vish Banthia, M.D., ZendyHealth | Image: Gan Khoon Lay, The Noun Project

to regulate the nerve signals in your body, says ZendyHealth. The natural muscle relaxant reduces pain and swelling and helps put an end to inflammation. Just add some Epsom salt in a hot bath and soak for 15-20 minutes. Repeat two or three times a week for effective results.

Magnesium-rich foods: Eating. foods high in magnesium would also help you manage your aching limbs. Eat bananas, tofu, walnuts, and whole grains to keep your magnesium levels up.

Apple Cider Vinegar: Apple cider vinegar has a natural anti-inflammatory property and helps to ease your leg pain away. There are many ways to use apple cider vinegar for pain relief. When consumed orally, apple cider vinegar makes up for nutrient deficiency. Another way of using apple cider vinegar for pain relief is to add it to a hot bath and soak your legs for 15-20 minutes.

Claudication is a common condition where leg pain occurs with exercise due to a reduction in the circulation. The cause is hardening of the arteries, or atherosclerosis. The common symptom is of a cramp-like pain in the calf muscles. The thigh and buttock muscles may also be involved. Symptoms are described as aching, burning, weakness or "dead weight" in their legs when walking, says McLeod Health based in Florence, SC [497] (medically reviewed by **Christopher G. Cunningham, M.D.** [498]). Claudication affects 10% of people over 70. Men are twice as likely as women to suffer this health issue. The pain can be easily treated, says Dr. Cunningham, but it could signal more serious issues, such as peripheral arterial disease or atherosclerosis.

Walking: Walking is the simplest way to strengthen leg muscles while building other blood vessels to feed the muscles, says Dr. Cunningham. Start slow – short walks several times a week. If discomfort arises, stop for a few minutes. Over time, try walking longer distances. In 3-6 months, you should be able to handle longer distances without aching.

"Doctor, Doctor!"

These trusted remedies are a great way to get relief from leg pain and boost your overall health. If pain persists even after following these self-care remedies, seek medical help to rule out more serious disorders such as peripheral arterial disease or atherosclerosis. [499]

COST-SAVINGS EXAMPLE:

All of these self-care remedies are inexpensive. What's costly is not finding a fix for your leg pain and allowing it to drag on, eventually reducing your mobility and curbing your independence. If these remedies aren't enough, seek medical help.

The long term cost of untreated leg pain is your mobility and independence. These trusted remedies can pay huge dividends. Use them before short-term pain becomes chronic.

---

[497] Leg Pain When You Walk? Claudication Defined, Easily Treated, mcleodhealth.org
[498] Christopher G. Cunningham, McLeod Health, Florence, SC, mcleodhealth.org
[499] How ZendyHealth Works, zendyhealth.com

MEMORY LOSS

Do an internet search for *home remedies for memory loss* and you'll get pages of "memory hacks," "genius tips", "brain breakthroughs," and other "amazing" fixes from a wide range of sources. It's not at all surprising, given that memory loss is such a common concern as we age. But with such a critical issue as your present and future mental wellness on the line, you want to at least begin your quest for effective memory care solutions with trusted remedies from knowledgeable, credentialed, grounded-in-science *physicians* – which is why you're reading this directory!

One such physician is **John La Puma, M.D.** [500] (drjohnlapuma.com [501]). Dr. La Puma's trusted remedies are useful for Alzheimer's or another dementia, as well as for memory loss caused by nutritional deficiency, medication interaction, sleep issues, a silent stroke or chronic stress. The news is all good, says Dr. Paluma: *all* these conditions are treatable with these trusted remedies:

Get enough sleep each night: Sleep apnea, stress, drug interactions and other issues that reduce the amount and quality of your sleep can also contribute to brain fog and memory loss. Getting a better night's sleep is essential to preserving and improving your recall. Turn to the section of this directory on **Insomnia** for physician-approved self-care remedies.

Eat less added sugar and inflammatory food: Memory loss is preventable with what you eat, says Dr. La Puma. According to Harvard Medical, foods to avoid are refined carbohydrates, such as white bread and pastries, French fries and other fried foods, red meat, processed meat (hot dogs, sausage), and soda and other sugary beverages. Many fruits have potent anti-inflammatory effects, says Harvard, especially berries, apples, stone fruits (cherries, peaches, apricots, and plums), pomegranates, and grapes. [502] In addition, Dr. La Puma reports that those who eat the most cruciferous and green leafy vegetables have the least memory loss. [503]

Get plenty of fish oil and vitamin D3: Eat sardines, wild salmon, trout and other toxin-free fish twice weekly, recommends Dr. La Pluma. [504] He also suggests Omega-3 supplements as well as D3 10,000 + K featuring vitamin D_3, the most bioactive form of supplemental vitamin D.

Garden: Seniors participated in gardening about 20 minutes a day. Nurses examined indicators of memory capacity before and after each session. Over time, reports Dr. La Pluma, participants' cognitive abilities improved. Garden programs provide strategies that reduce reliance on

---

[500] Your Brain On Nature: Natural Ways To Improve Memory | Image: Andrew Doane, The Noun Project
[501] John La Puma, M.D., Clinical Director and Founder of Chef Clinic, www.drjohnlapuma.com
[502] Foods that fight inflammation | Eat these fruits for their anti-inflammatory benefits, Harvard Health
[503] Food and Memory: What Can You Eat to Remember? Dr. John La Puma, drjohnlapuma.com
[504] Anti-Aging and Fish Oil: Time Capsule? | Vitamin D3 10,000 + K, Dr. John La Puma

medication while providing benefits like autonomy and mental stimulation, he explains.

Limit your alcohol consumption: Studies differ on the possible health benefits of light to moderate alcohol consumption. Heavy consumption, however, is clearly harmful to all aspects of health, including memory and recall. See the section on **Substance Abuse** in Part I of this directory, **Doctor-Trusted Remedies for the Top 10 Most Common Health Issues**.

Exercise Outside: While mental health walks are known to decrease stress and improve mood, there are other benefits to walking, including improved memory, according to Dr. La Pluma. Possibly the best news – it's never too late to start; even nursing home residents saw a big increase in verbal memory from walking outside and upper muscle strength training.

Rosemary: One plant you might want to include in your new garden is rosemary. It's been found to improve cognitive function whether you use it in aromatherapy or season your food with it. Rosemary was found to increase both the speed and accuracy of cognitive function.

"Doctor, Doctor!"

Some older adults have a condition called mild cognitive impairment, or MCI, meaning they have more memory or other thinking problems than other people their age, says the National Institute on Aging (NIA). People with MCI can usually take care of themselves and do their normal activities. MCI may be an early sign of Alzheimer's disease, but not everyone with MCI will develop Alzheimer's.

According to the NIA, signs that it might be time to talk to a doctor include: Asking the same questions over and over again; getting lost in places a person knows well; having trouble following recipes or directions; becoming more confused about time, people, and places; not taking care of oneself —eating poorly, not bathing, or behaving unsafely

COST-SAVINGS EXAMPLE:

All of these self-care remedies are inexpensive. What's costly assuming that memory loss is an unavoidable consequence of aging – it's not! Alzheimer's care is enormously expensive, so you want to do all you can to avoid or delay the need for such care.

The national average cost for memory care in the U.S. is $6,935 a month, or $83,220 per year. Do all within your power to eliminate or delay such costs, especially since doctor-approved remedies include fun hobbies such as gardening, reading, and walking outdoors. [505]

---

[505] Memory Care Costs, Average Costs of Dementia & Alzheimer's Care, seniorliving.org

MENOPAUSE

Menopause is not a disease, a disorder, or even a cause for alarm. It's a natural stage of life that you can choose to embrace, as many women have. Menopause offers real benefits to go along with its real challenges. Besides the obvious – no more menstrual periods or menstrual cycle side effects – you can look forward to less pelvic pain and a fresh outlook on life. Some have even referred to the phenomenon as 'postmenopausal zest.'

Whether you realized it at the time, your monthly cycle was emotionally and physically taxing, says Women's Health Specialists of Denton, TX [506] (**Marc Wilson, M.D.** [507]). Being free from the pressure that comes with reproductive years combined with emerging on the other side of menopause gives many women a newfound sense of empowerment and self-esteem, they explain. The North American Menopause Society (NAMS) (**Susan D. Reed, M.D., President-Elect** [508]) offers these trusted remedies for five common menopause symptoms: [509]

For mood changes: Relaxation and stress-reduction techniques, including deep-breathing exercises and massage, a healthy lifestyle (good nutrition and daily exercise), and enjoyable, self-nurturing activities may all be helpful. Some women try to treat their menopause symptoms with over-the-counter products such as St. John's wort or vitamin B_6.

For urinary incontinence: Incontinence is an unwelcome, unwanted annoyance. Fortunately, self-care remedies can improve incontinence without medication or surgery. Try drinking more water to keep urine diluted (clear and pale yellow). Limit foods or beverages with a high acid or caffeine content, which may irritate the bladder. These include grapefruit, oranges, tomatoes, coffee, and caffeine-containing soft drinks. Try Kegel exercises to strengthen your pelvic floor muscles. Also see the section of this directory devoted specifically to **Incontinence**.

For night sweats: To get relief from night sweats (hot flashes that occur during sleep), try different strategies to stay cool while you sleep: dress in light nightclothes; use layered bedding that can easily be removed during the night; cool down with an electric fan; sip cool water throughout the night; keep a frozen cold pack under your pillow and turn over the pillow often so that your head is always resting on a cool surface, or put a cold pack on your feet.

For trouble falling asleep: Wake up and go to bed at consistent times, even on weekends. Relax and wind down before sleep by reading a book, listening to music, or taking a bath. Milk and peanuts contain tryptophan, which helps the body relax. A cup of chamomile tea may also do the trick. Keep bedroom light, noise, and temperature at a comfortable level – dark, quiet, and cool are conditions that support sleep. Use the bedroom only for sleep and sex. Avoid caffeine and alcohol late in the day. Also see the section of this directory devoted specifically to **Insomnia**.

For sexual discomfort: With menopause come sexual function changes through decreases in hormone production, leading to vaginal dryness. To counteract these changes, try these remedies:

---

[506] 4 Benefits of Menopause: Women's Health Specialists | Image, Maxim Kulikov for The Noun Project
[507] Women's Health Specialists: OB/GYNs in Denton, TX, pro-lifeobgyn.com
[508] Susan D. Reed M.D., UW Medicine, Seattle, WA, obgyn.uw.edu
[509] Five Solutions for Menopause Symptoms, menopause.com

- **Vaginal lubricants:** Only water-soluble products designed for the vagina should be used; avoid hand creams and lotions containing alcohol and perfumes as well as warming/tingling and flavored lubricants which may irritate tender tissue. (Examples of appropriate vaginal lubricants include Astroglide, Moist Again, and Silk-E.)

- **Vaginal moisturizers:** These products improve or maintain vaginal moisture. They also help keep vaginal pH in a low and healthy range. (Examples include Replens and K-Y Long-lasting Vaginal Moisturizer.) These products can be used on a regular basis and offer a more lasting effect than vaginal lubricants.

- **Regular sexual stimulation:** Last but certainly not least, a woman can maintain vaginal health through regular painless sexual activity, which promotes blood flow to the genital area.

"Doctor, Doctor!"

Discussing mood issues and other menopause symptoms with your healthcare provider can help you decide on the most appropriate intervention, says NAMS.

COST-SAVINGS EXAMPLE:

Most self-care remedies for menopause symptoms are either free or inexpensive. The most common medical approaches to menopause are also relatively inexpensive – though some services offered to postmenopausal women can be very expensive.

The prevailing issue is your quality of life; with a life expectancy of about 79 years for women in the U.S., you could be postmenopausal for half of your adult life. Try physician-approved self-care first – they may be your best long term option, and may save you money.

Some women pay $200 - $500 per month for a therapy known as bioidentical hormone replacement therapy – medication, a customized treatment plan, and follow-up appointments. [510]

If these costs, along with the benefits, are acceptable to you, it's your call. However, you may also find you can avoid this recurring expense by consistently using the physician-approved remedies above.

Remember that throughout this directory you can find further information by using the sources at the bottom of every page and in the resources listing beginning on page 259.

---

[510] Does Health Insurance Cover Hormone Replacement Therapy for Women? Revitalizeyoumd.com

MOSQUITO BITES

Mosquitoes are a global public health concern, with more than 3,500 species worldwide. They are regarded as "the world's deadliest animal" due to the diseases they carry and the millions of people they infect every year. According to the Centers for Disease Control and Prevention (CDC) [511] (**Christopher Braden, M.D.,** acting director, National Center for Emerging and Zoonotic Infectious Diseases [512]), female mosquitoes bite people and other animals to get a blood meal. Most female mosquitoes cannot produce eggs without a blood meal. Males do not bite.

Mosquito bite signs include: a puffy and reddish bump that appears a few minutes after the bite; a hard, itchy, reddish-brown bump or multiple bumps that appear a day or so after the bite or bites; small blisters instead of hard bumps, or dark spots that look like bruises

More severe reactions can occur in: children; adults bitten by a mosquito species they haven't been exposed to previously; people with immune system disorders.

People experiencing more severe reactions have these signs: a large area of swelling and redness; low-grade fever, hives, or swollen lymph nodes. The CDC recommends these self-care remedies:

Wash: Wash the area with soap and water.

Ice: Apply an ice pack for ten minutes to reduce swelling and itching. Reapply as needed. Wrap your ice pack in a clean towel to avoid direct skin contact.

Baking soda: Apply a mixture of baking soda and water to further reduce the itch response. Mix 1 tablespoon baking soda with just enough water to create a paste. Apply the paste to the mosquito bite. After ten minutes, wash off the paste.

OTC creams: Use an over-the-counter anti-itch or antihistamine cream to relieve the itch. There are three types of anti-itch creams, according to Verywell Health [513] (by **Daniel More, M.D.** [514], medically reviewed by **Jurairat J. Molina, M.D.** [515]):

- *Topical steroids* work by reducing skin inflammation (redness, swelling, and itch).
- *Topical antihistamines* block histamine, the trigger of itch and other allergy symptoms.
- *Topical anesthetics* block nerve receptors in the skin and numb the skin.

All are available online or at any pharmacy without a prescription. Amazon offers highly rated anti-itch creams starting under $10, or ask your pharmacist for a recommendation.

<u>Do Not</u>: Do not scratch bites. They can become infected. An infected bite may appear red, feel warm, or show a red streak that will spread outward from the bite.

You can protect yourself and your family from mosquito bites. Use an Environmental Protection

---

[511] What is a Mosquito? Facts About Mosquitoes, CDC, cdc.gov

[512] Christopher Braden, M.D., National Center for Emerging and Zoonotic Infectious Diseases, CDC

[513] The 3 Best Anti-Itch Creams to Soothe Itchy Skin, verywellhealth.com

[514] Daniel R. More, M.D., Allergy Partners of the California Central Coast, allergypartners.com

[515] Jurairat J. Molina, M.D., Verywell Health, verywellhealth.com

Agency (EPA)-registered insect repellent. Wear long-sleeved shirts and long pants. Treat clothing and gear with permethrin. Control mosquitoes inside and outside. [516] Prevent mosquito bites when traveling overseas. [517, 518]

"Doctor, Doctor!"

Not everyone infected with a mosquito-borne virus or parasite gets sick. Viruses like West Nile and dengue, and parasites such as the one that causes malaria, can make you sick. Malaria symptoms start about 10-15 days after the infected mosquito bite. They include high fever, shaking chills, sweating, headache, diarrhea, fatigue, body aches, yellow skin (jaundice), kidney failure, seizure, confusion, bloody stools, and convulsions.

See a health care provider if symptoms of infection worsen. Also seek care if you get a high fever while living in or traveling to an area that has a high chance for malaria, says WebMD [519] (medically reviewed by **Dan Brennan, M.D.** [520]). These areas include Africa, South and Southeast Asia, The Middle East, Central and South America, and Oceania (Australasia, Melanesia, Micronesia, and Polynesia).

Given how quickly malaria can become life-threatening, it's important to get medical care as quickly as possible, but you should still get medical help even if you see symptoms weeks, months, or a year after your travel, says WebMD. Young children, infants, and pregnant women have an especially high chance for severe cases of malaria.

COST-SAVINGS EXAMPLE:

Self-care for mosquito bites is inexpensive. However, in certain parts of the world, mosquito bites are life-threatening. Globally, there were 241 million cases of malaria in 2020. And in that same year, there were over 620,000 malaria-related deaths. A vast majority of these cases were in sub-Saharan Africa. [521]

When traveling to an area where malaria and other mosquito-borne illnesses are endemic, plan ahead; know where you'll seek medical care, and know in advance how much you can expect to pay so you don't end up writing a blank check.

For detailed planning guidance, see the CDC page, "Getting Health Care During Travel." [522]

---

[516] The Best Ways to Get Rid of Mosquitoes, thisoldhouse.com
[517] Prevent Mosquito Bites, CDC
[518] Mosquito Bite Symptoms and Treatment, cdc.gov
[519] Malaria: Symptoms and Types, webmd.com | WebMD Care
[520] Daniel Brennan, M.D., Sansum Clinic Pediatrics, sansumclinic.org
[521] 6 Facts You Didn't Know About Malaria, ONE Campaign
[522] Getting Health Care During Travel, National Center for Emerging and Zoonotic Infectious Diseases

MOTION SICKNESS

Experts at Penn State Health Milton S. Hershey Medical Center [523] (**Sankar Bandyopadhyay, M.D.**, clinical neurologist [524]) say the best way to deal with motion sickness is to prevent it altogether. That means knowing your limitations and taking precautions.

Remedies can be as simple as rolling down the windows to get fresh air when traveling by car. Other approaches include:

- **Focus on a point in the distance**, or on the horizon, rather than on nearby objects.
- **Snag a window seat** on your next flight.
- **Make sure you are sitting facing the movement of a train** rather than backward.
- **Close your eyes** to block out visual stimuli.
- **Stay well-hydrated.**
- **Get a good night's sleep** before engaging in activities that could cause motion sickness.
- **Breathe deeply.**
- **Practice relaxation techniques.**

Ginger has long been used as an alternative medication to prevent motion sickness, says the American Journal of Physiology [525] . Danish scientists looked at 80 naval cadets – for whom seasickness is career-threatening – and found that those who took a gram of ginger powder suffered less than those given a placebo. **Natascha Tuznik, D.O.**, an infectious disease physician with UC Davis Health's Traveler's Clinic [526], suggests hard ginger candy as an effective remedy for motion sickness. [527] Other sources say even a serving of ginger ale may help.

If such strategies fail, consider trying over-the-counter medicines before talking to your doctor about a long-acting prescription patch.

"Doctor, Doctor!"

If the symptoms don't abate when the movement stops – or shortly thereafter – it could be a signal of something else, says Penn State Health. If you also have loss of hearing, ringing in the ears or excessive vomiting, seek medical attention immediately.

COST-SAVINGS EXAMPLE:

Motion sickness remedies are inexpensive; the real cost is the experiences motion sickness may deprive you of. If you're a seasick naval cadet, finding an effective remedy may save your career; if you're a traveler, it may save your vacation.

---

[523] The Medical Minute: Tips For Curbing Motion Sickness, Penn State University
[524] Sankar Bandyopadhyay, M.D., Penn State Health | Image: shashank singh, The Noun Project
[525] Effects Of Ginger On Motion Sickness, National Institutes Of Health, pubmed.ncbi.nlm.nih.gov
[526] Natascha Tuznik, DO, UC Davis Health, health.ucdavis.edu
[527] Travel and motion sickness: an expert weighs in on dramamine, ginger and more, health.ucdavis.edu

MUSCLE PAIN

Pain in muscles and joints can be annoying, discomforting, and debilitating, says Redirect Health Medical & Surgical Centers of Scottsdale, AZ [528] (**Janice Johnston, M.D.**, Chief Medical Officer [529]).

By instinct, you want to relieve pain the moment you feel it. Some forms of pain require more intense remedies, but there are some home remedies that you can use to help with muscle and joint pain. Here are a few you can try the next time you experience pain in your muscles or joints:

Apple Cider Vinegar: Many have found that drinking apple cider vinegar or rubbing it directly on the area of the sore muscle or joint can help to relieve pain.

Epsom Salt: Soaking in a tub of warm water with a couple of scoops of Epsom salt is a proven remedy for aching muscles, says Redirect Health. Epsom salt also helps reduce swelling by drawing excess fluids out of muscle and joint tissue. Try soaking for 15 minutes, 3 times a week.

Garlic: Garlic is rich in sulfur and selenium, both of which can help to relieve joint and muscle pain. The sulfur helps to relieve inflammation, while selenium has an anti-rheumatic effect. This can be helpful for those with arthritis who tend to have low levels of selenium.

Ginger: Drinking ginger tea is another way to relieve muscle pain. The anti-inflammatory properties in ginger make it an excellent remedy for both muscle and joint pain.

Heat and Cold: Using hot and cold compresses helps to ease joint pain, Redirect Health advises. Heat increases blood flow, relaxing muscles and joints and decreasing pain. Cold can cut inflammation and numb the aching area. Alternate between heat and cold for best results.

Turmeric: Containing an active ingredient called curcumin that is known for anti-inflammatory and antioxidant properties, turmeric is an excellent remedy for joint and muscle pain. Studies show that using turmeric is as effective as ibuprofen for pain relief for those with osteoarthritis.

"Doctor, Doctor!"

If you are experiencing pain on a regular basis, you may need medical help. Chronic joint pain could be a symptom of osteoarthritis; the sooner you address it, the sooner you'll get relief. Your doctor can steer you to treatment plans to manage the pain and symptoms. [530]

COST-SAVINGS EXAMPLE:

Apple cider vinegar, Epsom salt, garlic and other self-care remedies for muscle pain are very inexpensive. Give them a try before muscle pain becomes chronic and threatens to cost you everything – your mobility and your independence.

---

[528] Remedies for Muscle and Joint Pain, Redirect Health Medical & Surgical Centers, arrowheadhealth.com
[529] Janice Johnston, M.D., Redirect Health Provider Team | Image: Llisole, The Noun Project
[530] Healthcare on your terms – anytime, anywhere, 24/7/365, Redirect Health, redirecthealth.com

N

NAIL PROBLEMS

You have plenty of natural options to restore your nail health, says the lifestyle site mindbodygreen [531] (medical reviewed by **Keira Barr, M.D.** [532]). Here are some of the best physician-approved tips for longer, stronger, more beautiful nails:

Use a natural nail strengthener: Nail hardeners and strengtheners were once made with formaldehyde, a potentially dangerous ingredient, says mindbodygreen. Now we have plenty of safe, plant-based options using vitamin E, olive oil, garlic, and tea tree to feed the nail nutrients, rather than superficially strengthening the nail.

Take a collagen or biotin supplement: Studies indicate that collagen supplements can support healthy nail growth. One study found that when patients took collagen daily for 24 weeks, their nail health was better maintained, including faster growth rates, reduced breakage, and improved appearance. The same goes for biotin, a form of vitamin B that is often used in hair growth supplements. Biotin has been shown to support thickness and firmness of nails.

Avoid alcohol-based sanitizers: Hand sanitizers are often necessary, just know they might cause nail brittleness. Traditional sanitizers are very drying to your skin due to the high alcohol content. "Alcohol, the active ingredient in most sanitizers, will dry out your hands and strip the skin of its natural barrier," says dermatologist **Jeanine Downie, M.D.** [533] If your nails are consistently brittle, look for an alcohol-free option or just apply hand moisturizers more often.

Wear gloves while cleaning: In addition to the effects of water, many cleaning agents – soap, vinegar, lemon extract – are often drying and can be harsh on the hands and nails.

Keep them protected from the sun: Like the rest of your body, nails can get sun damage, too. They can yellow, turn brittle, or even develop vertical ridges that can last up to six months. You can also develop skin cancer under the nail. Mindbodygreen says that most colored nail polishes will act as a physical barrier to UV damage, but you can find clear or nude polish with UV protection (it will indicate so on the label).

Practice nail hygiene: Keep chips at bay by keeping nails clipped, filed, and cleaned "It's important to care for the entire nail area so that your nails stay healthy in general," says Dr. Barr.

Consider your diet: Nutritional deficiencies that contribute to brittle, damaged nails. Common

---

[531] 11 Research-Backed, Natural Remedies For Brittle Nails, mindbodygreen
[532] Keira Barr, M.D., Dermatologist, mindbodygreen.com | Image: Azam Ishaq, The Noun Project
[533] Dr. Jeanine B. Downie, image Dermatology ® P.C., Montclair, NJ

deficiencies are iron, vitamin B7, B12, magnesium, and proteins. It's not an immediate fix, but should help your nails over time. If you suspect a deficiency might be the cause of your brittle nails, see a doctor to get tested.

Limit the exposure to cold: When the temperature drops and there's less moisture in the air. This can dehydrate the nail bed in the same way that it can dehydrate skin. "The winter is drier, so that's when we need to focus on adding moisture, preventing water loss, and making sure the skin barrier is supported, as it becomes easily compromised when it's dry," says board-certified dermatologist **Howard Murad, M.D.** [534] While you can't control the weather, be sure to wear warm gloves or mittens when outdoors so as not to expose them to the elements.

Apply a cuticle oil daily: The cuticle is a vital part of nail health, as it overlaps the nail plate and rims the base of the nail. And dry, frayed cuticles—as well as the skin around your cuticles— can lead to picking. "[Picking] can damage the nail beds and matrix, which causes permanent indentations in the middle of your fingernails," says **Amy Wechsler, M.D.** [535], board-certified dermatologist and psychiatrist, who recommends applying a cuticle oil at least once a day. You can keep your cuticles hydrated with a variety of oils, like olive, coconut, or sweet almond. A lot of things you can find in the kitchen can be beneficial to cuticle health. And then just remember to rub the oil into the cuticles when you are applying your full-body moisturizer, she says.

Use a natural exfoliator: Sometimes nails need exfoliation, too. Don't take a scrub to your fingers, however (far too abrasive). Instead, opt for a gentle, natural chemical exfoliator. Research suggests that glycolic acid can help with restoring nail strength. It's a common skin care ingredient – in peels, pads, or serums – so simply rub it in your nails once a week.

Do Not: Don't soak nails in water: Water causes nails to expand and contract, making them weaker. (It's why you're told to avoid water or showers up to 24 hours after a manicure or pedicure.) Wear gloves while doing the dishes, and try to keep nails dry when possible, says mindbodygreen.

"Doctor, Doctor!"

If self-care isn't producing the results you desire, or if your nails are bleeding, painful, or you suspect an infection, call your doctor or a board-certified dermatologist.

COST-SAVINGS EXAMPLE:

Self-care for nail brittleness is generally inexpensive. Give them a try and you may be able to avoid the expense of a trip to the dermatologist. Or ask your physician to check your nails during your routine annual check-up or skin check; you'll get qualified medical advice without spending a dollar more.

---

[534] Dr. Howard Murad, El Segundo, CA, drhowardmurad.com
[535] Dr. Amy Wechsler Dermatology, New York, NY, dramywechsler.com

NAUSEA AND VOMITING

Nausea has many possible causes. No matter what's making you queasy at the moment, you want a dependable remedy that works fast, says Healthgrades, an online guide to finding the right doctors, hospitals, and care for you and your family [536] (medical reviewer, **Debra Rose Wilson, Ph.D.** [537]). They trust these self-care remedies to help their patients:

Apples: The fiber in apples helps your body get rid of the toxins that sometimes cause nausea. Fiber also slows down digestion, which could help soothe your stomach. Go with just one whole apple, 8 ounces of apple juice, or a cup of applesauce. Even apple syrup can sometimes do the trick, says Healthgrades.

Baking soda: Sodium bicarbonate, also known as baking soda, is a traditional remedy for upset stomach and nausea. It makes your stomach less acidic. Add just a half teaspoon of baking soda to 8 oz of warm water, stir, and drink.

Ginger: Ginger ale is a classic nausea remedy. Ginger is so effective, one study found it eases the nausea commonly experienced during pregnancy or while in chemotherapy. When possible, choose natural ginger in the form of ginger root, ginger tea, ginger candies, and powdered ginger.

Staying hydrated: Staying hydrated can help replace any fluids you lose through vomiting and diarrhea. Take small sips of soothing teas or carbonated drinks – but skip the carbonation if you are experiencing bloating, says Healthgrades. You may also want to try sipping a sports drink like Gatorade for extra electrolytes, but enjoy in moderation because the extra sugar could upset your stomach. Diluted juice is another way to get more water and less sugar. Stay away from caffeinated sports drinks or so-called "energy" drinks.

Lemons: Lemons and lemon water can also help relieve nausea. The neutralizing acids in lemon create compounds in your stomach that help soothe the upset. Just mix lemon juice with a pinch of salt in a glass of warm water and sip. The tang also distracts your brain from feelings of nausea. Sniffing a lemon may also work.

Meditation: Nausea may be due to – or worsened by – stress. A relaxation technique like meditation can help relax your stomach and diaphragm, as well as your mind. Take long breaths and put your attention on the feeling of air flowing in and out of your nose.

Peppermint: Peppermint has been scientifically proven to help soothe an upset stomach. The active ingredient, menthol, helps relax the stomach to calm cramping and nausea. Try drinking peppermint tea or sniffing peppermint essential oil.

Rest: Trying to "power through" can make a bout of nausea worse. Give yourself some downtime to let things settle; it can take a few days for a stomach virus or food poisoning to pass. Rest and avoid stressful or busy activities until you fully recover. Resting after each meal can also aid digestion to decrease nausea.

Saltines: Bland, easy-to-digest foods like saltine crackers are a good option if you have nausea.

---

[536] 20 Effective Home Remedies for Nausea, healthgrades.com | Image: Cahya Kurniawan, The Noun Project
[537] Debra Rose Wilson, Ph.D., Austin Peay State University School of Nursing, healthgrades.com

They move easily through the stomach without upsetting it any further. Any similar dry, mildly salty food can be beneficial to reduce feelings of nausea. Other simple foods like bananas, applesauce, rice, or toast are smart picks.

Sitting up straight: You might think you should lay down for comfort, but this actually makes your symptoms worse. Being in a horizontal position can cause stomach acid to come up; remaining upright keeps stomach contents where they belong. If you must lie down, prop your torso up on some pillows, or use a wedge-shaped pillow to elevate your head, neck, and shoulders. Digestive experts say that lying on your left side may soothe the upset faster.

Small, slow meals: When you're trying to recover from nausea, don't overwhelm your system with too much, too soon. Start with small, simple meals, says Healthgrades. Wait and see how the food settles before having seconds. Try not to skip meals when you have nausea.

Avoid spicy, fatty foods: When you're nauseated, your stomach needs foods it can digest easily. Avoid dairy, fried, overly sweet, very spicy, or strong-tasting foods and get plenty of liquids.

Loose clothing: Wearing tight clothes can compress your stomach and make nausea worse. Tight clothing may also make you feel warmer, especially if you are in a warm environment, also worsening nausea. Opt for loose-fitting clothing that makes you feel as comfortable as possible.

Fresh air: Deep breaths of some fresh air can help relieve nausea. Try opening a window or taking a gentle outdoor stroll, or simply stepping outside for a few minutes. A change in scenery may also help distract you from nausea. Just be sure to move and breathe slowly.

Popsicles: Try sucking on a frozen non-dairy treat. Any hard or gelatin-based sweet can release flavors into your mouth that can help relieve nausea. For example, you could try mint or lemon-flavored candies. However, avoid tart sweets if you have mouth sores as well as nausea.

Distraction: Focusing solely on nausea can make it worse and make you feel more stressed. Try distracting yourself with gentle, healthy activities that make you feel good while taking your mind off your nausea. For example, you could try listening to gentle music, watching your favorite TV program, and being with other people.

Ice chips: Ice chips help you stay hydrated without inundating your stomach with too much fluid at once. Let ice chips slowly melt in your mouth. This can also help you feel more comfortable due to the cold temperature. You can use frozen juice chips if you prefer some flavor.

Avoiding strong food smells: Aromas are common triggers of nausea. If someone else can prepare your food, this may help. Or try using prepared foods from the freezer, or preparing cold or room temperature meals.

Acupressure: One pressure point to help relieve nausea is located on your wrist, just below the palm of your hand. Use three fingers or your thumb on the opposite hand to locate two tendons in this area. Pressing gently on this spot could help relieve nausea. It's the same area that's worked by the wristbands people often use during pregnancy or to reduce seasickness. They're called sea bands, and you can find them on Amazon starting under $10.

"Doctor, Doctor!"

If someone may be vomiting due to poisoning, call Poison Control Centers at **(800) 222-1222** (available 24 hours every day). Reach out to your doctor if your nausea will not go away, you are unable to eat, or you cannot stop vomiting, says Healthgrades. A doctor can help you identify causes and recommend treatment. These may involve medications or other strategies, such as therapy. [538]

COST-SAVINGS EXAMPLE:

Home remedies for nausea are very inexpensive. Many are already in your kitchen. Others may be found in your grocery store, pharmacy, or online. In most cases, costly medical care is not needed.

NECK PAIN

With so many at-home treatment options for neck pain, how do you know which treatments are right for you? This wise approach is to start with physician-approved remedies. Spineuniverse.com offers these trusted at-home neck pain treatments [539] (medical reviewer, **Michael W. Hasz, M.D.,** assistant professor of surgery, Uniformed Services Health Science University, Bethesda, M.D. [540]).

Neck stretch: You can do this simple neck stretch almost anywhere, unless you are driving or operating equipment. Move your head toward your right shoulder until you feel a gentle stretch. You can use your right hand to gently guide your head toward the shoulder. Hold for 30 seconds, and repeat on the other side.

Schedule break time: It's common to hold one position for far too long, especially if you spend the day at a computer. When you hold a position for a long time, you strain your muscles – including your neck muscles. If you sit for hours at a time, remember to get up and stretch about every hour, says spineuniverse.com.

Ice and heat: Applying a cold pack can help reduce neck pain and inflammation, and a heat pack can soothe sore neck muscles. Alternate between heat and cold packs. Don't apply the pack directly to your skin; wrap in a towel. In general, apply a heat and/or cold pack several times a day for about 20 minutes each time, spineuniverse.com suggests.

Another physician offering trusted remedies for neck pain is pain management specialist **Akash Bajaj, M.D.** of Remedy Pain Solutions in Marina del Rey and Manhattan Beach, CA. He says that most of the time, neck pain is not serious initially and can be treated with some very simple remedies:

---

[538] Find a Doctor, Healthgrades.com
[539] At-home Treatments for Neck Pain, spineuniverse.com | Image, Llisole, The Noun Project
[540] Michael W. Hasz, M.D., Crowell Reconstructive Surgery, Reston, VA, spineuniverse.com

Water therapy: Hydrotherapy is another great remedy for neck pain, which can be easily done while taking a shower, explains Dr. Bajaj. The force of water reduces pain and soreness on the neck. Target the area of pain with warm water first for three to four minutes. Then follow the same with cold water for thirty to sixty seconds. The hot water therapy will ease stiff muscles and increase blood circulation, while cold water will help reduce inflammation in the neck.

Salt bath with Epsom: Epsom salt reduces stress, relieves muscle tension, and gives instant pain relief, says Dr. Bajaj. As Epsom salt has a mixture of magnesium in it, it acts as a natural muscle relaxant and reduces pain and swelling. To try this treatment at home, add two cups of Epsom salt to water, and soak your body, especially the aching neck area, in the water for 20 minutes.

Lavender oil: Massaging the neck with lavender oil also eases neck pain. After a hot water bath, gently rub some lavender oil on the pain affected area. Massage for 10 minutes. Repeat this daily until the neck heals completely.

"Doctor, Doctor!"

Neck pain can have a variety of causes, from overuse of your neck muscles or more serious spine conditions. But if you've tried at-home neck pain treatments for a few months and they haven't reduced your pain, call your doctor. He or she can recommend other neck pain treatments, such as prescription medications and physical therapy.

<u>COST-SAVINGS EXAMPLE:</u>

Self-care for neck pain is inexpensive or free. Use these remedies *before* neck pain becomes chronic. Americans spent an estimated $380 billion on low back and neck pain, as well as on joint and limb pain, and other musculoskeletal disorders in 2016. You don't want any part of that if you can possibly avoid it. [541]

Avoid taking on a share of $380 billion in costs for musculoskeletal disorders. Put physician-approved self-care remedies to work at the first hint of neck pain.

NIGHT BLINDNESS

Having good night vision is something many people struggle with, especially as they get older, says First Eye Care DFW [542] (**Craig C. Hughes, O.D.** [543]).

The editors of TrustedHealth.com (publisher of this directory) have a solution that works well for us: get up early and cut the number of hours in the day when

---

[541] Low Back And Neck Pain Tops US Health Spending, healthdata.org
[542] How To Improve Your Night Vision Naturally, First Eye Care DFW, firsteyecaredfw.com
[543] Craig C. Hughes, OD, First Eye Care, DFW | Image: Michael Wohlwend for The Noun Project

you rely on night vision. We are up at 5 a.m. and home by 5 p.m. almost every night. If this schedule doesn't work for you, just be aware of the need to be more cautious after dark. Simple and effective, if you can arrange it and stick to it. If you commute to a day job, ask your boss if you can swap your 9-5 hours for 7-3; she might say yes, and you may find you like leaving work early. You'll greatly reduce the number of hours you need to be out in the dark.

While poor night vision often keeps people from driving at night, there are self-care remedies that can help, says First Eye Care DFW. In fact, they have numerous ways you can improve your night vision naturally. Here are some remedies trusted by their physicians and patients:

Maintain a healthy diet: Eating foods rich in vitamin A can help night vision and protect the eyes from cataract formation, a common cause of night blindness. Vitamin A-rich foods include dark green leafy vegetables, carrots, potatoes, dairy products, broccoli, squash, and fish.

Do eye exercises: Doing eye exercises in the morning, before you go to bed, and anytime your eyes are tired can help improve your vision and strengthen your eye muscles.

Rest your eyes: When your eyes feel tired from looking at a computer screen or reading a book, give them a rest, says First Eye Care DFW. This will help your eyes recover and avoid any unnecessary strain, which can lead to weak eye muscles and poor night vision.

Avoid smoking: Studies have shown that nicotine can prevent your eyes from producing rhodopsin, the pigment responsible for night vision. One more reason to break nicotine's hold over your life. See the trusted remedies in Part I one of this directory under **Tobacco**.

Give your eyes a massage: Gently massaging your eyes for just five to ten seconds can help them adjust better to seeing in the dark.

Protect your vision: One of the most damaging things to the eyes is being exposed to bright sunlight without protection. The more often your eyes must adjust to bright sunlight, the harder time they will have adjusting to the darkness. Always wear sunglasses when outdoors and reduce the brightness of your computer screen or phone, especially in a dark room.

Vitamins: In addition to the above, there are numerous vitamins that can support your eyes, including vitamins A, B6, B9, and B12, C, and E; riboflavin; Omega-3 fatty acids; and niacin.

"Doctor, Doctor!"

To learn more about what you can do to improve your night vision naturally, contact your vision professional.

<u>COST-SAVINGS EXAMPLE:</u>

Self-care remedies for poor night vision are inexpensive or free. The cost of poor night vision can literally be *everything you have;* every year there's a spike in motor vehicle deaths when clocks "fall back" to Standard Time and commuters are plunged into darkness. Pedestrians die because drivers didn't see them in the dark. Use these remedies and see your way clear to better vision that could save a life.

NIGHT SWEATS

Night sweats can reduce your sleep quality, concern your partner, and provoke discomfort and sleep loss, says the Sleep Foundation [544] (medically reviewed by **Abhinav Singh M.D.,** sleep physician [545]). Here are some trusted remedies recommended by the foundation to banish the sweats and get some rest:

Sleep in a cooler bedroom: While a warmer bedroom is not the central cause of night sweats, it may facilitate or trigger them, the foundation says. Keeping the thermostat at a cooler setting can keep heat from building up around your body during the night.

Replace your mattress: Certain mattresses are more likely to retain heat than others, especially if they conform closely and restrict airflow. A cooling mattress can prevent heat retention and help you keep cool throughout the night. If you are experiencing menopause, a mattress that offers pressure relief and ample airflow may help reduce symptoms. (Also check the remedies in the section on MENOPAUSE just a few pages back in this directory.) A cooling mattress pad or topper is worth considering instead if you do not want to replace your mattress.

Invest in new bedding: In addition to assessing your current mattress, you may want to consider changing up your bedding. Lightweight, breathable sheets can help wick away moisture. You may also want to swap out a heavy duvet or comforter for a lighter quilt. No need to break a sweat running from store to store – Amazon and other online retailers have scores of choices.

Wear breathable clothing: Tight-fitting clothes trap heat, so it is best to wear lightweight, loose-fitting clothes made with materials that are breathable and airy. Dressing in layers makes it easier to make adjustments to maintain a comfortable temperature.

Avoid caffeine, alcohol, and spicy foods: All of these foods spike your body temperature and induce sweating. Avoiding them, especially in the evening, may cut down on night sweats.

Drink cold water: Having a small amount of cool water before going to bed may help you maintain a more pleasant temperature, the Sleep Foundation advises.

Maintain a healthy weight: Some research has identified a correlation between higher body weight and night sweats. Being overweight or obese can contribute to other health problems, including those that affect sleep, such as sleep apnea.

Utilize relaxation techniques: Finding ways to relax at night can make it easier to fall asleep. Controlled breathing may help to meaningfully reduce hot flashes and night sweats.

Many of these tips overlap with broader healthy sleep tips that can be gradually implemented to make your sleep-related habits work in your favor for more consistent and high-quality sleep, so be sure to see the section of this directory dealing with **Insomnia.**

---

[544] Night Sweats: Causes and Treatments, sleepfoundation.org | Image: Sewon Park, The Noun Project
[545] Abhinav Singh, M.D., Indiana Sleep Center, Greenwood, IN

"Doctor, Doctor!"

Underlying health issues may be responsible for your episodes of considerable sweating in your sleep, says the Sleep Foundation. [546] You should talk to your doctor if you have night sweats that are frequent or persistent. You should also mention them if they interfere with your sleep, negatively affect your daily life, or occur with other health changes.

Additional treatments for night sweats include cognitive behavioral therapy (CBT) and medications. Studies have found that cognitive behavioral therapy for hot flashes and night sweats can reduce their frequency and improve mood and quality of life in menopausal women.

Meeting with a doctor is important because she can help determine the most likely cause and work with you to create a treatment plan that takes your symptoms and overall health into account. It is also important to let the doctor know about any sleeping problems that you have. Sleep disorders, like obstructive sleep apnea (OSA), may be causing daytime sleepiness and, according to some research, may also be a factor promoting night sweats.

COST-SAVINGS EXAMPLE:

Insomnia costs the U.S. workforce $63 billion a year in lost productivity, says the American Academy of Sleep Medicine. Don't allow yourself to carry any part of this burden; try these trusted self-care remedies to end night sweats.

NOSEBLEED

If you have a history of nosebleeds, these trusted remedies may reduce their frequency, says Collin County (TX) Ear Nose & Throat (CCENT) [547] (**Keith E. Matheny, M.D.,** otolaryngologist [548]). Simply using a humidifier at night to add moisture to the air has helped many people. Cigarette use can increase the risk of nosebleeds, one more of the many reasons should kick the habit. (For help quitting, turn to the section on **Tobacco** in Part I of this directory, **Doctor-Trusted Remedies for the Top 10 Most Common Health Issues**.)

It may be helpful to keep the inside of your nose moist by using a saline nasal spray or applying petroleum jelly with a cotton swab, says CCENT. Use these remedies when a nosebleed occurs:

Elevate your head: Keep your head above the heart to slow the bleeding.

Lean forward slightly: This will keep the blood from draining down your throat.

Blow gently: Blow your nose gently to clear clotted blood that might be present

---

[546] Sleep Foundation, Creating A Healthy, Well-Rested World, sleepfoundation.org
[547] How To Treat Frequent Nosebleeds, Collin County Ear Nose & Throat, Frisco, TX, collincountyent.com
[548] Keith E. Matheny, M.D., Collin Co. ENT, Frisco, TX, collincountyent.com | Image: Rahul, The Noun Project

Apply pressure: Pinch your nose to put pressure on the bleeding point to stop the flow of blood.

Stay calm: A nervous response increases your heart rate and makes you bleed more.

<u>Do Not</u>: When the bleeding stops, be careful not to do anything that might make the bleeding start again, such as blowing your nose or bending over.

"Doctor, Doctor!"

According to CCENT, there are two scenarios where you might consider talking to a doctor about nosebleeds: inability to stop the bleeding, or frequency of the occurrence. Immediate medical treatment might be required if you experience any of these symptoms:

- You have a nosebleed that won't stop after 20 or 30 minutes
- A nosebleed is caused by injury or trauma, such as a car accident or hit to the face
- A greater than expected amount of blood is coming out
- Nosebleeds in children under the age of 2

If your symptoms aren't life-threatening, nosebleeds can be treated at most urgent care centers, says Revere Health Urgent Care, with locations throughout Utah. [549]

Try to have someone drive you to the doctor instead of driving yourself, says CCENT. If you are losing a lot of blood, then you might be at risk of passing out.

Smaller, frequent nosebleeds can also be a concern, even though emergency treatment usually isn't required. But it is smart to schedule a consultation with an experienced ENT to identify the underlying cause of the symptoms. The frequency of symptoms could indicate a more serious problem, such as a blood disorder, nasal tumor, and more. [550]

<u>COST-SAVINGS EXAMPLE:</u>

An emergency room visit can easily cost $1,000 or more. If these trusted home remedies can stop the bleeding within 20-30 minutes, that's substantial savings.

Avoid a $1,000+ emergency room bill to treat a nose bleed by trying self-care remedies for up to half an hour, unless blood flow is very heavy.

Remember that throughout this directory you can find further information by using the sources at the bottom of every page and in the resources listing beginning on page 259.

---

[549] Should You Go to the ER for a Bloody Nose? Revere Health, reverehealth.com
[550] Schedule Your ENT Doctor Appointment Today, CCENT, Frisco, Texas, collincountyent.com

O-P-R

OILY HAIR AND SKIN

 Many people struggle with overly oily hair and skin. If that's you, you may be wondering what it is that you're doing to cause this unwanted condition. **Marie V. Hayag, M.D.** is a board-certified dermatologist who practices on the Upper East Side of New York City. [551] Appearing on The Dr. Oz Show, she shared her most trusted self-care remedies for oily skin and hair: [552]

When you wash your hair: "If someone who has oily hair washes their hair every day and is still experiencing oily hair, they may be over-washing," Dr. Hayag explains. "Over-washing can strip the scalp of its natural oil and cause an overproduction of oil in order to rehydrate the scalp." Instead, aim to wash every other day.

How you wash your hair: Dr. Hayag recommends focusing the shampoo on the scalp, and the conditioner at the ends of the hair shaft. "It may also be helpful to condition first and then follow with shampoo to ensure there are no product residuals following a shower," says Hayag.

Clean your hairbrush: One thing that most people don't think about is cleaning the hairbrush, which Dr. Hayag says can harbor lots of product residue and dead skin.

Blow dry: You can also try blow-drying your hair. "The heat plumps up the hair cuticle, allowing it to better absorb scalp oil," says Dr. Hayag.

Apple cider vinegar & aloe: Dr. Hayag recommends applying apple cider vinegar to the scalp and letting it sit for a few minutes before washing to get rid of any product buildup and balance out the scalp's pH. She also loves aloe vera; mix one tablespoon of it along with three tablespoons of lemon juice into one cup of shampoo.

Choose shampoo carefully: If you'd rather just buy shampoo at the store, Hayag suggests looking for shampoos that contain detergents, like ammonium or sulfates, because these can dry out the excess oil. You can also find products that already contain apple cider vinegar.

Moisturize: Just because your hair is oily, that doesn't mean you can forgo all moisture. "Although it may seem counterintuitive to add more moisture to oily hair, it is actually important. This is because oily hair is likely caused by stripping away too many natural oils from the scalp, which then causes the body to overproduce oil," says Hayag. To combat dryness, Hayag suggests jojoba oil, which she says is super gentle.

Dr. Hayag also shares her most trusted self-care remedies for oily skin:

---

[551] Marie Hayag, M.D., Fifth Avenue Aesthetics, New York, mariehayagmd.com
[552] 10 Easy Ways to Treat Oily Hair & Skin, drozshow.com | Image: fauzan akbar, The Noun Project

Use products with acids: "It is important to incorporate acids that can combat oily skin and control the production of oils," she says. "Some acids to look for include salicylic acid, glycolic acid, beta-hydroxy acids and benzoyl peroxide."

Cleanse with the right ingredients: Dr. Hayag recommends looking for cleansers with sodium laureth carboxylate and alkyl carboxylates. She notes that these are great for oil control and tackling moderate acne. For a natural alternative, witch hazel, an astringent with high tannin levels, is good for removing excess oil without drying out the skin.

Moisturize: Managing oily skin and hydrating the skin are not mutually exclusive, says Hayag. Try to incorporate ingredients like hyaluronic acid, which helps balance the oil and water production in skin. In addition, look for products that are oil-free and non-comedogenic, meaning the product is specially formulated not to cause blocked pores.

"Doctor, Doctor!"

While oily hair and skin are generally cosmetic rather than medical concerns, you may want to consult a doctor if self-care remedies aren't enough and the condition is affecting your self-confidence.

COST-SAVINGS EXAMPLE:

Regular visits to a dermatologist can be expensive. Ask in advance if the treatments for your condition are covered by insurance. Some products for oily skin sell on Amazon for $200, $300, or more. [553]

Doctor visits and cosmetic products can quickly add up to thousands of dollars – all well and good if they help and you can afford it, but remedies like apple cider vinegar and aloe may be just as effective.

OSTEOPOROSIS

Learning about nutrient-rich foods that are important for your bone health and overall health will help you make healthier food choices every day, says the Bone Health & Osteoporosis Foundation [554] (**Kenneth W. Lyles, M.D.**, President [555]).

If you eat a well-balanced diet with plenty of dairy, fish, fruits and vegetables, you should get enough of the nutrients you need every day, the foundation says. But people who aren't getting the recommended amount from food alone may need to complement their diet with supplements.

---

[553] Amazon search results for "oily skin treatment"
[554] Osteoporosis Diet & Nutrition: Foods for Bone Health, bonehealthandosteoporosis.org
[555] Kenneth W. Lyles, M.D., Geriatric Medicine, DukeHealth.org | Image: VectorsLab, The Noun Project

Recent research has found that olive oil, soy beans, blueberries and foods rich in omega-3s, like fish oil and flaxseed oil, may also have bone boosting benefits, the foundation says. The foundation goes on to offer these trusted remedies:

Beans (legumes): While beans contain calcium, magnesium, fiber and other nutrients. Soak beans in water for several hours, then cook them in fresh water.

Meat and other high-protein foods: It's important to get enough, but not too much protein for bone health and overall health, the foundation explains. Many older adults do not get enough protein in their diets, and this may be harmful to bones. However, special high-protein diets that contain multiple servings of meat and protein with each meal can also cause the body to lose calcium. You can make up for this loss by getting enough calcium for your body's needs. For example, dairy products – although high in protein – also contain calcium that is important for healthy bones.

Limit foods that may contribute to bone loss, or consume them in moderation: According to the foundation, this includes salty foods; spinach and other foods with oxalates like rhubarb and beet greens; wheat bran, which may reduce the absorption of calcium in other foods eaten at the same time. If you drink alcohol, caffeine, and cola, do so in moderation.

To learn more about other foods that may be good for your bones, visit:

- *Food and Your Bones: Osteoporosis Nutrition Guidelines,* Bone Health & Osteoporosis Foundation [556]

- PubMed.gov, an online service of the US National Library of Medicine, to find research studies on nutrition and bone health. [557]

The foundation also recommends two types of exercise for building and maintaining bone density: weight-bearing and muscle-strengthening exercises. [558]

Weight-bearing Exercises: These are activities that make you move against gravity while staying upright. Weight-bearing exercises can be high-impact such as dancing, high-impact aerobics, hiking, jogging/running, jumping rope, stair climbing, and tennis; or they can be low-impact such as elliptical machines, low-impact aerobics, stair-step machines, fast walking on a treadmill or outside.

Muscle-Strengthening Exercises: These exercises include activities where you move your body, a weight or some other resistance against gravity. They are also known as resistance exercises and include: lifting weights, using elastic exercise bands, using weight machines, lifting your own body weight, functional movements, such as standing and rising up on your toes. Yoga and Pilates can also improve strength, balance and flexibility. However, certain positions may not be safe for people with osteoporosis or those at increased risk of broken bones. For example, exercises that have you bend forward may increase the chance of breaking a bone in the spine. A physical therapist should be able to help you learn which exercises are safe and appropriate for you.

---

[556] Osteoporosis Diet & Nutrition: Foods for Bone Health, bonehealthandosteoporosis.org
[557] PubMed, National Library of Medicine, pubmed.ncbi.nlm.nih.gov | Image: VectorsLab, The Noun Project
[558] Osteoporosis Exercise for Strong Bones, bonehealthandosteoporosis.org

"Doctor, Doctor!"

New technology is helping health care providers decide how likely it is that a patient will break a bone, says American Bone Health. Health care providers commonly diagnose osteoporosis using a scan to test bone mineral density, providing more information that can improve how health care providers diagnose and treat patients. Your doctor has additional options that can help you avoid life-changing fractures. For questions to ask your doctor about making a bone health plan, see the American Bone Health website at americanbonehealth.org. [559]

COST-SAVINGS EXAMPLE:

Osteoporosis is a very costly disease – costly to treat, and potentially very costly for your future health and independence. The American Journal of Managed Care reports total healthcare costs for each osteoporotic fracture were $34,855; even if insurance covers nearly all of it, you don't want to put your body through all that pain and treatment [560] (Dr. Richard J. Weiss, M.D.) [561] .

The same study said: "Osteoporotic fractures are associated with a significant economic burden, including costs of rehabilitation services and a high total all-cause cost of care ... Early identification and treatment of patients at high risk of fractures are of paramount importance to reduce risk and healthcare costs."

Avoid or delay the onset of osteoporosis by adopting bone-building habits starting at whatever age you are at today. You could save yourself having to endure tens of thousands of dollars in treatment, including hospitalization and rehab.

Remember that throughout this directory you can find further information by using the sources at the bottom of every page and in the resources listing beginning on page 259.

[559] How Testing Bone Structure Helps Predict Broken Bones, AmericanBoneHealth.org
[560] Economic Burden of Osteoporotic Fractures in US Managed Care Enrollees, ajmc.com
[561] Dr. Richard J. Weiss, M.D., Endocrinologist, Wayne, PA, US News Doctors, health.usnews.com

PHLEBITIS

Have you noticed an area on your leg that's dark with a lump? This is a symptom of phlebitis, says the Delaware Advanced Vein Center [562] (**Dr. Anthony Alfieri, D.O.,** cardiologist and vein specialist [563]). It refers to the inflammation of veins, which can cause blood clots called thrombophlebitis if left untreated.

Phlebitis has many causes but the most common causes include local trauma or injury to the vein, prolonged inactivities like long driving or plane rides, varicose veins, according to Dr. Alfieri. A short-term condition of phlebitis will subside in 1-3 weeks. Here are some trusted at-home treatments to relieve phlebitis symptoms:

Use warm/cold compresses: Apply heat or cold to the affected area. Do this for up to 10 minutes as often as directed. Heat: Use a warm compress, such as a heating pad. Cold: Use a cold compress, such as a cold pack or bag of ice wrapped in a thin towel. [564]

Elevate the affected leg for better blood flow: Elevating your legs places them above the level of your heart (Medically reviewed by **Angela M. Bell, M.D.** [565]). This means that gravity is now working in your favor. This may help improve blood flow in the veins in your legs. [566]

Wear compression stockings: When sitting for a long period of time during travel, swelling is likely to occur. To keep swelling down, try compression stockings or socks. Compression socks help keep oxygen flowing and prevent your legs from cramping. [567]

Use over the counter drugs: non-steroidal anti-inflammatory drugs (NSAID), such as ibuprofen (Advil, Motrin IB, others) or naproxen sodium (Aleve, others), are appropriate for phlebitis.

"Doctor, Doctor!"

Left untreated, phlebitis poses an increased risk of developing blood clots in deep veins, a condition known as deep vein thrombosis (DVT). The situation can be life-threatening. If phlebitis has caused DVT, hospitalization is often recommended along with anti-blood clot or blood thinner medications and monitoring. For all these reasons, let your doctor know about your symptoms, even if self-care appears to be helping.

COST-SAVINGS EXAMPLE:

Phlebitis can kill if it leads to deep vein thrombosis. That's why phlebitis calls for both medical care and home remedies; use both, save money elsewhere.

---

[562] Phlebitis: What Is It and How to Treat It, Delaware Vein Center, delawareadvancedveincenter.com

[563] Dr. Anthony Alfieri, D.O., Cardiologist & Vein Specialist, Delaware; treats venous insufficiency

[564] Superficial Thrombophlebitis, Fairview Health Services, Minnesota, fairview.org

[565] Dr. Angela M. Bell, M.D., Internist, Chicago, IL, US News Doctors, health.usnews.com

[566] Elevating legs: health benefits, how to, precautions, healthline.com | Image: Webtechops LLP, The Noun Project

[567] Compression Stockings, Delaware Vein Center, delawareadvancedveincenter.com

PHOBIAS AND FEARS

 The United States Navy has over 345,000 servicemen and women in its ranks. These sailors must cope with living and working conditions that are often highly stressful (such as living on an aircraft carrier, submarine, or battleship), while being fully prepared to go to war at any moment to defend the United States and its allies. So it's no surprise that Navy medical providers are skilled at assisting people dealing with phobias and fears.

A phobia is an irrational fear of a specific situation, activity or object, says the Navy's Bureau of Medicine and Surgery [568] (**Rear Admiral Bruce L. Gillingham, M.D., Surgeon General** [569]). The phobia compels the sufferer to avoid whatever is feared because with it comes a number of troubling symptoms, such as anxiety, rapid heartbeat, sweating, hot or cold flashes, dizziness, choking, shaking, faintness, smothering feelings, the need to flee the situation, and panic attacks.

Most of the time, simple phobias develop during childhood and often go away with time. Those that continue into adulthood may not go away without treatment.

Social phobia is the irrational fear of being embarrassed or humiliated in public. Examples of situations leading to this include: public speaking (the most common social phobia), stage fright, eating in public, talking to coworkers, or asking someone out on a date.

Agoraphobia is the irrational fear of being alone in public places from which the person:

- feels trapped with no way to escape (or thinks it would be difficult to escape)
- would be very embarrassed or helpless when phobic symptoms occur
- fears being totally unable to take care of himself or herself if help was not around

Agoraphobia can occur with or without panic disorder. It often comes after having panic attacks, as the person avoids the places where attacks occurred. He or she fears that something about the location caused the panic attack. The fear of having another panic attack results in avoiding going out in public; in severe cases, people with agoraphobia don't leave their home at all.

The Navy Bureau of Medicine and Surgery offers these trusted remedies to help with phobias:

List your irrational fears: Writing them down helps you to identify them. Try to figure out why you have the fears, what you think they mean, what they might symbolize, and what you can do to deal with them. Doing these things can give you some control over your fears.

Learn and practice relaxation techniques: These allow you to feel more comfortable and show that you can control the physical symptoms which result from your phobia. They also help you to overcome your phobia by allowing you to remain in the situation long enough to realize that you are not in any danger. Two important relaxation techniques to use are:

- **Controlled breathing:** When you panic, you over-breathe or hyperventilate, making you dizzy. This causes your heart to race, making you feel weak and tremble. Take a few deep breaths, hold each to the count of three, then exhale slowly to the count of three. This will

---

[568] Mental Health Phobias, U.S. Navy Bureau of Medicine and Surgery | Image: ic2icon, The Noun Project
[569] Rear Adm. Bruce L. Gillingham, M.D., Health.mil

f

- 198 -

help restore normal breathing, slow your pulse, and end the dizziness and shakiness.

- **Tension control:** When you panic, you tense your muscles, making them feel hard and uncomfortable. Concentrate on each muscle group (arms, legs, neck shoulders) and consciously relax them until you feel the tension subside. Practice this technique until you can relax your muscles simply by "thinking" about relaxing them

If you have a fear of speaking in public: Enroll in a public speaking course, such as Dale Carnegie or Toastmasters.

If you are afraid of flying: Take a course designed to help people conquer this fear.

What You Can Do for a Friend or Relative

Be supportive: Take their phobia seriously. A phobic person suffers an intense fear of something you most likely find harmless. Telling them they are being "silly" or "childish" will not help them. It will only serve to increase their feelings of anxiety and alienation.

Do not attempt "flooding" on your friend or relative: Forcing your friend or relative into a direct, sudden confrontation with their feared object, person or situation, etc. will only intensify their panic and physical distress. Only a trained professional should use this method.

"Doctor, Doctor!"

See a counselor if self-help does not help you deal with your phobia on your own, or if it causes you to be dependent on drugs, alcohol, or other additions.

COST-SAVINGS EXAMPLE:

Self-care for phobias and fears is typically free, and can be highly effective if you make a real commitment to using these trusted remedies on a regular basis.

Medical treatment for phobias can be expensive (though often covered by health insurance); may include drugs with serious side effects; and may turn into a lifetime commitment. Make a diligent effort to use trusted self-care remedies as long as the person's phobias and fears are not a threat to the safety of themselves or others.

Did one of these remedies help you?

Share your trusted remedies success with the publisher! We'd love to hear from you. **info@trustedremedies.com**

POISON IVY AND OAK

The leaves, vines, and roots of the poison ivy plant contain urushiol, an oil which causes an allergic reaction on your skin if you come in contact with it, explains Insider.com [570] (medically reviewed by **Sharleen St. Surin-Lord, M.D.,** [571] assistant professor of dermatology at Howard University). Poison oak and poison sumac contain the same oil, producing the same symptoms which respond to the same remedies.

About one in eight people are extremely allergic to poison ivy and should see a doctor if they touch the plant. For everyone else, medical attention is generally not needed. If you come into contact with poison ivy and have a skin reaction, the rash will show up in 12 to 48 hours and last one to three weeks. Try these trusted remedies to alleviate the itch and help the rash heal faster:

Wash the area: You may not always realize that you've come into contact with poison ivy. As soon as you suspect you have, wash the area thoroughly with soap and cold or lukewarm water. Avoid hot water, which can make your condition worse. You can also use rubbing alcohol while washing to remove urushiol from the skin or other affected areas. Also wash anything that might have contacted the plant's oil, such as your hands (including under your nails), clothing, any gear or equipment you were using, and even your pet. Once you've washed away all the urushiol, a poison ivy rash can't spread from person to person.

Soak in a bath: Taking a bath in lukewarm water can help soothe your skin. Just be sure to start with a quick shower, so you're not soaking in the same irritants you're trying to wash away.

Add oatmeal or baking soda to your bathwater: An oatmeal bath can help dry oozing blisters and soothe redness and irritation. Oatmeal has anti-inflammatory properties and can soothe inflamed skin. Soaking in an oatmeal bath for up to 30 minutes may help relieve itchiness. If you don't have oatmeal on hand, try adding a cup of baking soda to your bath.

Apply a common anti-itch cream: Over-the-counter hydrocortisone cream and calamine lotion can alleviate itching. You may have some on hand; go ahead and use them, as long as they don't have an expiration date (which is different from a best-by date). Still, for maximum effect, it may be worth picking up a fresh tube or bottle – inexpensive in supermarkets, drug stores, or online. Amazon Basics Anti-Itch Lotion Analgesic Skin Protectant, 6 fl oz, gets 4.5 out of 5 stars, has 5,329 reviews, and sells for just $4.92. [572] Hydrocortisone cream is similarly low-priced.

Baking soda paste: Until you can get your hands on some hydrocortisone cream or calamine lotion on hand, try mixing three teaspoons of baking soda with one teaspoon of water and apply the paste to the poison ivy rash. It should flake off naturally.

Cold compress: This can be as simple as wrapping a towel around a handful of ice cubes and holding it on your skin for 15 to 20 minutes. Don't put ice directly on the skin.

Aloe vera: Aloe vera gels or creams can reduce the hot, swollen skin of a poison ivy rash.

---

[570] 8 Ways To Treat Poison Ivy At Home And Relieve The Itchy Rash, Insider.com | Image: kindpng.com
[571] Dr. Sharleen St Surin-Lord, M.D., University of Maryland Medical System
[572] Amazon Basics Medicated Calamine Anti-Itch Lotion, Analgesic Skin Protectant, 6 Fluid Ounces

Oral antihistamines: These meds block the body's production of histamines, helping to stop the symptoms of your reaction, such as swelling, redness, and itchiness. Non-drowsy oral antihistamines (Zyrtec, Allegra) may be used during the day. Benadryl, which may induce drowsiness, is better for managing symptoms at night and allowing you to get better sleep.

Do Not: Do not use antihistamine creams for poison ivy, they can make it worse. Also avoid creams that contain anesthetics, like benzocaine, or antibiotics like neomycin or bacitracin, as these can further irritate the skin.

Make an aluminum acetate soak: Aluminum acetate is an astringent, which means it causes skin to contract and dry out. Find it at drugstores or on online in ready-to-use packets from brands like Domeboro (under $15 for a twelve-pack on Amazon). Simply mix according to package directions, and soak the rash directly or apply the mixture with a cloth for up to 30 minutes.

Smooth on a bentonite clay mask: Bentonite is a natural clay that is used to draw impurities out of the skin and body. It may be helpful in treating an allergic reaction from poison ivy. Buy the dry clay from health food stores and some drugstores. Molivera Organics Bentonite Clay, 16 oz. is highly rated on Amazon and sells for under $15. Mix it with water and apply the paste to your rash. Let it dry, then rinse it away with water. Before applying it to your poison ivy rash, test on a small patch of skin to make sure it won't cause more irritation.

"Doctor, Doctor!"

A poison ivy rash will usually clear up on its own, in as quickly as four hours or as long as three weeks. You should see a doctor, though, if you exhibit symptoms of a severe poison ivy allergic reaction, which can include:

- Difficulty breathing – this is an emergency, dial 9-1-1
- Fever
- Severe swelling of the afflicted area
- A rash that covers more than a quarter of your body
- The rash occurs on your face, eyes, lips, or genitals
- The rash appears infected; the blisters ooze yellow fluid or have a foul odor

Your doctor can then prescribe the best course of treatment to hinder the body's extreme allergic response or to control any infection in the skin or body.

COST-SAVINGS EXAMPLE:

The best poison ivy treatment is free: prevention. Learn to identify and avoid poison ivy, oak, and sumac; do a Google search for images of these plants, learn about where and when they grow, and teach this information to your family. Or watch and share "Mayo Clinic Minute: How to treat poison ivy rash." [573] **(Dr. Summer Allen** [574]**)**

The next best option is soap and water – it doesn't get much cheaper than that! But for

---

[573] Mayo Clinic Minute: How To Treat Poison Ivy Rash
[574] Summer V. Allen, M.D., Mayo Clinic

this to work, you must act immediately after exposure, which means paying attention in wooded areas.

Medications for poison ivy include oral corticosteroid, such as prednisone, to reduce swelling. If the rash is infected, your doctor may prescribe an oral antibiotic. These are inexpensive drugs, but by the time you get to the point of needing them, you're likely to have endured hours, days, or weeks of suffering.

Avoid the cost of medical treatment for poison ivy and along with the agony and the itch by avoiding the plant and by using these remedies as soon as exposure is suspected.

PORTUGUESE MAN O' WAR STINGS

First things first – a Portuguese man o'war is not a jellyfish. It's not related to jellyfish, it's not even correct to call it an organism. Portuguese man o'war is a floating colony composed of thousands of genetically identical organisms operating as a single individual. Still, many scientific sources will mention Portuguese man o'war and true jellyfish in the same discussion because of their similar distribution, general appearance ("blob" on top, tentacles below), and health dangers to humans.

Now that we have the biology out of the way, this is not a life form you ever want to come into physical contact with. They will hurt you. The stinging, venom-filled cysts in the tentacles of the Portuguese man o' war can paralyze small fish and other prey. Detached tentacles and dead specimens (including those that wash up on shore) can sting just as painfully as those of the live organism in the water, and may remain potent for hours or even days after the death of the organism or the detachment of the tentacle. [575]

Portuguese man o' war are among the most recognizable stinging jellies with their bright blue tentacles and colorful inflated floating sails. Strandings of bluebottles are common in Hawai'i as the onshore winds push thousands of these small, painful critters onto the beaches. Similar mass strandings are frequent with the Atlantic species too, and have been known to cause hundreds of stings in a single day on beaches from Florida to France.

Stings usually cause severe pain to humans, leaving whip-like red welts on the skin that normally last two or three days after the initial sting. The pain normally subsides after about one to three hours. However, the venom can travel to the lymph nodes and cause symptoms that mimic an allergic reaction, including swelling of the larynx, airway blockage, cardiac distress and trouble

[575] Wikipedia. Sources: "Fatal Portuguese Man-O'-War Envenomation," Annals Emergency Medicine; "Dive First Responder," By Richard A. Clinchy, Ph.D.; "Worldwide Deaths And Severe Envenomation From Jellyfish Stings," Medical Journal of Australia | Image: svgsilh.com, CC0

breathing. Other symptoms may include fever and shock and, in some extreme cases, death.

In past decades, trusted first aid resources have recommended stings from man o' war be treated differently from actual jellies, say researchers at the University of Hawai'i – Mānoa (UHM) [576]. (**Christie Wilcox, Ph.D.** [577]). But when they dug into the scientific literature, they found scant evidence to support this theory.

Rinse with vinegar to remove any residual stingers: Recent studies suggest that man o' war stings should be treated no different from true jellyfish stings; the best first aid is to rinse with vinegar to remove any residual stingers or bits of tentacle left on the skin.

Apply heat: Immerse the area in 113° F (45° C) hot water or apply a hot pack for 45 minutes.

Do Not: Seawater rinsing, once considered a remedy for man o' war stings, actually spreads stinging capsules over more areas and makes stings much worse.

Do Not: The application of ice packs also makes stings worse.

"Doctor, Doctor!"

Medical attention for those exposed to large numbers of tentacles may become necessary to relieve pain or open airways if the pain becomes excruciating or lasts for more than three hours, or if breathing becomes difficult. Instances in which the stings completely surround the trunk of a young child are among those that may be fatal (**Richard A. Clinchy, Ph.D., Chief Executive Officer at Emergency Medical Resources, LLC** [578]).

COST-SAVINGS EXAMPLE:

Considering most man o' war strings can be treated with self-care and are largely resolved within three hours, avoid a potentially huge bill from the emergency room except under the conditions described above.

In 2019, the average ER visit by an insured patient cost $1,082. Those who were uninsured spent an average of $1,220. Costs vary by state and illness, but range from $623-$3,087. These are only averages; individual bills can be much higher. [579]

You may be able to avoid an emergency room bill of up to $3,087 or even higher by treating Portuguese man o' war stings with trusted self-care remedies. Save the ER for actual emergencies.

---

[576] "Scientists scrutinize first aid for man o' war stings," School of Ocean and Earth Science and Technology at the University of Hawai'i at Mānoa
[577] Christie Wilcox, Ph.D.
[578] Richard A. Clinchy, Ph.D., Emergency Medical Resources, Facebook
[579] How Much Does an ER Visit Cost in 2022? What to Know, by Latifa deGraft-Johnson, M.D., K-Health

PMS – PREMENSTRUAL SYNDROME

As your hormones rise and fall during your menstrual cycle, you may experience a variety of emotional and physical symptoms, say the women's health experts at Rose Wellness Center for Integrative Medicine of Oakton, VA [580] (**Andrew David Shiller, M.D., Integrative Medicine Physician** [581]).

These symptoms include bloating, breast tenderness, abdominal pain, change in appetite, fatigue, mood swings, and even anxiety and depression – all signs of premenstrual syndrome or PMS, says Rose Wellness. If you are suffering from PMS, there are several trusted remedies that can help relieve or eliminate your symptoms:

Acupuncture: Acupuncture reduces pain and inflammation, improves circulation, relieves anxiety and stress, and regulates your cycle. Acupuncture has been shown to relieve cramps better than non-steroidal anti-inflammatory drugs (ibuprofen, aspirin, naproxen, etc.), and has also been shown to help regulate menstrual cycles and prevent heavy and prolonged bleeding.

Aromatherapy: Aromatherapy is the practice of inhaling the aroma of essential oils. The practice can help reduce stress levels, relieve menstrual pain, and improve your sleep naturally. Some favorite essential oils for PMS include:

- Chamomile – used for centuries to promote relaxation and sleep.
- Clary sage – can help relieve stress and ease menstrual cramps.
- Lavender – promotes relaxation and a good night's sleep.
- Rose – the calming scent can help relieve PMS and reduce stress.

Calcium: Many women who do not get in the recommended daily amount of calcium experience PMS symptoms. Calcium supplements may help relieve fatigue, bloating, anxiety, and mood swings caused by PMS. For best results, consume at least four servings of calcium rich foods like milk, fortified orange juice, yogurt, spinach, dairy products, or green leafy vegetables each day.

Chaste Berry: Multiple studies support the effectiveness of chaste berry for PMS, including both physical and psychological symptoms. Before taking chaste berry, consult a doctor as chaste berry may interact with certain medications, says Rose Wellness.

Diet: Foods high in salt can contribute to bloating. Refined carbs and sugary foods can cause significant blood sugar fluctuations, which can worsen mood swings and fatigue levels. Finally, high fat foods and red meats can increase the severity of abdominal cramping and back pain. To help combat PMS symptoms, eat small meals frequently, opt for complex carbs, and choose healthy vegetables and fruits. Finally, avoid eating sweet or salty snacks, limit your alcohol consumption, and avoid consuming excess caffeine to reduce the risk of PMS symptoms.

Exercise: When you are bloated, depressed, in pain, and suffering from the many other symptoms of PMS, the last thing on your mind is exercise; however, regular exercise can help improve the symptoms of PMS naturally. Try to get at least 30 minutes of exercise each day to help boost your mood, improve your sleep, and enhance your energy levels. Regular exercise increases the release

---

[580] Natural Remedies for PMS, Rose Wellness, Oakton, VA | Image: Olena Panasovska, The Noun Project
[581] Andrew David Shiller, M.D., Integrative Medicine Physician, Rose Wellness

of dopamine, serotonin, and endorphins, which helps relieve many of the symptoms of PMS, says Rose Wellness.

Ginkgo Biloba: Many people know that Ginkgo biloba can help improve memory; however, this herb can also relieve many PMS symptoms. Ginkgo biloba can help reduce inflammation in the body, soothe achy muscles, regulate the mood, reduce bloating, prevent weight gain, ease anxiety, and boost circulation. It may also help relieve brain fog and fatigue caused by PMS.

Magnesium: Women who have low levels of magnesium are at an increased risk of suffering from PMS. Magnesium rich foods include peanuts, almonds, and green leafy vegetables. Magnesium has been shown to ease a plethora of unpleasant PMS symptoms, including headache, water retention, anxiety, depression, breast tenderness, and insomnia.

Massage: Massage is a hands-on approach that relieves PMS symptoms. Massage helps to reduce the stress hormone cortisol to improve the mood, release natural endorphins to reduce cramping, and relax your body to counteract the effects of PMS on the body. Furthermore, massage therapy can reduce bloating and water retention by its ability to increase circulation. It can also help regulate your mood and improve skin health, which can help reduce acne outbreaks and other skin issues, says Rose Wellness.

Sleep: If you are not getting between 7 and 9 hours of sleep each night, a lack of sleep could be causing many of your symptoms. Insomnia can increase the risk of fatigue, irritability, depression, and anxiety. Practicing good sleep hygiene that includes going to bed at the same time, avoiding naps, turning all electronics off a couple of hours before bedtime, dropping your bedroom temperature a few degrees, and participating in relaxing activities like reading before bedtime can help you get a full night's sleep and minimize the symptoms of PMS.

St. John's Wort: This powerful herb that can affect norepinephrine and serotonin in the brain. When St. John's wort is taken for PMS, it can relieve your mood swings, including depression and anxiety. In addition to this, St. John's wort can help relieve the pain associated with PMS thanks to its ability to reduce the number of proinflammatory cytokines in the body.

Stress Management: When you are experiencing the symptoms of PMS, your stress levels can increase significantly. Stress management is designed to promote relaxation and reduce your stress naturally. Some of the most common stress management tools are meditation, deep breathing exercises, journaling, prayer, and yoga. These stress management techniques are designed to help you relax, embrace your emotions, and reduce the symptoms of PMS.

Vitamin B-6: This potent, water-soluble vitamin is used in the production of the body's neuro-transmitters. This vitamin can be found in organ meats, starchy veggies like potatoes, chickpeas, and fish like tuna and salmon. Vitamin B6 may help relieve anxiety, depression, irritability, and moodiness. Vitamin B-6 cannot be stored by the body; therefore, ensure you are getting enough of this vitamin from your diet, says Rose Wellness.

Vitamin D: The body uses vitamin D to help improve calcium absorption and regulate calcium metabolism from calcium rich foods. Although vitamin D in and of itself does not help reduce the risk of PMS symptoms, it helps relieve specific menstrual symptoms, including breast tenderness, constipation, depression, diarrhea, and fatigue.

"Doctor, Doctor!"

Menstruation is not a disease or a disorder; in fact, it's a sign of health. However, if you are experiencing symptoms of PMS, your doctor can help. Many of today's therapies utilize a holistic approach to help relieve the symptoms of PMS.

COST-SAVINGS EXAMPLE:

The largest cost of PMS may be lost productivity and missed work days. No one wants to give up well-earned vacation and personal days to deal with PMS. At $15 an hour, a lost day's wages comes to $120. A typical woman's salary is $52,000 a year; miss a week's work over the course of a year and you may be out $1,000.

Save $1,000 or more per year in lost productivity by using trusted self-care remedies to take charge of your PMS symptoms.

PROSTATE PROBLEMS

For such a small gland (about the size and shape of a walnut), the prostate can be quite a troublemaker, says bensnaturalhealth.com [582] (**Ahmed Zayed, M.D.** [583]). The most common prostate troubles are enlarged prostate, prostatitis, and prostate cancer. Let's take a brief look at each.

Enlarged prostate (BPH) –Your risk for getting BPH increases with age, says Dr. Zayed. When you don't take care of the enlarged prostate with adequate treatment, you can have troubling symptoms like the sudden inability to get normal urine flow. This may result in kidney or bladder damage, as well as susceptibility to urinary tract infections.

Prostatitis – Prostatitis, the inflammation of the prostate, may be caused by infection, injury, or an immune disorder. Symptoms may include pain in the genitals, pelvic area, or groin. Prostatitis can obstruct urine flow. If left untreated, acute prostatitis can lead to infertility, semen abnormalities, inability to urinate, and bacteria in the blood. With chronic bacterial prostatitis, symptoms are less intense, but can still lead to urinary tract infections, says Dr. Zayed.

Prostate cancer – Roughly 1 in 8 men are estimated to be diagnosed with prostate cancer in their lifetime. Symptoms include urinary hesitancy, trouble with urine flow, urgency, and blood in semen or urine. Many men also feel as though they can't empty their bladder completely. Some lose their sex drive after prostate cancer, or face erectile dysfunction after chemo or other cancer treatment. Even the diagnosis itself can feel devastating and force your sexual desire to plummet.

Doctors often recommend healthy lifestyle changes, supplements, and physical activity to keep

---

[582] 11 Home Remedies for Prostate Issues That Are Side Effect Free, bensnaturalhealth.com
[583] Dr. Ahmed Zayed, bensnaturalhealth.com | Image: onlinewebfonts.com

the prostate in good condition. Dr. Zayed recommends these trusted self-care remedies:

Take a warm bath or shower: A hot bath can temporarily relieve prostatitis symptoms. In comparison, cold creates the exact opposite effect.

Skip spicy meals: Spicy foods make spicy urine, aggravating your bladder and prostatitis symptoms. Skip or limit the use of hot peppers and pepper-based sauces and condiments.

Drink more caffeine-free fluid: The solution to pollution is dilution. When you drink 6 to 8 glasses of water a day, you help the urinary pathways flush out all the toxins. In comparison, caffeinated drinks irritate the bladder and make urination worse. In the case of an overactive bladder, you will know you are drinking enough if the urine is almost colorless.

Avoid alcohol for some time: Ethanol can make it difficult for the prostate muscle to relax, further irritating BPH symptoms.

Take a comfortable sitting position on a cushion: When you sit on a hard surface for a very long time, you can put a lot of pressure on the prostate. It's best to stand up when you can. But, if you need to sit for a while, then use a comfy cushion to reduce that pressure.

Drop activities that create a lot of strain on the prostate: This includes cycling, squatting, and climbing. Cycling can worsen BPH symptoms, chronic prostatitis, and erectile dysfunction; if you are a cyclist, opt for a seat that puts the pressure on your thighs, not the area between them.

Pygeum: Studies show that the Pygeum africanum could be a practical treatment for men with BPH. Men who took it were twice as likely to notice an improvement in overall BPH symptoms.

Saw Palmetto: Capsules with saw palmetto extract are one of the best natural remedies for enlarged prostate. Data shows that saw palmetto may have a similar effect to finasteride, a medicine for BPH, but it is better tolerated and much cheaper, according to Dr. Zayed.

Stinging nettle: This is another of the most trusted remedies for enlarged prostate. It is packed with anti-inflammatory and antioxidant components. The root can diminish the size of the prostate and curb some of the urinary incontinence. That's why it is sometimes used together with saw palmetto. But, more studies are necessary to evaluate its full impact on prostate health.

Ryegrass pollen extract: Many men use this extract to ease prostate symptoms. They report not having to get up as often at night; more research is needed to fully evaluate its effect.

Green tea: If you're cutting back on alcohol and caffeine, consider the benefits of green tea. Experts say that polyphenols in green tea promote prostate health and could even slow prostate cancer.

"Doctor, Doctor!"

Don't wait until you can't urinate comfortably to speak with your doctor about prostate health. It's definitely a topic to bring up at your next check-up. Since Dr. Zayed describes the above remedies as side effect-free, why not incorporate some of them into your lifestyle *before* any problems begin. But if you are experiencing pain in the area or are having difficulty urinating, call your doctor right away. The earlier you are diagnosed, the sooner you can begin treatment and the better your options in most cases.

COST-SAVINGS EXAMPLE:

These trusted remedies are very inexpensive. It's not really necessary to put a dollar figure on the impact that prostate problems can have on a man's urinary or sexual health – these are trouble spots you want to avoid at all costs.

Save yourself some nightly bathroom trips, your sexual health, and possibly even your life by taking full advantage of trusted self-care remedies plus regular medical check-ups for your prostate health.

PSORIASIS

People are successfully using self-care for temporary relief of psoriasis, says psoriasis.com [584] (**Thomas J. Hudson, M.D.,** Senior Vice President, R&D, and Chief Scientific Officer [585]). These home shampoos and salves may help to temporarily relieve symptoms. These trusted remedies are not meant to substitute for your prescribed treatment plan.

Some herbal remedies may cause dangerous interactions with your medications. So, before taking any home remedies for your psoriasis, speak with your doctor. Here are five of the most trusted solutions from psoriasis.com:

Apple cider vinegar: Apple cider vinegar may be used to help relieve the symptoms of psoriasis, says psoriasis.com. Try applying it to your scalp several times a week. If it burns, you can dilute it with a 1:1 ratio of water. Be careful not to apply apple cider vinegar to open wounds. It might burn. Some people even add a cup of apple cider vinegar to a warm bath for all-over relief. If you want to use it as a compress, soak a washcloth in a solution of 1 part vinegar to 3 parts warm water and apply to your skin for at least 1 minute. Test a small area first.

Aloe vera: It's no surprise that aloe vera makes our list for its soothing characteristics. Aloe vera is a type of succulent with gel-filled leaves that may have a soothing effect and improve hydration. That's why applying pure aloe vera gel could be beneficial in helping your psoriasis symptoms temporarily, psoriasis.com explains.

Oats: Oats have long been considered a safe way to soothe irritated skin. You might have heard of people taking oatmeal baths for chicken pox, and the same philosophy applies here. You'll want to use colloidal oatmeal, which is ground into a fine powder, to avoid clogging your drain. Try adding half a cup at a time to your bath until you find the right consistency. You can even apply it as a salve if you don't want to take a full bath.

Tea tree oil: It's all-natural, antibacterial, AND antifungal. This multipurpose solution can be mixed with water and applied to the skin overnight, added to a warm bath, or even mixed with

[584] Natural & Home Remedies for Psoriasis, psoriasis.com
[585] Thomas Hudson, M.D, AbbVie

shampoo. A little goes a long way, so make sure not to add too much.

Epsom salts: Epsom salt is a naturally occurring mineral made up of magnesium and sulfate. While that may sound intense, these minerals can be beneficial to your body, and even reduce irritation and inflammation in some cases. You can find Epsom salts in any grocery store. Try adding them to a warm bath and soaking in the soothing qualities.

These are just a few of the many self-care remedies out there for psoriasis symptoms, but not all are guaranteed to work for you, reminds psoriasis.com. Remember, these alternatives only address the symptoms of your psoriasis and not the cause.

"Doctor, Doctor!"

It is important to talk to your doctor about the management and treatment of your psoriasis. While self-care remedies have been shown to offer temporary relief, they shouldn't take the place of your treatment plan. [586]

COST-SAVINGS EXAMPLE:

These trusted remedies are very inexpensive. If they delay or reduce your need for more advanced psoriasis treatment, that could be money in your pocket. Still, like most conditions, early diagnosis and early treatment is better than late diagnosis and late treatment.

RASHES

Itchy skin has many causes, says the American Academy of Dermatology Association [587] (**Mark D. Kaufmann, M.D.**, president [588]). It may be the result of a skin condition, like eczema, shingles, hives, or psoriasis (each covered in its own section of this directory), or it could be a sign of a contagious disease, like scabies or ringworm. Dermatologists trust these remedies to soothe itchy skin:

Apply a cold, wet cloth or ice pack: The itch should subside in 5-10 minutes.

Take an oatmeal bath: This can be very soothing, especially for blisters or oozing skin due to chickenpox, hives, poison ivy or sunburn.

Moisturize your skin: Always choose a moisturizer free of additives, fragrances and perfumes.

Apply topical anesthetics that contain pramoxine: this over-the-counter product is sold under the brand names Aveeno Anti-Itch Cream and CeraVe Itch Relief Moisturizing Lotion.

Apply cooling agents, such as menthol or calamine. You could also place your moisturizer in

---

586 Psoriasis.com
587 How To Relieve Itchy Skin, American Academy of Dermatology Association, aad.org
588 Mark Kaufmann, M.D., Advanced Dermatology, Fort Lauderdale, FL | Image: The Icon Z, Noun Project

the refrigerator to help achieve this cooling effect.

Avoid scratching: scratching further irritates your skin and may increase your risk of infection.

To help prevent itching, AADA recommend the following trusted remedies:

Bathe with lukewarm – not hot – water: Try to limit your bath or shower to just 10 minutes.

Use "fragrance-free" lotions, soaps and detergents only: Be wary of products labeled "unscented," as they might still have chemicals that can irritate your skin.

As directed by your dermatologist, apply medications before moisturizing. Then, apply your moisturizer to all areas of your skin, including areas treated with medication.

Wear loose-fitting, cotton clothes: Wool and other rough-feeling fabrics can irritate your skin, causing intense itching.

Avoid extreme temperature changes: Maintain a relatively cool, neutral humidity environment in your house. Use a humidifier during winter if you are prone to dry skin and eczema.

Reduce stress: stress makes a lot of conditions worse, including your itch.

"Doctor, Doctor!"

If your itch does not go away with home treatment, see a board-certified dermatologist. Some people have more than one reason to scratch, and a dermatologist can work with you to find the cause and relieve your itching.

COST-SAVINGS EXAMPLE:

Many drugs are used to treat skin rash. Some may be expensive even with insurance, and many can cause unwanted side effects. GoodRx lists 71 drugs for skin rash; eight are priced between $500 - $5,000, while one is listed "as low as $5,741." [589]

Save yourself a trip to the dermatologist and the potential cost and side effects of Rx; trying these trusted remedies first.

Remember that throughout this directory you can find further information by using the sources at the bottom of every page and in the resources listing beginning on page 259.

---

[589] Skin Allergy Medications, goodrx.com

RAYNAUD'S SYNDROME

Raynaud's phenomenon, also called Raynaud's syndrome or disease, happens when blood vessels in the fingers and toes – and sometimes in the earlobes, nose, and lips – narrow and cause the skin to turn pale or patchy red to blue, says St. Louis-area St. Luke's Hospital [590] (**Lawrence Samuels, M.D., Chief of Dermatology** [591]). The affected body part may feel numb and cold.

Episodes are usually triggered by cold or stress. They come and go and may last minutes or hours, says St. Luke's. Women are much more likely than men to have the condition. It usually happens between ages 20 to 40 in women and later in life in men. When it happens by itself, it's called primary Raynaud's. It can also happen along with other conditions, such as scleroderma, lupus, and rheumatoid arthritis. In those cases, it's called secondary Raynaud's. These trusted remedies may help reduce or manage flare-ups:

Omega-3 fatty acids: Found in fish oil, Omega-3s may reduce symptoms in people with primary Raynaud's; it did not help in people who had secondary Raynaud's. High doses of fish oil can increase your risk of bleeding, so ask your doctor before taking it, says St. Luke's.

Evening primrose oil (EPO): EPO contains another type of fatty acid that stops the body from making chemicals that narrow blood vessels. People with a history of seizures should not take EPO. Ask your doctor before taking it, especially if you already take blood thinners.

Niacin: One specific form of niacin, vitamin B_3, may reduce the frequency of Raynaud's attacks. Inositol hexaniacinate (sometimes called inositol hexanicotinate) is a natural compound with a proven beneficial effect of widening of blood vessels, which improves blood flow in conditions where it is compromised, says **Dr. Tomislav Mestrovic, M.D., Ph.D.**, a researcher with the University of Washington School of Medicine [592]. In Europe, the vitamin is often prescribed for relief of Raynaud's symptoms. Ask your doctor to determine the right dose for you; a common dose is 3 grams per day. Find it on Amazon as Nature's Bounty Niacin 500 mg Flush Free.

Magnesium: Some doctors suggest taking a magnesium supplement, says St. Luke's. Take with meals and reduce dose if diarrhea occurs. Magnesium can interact with some medications, so ask your doctor before taking it.

Herbs: Herbs are known to tone the body's systems. As with any therapy, work with your doctor to diagnose your problem before starting treatment. You may use herbs as dried extracts (teas, capsules, or powders), glycerine extracts, or tinctures (alcohol extracts). Unless otherwise indicated, make teas with 1 tsp herb per cup of hot water. Steep covered 5 to 10 minutes for leaf or flowers, and 10 to 20 minutes for roots. Drink 2 - 4 cups a day. You may use tinctures alone or in combination. Tell your doctor if you are pregnant or nursing before taking any herbs.

Ginkgo: Ginkgo may improve circulation in the fingers. Ginkgo can interact with herbs and medications, and can increase your risk of bleeding, so talk to your doctor before taking it. Don't take it if you have a history of seizures. There's also some concern linking ginkgo to infertility.

---

[590] Raynaud's Phenomenon, Complementary and Alternative Medicine, St. Luke's Hospital, St. Louis, MO
[591] Dr. Lawrence Samuels, Dermatology & Cosmetic Medicine, saintlouisderm.com
[592] Tomislav Meštrović, M.D. | Image: Vector Bakery, The Noun Project

Acupuncture: Although no major studies have looked at acupuncture to treat Raynaud's syndrome, some people may find that acupuncture increases blood flow and decreases pain.

Mind-body medicine: Although there have not yet been any clinical trials, some people with Raynaud's say they have used guided imagery to reduce symptoms. More research is needed.

Note that according to the Raynaud's Association, Inc. while some Raynaud's sufferers may have had a positive experience with some of these remedies, there's no clinical proof that any of these options will improve Raynaud's symptoms [593] (**Maureen D. Mayes, M.D., M.P.H.** Medical Advisor [594]). So it's really a matter of trying these remedies and seeing if they help you.

Self-heating gloves and socks: The Raynaud's Association recommends and sells self-heating gloves and socks made with a special inner liner fabric. The design uses a combination of hi-tech fibers that work together in a patent-pending process to power a unique self-heating capability when interacting with the wearer's skin. It's important to put them on before cold exposure and to avoid getting them wet. [595] Other trusted remedies come from Mayo Clinic: [596]

Avoid smoke: Smoking or inhaling secondhand smoke causes skin temperature to drop by tightening blood vessels, which can lead to an attack.

Exercise: Exercise can increase circulation, among other health benefits. If you have secondary Raynaud's, talk to your doctor before exercising outdoors in the cold.

Control stress: Learn to recognize and avoid stressful situations to reduce the number of attacks.

Avoid rapidly changing temperatures: Try not to move from a hot environment to an air-conditioned room. If possible, avoid frozen-food sections of grocery stores.

"Doctor, Doctor!"

Be sure to tell your doctor about any herbs, supplements, or home therapies you are using, says St. Luke's. Some alternative therapies can interfere with conventional medical therapies. Work with a doctor who is experienced in alternative therapies to find the combination of treatments that is right for you. Depending on the cause of your symptoms, medications, surgery or injections might help, says Mayo Clinic. If your symptoms don't respond adequately to trusted self-care remedies, consult a doctor. [597]

COST-SAVINGS EXAMPLE:

Members of The Raynaud's Association get discounts on self-heating gloves and socks and other products. It's free to join the association. [598]

---

[593] Natural Remedies for Raynaud's Lack Scientific Support, The Raynaud's Association, raynauds.org
[594] Dr. Maureen D. Mayes, M.D., Rheumatologist, Houston, TX, US News Doctors
[595] FibreHeat™ Self-Heating Gloves, Raynaud's Association, raynauds.org
[596] Raynaud's disease, Diagnosis and treatment, Mayo Clinic
[597] Appointments at Mayo Clinic
[598] Become A Member & Profile Update, Raynaud's Association, raynauds.org

RECTAL ITCH AND ANAL FISSURES

 Yes, we're going to go there – to one of those itches you simply can't scratch in public – because having this problem is maddening and embarrassing, and you just want to know how (asking for a friend) to make it go away. UPMC Susquehanna (formerly University of Pittsburgh Medical Center, **Jasneet Bhullar, M.D.**, [599] colorectal surgery) explains:

A fissure most commonly occurs after an episode of constipation, but it can happen after an attack of diarrhea. A fissure begins on the surface and usually heals rapidly on its own. Fissures may deepen to reach the underlying sphincter muscle (the muscle around the anal canal).

It is not completely understood why some fissures heal and others do not. One major factor is persistent constipation or diarrhea, which can prevent healing. In addition, each time stool passes, the muscle goes into spasm, tightening the anal canal. If the sphincter muscle does not relax and the anal canal remains too tight, the fissure opens again with each bowel movement. [600]

We get that you don't actually want to read another word about this topic; you just want the symptoms to go away – the pain, rectal bleeding, and most of all, the itch. UPMC suggests:

Dietary fiber: Most superficial fissures heal without treatment, but some become chronic and cause ongoing discomfort. The first step is to correct the constipation or diarrhea and treat any underlying disease. A high-fiber diet or dietary bulk agent with plenty of fluids is recommended.

A topical anesthetic ointment may help relieve the pain. You can also relieve the spasms by sitting in a warm bath several times a day. These measures usually result in healing. If they do not, surgery may be required. Your doctor will discuss this with you.

If constipation is a problem, eat foods high in fiber. Drink 8 to 10 glasses of fluid that do not contain caffeine or alcohol. Your doctor may recommend a commercially available natural fiber product to increase your fiber intake.

If symptoms do recur, take warm baths. This will help to reduce the spasms and lessen the pain. If your doctor recommends an ointment, apply it directly to the painful area.

Mayo Clinic (**Darrell S. Pardi, M.D.**, chair, Division of Gastroenterology and Hepatology [601]) recommends these self-care measures for anal itching: [602]

Cleanse gently: Clean the area around the anus with plain water or mild soap and a soft (non-terry) washcloth once daily. Avoid scrubbing. Pat dry or use a hairdryer set on low. If you have fecal incontinence or diarrhea, clean the area with moist cotton balls or a squirt bottle of plain water. It may also help to apply a moistened or dry cotton ball to the outside of the anus.

Don't scratch: Scratching further irritates your skin. You may find relief by applying a moist, room-temperature compress to the area or taking a lukewarm oatmeal bath. Trim your nails short

[599] Jasneet Bhullar, M.D., cornerstonemedgroup.com
[600] Anal Fissures, susquehannahealth.org
[601] Darrell S. Pardi, M.D., Mayo Clinic
[602] Gastroenterology and Hepatology, mayoclinic.org

and wear cotton gloves while you're sleeping to help prevent scratching.

Wear white cotton underwear that doesn't bind: This helps keep the area dry. Avoid wearing pantyhose and other tight-fitting garments because these can trap moisture.

Avoid irritants: Avoid bubble baths, genital deodorants, harsh or perfumed soaps, and moist wipes. Use white, unscented toilet paper.

Change your diet: Cut back on or avoid coffee, cola, alcohol, citrus fruits, chocolate, spicy foods, tomatoes, and foods that may cause diarrhea. Avoid overuse of laxatives.

Apply ointments or gels: Protect the affected skin from moisture by applying a thin layer of a zinc oxide ointment (Desitin, Balmex) or petroleum jelly (Vaseline). If needed, apply hydrocortisone 1% cream 2-3 times a day for a brief period to relieve symptoms.

Maintain regular, firm bowel movements: If soft stools or frequent bowel movements are a problem, gradually adding fiber to your diet may help. Fiber supplements such as psyllium (Metamucil) and methylcellulose (Citrucel) also may help. [603]

"Doctor, Doctor!"

Call a doctor about your anal fissures and itching if pain or itching is severe or lasts over 3 days, you think you need to be seen, or you get worse, says MedNow Clinics (**Nathan Moore, M.D.**, President/CEO [604]).

COST-SAVINGS EXAMPLE:

Petroleum jelly is cheap, cleanliness is free, and both can make a significant difference. Combining these two remedies may allow the area to heal on its own.

The estimated national average cost for anal fissure removal (fistulectomy) is $9,248. While insurance may pay for this, the mere thought of this procedure is likely enough to encourage you to explore all possible self-care options. [605]

Potential savings: $9,000 or more

Remember that throughout this directory you can find further information by using the sources at the bottom of every page and in the resources listing beginning on page 259.

---

[603] Anal itching, mayoclinic.org
[604] Dr. Nathan Moore, mednowclinics.com; Rectal Symptoms, mednowclinics.com
[605] Anal Fissure Removal, mdsave.com

RESTLESS LEGS

 Restless leg syndrome (RLS) is the irresistible urge to move your legs in an effort to relieve uncomfortable sensations, says Missouri Vein Specialists of Kansas City, MO. [606] (**Scott Darling, D.O.,** American Board of Venous and Lymphatic Medicine [607]). Symptoms can intensify after you've been lying down or sitting for an extended period of time, so they tend to worsen at night as you're trying to sleep. Several medical options are available for treating restless leg syndrome, but you can also try trusted self-care remedies, says Dr. Darling, and hopefully get a good night's sleep.

Dark leafy greens: Studies suggest that eating iron-rich food and taking iron supplements may reduce RLS symptoms. Try adding plenty of dark leafy greens to your diet – spinach, kale, collard greens, and beet greens. You may also want to pair your green leafy veggies with fruits that are high in vitamin C, such as citrus and berries, since vitamin C improves iron absorption. Ask your vein doctor how much iron you should take if supplements are recommended for you.

Dark chocolate and nuts : Evidence also suggests that a dopamine imbalance could contribute to restless leg syndrome. Dopamine is a brain chemical that is responsible for smooth and purposeful muscle movement, so a lack of dopamine may affect control in your leg muscles. To help with dopamine balance, enjoy eating dark chocolate and nuts like almonds and walnuts.

Try massage and compression therapy: Some studies show that restless leg syndrome may be linked to poor blood circulation. Getting a massage can help to promote blood flow and release muscle tension, easing RLS symptoms. Massage therapy can also relieve some stress and make it easier for you to fall asleep and stay asleep. Similarly, wearing compression socks or compression stockings can foster proper blood flow in the legs.

Exercise: Staying active can provide relief from RLS symptoms, so try to get about 30-60 minutes of exercise per day, Dr. Darling recommends. Keep the intensity low, as you don't want to push your body too hard – since it may worsen your restless leg syndrome. Stick to no- and low-impact activities like swimming and walking, and be sure to include gentle stretching.

"Doctor, Doctor!"

While natural remedies can help to ease the symptoms of restless leg syndrome, it may be necessary to visit a medical professional for treatment that works for you. A board certified vein specialist can diagnose and treat circulatory conditions and craft an effective treatment plan to tamp down your RLS symptoms. [608]

COST-SAVINGS EXAMPLE:

Trusted self-care remedies for rest leg syndrome are inexpensive. As for prescription medications, GoodRx lists five options for restless leg syndrome, starting at just $8 per prescription, but going as high as $142, $449, or $754 for a 30-day supply.

---

[606] Natural Remedies for Restless Leg Syndrome, Missouri Vein Specialists, Liberty, MO
[607] Dr. Scott Darling, Vein Doctor in Kansas City and Marshall, MO | Image: Nicole, The Noun Project
[608] Contact Us | Vein Doctor, Kansas City, Liberty & Marshall, MO & Leavenworth, KS

Delay or avoid the need for drugs costing as much as $9,048 per year by controlling restless leg syndrome with physician-trusted remedies.

ROSACEA

 Many people are affected by rosacea, an inflammatory skin condition that results in facial flushing, itching and small pimple-like bumps, says **Dr. Leslie Baumann, M.D.** [609] of Baumann Cosmetic and Research Institute, Miami, FL [610]. So it's no surprise there are so many "tips and tricks" on the internet claiming to alleviate symptoms. What you really need are *trusted, physician-approved remedies* for your health concerns, and Dr. Baumann has shared hers for rosacea:

Identify and avoid triggers: It can be helpful to determine and avoid the triggers that tend to cause your rosacea flare-ups. Some of the most common triggers include very hot or cold temperatures, exercise, sun exposure, spicy foods and alcohol.

Anti-inflammatory foods: Adding anti-inflammatory foods like flaxseed oil, nuts, and seeds to your diet may help to calm redness and flushing.

Essential oils: Tea tree oil, sage oil, and peppermint oil have gained attention as rosacea remedies, says Dr. Baumann, because they may reduce the number of Demodex on your skin. Demodex is a species of microscopic mite that is naturally present on human skin, whether you have rosacea or not. In most cases, Demodex is harmless and may even be beneficial. However, many people with rosacea have greater numbers of this mite. If you are thinking about trying essential oils to help reduce inflammation caused by mites, ask your dermatologist first.

"Doctor, Doctor!"

Rosacea is *not* a purely cosmetic condition. It has been linked with a higher risk for heart disease, certain cancers, and gastrointestinal disorders. For these reasons, it is important to see a doctor and get rosacea under control. While it can be tempting to try the latest natural remedies for conditions like rosacea, see a dermatologist for an accurate diagnosis and professional treatment recommendations.

COST-SAVINGS EXAMPLE:

Self-care remedies for rosacea are very inexpensive and may help in the management of your symptoms. But since the condition is linked to heart disease and cancer, at least having an initial consultation with a dermatologist is probably wise.

---

[609] Dr. Leslie Baumann | Image: Adrien Coquet, The Noun Project
[610] Baumann Cosmetic Dermatology, Miami, FL

S-T-U

SCARS

It is possible to assist in your body's healing of scars or unwanted marks, says **Dr. Nathan Brought, D.O.,** [611] of Southern Plastic & Reconstructive Surgical Institute in Franklin, TN. [612] Here are some self-care remedies he trusts to help heal scars without surgery:

Aloe Vera: Pull back the dark green skin of an aloe leaf or purchase a topical gel. Gently apply the clear gel to scars twice a day in a soft, circular motion. Rinse off the gel after about 30 minutes with cool water.

Vitamin E: Pour a vitamin E capsule over a scar and massage for several minutes. Wash off the oil and repeat this process multiple times a day.

Apple cider vinegar: Make a solution by combining a few tablespoons of distilled water with one tablespoon of apple cider vinegar. Dip a cotton ball into the solution and place it on top of your scar. Cover the cotton ball with a Band-Aid or piece of medical tape to hold it in place. Wash off the solution after a few minutes, and be sure to moisturize to replenish the skin.

Lavender essential oil: Place three drops of lavender essential oil into about three tablespoons of extra-virgin olive oil, says Dr. Nathan Brought. Massage this mixture on the scar for five minutes. Leave the oil in place for thirty minutes and rinse.

Honey: Spread honey on the scar and cover with a Band-Aid overnight. Wash off the scar in the morning and repeat nightly.

Coconut oil: Heat the oil slightly so it melts. Massage the scar with oil for 10 minutes and rinse.

Lemon/lime juice: Place lemon or lime juice on the scar with a cloth. Let this sit for a few minutes on the skin before washing it off. The acidic qualities of the juice help remove dead skin cells along the scar and can lessen the redness or appearance of scars.

Drink water: Drinking plenty of water promotes hydrated and healthy skin. Be sure you are drinking plenty of water each day to assist these self-care remedies in the healing of your scars.

"Doctor, Doctor!"

If these remedies aren't producing the results you hoped for, it's time to consider your options. Ask yourself what difference it will make in your life to reduce the appearance of your scars, and what cost you are willing to bear. It may be that your scars are not as

---

[611] Dr. Nathan Brought, Plastic Surgeon, sprsi.com | Image: José Manuel de Laá, The Noun Project
[612] 8 Natural Remedies for Scar Removal, Southern Plastic & Reconstructive Surgical Institute, sprsi.com

noticeable or concerning to others as they are to you. Of course, if your scars are truly disfiguring or greatly affect your self-confidence, then consult a dermatologist. A doctor can evaluate your individual situation and help you select the best treatment options.

COST-SAVINGS EXAMPLE:

Dermatology care can be expensive. For example, Dermal fillers for acne scar treatment can cost $570 - $900 per treatment. A chemical facial peel for acne scars can be $400, while laser skin resurfacing may cost more than $1,400. The cost of laser treatment can range from $200 to $3,400. [613]

Be sure to discuss with your doctor whether procedures you are considering are deemed medically necessary, meaning they'll be covered by insurance, or purely cosmetic, which may mean you'll have to pay out of pocket.

If your scars are purely cosmetic, consider whether you would rather save thousands of dollars by using self-care remedies and working toward being more accepting of your condition. But if the expense is worth it to you, today's treatment options are better than ever before.

SCIATICA

Sciatica is low back pain that radiates downward from the buttock into the leg, sometimes all the way to the foot, says **Neel Anand, M.D.** [614] of Spine Universe. [615] In some cases, the pain can be excruciating; even so, sciatica often goes away within 3 months with trusted remedies you can do at home.

The self-care remedies below are good options for people who recently started experiencing sciatic nerve pain or whose pain is not severe, but Dr. Anand still urges people to get a doctor's approval before trying any of these remedies.

It's okay to exercise: It may feel unnatural to exercise when you're in pain, but research suggests that resting too much can aggravate your back and leg symptoms, says Dr. Anand. Instead of total rest, incorporate gentle exercise into your day to ease your sciatica. A walk around the block is an ideal way to keep your spine strong without doing any additional damage. Exercise also triggers the release of endorphins to reduce your perception of pain.

Stretch It Out: Add gentle stretching to your daily routine. Stretching is a great way to improve spine flexibility and range of motion, while also building core and spine strength. Most stretches

---

[613] Acne Scar Treatment, AEDIT; Laser Scar Removal, Goodrx; Laser Treatment For Scars, Healthline
[614] Dr. Neel Anand, Cedars-Sinai Spine Center, spineuniverse.com | Image: Langtik, The Noun Project
[615] Sciatica Self-care: 5 At-home Remedies for Low Back and Leg Pain, spineuniverse.com

are simple enough to be done while watching the news or the ballgame.

Grab the ice pack and heating pad: Alternating heat and ice can provide fast relief of sciatic nerve pain, Dr. Anand advises. Ice helps reduce inflammation, while heat encourages blood flow to the painful area to speed healing. Heat and ice may also help ease painful muscle spasms that often accompany sciatica. Apply an ice pack to the painful area for 15 minutes once every hour, and then apply heat for 15 minutes every 2 or 3 hours. Always use a barrier (like a towel) to protect your skin when using heat or ice, and never sleep while using heat or ice therapy.

Refresh Your Posture: Whether you are working at your desk or relaxing at home, staying in one position for too long may spike your sciatica. Vary your posture every 20 minutes and use proper posture to help take pressure off your spine and reduce your sciatica symptoms.

Over-the-counter non-steroidal anti-inflammatory drugs: OTC NSAIDs may help ease sciatica symptoms when they strike. NSAIDs can be a good option because they relieve both inflammation and pain, unlike acetaminophen (Tylenol) that only reduces pain. Examples of OTC NSAIDs include ibuprofen (Advil, Motrin), aspirin (Ecotrin), and naproxen (Aleve). NSAIDs have their own health risks, so make sure to discuss their safety with your doctor first.

"Doctor, Doctor!"

Some sciatica symptoms are truly medical emergencies. In rare cases, delaying medical care could lead to or cause permanent nerve damage. If you experience any of the following, please see a doctor as soon as possible:

- You have severe pain in your low back and legs
- You experience nerve-related symptoms, such as weakness, numbness, tingling, or electric shock-like pain
- Your pain doesn't improve after 2 weeks
- Your pain gets worse, even when using at-home therapies
- You have loss of bowel and/or bladder control.

Easing the extreme pain of sciatica doesn't always require an extreme treatment approach. Relieving the pain at home with trusted remedies may be all you need. But the most important thing you can do for your low back and leg pain is to take it seriously—always call your doctor if you aren't experiencing relief. [616]

COST-SAVINGS EXAMPLE:

Because some sciatica symptoms are truly medical emergencies, don't risk your future health; consult a doctor about your sciatica. Once you rule out an emergency, you may be able to recover using these trust remedies above.

---

[616] Neel Anand, M.D., Orthopaedics | Cedars-Sinai, Los Angeles, CA, cedars-sinai.org

SCRATCHES, BITES, AND STINGS

In addition to the general guidance below, see individual entries elsewhere in this directory for: **BEE AND WASP STINGS | FIRE ANTS | JELLYFISH STINGS | MOSQUITO BITES | PORTUGUESE MAN O' WAR | SNAKEBITES | SPIDER BITES | STINGRAY STINGS | TICK BITES**

Bug bites, pet scratches, insect stings, and such are a fairly common part of life. While many or most are easily treated or go away on their own, these seemingly mundane events can become itchy, inflamed, or very serious – even leading to amputation or life-threatening complications.

Urgent care clinics see such cases daily. These clinics close the ever-widening gap between personal care physicians, who often expect you to make an appointment weeks in advance, and hospital emergency rooms, which can be massively expensive and often very slow and crowded.

Here's general help for any bite, scratch, or sting from Medfast Urgent Care Centers [617](**David Williams, M.D., Chief Medical Officer** [618]), with a dozen Florida locations – then check the other entries in this directory based on what type of animal inflicted the damage.

Any type of animal bite and scratch (pet, insect, spider, tick, wildlife) can potentially lead to unpleasant or even serious complications. Any animal scratch or bite, even a small one, can carry disease, no matter if it is the family pet, a neighbor's pet, or an unknown or wild animal.

Some bites can become infected by bacteria transmitted from the animal's mouth; this is especially true with cat bites. A serious bacterial infection known as Cat Scratch Disease can sometimes be transmitted by a cat scratch (most often from kittens) and may be present even if the scratch doesn't look infected.

Certain wild animals such as bats, raccoons, and foxes can carry and transmit rabies; in theory, any mammal can have rabies. Any child who is bitten, and whose tetanus shots are not up-to-date, will need a shot to prevent tetanus. Use these remedies for an animal bite or scratch:

Take a picture and note the location: If bitten or scratched by a stray or wild animal, take a picture of the animal if you can do so quickly and safely. It also is essential to note the location of the animal, so it can be captured, confined, and observed for rabies. (While not actual remedies, these steps will help professionals help the victim.) DO NOT try to capture a wild or unknown animal yourself; contact animal control or call 9-1-1.

Apply pressure: If the wound is bleeding, apply pressure with clean gauze or cloth until it stops.

Wash: If there's no bleeding, clean the area with soap and water; hold it under running water until clean.

Antibiotic ointment: Pat the wound dry, apply antibiotic ointment, then cover with clean gauze.

---

[617] MedFast Urgent Centers, Cocoa Beach, Florida area, medfastcare.com/
[618] MedFast Urgent Centers, Dr. David Williams, Founder | Image: Llisole, The Noun Project

"Doctor, Doctor!"

Any bite or scratch to a child should be evaluated by a doctor as soon as possible. Bites to the face, hand, or foot are particularly prone to infection and need medical attention. Seek immediate medical care if:

- The injury broke or punctured the skin, which can lead to an infection
- The wound doesn't stop bleeding after ten minutes of direct pressure
- The wound is deep or large
- The wound is to the face or neck, hand or foot, or is near a joint
- The wound becomes red, hot to the touch, swollen, or increasingly painful – all signs of an infection that needs treatment
- The animal was wild, unknown to you, or acting strangely – all concerns for rabies

Urgent care centers offer fast, professional medical treatment for animal bites and scratches. Typical wait times to see patients are less than an hour, compared to hospital emergency rooms, which can sometimes take longer than three to four hours and are much more expensive. [619]

COST-SAVINGS EXAMPLE:

Looking only at dog bites, the costs are staggering. In 2019, insurance companies settled 17,802 dog bite claims for a total of $796 million, or $44,760 per claim. [620]

A 53-year-old Florida woman was billed $12,000 for emergency room care when she was stung by a single bee in 2015. Her ER visit lasted less than two hours. The hospital was out of network, her insurer refused to help, and she had to pay it all. [621]

Avoid contact with wild animals, even if they are injured or sick and you want to help. Call animal control; they have the training and the tools to handle wildlife safely.

While the self-care remedies above are important and effective, seek medical care to avoid infections and potentially serious consequences. Urgent care is often the fastest and most cost-effective medical care option for scratches, bites and stings.

Try to avoid situations where you could be bitten, stung, or scratched. Know the risks of pet ownership and choose your pet wisely; many victims are attacked by their own adorable "fur babies" and "lovable" reptiles. Use the appropriate remedy a.s.a.p. based on the species involved.

---

[619] Animal Bites And Scratches, Medfastcare.Com, Urgent Care In Brevard Co. And Edgewater, FL
[620] Spotlight On: Dog Bite Liability, Insurance Information Institute, iii.org
[621] $12,000 For A Bee Sting? Emergency Room Visits Get Even Pricier, Money.Cnn.Com

SAD – SEASONAL AFFECTIVE DISORDER

 In winter months when daylight hours are short, many people notice their moods begin to change, says the Women's Health Network [622] (reviewed by **Dr. Amber Anderson, D.O.**, family practice physician [623]). They feel more tired, want to sleep and eat more, or feel sad much of the time. They tend to spend more time inside, eat heartier foods, and slow down a little. When these changes interfere with your life, doctors call the condition seasonal affective disorder (SAD).

These "winter blues" are experienced by about 5% of the US population for up to 40% of the year. Here are some of the physician-trusted remedies they suggest for coping with SAD:

Get outside every day: Being outside for as little as 15 minutes a day will expose your body to the sun's healthful rays, help you produce your own vitamin D and reconnect you with nature. If possible, move your desk or workspace near a window with natural light.

Get vitamin D testing and supplement with vitamin D: If you suspect low vitamin D levels, work with your healthcare provider to have your blood levels tested and supplement with vitamin D as needed. Some women may need to take 2000-6000 IU per day for several weeks to reach adequate levels. Amounts higher than 2000 IU daily should be ordered by a health practitioner because vitamin D is toxic at very high levels, says the Women's Health Network.

Enjoy some exercise: Daily exercise is vital to your overall well being, particularly if you are sad or depressed. It's the healthiest way to increase your serotonin levels and you can start small. Try short bursts of intense activity – walking up and down stairs or skipping rope for 1-3 minutes, four times a day, three times per week. Work up to at least 30 minutes of activity a day, 5 days per week. You can walk, swim, dance – the key is to find something you enjoy!

Consider phototherapy: Light therapy is an effective treatment for SAD. A light box costs as little as $30 on Amazon. Light boxes can emit some UV radiation, so get one with a UV filter or diffusing screen to protect your skin and eyes; better yet, choose one that's UV-free.

Keep a regular schedule: You want to establish an internal rhythm that's in sync with nature. Research shows that people who work long hours or split shifts develop imbalanced melatonin cycles, especially if they work at night or have limited access to sunlight. Try to go to bed and get up at the same time every day, and get at least 8 hours of sleep per night.

Pay attention to what you eat: Avoid highly processed foods, as they throw your body out of balance. Choose whole, minimally processed foods with little or no artificial ingredients. Often with SAD, your body craves foods that quickly raise serotonin levels, such as sugars and refined carbohydrates. These foods set you on a cycle of ups and downs with negative effects on your mood and weight. Stick to whole grains and complex carbs and those cravings will go away.

Take high-quality nutritional supplements: SAD affects the whole body, which means you'll need to support all of your body's systems. Modern food processing strips food of its nutritional

---

[622] Natural Remedies for Seasonal Affective Disorder, womenshealthnetwork.com | Image: SAM Designs, The Noun Project
[623] Amber Anderson, DO, Cabarrus Family Medicine, Harrisburg, NC, womenshealthnetwork.com

value, which is why everyone can benefit from taking high-quality vitamin and mineral supplements, such as omega-3 fatty acids, which can play a key role in treating depression.

With guidance from seven doctors, the Women's Health Network empowers women with health knowledge as well as physician-trusted products and remedies for concerns like depression, anxiety, mood and much more. They offer a 15% discount for signing up for their free newsletter.

"Doctor, Doctor!"

If your seasonal affective disorder is edging toward depression, excellent help is available. According to Advent Health, call a doctor if: [624]

- you feel sad, empty or hopeless most of the time
- your emotional life changes significantly when you have depression.
- your weight and appetite has gone up or down
- you don't sleep very well, or you have little or no energy most of the time

Treatments for these symptoms are generally covered by insurance. Self-help can be highly effective for depression, anxiety and mood disorders, but if you aren't getting better on your own, definitely reach out for help.

COST-SAVINGS EXAMPLE:

What is your happiness worth? Probably more than any earthly possession. Start with the belief that you deserve to be happy, then use the trusted remedies above like your life depended on them. If that doesn't turn things around for you, schedule a visit with your doctor. It's worth it, and you're worth it.

A word of caution: get a second opinion if your doctor suggests a prescription drug for anxiety, depression, or SAD. Drugs may be expensive and can have severe side effects. While waiting for your second opinion, double down on the trusted remedies above.

SAD is not considered a major depressive disorder (MDD), but it could be the start of one. The economic burden of MDD was $326 billion in 2018; that's one statistic you don't want to be any part of. Instead, put physician-trusted remedies to work and beat the winter blues. [625]

Remember that throughout this directory you can find further information by using the sources at the bottom of every page.

---

[624] 5 Signs You Should Talk With Your Doctor About Depression | AdventHealth Orlando, adventhealth.com
[625] Depression Cost the US $326 Billion Per Year Pre-Pandemic, a 38% Increase Since 2010, prnewswire.com

SHIN SPLINTS

 Shin splints are an inflammation of the muscle attachments along the tibia (shinbone), explain podiatrists **Dr. Douglas S. Hale** and **Dr. Lawrence Z. Huppin** [626] of Foot & Ankle Center of Washington in Seattle [627] . Shin splints may also be referred to as medial tibial stress syndrome (MTSS) or tibial fasciitis.

Shin splints can be very painful and resistant to treatment. If you want to treat your shin splints at home, Drs. Hale and Huppin suggest following this plan rigorously for four weeks.

Use a compression sleeve: For the first two weeks, wear a shin splint compression sleeve throughout the day. Then for the next two weeks, wear the sleeve for athletic activities. It applies gentle compression forces while firmly supporting the lower leg muscles and soft tissue. The sleeve also tends to stimulate circulation and maintain warmth, which controls fluid build-up.

Use a good arch support: A medical grade orthotic arch support will act to decrease painful joint motion by preventing arch collapse. One with a higher arch and some rigidity will work best. OTC arch supports will not work as well as a quality custom orthotic, but will help.

Wear slippers with an arch support: Around the house, use a slipper with arch support to reduce tension on your leg muscles. Avoid sandals or flip-flops unless they have arch support.

Wear stable shoes: Always wear a stable shoe, particularly during any weight-bearing activities.

Pain relief measures: Use a cold therapy roll-on as needed to reduce pain. Ice the painful areas for 10 minutes each evening. Find further information on all of these products at footankle.com.

"Doctor, Doctor!"

If you don't see improvement in two to four weeks, see a podiatrist who specializes in sports medicine. You should also see a healthcare provider if you notice pain in just one specific spot on your shin instead of along most of your shinbone. These may be signs of a stress fracture. You should also see a doctor if you have these symptoms in your lower leg or foot: cramping, numbness, tingling, redness, swelling. Shin splints should not cause any of these symptoms; they could be signs of another medical condition.

COST-SAVINGS EXAMPLE:

Since shin splints typically do not require prescriptions, surgery, or hospitalization, treatment cost studies are hard to find. Most of the remedies given above are quite affordable. If shin splints are affecting your athletic performance or favorite pursuits, you might find yourself spending a few hundred dollars a year on shoes, orthotics, and other devices along with occasional doctor visits.

---

[626] Dr. Douglas S. Hale, DPM, footankle.com | Dr. Lawrence Z. Huppin, DPM, footankle.com
[627] Shin Splints Treatment Plan, Foot & Ankle Center of Washington, footankle.com

SHINGLES

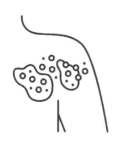

Shingles is a skin condition caused by the varicella-zoster virus, says emedihealth.com [628] (**Sarita Sanke, M.D.** [629]). The virus can remain inert in the body for a long time after an infection and may get reactivated by certain factors, leading to shingles.

The varicella-zoster virus causes chickenpox in children and may cause herpes in adults. It commonly causes shingles in middle-aged and elderly people. Certain self-care remedies can help you heal from shingles fast. However, they are not a substitute for medical treatment and should be used only to help relieve the symptoms.

Capsaicin-based ointment: Capsaicin is an effective pain relief agent and can be used to soothe the pain associated with shingles rash and blisters. A natural compound derived from chilies, capsaicin is available over the counter or online. Apply a small amount of capsaicin cream to the blisters and rash at least 2–3 times a day. Wash your hands with soap afterward.

Licorice: Licorice has a compound called glycyrrhizin, which has viral-inhibiting properties and can help stop the replication of the varicella-zoster virus. Add a few drops of water to 1 teaspoon of licorice powder. Apply this paste to affected areas; wash it off after drying.

Eucalyptus oil: Eucalyptus oil is well known for inhibiting viral replication. It has potent antimicrobial properties that help fight infections. Add ½ teaspoon of eucalyptus oil to 2 tablespoons of a carrier such as coconut or grapeseed oil. Apply to the affected area twice a day.

Calendula: Calendula flowers are widely known for their medicinal properties. Calendula can help soothe the itching and pain in the shingles rash, as well as help decrease viral replication. Apply a small amount of calendula lotion or gel to the affected area twice or thrice a day.

Apple cider vinegar: ACV is another natural agent that exhibits strong antiviral and anti-inflammatory properties. It helps soothe the rash and fight the infection. Apply an apple cider vinegar compress to the affected area. Alternatively, you can add a couple of cups of apple cider vinegar to your bath water and soak in it.

Neem: Neem leaves have traditionally been used as a shingles cure in Ayurvedic medicine. They have antiviral properties and can help decrease the infection and inflammation associated with the condition. Crush a few neem leaves to make a paste, and apply it to the affected area. Alternatively, you may take a bath in neem leaves soaked in water.

"Doctor, Doctor!"

Shingles is a common condition but can lead to serious complications in immunocompromised individuals, warns Dr. Sanke. It is important to seek medical treatment as soon as possible to prevent the rash from spreading.

---

[628] 6 Home Remedies for Shingles and How to Use Them, eMediHealth
[629] Sarita Sanke, M.D., Dermatologist, eMediHealth | Image: Amethyst Studio, The Noun Project

COST-SAVINGS EXAMPLE:

According to the U.S. Department of Health & Human Services, the average total cost to treat shingles is about $525 per patient. [630] Most of your costs should be covered by insurance. Since shingles can be very painful, do not hesitate to get medical treatment if the doctor-trusted remedies above are not enough.

SINUSITIS

These remedies can help relieve sinusitis symptoms, says Mayo Clinic: [631]

Drink fluids: Water or juice will help dilute mucous secretions and promote drainage. Avoid beverages that contain caffeine or alcohol, as they can be dehydrating. Drinking alcohol can also worsen the swelling of the lining of the sinuses and nose.

Moisten your sinus cavities: Drape a towel over your head as you breathe in the vapor from a bowl of hot water. Direct the vapor toward your face. Or take a hot shower, breathing the warm, moist air. This helps ease pain and helps mucus drain.

Apply warm compresses to your face: Place warm, damp towels around your nose, cheeks and eyes to ease facial pain.

Rinse your nasal passages: Use a specially designed squeeze bottle or neti pot. This self-care remedy, called nasal lavage, can help clear your sinuses. If you make your own rinse, use water that's contaminant-free – distilled, sterile, previously boiled and cooled, or filtered using a filter with an absolute pore size of 1 micron or smaller – to make the solution. Also be sure to rinse the irrigation device after each use with contaminant-free water and leave open to air-dry.

Rest: This will help your body fight infection and speed recovery.

Sleep with your head elevated: This will help your sinuses drain, reducing congestion.

To reduce your risk of getting acute sinusitis: avoid upper respiratory infections; manage your allergies; work with your health care provider to keep symptoms under control; avoid cigarette smoke and polluted air; use a humidifier.

"Doctor, Doctor!"

Most people with acute sinusitis don't need to see a health care provider but you should seek medical care if you have any of the following:

- Symptoms that don't improve in a few days or worsen

---

[630] Shingles Treatment Cost, Costhelper.com
[631] Home Remedies: Steps To Help Relieve Sinusitis, Mayo Clinic | Image: Caputo, The Noun Project

- A persistent fever
- A history of recurrent or chronic sinusitis. You may have several episodes of acute sinusitis, lasting less than four weeks, before developing chronic sinusitis.

COST-SAVINGS EXAMPLE:

Sinusitis treatment in early stages is inexpensive. However, chronic conditions can lead to the need for endoscopic sinus surgery, ranging from about $3,600 to more than $10,500. One reason charges vary is because endoscopic sinus surgery can include multiple procedures. So besides saving the cost, you'll want to avoid the discomfort and recovery period of having to go through the procedures.

Save $3,600 more on sinus surgery in the future by taking care of your sinusitis promptly with these trusted remedies.

SLEEPLESSNESS – SEE INSOMNIA

SNAKEBITES

Despite fears you may have picked up watching old Western movies, snakebites are not common in the U.S. and are rarely fatal, says Medical News Today [632] (**Elaine Hanh Le, M.D.**, senior director of Medical Affairs [633]).

Not all snake species are venomous. Knowing which snake has bitten a person helps with treatment, says Medical News Today. Snakebite injuries range from mild to severe, but deaths from snakebites in the U.S. are rare, about five per year. [634]

People can usually survive venomous snakebites if they seek immediate medical attention. Never assume that a snake is nonvenomous without first consulting an expert. The misclassification of snake species could be fatal. Snakes will not bite humans unless they feel threatened, so leaving them alone is the best strategy for preventing a bite, says Medical News Today.

One fact you may have picked up from those old Western movies – dead snakes can still bite, so avoid handling any snake in the wild. If despite the odds you do find yourself the victim of a snakebite, Medical News Today offers these remedies, all of which require calling for help:

If someone gets a snake bite, take the following steps –

---

[632] How To Identify And Treat Snake Bites, Medicalnewstoday.Com
[633] Dr. Elaine Hanh Le, doctor.webmd.com | Image: publicdomainvectors.org
[634] Venomous Snakes, National Institute for Occupational Safety and Health, CDC, cdc.gov

Take a picture: Grab your phone and snap a picture of the snake, provided you can do so quickly and safely.

Remain calm and call 9-1-1 immediately: You may also call the National Poison Control Center at **1-800-222-1222** about a snakebite. Provide your picture or describe the snake as best you can.

Gently wash the area with soap and water if possible. This may help prevent an infection.

Remove tight clothing or jewelry: This is because the area around the bite is likely to swell.

Keep the bite area below the heart if possible: this will slow the movement of venom into the bloodstream.

If a doctor suspects that someone has received a bite from a venomous snake, he or she may give them antivenom medication, if available. It helps if the person knows which species of snake bit them, as different snake bites require different types of antivenom.

There are many misconceptions about first aid for snake bites. The following list describes what *to avoid* doing after a snake bite:

Do Not: attempt to catch or kill the snake

Do Not: cut into the bite wound

Do Not: wrap a cloth above the wound to restrict blood flow

Do Not: apply ice to the wound

Do Not: attempt to suck the venom from the wound or use a suction device

Do Not: give medication unless a health care professional gives this instruction

"Doctor, Doctor!"

Always call 9-1-1 about a snake bite.

COST-SAVINGS EXAMPLE:

Going to an emergency room for a snake bite may result in a large bill. Not going to an emergency room for a snake bite may result in death. *Save money elsewhere.*

If still unsure, call the National Poison Control Center toll-free at 1-800-222-1222.

> **Did one of these remedies help you?**
>
> Share your trusted remedies success with the publisher! We'd love to hear from you. **info@trustedremedies.com**

SNORING

There are many reasons people snore, and just as many snoring remedies, says **Michael Breus, Ph.D.** [635] of TheSleepDoctor.com [636]. Some methods may not work for everyone – you just need the one that works for you. Dr. Breus says that identifying the underlying cause is the key to finding your snoring solution.

If your snoring is mild or infrequent, you may be able to reduce or stop snoring with home care. Dr. Breus's trusted snoring remedies are easy to implement, don't require medical supervision, and may be successful in reducing snoring for some people.

Saline rinse: Clearing your nasal passages can help improve nasal breathing and reduce mouth breathing. Grab a four-finger pinch (thumb plus three fingers) of non-iodized salt. Mix with one cup of distilled water. Rinse nasal passages using a clean neti pot or nasal rinse bottle.

Change your sleep position: Your sleep position can cause snoring or make it worse. People who sleep on their back tend to snore the most, while side sleepers snore less. Half of people with obstructive sleep apnea find that their symptoms are exacerbated by back sleeping, while about 65% of those without sleep apnea may snore less just by changing their sleeping position.

Assistive devices: Products that can help you change your sleep position include vibrating devices to prevent back sleeping, and special pillows designed to encourage side sleeping. Propping up the upper body with a wedge pillow may also help reduce snoring.

Prioritize sleep: Sleep hygiene is a series of protocols meant to encourage restful sleep, Dr. Breus explains. For example, sleep hygiene recommendations call for the bedroom to be as dark as possible; evidence suggests that sleeping in a more brightly lit bedroom may cause a stress response that exacerbates sleep apnea. Other tips include keeping a consistent evening routine, avoiding electronics before bedtime, and getting plenty of daytime exercise.

Avoid alcohol and other sedatives before bed: Alcohol and sedatives relax muscles in the airway, which may increase snoring and sleep apnea symptoms. It takes about two hours to metabolize one alcoholic drink, so people who have more than one drink may need to stop drinking several hours before bedtime. Some people who take medication with sedating side effects do so at night to avoid daytime drowsiness or to help them sleep, but this may also increase snoring; your doctor may be able to help you adjust your dosing schedule.

Address nasal congestion: Nasal congestion is a common reason for snoring. It blocks air from flowing freely and may lead to breathing through your mouth, which promotes snoring. Things that block the nasal passages include nasal polyps, a deviated septum, and sinus inflammation caused by colds, allergies, and bacteria. The treatment for nasal congestion depends on the cause, and may include sprays, antihistamines, saline irrigation, decongestants, and using an air purifier.

Maintain a healthy weight: Snoring is closely linked with excess body weight, says Dr. Breus. The extra weight presses on the airway, narrowing the breathing passage and interfering with airflow. Losing weight can significantly reduce snoring and obstructive sleep apnea, especially in

---

[635] Dr. Michael Breus, Diplomate of the American Board of Sleep Medicine, thesleepdoctor.com
[636] How to Stop Snoring, The Sleep Doctor | Image: DvM Design, The Noun Project

those under age 50. For individuals who have obesity and obstructive sleep apnea, experts recommend implementing a healthy diet and beginning regular exercise to reduce symptoms.

Nasal dilators: Nasal dilators are designed to widen your nasal passages. External nasal dilators, or nasal strips, are adhesive bands that are placed on the nose. Internal nasal dilators are placed in the nostrils. Although over the counter nasal strips are inexpensive and readily available, their effectiveness is unclear. Internal nasal dilators (one type is called nose cones) may work better.

Practice Mouth Exercises: Also known as myofunctional therapy, certain mouth exercises are designed to improve the function of the mouth and upper respiratory tract to reduce snoring. For example, these movements may include pronouncing vowel sounds, swallowing and chewing motions, and moving the tongue against the teeth to strengthen the surrounding muscles. You can learn how to perform these exercises using videos and apps. Talk to your doctor for additional information about myofunctional therapy.

"Doctor, Doctor!"

While these strategies can benefit anyone who snores, they aren't a substitute for professional treatment, says Dr. Breus. It's important to consult a provider, especially if home care approaches don't help your snoring or if your snoring is severe.

People with sleep apnea and structural problems especially need to discuss these issues with a medical provider. For example, if you have a structural problem that is obstructing your airway, your doctor may recommend having nasal or sinus surgery. For some, medical weight loss options may be appropriate. Talk to your healthcare provider to decide the best treatment plan for your situation. [637]

COST-SAVINGS EXAMPLE:

Snoring is very common, and the number of affordable and trusted remedies is large. Take your snoring problem seriously because it can negatively impact your health in many ways. If after a few months of trying self-care remedies your condition does not improve, the cost of medical treatment is likely very worthwhile.

From pricey therapies to lost wages, the costs of sleep apnea can add up. The American Academy of Sleep Medicine found that people with sleep apnea pay about $2,105 per year for testing, medical appointments, treatment devices, and surgery if necessary. [638]

The average cost of sleep apnea surgery without insurance is $6,400 to $10,000. This cost represents minor surgical procedures on the nose, throat or mouth. [639]

Reducing or eliminating your snoring before it reaches the point of needing medical intervention may save you thousands of dollars.

[637] How Sleep Works; Common Sleep Issues; Sleep By Age; Sleep Products, thesleepdoctor.com
[638] The Cost of Sleep Apnea, Webmd.com
[639] Sleep Apnea Surgery Costs and Financing, Carecredit.com

SORE THROAT

Whether you got it from a cold, allergies, or cheering on your favorite team, a sore throat is a "pain," says *Eat This, Not That!* [640] (**Lisa Young, Ph.D., RDN, medical board expert** [641]). The scratchiness, the aches when you swallow, and the effort it takes to speak are bad enough. The worst part? It can prevent you from eating or drinking, which you need to do when you're sick to help you heal from whatever it is that's causing your symptoms.

Dr. Young offers her most trusted remedies for soothing a sore throat.

Oatmeal: Foods that have a soft texture and are easy to swallow are the best bets. Oatmeal provides an abundance of nutrients, so you will remain healthy while you heal. Oatmeal's benefits include reducing inflammation and increasing energy.

Yogurt: Yogurt is also another nutrient-dense food that's easy to swallow. Besides being a great source of calcium and protein, yogurt contains probiotics to help support the immune system. Probiotics can help prevent the growth of harmful bacteria, potentially helping to prevent colds.

Chicken broth: Warm foods soothe your throat, advises Dr. Young. She says chicken broth is a perfect food to help reduce irritation. Besides being very hydrating, it has fairly high amounts of sodium, making it a natural way to help replenish the body's electrolytes. This is great if your sore throat is tied with the flu, cold, or anything causing your body to lose water and electrolytes.

Ice pops: If you ever had your tonsils out, the doctor probably told you you could eat Popsicles for three meals a day. Popsicles are hydrating and soothing to the throat, says Young.

"Doctor, Doctor!"

In most cases, your sore throat will improve with at-home treatment, says the American Osteopathic Association (**Ernest Gelb, D.O.,** President [642]) . However, call your doctor if a severe sore throat and a fever over 101 degrees lasts longer than one to two days; you have difficulty sleeping because your throat is blocked by swollen tonsils or adenoids; or a red rash appears. Any of these symptoms could mean you have a bacterial infection. In that case, your doctor may prescribe an antibiotic to treat your infection. [643]

COST-SAVINGS EXAMPLE:

Both self-care and a doctor's prescription for sore throat are inexpensive. You may be able to save time and money by going to urgent care, depending on your insurance situation and how long it takes to get an appointment with your doctor.

---

[640] 4 Best Foods to Eat for a Sore Throat, Eat This, Not That! | Image: Stefania Servidio, The Noun Project
[641] Dr. Lisa Young, Internationally Recognized Nutritionist & Portion-Control Expert, drlisayoung.com
[642] Ernest Gelb, DO, American Osteopathic Association, osteopathic.org [see next page, "What is a DO?"]
[643] Sore Throat: When to See a Doctor, American Osteopathic Association, osteopathic.org

What is a DO?

Accounting for 11% of all physicians in the United States, Doctors of Osteopathic Medicine, or D.O.s, bring a unique, patient-centered approach to every specialty across the full spectrum of medicine. They are trained to listen and partner with their patients to help them get healthy and stay well.

Doctors of Osteopathic Medicine use a unique whole-person approach to help prevent illness and injury. D.O.s practice in all medical specialities – primary care, pediatrics, OBGYN, emergency medicine, psychiatry and surgery. Moreover, D.O.s hold some of the most prominent positions in medicine today, including overseeing care for the President of the United States, the NASA medical team, Olympic athletes and many who serve in the uniformed services.

From their first days of medical school, D.O.s are trained to look beyond your symptoms to understand how lifestyle and environmental factors impact your well-being. They practice medicine according to the latest science and technology, but also consider options to complement pharmaceuticals and surgery. D.O.s receive special training in the musculoskeletal system, your body's interconnected system of nerves, muscles and bones. By combining this knowledge with the latest advances in medical technology, they offer patients the most comprehensive care available today.

SPIDER BITES

All spiders contain venom, but the biting parts of most spiders cannot puncture human skin, says the National Poison Control Center. That leaves the brown recluse and the black widow as the two most concerning spiders. The brown recluse is one of the most deadly spiders in the U.S., says Dengarden, a home and garden design company. [644] The species is also known in some areas of the country as the violin or fiddleback spider because of the markings on its back.

The brown recluse is aptly named; the spider is rarely seen or identified. It's just half an inch long and is further distinguished by its six eyes instead of the usual eight found in most spiders. A brown recluse spider bite is often not felt when it happens. The complex venom causes injury and death (necrosis) of the surrounding tissues. In severe cases, the venom can damage deeper tissues. *There is no antidote;* treatment includes treating the wound and preventing infection.

If one source knows all about spider bites, it's Terminix, a leading supplier of pest-control services. The company has 2.7 million residential and commercial customers – as well as 8,500 employees – to protect in forty-seven U.S. states and twenty-two countries. Terminix cautions that while recluse spiders are found primarily in the Southern and Southeastern U.S., they have been known to migrate to other areas of the country. They generally prefer to live in buildings, and they typically hunt for their prey at night.

The brown recluse web is usually not produced in open areas where it can be easily identified.

---

[644] U.S. Venomous Spiders: Black Widow, Brown Recluse, & Hobo, Dengarden, dengarden.com

Terminix says the recluse is a fast runner and will likely evade pursuit if seen within a household. The brown recluse is often confused with the wolf spider, of which there are over 200 species living in the U.S. However, wolf spiders lack the "fiddle shape" that is a characteristic of the brown recluse and have distinguishing stripes and/or bands on their bodies and legs.

If you have been bitten by a brown recluse spider, Mayo Clinic (**Laura Walker, M.D.**, emergency medicine [645]) recommends the following trusted remedies:

Clean: Clean the bite with mild soap and water, and apply an antibiotic ointment.

Compress: Apply a cool compress to the bite to help reduce pain and swelling.

Elevate: If the bite is on the arm or leg, elevate it.

Medicate: Take over-the-counter pain medications as needed.

Call: You may call the National Poison Control Center at **1-800-222-1222** about a spider bite.

The other problem spider species is the black widow. Its bites can be dangerous, but fatalities are rare. Black widow spider bites often are painful right away. Severe pain and muscle cramps can start in a couple of hours, but can be treated. Antivenom is available, but is needed only rarely.

"Doctor, Doctor!"

If you think you may have been bitten by a brown recluse or a black widow, call Poison Control – **1-800-222-1222**. For *any* spider bite, observe the area for signs of infection – redness, swelling, warm to the touch. Consult your doctor if the bite becomes infected. [646]

COST-SAVINGS EXAMPLE:

Going to the emergency room for a spider bite may be very expensive. One patient received an emergency room bill of $4,348.44 for treatment of a spider bite. [647]

A call to Poison Control (1-800-222-1222) is free, and doesn't require waiting in line.

Call Poison Control toll-free at 1-800-222-1222. It could save you a costly emergency room bill.

Remember that throughout this directory you can find further information by using the sources at the bottom of every page and in the resources listing beginning on page 259.

---

[645] Laura E. Walker, M.D., Emergency Medicine Physician, Mayo Clinic | Appointments at Mayo Clinic
[646] Spider Bites: First Aid, Mayo Clinic, mayoclinic.org
[647] A Spider Bite, And $4,348.44 Dollars Later: 'I Don't Have The Willpower To Argue Any Of It', clearhealthcosts.com

SPLINTERS

Splinters are another seemingly trivial malady – until you get one, and all you can think about is getting it out! Mountain Peaks Family Practice in Orem, Utah [648] (**Dr. Robert Durrans, M.D.** [649]) trusts these remedies to get that small but offensive foreign object out of your body *f-a-s-t*; if nine ways to remove a splinter seem like overkill, remember you only have to find one that works:

Tape: Wash the area with soap and water. When dry, apply adhesive tape over the splinter. Gently press down to secure the tape to the splinter. After 30-45 seconds, pull tape off in one smooth movement. The splinter will hopefully come off, too.

Glue: If tape didn't work, try glue; Elmer's works well. Apply a drop of ordinary glue over the splinter and allow it to dry. Peel off the glue, and the splinter should become loose and pop out. **Do Not:** Do not use superglue, epoxy, or other types of adhesives meant for permanent adhesion.

Baking soda and water: Mix baking soda and water to make a paste. Apply to the affected area. Let it sit for two to three hours. Wash off the paste, and gently remove the splinter with tweezers.

Epsom Salt: Place Epsom salt on the sticky side of an adhesive bandage, and wrap around the affected area. The salt will cause swelling, and help push the splinter out. Remove with tweezers.

White vinegar: Soak the area in a bowl of white vinegar for 30 minutes. The vinegar will help the splinter break through the surface of the skin, then gently pluck it out with tweezers.

Bacon Fat: Cut a small amount of fat off a fatty piece of raw bacon. With a band aid, secure the bacon fat on the affected area. Leave it overnight. The fat will draw the splinter out.

Hydrogen peroxide: Coat the area around the splinter to create a cleansing reaction and improve visibility of the splinter. Then 86 that splinter with tweezers.

Clear nail polish: Every lady will have clear nail polish on hand! Apply the polish over the affected area. Let it dry. Peel off polish in the opposite direction of the splinter.

Honey: Apply to the affected area and let sit. Cover with a bandage if you wish. The honey will draw the splinter out to create better visibility, and you can remove the splinter with tweezers.

"Doctor, Doctor!"

If these remedies don't work or you notice the splinter is becoming infected, visit urgent care or call your doctor. But if it is infected, do make that call to a healthcare provider.

COST-SAVINGS EXAMPLE:

Use physician-trusted remedies promptly to treat a splinter, before it can become infected and require a doctor visit.

---

[648] 9 DIY Home Remedies for a Splinter, Mountain Peaks Family Practice, Orem, Utah
[649] Dr. Robert Durrans, M.D., Orem, Utah, mountainpeaksfamilypractice.com

SPRAINS

A sprained ankle refers to ligaments in the ankle becoming torn or pulled, says Elite Sports Medicine + Orthopedics of Nashville, TN [650] (**Burton F. Elrod, M.D.**, sports medicine specialist [651]). When you roll your ankle while running or playing sports, it may be painful to bear weight on the foot, suggesting a sprained ankle injury. If you think you may have sprained your ankle, these trusted remedies may help:

Stay off it: Avoid bearing any weight on the ankle. After that, use the R-I-C-E method below.

R - Rest: Resting the injured ankle will help give your body time to heal. Avoid participating in activities that cause pain or inflammation to the affected area. Limit movement such as walking for a few days to see if the pain gradually subsides.

I - Ice: Ice therapy is a great way to reduce the inflammation caused by a sprained ankle. Use an ice pack and make sure to not place it directly on the skin by using a towel underneath. Ice the ankle for 15-20 minutes every 2-3 hours as needed.

C- Compress: To help stop further swelling, compress the ankle with bandages until the swelling stops. We advise not taking your shoe off after an injury, as this helps to compress the ankle and prevent further injury.

E - Elevate: Elevate the ankle above heart level by laying down and putting pillows or cushions under your leg.

NSAIDs – Doctors recommend starting with anti-inflammatory medications (NSAIDs) within the first day of injury. This helps to get ahead of the inflammation and prevent further pain. Both pills and topical treatments will help inflammation after a sprained ankle.

Once you have taken a couple of days to rest, mild exercise can help heal a sprained ankle, says Elite Sports Medicine + Orthopedics. Exercise helps increase blood flow, strengthens the muscles around the ankle, and jumpstarts the healing process. Decreasing activity has been shown to worsen the injury. Focus on strengthening your calf muscles. Simple exercises like a calf raise, standing on one foot, and walking help build calf muscles and strengthen your ankle. Stretching before and after exercise helps keep the ligaments lubricated and increases mobility. This will also help if you are feeling sore from your workouts. Ankle circles, Achilles stretches, and standing calf stretches are all great options after spraining your ankle. If you feel pain after a week of rest and exercise, seek medical attention from an orthopedic doctor.

"Doctor, Doctor!"

Depending on the severity of your ankle sprain, it may be best to seek medical attention immediately, says Elite Sports Medicine + Orthopedics. Severe swelling, bruising or pain are all good indicators that you should see a doctor. A trip to urgent care or schedule an appointment with an orthopedic doctor is always recommended to avoid further injury and ensure proper diagnosis.

---

[650] How to Heal a Sprained Ankle: Elite Sports Medicine + Orthopedics, Nashville, TN
[651] Burton F. Elrod, M.D., Knee, Shoulder & Elbow Doctor, Nashville, TN, eliteorthopaedic.com

COST-SAVINGS EXAMPLE:

The cost savings of self-care remedies really depends on the severity of the sprain. In the minutes after the injury first occurs, put these remedies into practice. Trust your body to tell you if self-care is sufficient; however, if there's any doubt, calling a doctor may result in faster healing and lower risk of longer-term injury.

STINGRAY STINGS

Stingrays have long, whip-like tails equipped with up to three barbed venomous spinal blades, reports the National Capital Poison Control Center (Serkalem Mekonnen, R.N., M.P.H., certified specialist in Poison Information; **Cathleen Clancy, M.D.**, associate medical director).[652]

Though stingrays are generally shy, they may strike when stepped on. Their venom causes intense pain, but the main risk is the puncture wound. The best way to prevent being stung by a stingray is to avoid stepping on it when in the ocean by shuffling through the sand rather than lifting your feet and walking normally (commonly referred to as the "stingray shuffle""), says the NCPC. This will warn a stingray of your approach, and it will likely swim away. A pole or stick can also be used ahead of your feet.

Divers should be cautious and avoid swimming close to the seafloor. It is also important to know where stingrays are and never to provoke them.

Wash: Treatment of stingray injuries starts with first aid. Because the puncture is often deep and considered dirty, there is high risk of infection. Wash and disinfect the area immediately, and get a tetanus vaccine or booster if needed. The wound should be inspected for any retained spines.

Hot water: The standard treatment for the pain is hot water immersion.

Call for help: If you have a stingray injury, check the webPOISONCONTROL® online tool – say, "Hey, Siri, get webPOISONCONTROL® online tool" (see link in footnote [653] for guidance), or call Poison Control at **1-800-222-1222.** [654] Stay calm and let them guide you. Take the time to provide accurate information.

<u>Do Not</u>: Never attempt to suck out venom by mouth.

"Doctor, Doctor!"

Medical evaluation and treatment in a hospital are necessary if there are any retained spines, if the puncture is deep, or if it involves the chest, abdomen, or neck.

---

[652] Cathleen Clancy, M.D., National Capital Poison Center, gwdocs.com | Image: Yandi RS, The Noun Project
[653] Webpoisoncontrol.Org | Prefer To Talk? It's Always Ok To Call Poison Control At 1-800-222-1222.
[654] How to Prevent and Treat Stingray Injuries, National Capital Poison Control Center, poison.org

COST-SAVINGS EXAMPLE:

Keep your treatment case – and costs – from escalating by using all three remedies above at once. A stingray killed famed outdoorsman Steve Irwin; all stings should be treated immediately and aggressively; do not take a wait-and-see approach.

STOMACH FLU – SEE NAUSEA AND VOMITING, DIARRHEA

STRESS

Anxiety affects some twenty percent of Americans each year, says **Dr. Jill Kapil, Licensed Clinical Psychologist** [655] at K-Health.com. [656] Here are several trusted, evidence-based remedies for managing stress:

Exercise: Routine physical activity is one of the best ways to improve your overall mental health and naturally reduce symptoms of anxiety. Healthy activity can serve as a helpful distraction from your worries, but exercise also works with your body's chemistry to physically reduce anxiety. Exercise increases the availability of neurotransmitters serotonin and gamma-aminobutyric acid (GABA), which your brain uses to reduce anxiety.

Reduce caffeine: Caffeine may increase alertness, but it can also mimic anxiety symptoms – and in high doses, may actually trigger anxiety. If you're someone who experiences anxiety, and especially if you're noticing that morning (or afternoon) cup is doing you more harm than good, it may be a good idea to limit your caffeine intake. Try half-caf or decaf options. Herbal teas, which don't contain any caffeine (e.g., green tea), are another option for a hot morning drink. Also drink more water, which can also improve your physical and mental well-being.

Herbal teas and supplements: Nutrition and herbal remedies can actually impact your mental health—and supplementing with vitamins and minerals under a doctor's supervision is one way to improve anxiety. The following dietary supplements have been linked with decreased anxiety symptoms and overall improved mental health:

- **Magnesium:** Magnesium is an important mineral that plays a key role in brain health, heart health and bone structure. Some research connects magnesium deficiency to anxiety, and taking magnesium supplements may be able to assist with anxiety episodes.
- **Vitamin D:** Low vitamin D levels have been associated with anxiety, so boosting your vitamin D with a supplement may help your overall mood.
- **L-theanine:** This amino acid has been shown to reduce the effects of stress, helping with symptoms of both anxiety and depression.
- **Omega-3 fatty acids (fish oil):** A number of studies have suggested that Omega-3s can reduce anxiety, especially acute episodes.
- **Chamomile:** Scientific research has found chamomile, including chamomile tea, to have

---

[655] Jill Kapil, Psy.D., Author at K Health | Image: Rolas Design, The Noun Project
[656] 15 Natural Remedies for Anxiety: Ways to Find Relief, K-Health, khealth.com

positive effects on sleep quality and general anxiety disorder (GAD).

Stop Smoking: Like caffeine, nicotine is a stimulant, which can cause symptoms similar to anxiety or panic attacks. At the same time, stopping smoking suddenly can cause nicotine withdrawal, which can also cause anxiety attacks. If you smoke and experience anxiety, quitting could improve your health in many ways. Ask your medical provider about tools that could help you quit safely and effectively, and see the section on **Tobacco** in Part I of this directory, **Doctor-Trusted Remedies for the Top 10 Most Common Health Issues**.

Avoid Alcohol: Alcohol is both a stimulant and a depressant, which means it affects the nervous system. Alcohol may provide temporary comfort, but it's not helpful for managing anxiety in the long term, says Dr. Kapil. Many people with alcohol use disorders also have anxiety disorders. Alcohol withdrawal can also cause both anxiety and panic attacks. Even if you aren't misusing alcohol, you may experience negative mental health consequences. Alcohol alters levels of serotonin, a neurotransmitter linked to anxiety. So while you may feel relaxed while sipping a cocktail, you might feel more anxious the next day, even if you only have one or two drinks. If you do drink alcohol, do so in moderation, and don't use drinking to self-medicate. Also see the guidance in Part I of this directory under **Substance Abuse**.

Aromatherapy: Aromatherapy, or the smelling of essential oils, may be one of the effective natural ways to manage anxiety and improve sleep quality. Try using an essential oil diffuser with a calming scent, or simply inhale the aroma of the oil straight from the bottle. Common essential oils used for relaxation include: lavender, orange, roman chamomile, lemon, and clary sage. Do not apply essential oils directly to your skin or ingest them, and talk to a doctor before using these natural products around children.

Journaling: Writing about your feelings in a journal can have a positive effect on your mental health. It can help you process feelings, understand situations, or just get things off your chest. Journaling can also help you recognize cognitive distortions, or ways of thinking that might be contributing to your anxiety. Make a habit of journaling about your emotions on a regular basis, or grab a notebook and pour out your feelings when you're anxious or stressed. If you're concerned about privacy, do your writing in a password-protected computer file.

Meditation: Mindfulness meditation, or training your mind to stay present (as opposed to obsessing about the past or worrying about the future), can improve anxiety, help with sleep, and even support a healthy immune system. You can practice mindfulness meditation anywhere, at any time. Apps like Headspace and Calm provide useful resources and can make it easier to integrate meditation into your daily life.

Breathing exercises: Your breath is a powerful tool to ease stress and make you feel less anxious, says WebMD [657] (medically reviewed by **Nayana Ambardekar, M.D.** [658]). Simple breathing exercises can make a big difference if you make them part of your daily routine.

Dr. Kapil explains that deep breathing has been shown in scientific literature to promote a bodily sense of calm by reversing the stress response. Also called "fight or flight," this response is your nervous system's natural reaction to anxiety. When you're anxious, focus on taking slow, deep

---

[657] Deep Breathing Exercises & Techniques for Stress Management and Relief, webmd.com
[658] Nayana Ambardekar, M.D., Board-Certified General Internist, Atlanta VA Medical Center, webmd.com

breaths through your nose, and make sure you're using your diaphragm and expanding your belly as you breathe. This can help soothe your mental and physical health.

Getting enough sleep: Anxiety can make it hard to sleep, but poor sleep can also contribute to anxiety, either causing or worsening anxiety disorders. In general, sleep deprivation can take a toll on mental health, including triggering anxiety. Research shows people who already have anxiety experience heightened anxiety when they get less sleep.

Weighted blankets: Users say these heavy bed covers feel like a cozy, all-over hug. Weighted blankets can have a calming effect, promoting healthy sleep and helping to manage anxiety. One reason they feel so good is that they push your body downwards, which is called grounding. Studies suggest grounding can decrease the body's levels of cortisol, a stress hormone that can cause anxiety. Grounding can also improve sleep quality – which can improve anxiety symptoms. If you buy a weighted blanket, aim for one that's about 10% of your body weight.

Eating a healthy diet: A balanced diet rich in fruits, veggies, whole foods, and lean proteins can support brain health. Reducing sugar intake can help, too; sugar can cause your blood sugar to spike and then crash, leading to feelings of anxiety. Skipping meals can have similar effects. Foods rich in omega-3 fatty acids, zinc, and magnesium have been shown to help with anxiety.

Spending time outdoors or with animals: Spending time in nature can help relieve stress and anxiety, improve your mood, and boost feelings of happiness and wellbeing, says the American Heart Association [659] (**Michelle A. Albert, M.D., President** [660]).

Being in nature has been linked with many mental health benefits, including alleviating anxiety, says Dr. Kapil. Going outdoors can help lower heart rate and blood pressure, two common effects of anxiety. A simple ten-minute walk around the block or a few deep breaths in your yard can help zap the effects of stress. Look for something calming and soothing to focus on, like a beautiful sunset or waves washing up on the beach. Spending time with animals can also help. Research suggests that furry friends can lower cortisol, a stress hormone that's associated with anxiety. The effects are even better if you can pet an animal – one experiment found people who did so experienced lower anxiety symptoms. This explains why 'goat yoga' is a thing!

Time Management Skills: Sometimes, the stressors of everyday life – like a busy schedule – can cause symptoms of anxiety. Implementing time management skills is an important component of staving off stress. Keep a digital or paper calendar to manage your day. When you can see what's coming up, you'll be able to plan ahead, helping events feel less stressful.

"Doctor, Doctor!"

Make a diligent effort to use these trusted remedies. If you aren't seeing the results you hoped for, make a call to your doctor. Don't be embarrassed to discuss emotional issues with your doctor; most will say that they wish their patients were more open about stress and anxiety – because these issues have a profound impact on health, and because we have better ways than ever to treat them. There are different ways to treat anxiety in different

---

[659] Spend Time in Nature to Reduce Stress and Anxiety | American Heart Association, heart.org
[660] Michelle A. Albert, M.D. | American Heart Association, heart.org

people. Your doctor can help you choose the right options for you.

Alcohol, herbs, supplements, and such can negatively interact with antidepressants, antibiotics, blood thinners, and other medications. Always consult a doctor before trying a new supplement, especially if you have preexisting health conditions or are on any prescription drugs; always follow doctor's instructions about prescription medication. You can also find free assessments online, like the one offered by K-Health.com. [661]

COST-SAVINGS EXAMPLE:

In some cases, counseling or medical intervention over a limited period of time can set things straight in terms of stress and anxiety. However in other cases, professional treatment for stress and anxiety disorders becomes a lifetime commitment. While this may be the best option in some cases, try to avoid the costs – financial and personal – with physician-trusted remedies to control your stress.

You may wish to get a second opinion before starting any anti-anxiety medication. Read the warning insert thoroughly and discuss any concerns with your pharmacist. You can often find the warning inserts online without having to fill the prescription. Then you can make an informed decision about the risks versus the benefits.

SUNBURN

If your skin is unprotected, it can burn in only a few minutes, says Allina Health [662] (Jessica Dehler, PA-C, **Hsieng Su, M.D., Senior Vice President, Chief Medical Executive** [663]). Use these doctor-trusted remedies to treat sunburns and soothe the sting:

Get out of the sun immediately: Find some shade, go indoors, or at least cover your exposed skin with clothing, an umbrella or anything else that will block the sun.

Hydrate: A sunburn draws water away from other parts of the body toward your skin. Drink plenty of water—right away and for a few days after—to avoid becoming dehydrated.

Take a cold shower or bath: While it might sting a little, a brief cold shower will lower the temperature of your skin and reduce inflammation.

Apply cold compresses or moisturizer to blisters: Do not break open any blisters intentionally, as this can cause infection. If a blister does break open, clean the area with mild soap and water. Then apply an antibiotic ointment and cover the area with gauze.

Avoid scratching: Scratching the itch will delay healing and could lead to a skin infection. Try a one-percent hydrocortisone cream or take an antihistamine.

---

[661] Peace of Mind Starts Here: K Mental Health | app.khealth.com
[662] How to treat a sunburn, Allina Health, allinahealth.org | Image: Chanut is Industries, The Noun Project
[663] Hsieng Su, M.D., Senior Vice President and Chief Medical Executive, Allina Health, allinahealth.org

Take NSAIDs: Take aspirin or ibuprofen for the pain.

Aloe vera: Don't pick or pull at peeling skin. Use a moisturizer such as 100% aloe vera. Aloe contains compounds that have antibacterial and anti-inflammatory properties.

Apple cider vinegar: Cider vinegar can promote healing and restore pH balance. To use this, add one cup of cider vinegar to a bath.

Essential oils: Peppermint, lavender, chamomile, and tea tree oil can reduce inflammation and cool your skin. Dilute the essential oils with a "carrier" oil such as almond oil, or add the essential oils to a moisturizer such as aloe vera.

Oatmeal: Oatmeal is a natural anti-inflammatory. You can make a paste of oatmeal and cold milk and apply it to your skin, or add oatmeal to a cool bath and soak in it.

Coconut oil: This oil is rich in natural fats like linoleic and lauric acids, which have moisturizing and antimicrobial properties. It's best for later in the healing process to keep skin hydrated.

Witch hazel: Witch hazel applied to the skin can provide anti-inflammatory relief.

Cucumbers: These cool veggies are a natural antioxidant and analgesic (pain reliever). You can chill cucumbers, mash them in a blender and apply the paste to your skin.

Shaving cream. Think about it – shaving cream is all about soothing irritated skin. Perhaps you remember tv commercials for "the medicated, comfort shave." Shaving cream with menthol can soothe mild sunburn. Apply a thin layer to the affected area, let dry for 30 minutes and rinse.

"Doctor, Doctor!"

Get medical care if you have any of these symptoms: blistering on more than 20 percent of your body; fainting or weakness; high fever, headache, dehydration, confusion or nausea; skin infection; sunburn doesn't respond to treatment.

<u>COST-SAVINGS EXAMPLE:</u>

With sunburn, the key to cost saving is prevention. A 6.7 oz. tube of SFP 70 sunscreen is under $10 on Amazon. [664] Even if you have to "overpay" at a beachside convenience store, it's still worth every penny to avoid the burn and the pain.

Actual treatments for sunburn are mostly inexpensive, but losing a day or two of work for a sunburn could make a dent in your paycheck or cost you vacation days.

Save lost productivity and lost wages by preventing sunburn with a few dollars' worth of sunscreen.

---

[664] Neutrogena Beach Defense Water Resistant Sunscreen Lotion with Broad Spectrum SPF 70, 6.7 oz

TACHYCARDIA (Heart Palpitations)

 Tachycardia is the medical term for a heart rate over 100 beats a minute, [665] though you may be more familiar with the term palpitations. Although heart palpitations can be a warning sign that you have a thyroid or heart issue, palpitations can also occur organically and often do not require medical treatment, says the Integrative Cardiology Center of Long Island [666] (**Regina Druz, M.D.,** board-certified in cardiovascular disease and internal medicine [667]).

There are many ways to relieve heart palpitations, says Dr. Druz. In the majority of cases, these trusted remedies bring relief to the heart and help it operate normally.

Reduce stress: Stress inhibits our minds and even our bodies from functioning properly. When you feel heart palpitations, you should take a moment or two to relax and let any tension ease from your body. Practicing yoga, meditation, journaling, or deep breathing can help keep your heart working well and can be used in the moment to relieve heart palpitations. See the section on **Stress** just a few pages back in this directory.

Avoid stimulants: Your heart doesn't need to work overtime, but many of the things we do in everyday life make our heart work twice as hard. From smoking tobacco, drinking alcohol, and illegal drug use, to caffeine and some medications, these stimulants make it harder for the heart to function, leading to palpitations.

Stimulate the vagus nerve: The vagus nerve connects your brain to your heart. Re-stimulating the connection through coughing, gagging, taking a cold shower, or holding your breath while pushing out, like making a bowel movement, will help the heart synchronize with the brain, as it usually does.

Food and water: Eat foods with magnesium, potassium, and calcium, while staying hydrated. This boosts your heart function by providing electrolytes. Electrolytes help transfer electrical signals, which is directly linked to your heart rate. Potatoes, bananas, and avocados have lots of potassium, while dark leafy greens and dairy foods are high in magnesium and calcium.

"Doctor, Doctor!"

Even if some of these natural remedies for heart health help relieve the pain, feeling palpitations for more than a few seconds, or a prolonged period is a sign that you should see a specialist, advises Dr. Druz. While heart failure is uncommon with these symptoms, it can occur. If you are unsure of what to do about your heart palpitations, contact a cardiologist to learn more about your condition. [668]

COST-SAVINGS EXAMPLE:

The above trusted remedies for heart palpitations are very inexpensive. Since

---

[665] Tachycardia, Symptoms and causes, Mayo Clinic, mayoclinic.org | Image: Vectors Point, The Noun Project
[666] Home Remedies For Relieving Your Heart Palpitations, Integrative Cardiology Center of Long Island
[667] Regina Druz, M.D., Integrative Cardiology Center of Long Island, Greenvale, NY, iccli.com
[668] Register as a patient, Integrative Cardiology Center of Long Island, holisticheartcenter.md-hq.com

palpitations can be a warning sign that you have a thyroid or heart issue, you should see a doctor even if these remedies are completely effective. As with most conditions, the earlier they are detected, the more treatment options are available, which could save you money as well as improving your health.

TMJ

TMJ stands for temporomandibular joint, the two joints that connect your lower jaw to your skull. If you have pain when you chew or yawn, you know the discomfort of TMJ disorders, says the TMJ Association [669] (**Allen W. Cowley, Jr., Ph.D.,** Scientific Advisory Board Chairman [670]). You may find relief with some or all of the following therapies to manage TMJ symptoms at home.

Moist heat and cold packs: A survey of TMJ patients showed the most frequently used intervention (65% of respondents) was thermal therapy (hot or cold compresses) to the jaw. 74% of respondents said that use of compresses resulted in a reduction of their symptoms.

Moist heat: If you have a dull, steady ache rather than sharp pain, heat may help increase blood circulation to the area, relax jaw muscles, and improve function. Soak a couple of washcloths in warm water and hold them to your face for 20 minutes or so. Run them under hot water a few times to keep them hot. Moist heat from a heat pack or a hot water bottle wrapped in a warm, moist towel can also be effective. Be careful to avoid burning yourself when using heat.

Cold packs: When you feel occasional sharp pain in your jaw joints, apply a pair of cold packs to decrease inflammation, numb pain and promote healing. Wrap a couple of cold packs in thin towels and hold them on both sides of your face for about 10 -15 minutes, but not longer than 20 minutes or you could cause mild frostbite. Repeat every two hours as needed. Do not place a cold pack directly on your skin. Keep the pack wrapped in a clean cloth while you are using it.

Soft foods: Temporarily eating soft or blended foods may help by allowing the jaws and surrounding muscles to rest. Especially avoid extremely hard, crunchy and chewy foods, or foods that require you to open your mouth wide, such as apples or corn on the cob. Choose soups, pastas, and other easy-to-eat foods.

NSAIDS: Short-term use of over-the-counter pain medicines or non-steroidal anti-inflammatory drugs, such as ibuprofen, may help.

"Doctor, Doctor!"

Routine dental care to maintain your teeth and gums is important in the overall management of TMJ disorders, says the TMJ Association. Their guide, *Temporomandibular Disorders – Dental Care and You,* [671] provides oral hygiene self-care

---

[669] Self Care, The TMJ Association, tmj.org | Image: Gan Khoon Lay, The Noun Project
[670] Allen W. Cowley, Jr., PhD, Medical College of Wisconsin, mcw.edu
[671] Temporomandibular Disorders, Dental Care and You - The TMJ Association, tmj.org

tips that you can do at home, as well as suggestions for dental appointments.

After you have used home therapies, if your symptoms don't improve within several weeks or months, you should discuss your concerns with your doctor. It is important that your doctor rule out any other conditions which could be causing your symptoms. Your doctor may prescribe stronger pain or anti-inflammatory medications, muscle relaxants, or antidepressants to help ease symptoms. The TMJ Association also offers a list of questions to ask your doctor before consenting to any treatment (see footnote). [672]

COST-SAVINGS EXAMPLE:

The cost of TMJ surgery can vary widely depending on the severity of the case and the root cause, says Lake Norman Oral & Facial Surgery [673] (Raymond J. Haigney II, DDS, FACS [674]) Overall patients can expect to pay between $5,000 and $50,000.

If physician-trusted remedies correct your condition, you may avoid thousands – or tens of thousands – of dollars in surgical treatment costs.

TENDONITIS

Tendons are what connect your muscles to your bones, explains Missouri Orthopedics & Advanced Sports Medicine [675] (**David W. Irvine, M.D.** [676]). When a tendon becomes inflamed, as a result of overuse, it's known as tendonitis (sometimes spelled *tendinitis*). The most common areas for the condition are your elbow, shoulder, hip, knee, Achilles tendon and base of your thumb. If you have been experiencing this pain, due to a sports injury or daily tasks, here are five self-care remedies to help reduce tendonitis.

Ice and heat: To help reduce swelling, apply an ice pack, or frozen bag of vegetables, wrapped in a towel, for at least half an hour, 3 to 4 times a day. Never place an ice pack or bag directly on the skin as this can cause damage to skin tissue if left on too long. Applying a warm compress, like a heating pad or heating pods, helps to increase the blood flow and speed up the healing process. This not only feels good on the injury, but it helps relax tight muscles and relieves pain.

Compression: As mentioned in the above, a warm compress helps to increase blood flow. Compression alone helps to prevent buildup of other fluids in your body and limits swelling. It can give the affected area more support while continuing to exercise safely. Look for compression aids such as compression socks, elbow to ankle braces, supports and straps.

---

[672] Educate Yourself, Questions You Should Ask, The TMJ Association, tmj.org
[673] TMJ Surgery Cost, Lake Norman Oral & Facial Surgery, lakenormanofs.com
[674] Raymond J. Haigney II, DDS, FACS, Huntersville, NC, lakenormanofs.com
[675] 5 Home Remedies to Help Reduce Tendonitis, Missouri Orthopedics & Advanced Sports Medicine, mosportsmed.com | Image: karina, The Noun Project
[676] David W. Irvine, M.D., Missouri Orthopedics & Advanced Sports Medicine

Herbs: When dealing with tendonitis, you might think of trying herbs. One herb that Missouri Orthopedics trusts to reduce inflammation is curcumin, a yellow pigment found primarily in turmeric and best known as a spice used in curry. Curcumin has anti-inflammatory properties and the ability to increase the amount of antioxidants that the body produces [677]. Other herbs for tendonitis include white willow, ginger, devil's claw and bromelain. Remember when taking herbs to treat them like any medication and only take the recommended dosage.

Food: Eating the right foods, such as adding more brightly colored vegetables to your diet, can provide your body with vitamins and minerals to also help reduce tendonitis. Salmon, flaxseeds and certain kinds of nuts have Omega-3 fatty acids, which carry strong anti-inflammatory ingredients. When you balance your eating habits with plenty of protein and iron-enriched foods this will strengthen your body and lessen the risk of injuries that could lead to tendonitis.

Rest: Lastly, but certainly not the least important, is to make sure you give yourself ample amounts of rest. Take a few days off from your regular exercising or lower the intensity level to allow the tendonitis to subside. Be sure to get the recommended amount of sleep, 7-8 hours, as this is the best time when your body is rebuilding and repairing your muscles and tissues. It also allows pressure to be released from your tendonitis pain.

"Doctor, Doctor!"

If you have tried these self-care remedies but the pain is still persisting, contact an orthopedist for more options to reduce and treat your tendonitis. They'll help you get back to the sports you love and the daily activities you enjoy. [678]

COST-SAVINGS EXAMPLE:

Tendon or muscle repair in the forearm or wrist has an estimated national average cost $11,393. [679] Costs will vary based on your individual case, where you live, and your insurance plan. You might also miss time from work, resulting in lost wages.

Try these trusted remedies before your tendonitis becomes chronic, possibly saving yourself the expense – and the experience – of having to go through surgery.

TICK BITES

Prevention is the key to avoiding tick-borne diseases. Deer ticks live in grassy or wooded areas in all eastern and central states and as far west as Texas, Oklahoma, Kansas, Nebraska, South Dakota, and North Dakota, says Norton Healthcare of

[677] Curcumin: Health Benefits, Dosage, Safety, Side-Effects, And More, Supplements, Examine.Com
[678] Missouri Orthopedics & Advanced Sports Medicine, St. Louis, mosportsmed.com
[679] Tendon or Muscle Repair in Forearm or Wrist, MedSave.com

Louisville, KY [680] (**Steve Heilman, M.D.,** [681] Senior Vice President, Chief Health Innovation Officer).

When heading for fields and forests, treat clothing with permethrin, an insecticide that can kill ticks on contact. The product is available at REI, Dick's Sporting Goods, Walmart, Amazon, and other retailers. Wear long sleeves and long pants when outdoors. As soon as you come indoors, check your entire body, clothing and any gear for ticks. However if you're reading this, it may be too late for prevention. Here's what doctors recommend to treat a tick bite.

Remove it immediately: If you find a tick, remove it as soon as possible. Using fine-tipped tweezers, grasp the tick as close to the skin as possible and pull the tick upward in a steady motion. To increase the chances of removing the entire tick and not leaving parts behind, do not use twisting or jerking movements. If you don't have fine-tipped tweezers, dental floss may be used to "lasso" the tick, or a coating of liquid soap may convince it to let go.

Clean: Clean the area with rubbing alcohol or soap and water.

"Doctor, Doctor!"

See a provider if you can't remove the tick completely. A tick-borne disease can be a lifetime ailment, while a trip to urgent care is a one-time expense. If in doubt, go to urgent care.

See a provider if you develop a rash, especially one that looks like a bullseye.

See a provider if you have pain or swelling at the site of a bite, or any of these symptoms: difficulty breathing, headache, nausea, weakness, chills, swollen lymph nodes.

Your health care provider may prescribe doxycycline, says Norton Healthcare. The provider may start you on an antibiotic if it's within 72 hours of the tick removal. If you can retain the tick, or take pictures with your phone, it may be possible to determine if it is a species that carries Lyme disease. Estimating the amount of time the tick was attached may also help your health care provider determine treatment options.

COST-SAVINGS EXAMPLE:

Lyme disease can take an incredible toll on patients and families, says the Global Lyme Alliance. [682] **Do not take chances or cut corners when it comes to a tick bite. A phone call to your doctor or a visit to urgent care is probably a wise precaution. Save money elsewhere.**

Remember that throughout this directory you can find further information by using the sources at the bottom of every page.

---

[680] Rash, Bug Bites And Tick Bite: How To Care For 3 Common Skin Issues, NortonHealthcare.com
[681] Dr. Steven Heilman, M.D., Emergency Medicine Specialist in Louisville, KY | Healthgrades
[682] The True Cost of Lyme Treatment, globallymealliance.org

TOOTH PAIN

 Toothaches can be caused by tooth decay, gum irritation, a broken tooth, repetitive motions such as chewing, or an abscessed tooth, says Klement Family Dental of St. Petersburg, FL [683] (**Stephen M. Klement, DMD** [684]). While these are all possibilities, the leading reason people get toothaches is that there's an irritation of the nerve in the root of the tooth.

Most toothaches are preventable by regular flossing, brushing with fluoride toothpaste, and having regular dental cleanings. Many of the remedies below work by calming inflammation in your mouth, killing harmful bacteria, or acting as a numbing agent, says Dr. Klement.

Ice: Applying ice to the area of the painful tooth can help to numb the pain. You can try different versions of this technique. Wrap some ice in a towel and apply it to the affected area. Keep the compress in place for 15 minutes at a time. Also, you could try holding ice water in your mouth for several seconds at a time. Don't bite the ice, however, as it could break your teeth.

Elevate your head: Though it may be difficult to get to sleep when you have a toothache, lying down can make your pain worse. When going to sleep, try propping your head up with pillows or sleep in a recliner with your head up, if possible.

Over the counter medications: Aspirin and ibuprofen target inflammation and can give you some pain relief. Alternating acetaminophen (Tylenol) and ibuprofen (Advil) can give better pain relief. Oral gels can also be applied directly to your tooth and gums to ease your pain.

Salt water rinse: Rinsing with salt water serves two purposes. The rinsing action can dislodge substances stuck between your teeth. Salt can also help draw out any infection and reduce inflammation. Mix a ½ teaspoon of salt with warm water and gargle like a mouthwash.

Hydrogen peroxide rinse: Hydrogen peroxide is also useful for attacking inflammation and bacteria. When using a hydrogen peroxide rinse, mix 1 part three percent hydrogen peroxide with 2 parts water. Do not swallow the solution; it's not a problem if you swallow a few drops, just dilute it by drinking a glass of water.

Tea Bags: You can apply either a cold or warm tea bag to your tooth. If applying a used tea bag, make sure that it has cooled down so that it is not hot but is still warm. If you prefer the cold option, try placing a used tea bag in the freezer for a few minutes, then apply it to your tooth. Peppermint tea may be especially good for toothaches due to its bacteria-fighting properties. However, tea can stain your teeth, so don't use this method often.

Garlic: In addition to combating bacteria, garlic is also a pain reliever. You can make a paste out of crushed garlic that you can apply to your tooth. You can also chew on a piece of fresh garlic clove or soak a cotton ball in garlic oil and place it on your tooth.

Vanilla Extract: Another natural anti-inflammatory, vanilla, can also help to numb the pain caused by a toothache. Try putting a small amount on your finger or a cotton swab and applying it

---

[683] 12 Home Remedies for Toothaches, Klement Family Dental | Image: Nur Achmadi Yusuf, The Noun Project
[684] Dentists in St. Petersburg, FL, Stephen M. Klement, DMD, Klement Family Dental, stpetedentist.com

to the affected area a few times a day.

Clove: There are several ways you can use this spice to treat your toothache. Since clove is an antiseptic, it is useful for reducing inflammation and pain. You can put clove oil on a cotton ball and apply it to the painful area, or place a drop of the oil directly on your tooth. Alternatively, you can also put a drop of clove oil into a glass of water and use it as a mouthwash.

Guava leaves: Guava leaves have anti-inflammatory and anti-microbial properties that can help to soothe your aching tooth. You can use the leaves to make a tea that you allow to cool and use as a rinse, or simply chew on the leaves to get some relief.

Wheatgrass: There are many benefits of wheatgrass that make it a useful means of treating your toothache. Like many of the other methods mentioned, it is great for addressing infections caused by bacteria. So, simply get some wheatgrass juice and rinse it in your mouth a few times a day.

Thyme: Thyme oil can be used as a rinse or applied directly to your tooth. To rinse, add a drop of oil to a glass of water and use it as a mouthwash. To apply to your tooth, dilute some oil with water, place a few drops on a cotton ball, and put on your tooth.

"Doctor, Doctor!"

These tips are meant to provide temporary relief to get you through the day (or night), not to permanently cure a toothache that is causing you extreme pain, says Dr. Klement. Tooth decay can progress into the nerve, creating sensitivity to hot and cold. If left unattended, it can progress into pain or throbbing sensation. If you're experiencing an intense toothache, it will need treatment right away. Putting it off will only make things worse and prolong your pain. Contact your dentist and book an appointment.

COST-SAVINGS EXAMPLE:

For reasons that defy logic, dental care is not usually covered by medical insurance, even though tooth decay and tooth loss are directly tied to heart disease, dementia, poor nutrition in the elderly, and other serious health concerns. You'll either need dental insurance or the ability to pay out of pocket.

Take care of your dental health by flossing (very inexpensive), brushing (also inexpensive), and getting regular check-ups (likely the lowest cost service your dentist offers).

Dental care can be costly. But as long as you have a trustworthy provider, it's probably worth it. Proper care will end your pain, keep oral health from getting worse, and may save your teeth. Dental enamel is the most valuable commodity on earth; you can't regrow it, so take care of it.

ULCERS

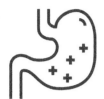

Stomach ulcers (gastric ulcers) are open sores within the lining of the stomach, explains Healthline [685], one of the internet's best sources for physician-approved remedies (medically reviewed by **Judith Marcin, M.D.** [686]). If you have one, you know an ulcer is as painful as it sounds; an open wound bathed 24/7 in stomach acid is not a happy combination.

The most common cause of stomach ulcers is the bacterium *Helicobacter pylori*, or *H. pylori*. Ulcers may also be caused by overuse of painkillers, such as aspirin and other non-steroidal anti-inflammatories, such as ibuprofen (Advil, Motrin) or naproxen (Naprosyn). Research supports several natural trusted home remedies for managing a stomach ulcer. Talk with your doctor about adding these foods to your diet:

Flavonoids: Flavonoids, also known as bioflavonoids, may be an effective treatment for stomach ulcers, says Healthline. Flavonoids occur naturally in many fruits and vegetables. Foods rich in flavonoids include: soybeans, legumes, red grapes, kale, broccoli, apples, berries, teas, especially green tea. Flavonoids are referred to as gastroprotective, as they defend the lining of the stomach and could allow ulcers to heal. You can get flavonoids in your diet or take them as supplements.

Licorice: One study showed that licorice might help ulcers heal by inhibiting the growth of *H. pylori*. Specifically, you want deglycyrrhizinated licorice, which is just licorice with the sweet flavor extracted. Deglycyrrhizinated licorice is available as a supplement. You can't get this effect from eating licorice candy, though, says Healthline.

Probiotics: Probiotics are living bacteria and yeast that provide important microorganisms to your digestive tract. They are present in many common foods, particularly fermented foods. These include: buttermilk, yogurt, miso, kimchi, kefir. You can also take probiotics in supplement form. Studies show that probiotics may be helpful in wiping out *H. pylori* and increasing the recovery rate for people with ulcers when added to a regimen of antibiotics.

Honey: Honey is a powerful antibacterial and has been shown to inhibit *H. pylori* growth. Depending on the plant it's derived from, honey can contain up to 200 elements, including polyphenols and other antioxidants. As long as you have normal blood sugar levels, you can enjoy honey as you would any sweetener, with the bonus of perhaps soothing your ulcers.

Garlic: Garlic extract has been shown to inhibit *H. pylori* growth in lab, animal, and human trials. If you don't like the taste of garlic, you can take it in supplement form. Garlic acts as a blood thinner, so ask your doctor before taking it if you use blood thinners or aspirin.

Cranberry: Cranberry has been shown to help decrease urinary tract infections by preventing bacteria from settling on the walls of the bladder. Cranberry and cranberry extract also may help fight *H. pylori*. You can drink cranberry juice, eat cranberries, or take cranberry supplements. Start with modest amounts and increase gradually. Many commercial cranberry juices are heavily sweetened with sugar or high fructose corn syrup, which can add empty calories. Avoid those juices by buying juice sweetened only by other juices.

---

[685] The Best Natural and Home Remedies for Ulcers, Healthline.com | Image: Becris, The Noun Project
[686] Dr. Judith L. Marcin, M.D., Family Medicine Doctor, Cornelius, OR, health.usnews.com

Mastic: Mastic is the sap of a tree grown in the Mediterranean. Studies of the effectiveness of mastic are mixed, but at least one study shows that chewing mastic gum may help fight *H. pylori.* You can chew the gum or swallow mastic in supplement form.

Fruits, vegetables, and whole grains: A diet centered on fruits, vegetables, and whole grains is good for your overall health. According to Mayo Clinic, a vitamin-rich diet can also help your body heal your ulcer. Foods containing polyphenols may protect you from ulcers and help ulcers heal. Polyphenol-rich foods and seasonings include: dried rosemary, flaxseed, Mexican oregano, dark chocolate, blueberries, raspberries, strawberries, elderberries, blackberries, and black olives.

"Doctor, Doctor!"

Stomach ulcers are often treated with antibiotics to kill the bacteria and medications to reduce and block stomach acid, says Healthline. Stomach ulcers don't stop at abdominal pain, says Healthline. If left untreated, they can create a hole in the stomach, which requires surgery. On rare occasions, ulcers might signal larger problems, like cancer. If the above remedies are not enough to relieve your discomfort, call your doctor. [687]

COST-SAVINGS EXAMPLE:

Some medicines for stomach ulcers are inexpensive, like Prilosec, just $12 with GoodRx. However, others are priced at $500 to $1,000 or more per prescription. [688]

Save up to $1,069 per prescription on ulcer medications by using trusted remedies in consultation with your doctor.

URINARY TRACT INFECTION

While antibiotics are the fastest and most recommended way to treat urinary tract infections, they sometimes don't work, says the National Association for Continence (NASC) [689] (**Donna Deng, M.D., Chair** [690]). You may also be wary of taking an antibiotic due to certain risks that accompany that treatment. Fortunately, self-care remedies for urinary tract infections are often effective.

Drink lots of water: Repeat after us: *"the solution to pollution is dilution."* Drinking lots of water, and emptying your bladder regularly, will help flush harmful bacteria from your system, says the NASC. You may be hesitant to drink water due to the burning sensation you may have when peeing, but getting your recommended 8 glasses a day will do you a world of good.

---

[687] The Best Natural and Home Remedies for Ulcers, Healthline.com
[688] Compare Duodenal Ulcer Medication Prices for Brand and Generic Drugs, GoodRx.com
[689] 5 Home Remedies For UTIs, National Association For Continence | Image: Icon Market, The Noun Project
[690] Donna Deng, M.D., Board Member, National Association For Continence, nafc.org

Unsweetened cranberry juice: Cranberries have been used to prevent UTIs for generations. Studies show that cranberries make it harder for bacteria to stick to the urinary tract walls. "Unsweetened" is key here – consuming added sugars may make your infection worse.

Don't "hold it": We all get busy, but holding off bathroom breaks gives any bacteria already in your bladder the chance to grow and multiply, potentially resulting in infection. Drink lots of water and when you have to go, go. Another good prevention measure – be sure to pee after sexual activity to wash away any harmful bacteria and prevent it from spreading.

Take a probiotic: Introducing a probiotic to your system may help to replenish the naturally occurring, healthy bacteria that live in the gut, says the NASC. Probiotics are found in supplement form or they occur naturally in certain foods including yogurts, kombucha, and kefir.

Eat garlic: A study showed that garlic may be effective in reducing the bacteria that cause UTIs.

Add vitamin C to your diet. Not only does vitamin C help strengthen your immune system, it may also acidify your urine, limiting the growth of bacteria and preventing UTIs. Just be careful of eating too many acidic foods when you have a UTI, as they can potentially irritate your bladder and make UTI symptoms worse. Again, plenty of water helps neutralize everything.

Avoid bladder-irritating foods: Certain foods are known bladder irritants – acidic foods, artificial sweeteners, caffeine, and alcohol – leading to bladder leaks. Try to watch out for these common bladder irritants to prevent further irritation to your bladder and UTI.

Wipe from front to back: You already know this, but here's a reminder. UTIs often develop from the spread of bacteria from the rectum. Always wipe from front to back to avoid spreading bacteria to the urethra, and on to the urinary tract.

Wear loose clothing. The idea is to prevent moisture from accumulating in the pelvic region, which could make your infection worse. Cotton and other natural materials are best – they help keep moisture at bay and will help you feel more comfortable.

Apply heat: Use a heating pad, a warm washcloth, or a hot water bottle to apply heat to your pelvic area if you're feeling pain or discomfort there from your UTI. You may also wish to take a warm bath to help relieve any pain and to help your muscles relax, the NASC suggests.

Take an OTC pain reliever: Over-the-counter pain medications can temporarily relieve pain caused by a UTI. Use caution here, and always speak with a doctor first, as some UTIs can turn into kidney infections. In these cases, patients should avoid taking non-steroidal anti-inflammatory drugs (NSAIDs), which could make the infection worse.

"Doctor, Doctor!"

If symptoms persist beyond a few days with no sign of improvement, or if your infection continues to recur, the National Association for Continence says it's best to see a doctor. While trusted self-care remedies may ease symptoms for a time, your doctor can find the cause and prescribe a course of antibiotics to take care of your UTI for good.

COST-SAVINGS EXAMPLE:

For patients not covered by health insurance, treatment for an uncomplicated urinary tract infection typically costs less than $300 for a doctor visit, urine culture, antibiotics and an analgesic for pain, says CostHelper. [691]

However, for a severe infection in which the kidneys have become involved and hospitalization is needed, costs can be high. For example, at Baptist Memorial Health Care in Memphis, a urinary tract/kidney infection costs about $13,600-$21,800.

Like most conditions, the longer you wait to cure your UTI, the more it is likely to cost.

Avoid a possible $20,000 hospital bill and days of discomfort by using trusted remedies and consulting a doctor sooner rather than later.

URTICARIA – SEE HIVES

Remember that throughout this directory you can find further information by using the sources at the bottom of every page and in the resources listing beginning on page 259.

> ### Did one of these remedies help you?
>
> Share your trusted remedies success with the publisher! We'd love to hear from you. **info@trustedremedies.com**

---

[691] Cost of Urinary Tract Infection Treatment, CostHelper.com

VARICOSE VEINS

Sixty percent of adults are affected by varicose veins, reports Vantage Radiology & Diagnostic Services [692] (**Philip Lund, M.D., President** [693]). Left untreated, the condition may lead to bleeding, blood clots, infections, rashes, or sores.

You can successfully reduce or eliminate the effects of varicose veins with remedies right at home. These popular, simple self-care remedies can help prevent worsening symptoms of your varicose veins:

Compression stockings: Compression stockings can improve your circulation, whether you already have varicose veins, or need relief from the effects of prolonged sitting or standing. Check an online resource such as Discount Surgical to select the best size for your needs. [694]

Eat flavonoids: Fruits and vegetables loaded with antioxidants will support your varicose veins by strengthening your blood vessels and improving their function. These foods include apples, berries, broccoli, garlic, green tea, onions. These foods can also reduce and eliminate inflammation, which leads to varicose veins, says Vantage.

Eat high-fiber foods: High-fiber foods like beans, fresh fruits, lentils, nuts, seeds, vegetables, and whole grains make your veins and arteries stronger and more flexible.

Epsom salt: Soak in a bath with Epsom salt to reduce inflammation and swelling. You can use Epsom salt daily to reduce symptoms from your varicose veins.

Exercise: When you regularly exercise, you improve your blood circulation while lowering your blood pressure, thus reducing the likelihood of experiencing varicose veins. Here are some examples of exercises you can do: Cycling, Swimming, Walking.

Yoga: Exercise will help you to feel better, and you'll also mitigate the appearance and worsening effects of your varicose veins.

Hot & cold compresses: Use compresses to reduce the inflammation and swelling in your feet and legs. You can alternate hot and cold to relax your muscles and improve circulation.

Massage: Proper massage techniques can help improve your circulation while reducing the pain and discomfort in your legs and feet. It can also help you reduce stress levels, which can affect your varicose veins.

---

[692] Top varicose vein home remedies to help relieve discomfort in legs, Vantage, Seattle, WA, vrads.com
[693] Philip Lund, M.D., FACR, vrads.com | Image: Pike Picture, The Noun Project
[694] What Size Compression Socks Do I Need? Discount Surgical, Brooklyn, NY, discountsurgical.com

Stop smoking: Smoking reduces the flow of blood and increases plaque buildup. Stop smoking and you will positively affect your varicose veins and the rest of your body as well.

"Doctor, Doctor!"

While physician-trusted self-care remedies can help significantly with your symptoms, often are they not enough to cure your varicose veins. A vein health expert can assess and help you understand your condition, and offer recommendations for helping to mitigate the pain and discomfort. [695]

COST-SAVINGS EXAMPLE:

Because varicose veins are usually caused by an underlying medical condition called venous insufficiency, treatment should be covered by insurance, Advanced Interventional Vein and Vascular Center says. [696] **The exception is in cases where the condition is merely cosmetic, such as sclerotherapy for small varicose veins.**

The leading treatments for varicose veins – vein ablation and sclerotherapy – cannot be achieved with self-care. Ablation procedures usually cost between $3000 and $5000, depending on the practice location. If the above remedies do not produce satisfactory results for you, consult a specialist. As mentioned above, untreated varicose veins may lead to blood clots and other serious conditions, so try self-care remedies, but don't put off getting medical attention.

WARTS

Warts are caused by viruses and typically go away on their own in a year or two, says GoodRx Health [697] (reviewed by **Sophie Vergnaud, M.D.** [698]). But if your warts are uncomfortable, unsightly, or you just want to get rid of them faster, these doctor-trusted self-care remedies may help.

Duct tape: Though it's one of the most popular wart removal remedies, research is unclear. It may or may not help. This remedy consists of covering the wart with a piece of duct tape and changing the tape every few days. It may take a few weeks to see results, if any. So might help, can't hurt.

Salicylic acid: Salicylic acid is available over-the-counter and works by wearing down the layers of the wart over time, explains GoodRx Health. Sometimes, salicylic acid can cause irritation to the surrounding skin, so apply with care. Overall, studies show that this may be one of the

---

[695] About Vantage Radiology & Diagnostic Services, vrads.com
[696] Are Varicose Vein Treatment Costs Covered by Insurance? Advanced Interventional Vein and Vascular Center, Woodbridge and Alexandria, VA, vaveinandvascular.com
[697] What Are the Best Natural Remedies and At-Home Treatments for Warts and Verrucas? GoodRx.com
[698] Sophie Vergnaud, M.D., GoodRx.com | Image: Shital Patel

most-effective self-care remedies, especially for plantar warts.

Garlic: Garlic extract has antiviral properties and can be used to remove warts. One study showed that garlic extract helped treat warts without recurrence after 3 to 4 months.

Apple cider vinegar: Some people swear by apple cider vinegar banishing warts. However, there is no current research that proves it's effective. It's relatively safe to try at home, but stop using it if it causes skin irritation. Other than that, it's another case of might help, can't hurt.

Nail polish: Using clear nail polish on warts is another popular if unsupported home remedy. The idea is that the nail polish "suffocates" the wart and makes it go away faster. As with other remedies, apply carefully to reduce contact with surrounding healthy skin. Might help ….

"Doctor, Doctor!"

You'll have to decide if your warts are bothersome enough to justify a visit to the dermatologist. If they are on your face or your genitals, that's probably reason enough to see a doctor – these aren't areas where you want to be applying duct tape or nail polish. Of course, if you're going for a skin check-up anyway, go ahead and ask about treatment for your warts.

COST-SAVINGS EXAMPLE:

Wart removal typically costs about $190 total for intralesional immunotherapy, says CostHelper; about $360 total for pulsed dye laser therapy, which usually requires one to three treatments; or $610 total for cryotherapy, or freezing, which may include an initial visit and three to four follow-up treatments.

Duct tape, nail polish, and patience may be all it takes to cure your warts for next to no cost, saving you several hundred dollars. On the other hand, if the condition is on your face or genitals, you may be happy to pay to get a cure as quickly and as painlessly as possible.

WEIGHT PROBLEMS – SEE PART I, OVERWEIGHT AND OBESITY

WRINKLES

The health and lifestyle site Stylecraze [699] (medically reviewed by **Dr. Nicholas Jones, M.D.** [700]) offers dozens of doctor-trusted remedies to reduce the appearance of wrinkles without spending a small fortune on skin care products. Try some of these ingredients from your pantry to combat the signs of aging skin:

Organic coconut oil: Coconut oil will give your skin a natural glow and radiance. Using it will often help fade wrinkles as coconut oil is moisturizing and hydrating for the skin. Massage coconut oil under the eyes and other affected areas for a few minutes. Use gentle circular motions. Leave it on overnight. Repeat every night before going to bed.

Grape seed extract or grape seed oil: The seed of this little fruit will help to tighten your skin and impart a healthy glow to it. It does this by supplying the skin with fatty acids, polyphenols, and vitamin E. Massage the oil into the affected area. Leave it on for as long as you can and then wash off. A few re-runs over the next few weeks, and your skin will be supple and wrinkle-free.

Vitamin E: Vitamin E moisturizes and refreshes your skin with antioxidants and hydrating effects, plus anti-inflammatory and photoprotective effects to renew the skin's vigor and reduce wrinkles. Pierce a vitamin E capsule and pour the oil into a small bowl or the palm of your hand. Use as many capsules as needed to cover the area you wish. Apply and massage the area for a few minutes. Leave it on for a couple of hours. This is best done at night before going to bed.

Cucumber juice: This one is another trusted wrinkle remedy that is simply fail proof. Cucumber contains 95% water and many minerals and vitamins. Within a few applications, you will see that the wrinkles and dark circles have visibly reduced. Scoop out the seeds from the cucumber and grate the rest. Squeeze the grated cucumber to extract the juice. Gently cleanse your skin and apply this all over your face. Let it dry naturally and then rinse with water.

Honey: Heavy work really tells around your eyes, and with age, you get wrinkles and your eyes look very tired. Counter this by applying honey near your eyes. It balances the skin's pH and conditions it to decrease the appearance of wrinkles and fine lines. Apply honey on your skin and massage for a minute or so. Leave it on for a half an hour and then rinse with lukewarm water. Shred a small piece of ginger and add it to the honey for added benefits.

Rosehip oil: This essential oil is excellent for deep wrinkles and other signs of premature aging. The Duchess of Cambridge (Catherine, Princess of Wales) swears by the anti-aging effects of this oil. The vitamin A, vitamin E, and fatty acids in it penetrate into the deeper layers of skin and lighten scars and banish wrinkles. Apply the oil on your face and massage until it is absorbed. Leave it on overnight.

In addition to these natural, physician-trusted facials, Stylecraze and Dr. Jones offer these trusted remedies to reduce the appearance of wrinkles:

Sleep: Nothing can be more effective than sleep to ease out those fine lines appearing on the skin. As you sleep, the body goes into the restoration mode, which includes keeping your skin more

---

[699] 30 Effective Home Remedies To Get Wrinkle-Free Skin, Stylecraze.com
[700] Dr. Nicholas Jones, M.D., FACS, Stylecraze.com | Image: Катя Гнидаш, The Noun Project

elastic and less prone to wrinkles. If your body is deprived of rest, it results in an increase in cortisol, which breaks down the skin cells, triggering wrinkle formation. Try to sleep on your back. Sleeping on your side can cause wrinkles on that side to increase. In addition, look under **Insomnia** earlier in this directory for more than a dozen doctor-trusted sleep remedies.

De-stress: Lighten up, for stress can have adverse effects on your beauty. Stress, along with anxiety and tension, could make your skin thin and weaker and prone to wrinkles. Indulge in recreational activities so that stress does not get to you. Think about all the good things in your life – and smile. A smile will help you beat the stress and banish those wrinkles. Life often springs unexpected situations at you. You need to learn the technique of keeping calm, no matter how challenging or adverse the situation may be. Stay relaxed all the time, and maintain a healthy lifestyle. Also check the section on **Stress** just a few pages earlier in this directory.

Water: An adult is advised to drink at least 8 glasses of water in a day. However, says Stylecraze, studies indicate that you should drink two or three times that much water in a day to keep your organs (that includes your skin) healthy. Drinking ample amounts of water helps your body flush out toxic waste; as stated elsewhere in this directory, "the solution to pollution is dilution." A clean inside reflects on the body outside.

Stay out of the sun: Yes, the sun is the most crucial factor that contributes to the generation of wrinkles. The harmful UV rays of the sun are extremely damaging for the skin and deplete it of its natural moisture. The weakened collagen fails to protect the skin from further damage. The risk of skin cancer also increases if you step out in the sun every day without any protection. So, do not forget to use an umbrella or a hat the next time you step out.

Quit smoking and reduce alcohol: Smoking is hazardous to your health in every way, and that includes causing wrinkles. The carcinogens in cigarettes act as a toxic plastic bag around your pretty face, blocking and depriving it of oxygen. This exaggerates the pace with which wrinkles appear on your skin. So, say goodbye to smoking. Also eliminate or cut back on alcohol to reduce skin aging.

"Doctor, Doctor!"

You'll have to decide if your wrinkles are bothersome enough to justify a visit to the dermatologist. The above self-care remedies come from respected dermatologists and should be very helpful. Since wrinkles are a cosmetic issue, not a medical disorder, health insurance is not going to cover the costs of treatment. [701] If the costs are not as important to you as putting your best face forward, call a dermatologist.

COST-SAVINGS EXAMPLE:

Dermatology treatments come at very high costs. Make a concerted effort to use these trusted remedies and your savings could be substantial.

---

[701] Does Health Insurance Cover Dermatology? | ehealthinsurance.com

Folklore remedies only put you at greater risk for dangerous diseases.

*– **Good Housekeeping,** May 3, 2022*

Use physician-trusted remedies instead!

Y-Z

YEAST INFECTION

When it comes to your vagina, anything that seems different can cause alarm, says K-Health, [702] an online network of board-certified doctors with over six million users, available 24/7, in 48 states (**Neil Brown, M.D., Chief Medical Officer** [703]).

If you experience itch, irritation, or soreness and have thick white discharge, take a deep breath, says K-Health – you likely have a vaginal yeast infection. While in some cases you need to see a doctor for help, if your symptoms are mild, these natural remedies, over-the-counter (OTC) treatments, and other medications may help you find relief.

Patience: Mild yeast infections often clear up in a few days. Persistent infections can take up to two weeks to heal completely. During that time, try more of the trusted remedies below.

Boric acid: Boric acid has antifungal and antiviral properties and can be used for homemade vaginal suppositories. It seems to help, particularly in cases when other traditional treatments have failed. One word of caution: Boric acid is toxic to a fetus, avoid it if you may be pregnant.

Probiotics: Early research suggests that taking a probiotic supplement may re-introduce helpful bacteria like *lactobacillus acidophilus* into your body. And some women's health experts believe these supplements help re-establish a more balanced vaginal pH. The science is inconclusive, though, so if you want relief quickly, seek a proven treatment instead, says KHealth.

Yogurt: *Eating* yogurt with live cultures may support immune health. However, it's unclear if this means that consuming yogurt can fight or treat yeast infections. In any case, never smear yogurt *on* your vagina; you'll only feed the fungi and make the infection worse.

Baking soda: Adding up to 1 tablespoon of baking soda to bathwater may help relieve some of your symptoms. Baking soda is reputed to help to soothe ailments like athlete's foot, poison ivy, and hives. Check with your doctor before using baking soda for vaginal yeast infection.

Oil of oregano: Oil of oregano can be used to treat a yeast infection at home. It's easy to obtain from most health food stores or grocery stores. The best way to use this as a treatment is in capsule form, inserting at night. If capsules aren't an option, oil will do just as well. Apply 2-4 drops to the inside of the genital area. This oil can also be applied to a tampon, with or without coconut oil, to achieve the same medicinal effects.

Lemongrass: Lemongrass is an effective remedy for a yeast infection. Studies have found that lemongrass interacted with Candida biofilm formation in a way that would remedy a yeast

---

[702] 13 Home Remedies for Yeast Infections, K-Health, khealth.com
[703] Dr. Neil Brown, Emergency Medicine, K-Health, khealth.com

infection. This essential oil can be applied topically or as a capsule. When using it topically, it's a good idea to use a carrier oil (such as coconut oil) when applying to the affected area.

Vitamins C and E: Both vitamins can be beneficial in treating yeast infections. Because vitamin C boosts the immune system and vitamin E is soothing on the skin, they make a great duo. While the C is giving a boost to your body to fight off the infection, the E boasts anti-inflammatory properties to help reduce the itchiness that often accompanies a yeast infection.

Do Not: Apple cider vinegar is useful for many ailments, but researchers say yeast infection isn't one of them. Never douche with any vinegar; it irritates the skin and aggravates symptoms. There's no evidence that adding apple cider vinegar to a bath will help, either.

Do Not: Garlic has many health benefits; taken orally, it is a reputed yeast infection treatment. Always consult your doctor to understand how much garlic to take. Though some tout garlic as a cure for all kinds of medical conditions, do not use cloves as vaginal suppositories to treat a yeast infection; you may end up burning your vagina or making your condition worse.

Do Not: Douching with hydrogen peroxide might seem like a good idea – after all, it is famously antiseptic and used regularly to clean open wounds of invasive microbes. However, self-treating your vagina with hydrogen peroxide can throw off its pH balance even further, exacerbating a yeast infection.

Do Not: People often use salt water to treat fungal infections like athlete's foot and oral thrush. Some suggest adding salt to bathwater as a gentle way to kill candida albicans, but more research is necessary to show this works.

"Doctor, Doctor!"

Nearly 1.4 million American women seek medical help for a yeast infection every year. If you have symptoms for more than three days, talk to a provider. Also see a doctor if you are pregnant, have chronic yeast infections, have STD-related symptoms, or are unsure if you have a yeast infection. On the other hand, if your symptoms are mild and want some relief, the physician-trusted remedies above may be "just what the doctor ordered."

COST-SAVINGS EXAMPLE:

Yeast infections are inexpensive to treat as long as they don't go on too long. Get started right away with these trusted remedies, but call a doctor after three days. Restoring your vaginal health is more important than saving the cost of a doctor's visit.

ZOSTER – SEE SHINGLES

RESOURCES

Here's a state-by-state list of the dedicated doctors and providers who have made the effort to share their trusted self-care remedies with the public. Use it to find services that may suit your needs for professional care. Included for each provider is the section(s) in this directory where you'll find their remedies. *Keep in mind that they likely treat other conditions beyond those listed here; check their websites to learn more.* Also bear in mind that individual practitioners may have changed positions; you may wish to ask for their new contact information or who has taken their place. Only providers of patient healthcare who are accepting new patients at the time of publication are listed. In addition, find other sources of goods and services to meet your personal healthcare needs by using the footnotes with each entry in this directory – nearly 700 footnotes in all.

VIRTUAL, REMOTE, and NATIONWIDE RESOURCES

Cedrina Calder, M.D. | Fitdocofficial.com
Helping women improve their health, transform their lives, and become the best version of themselves
See their remedies under Overweight and Obesity (Part I)

Craft Medical | Virtual Clinic For Men's Health
Robert Mitchell, M.D., Medical Advisor
Available in Arkansas, Colorado, Missouri, Okla., Texas; coming soon in Ohio, Pennsylvania and more
Appointments: (800) 405-5020 | craftmedical.com
See their remedies under Herpes

Healthgrades Marketplace, Find a Doctor
Dr. Debra Rose Wilson, School of Nursing, Austin Peay State University, McCord Hall 324, Clarksville TN 37044
Learn more: healthgrades.com | *See their remedies under Ingrown Hair, Insomnia, and Nausea And Vomiting*

K-Health | Dr. Neil Brown, Chief Medical Officer
Jill Kapil, Psy.D., Clinical Psychologist
24/7 board-certified doctors, available on your phone
Learn more: Khealth.com | *See their remedies under Food Poisoning, Stress, and Yeast Infection*

MDacne | Yoram Harth, Dermatologist
Full analysis of your acne condition, totally free of charge, via selfie and app | Learn more: Mdacne.com
See their remedies under Acne

Resilient Health Institute | Keira Barr, M.D., Dermatologist and Menopause Specialist
Learn more: Drkeirabarr.com
See their remedies under Nail Problems

Dr. Amy Shah | Online Counseling for Diet, Inflammation, Food Sensitivities, Weight Loss
Scottsdale, AZ | Learn more: AmyMDWellness.com
See their remedies under Cuts and Scrapes

ZendyHealth | Vish Banthia, M.D. | Cosmetic, Dental, Health Procedures, and Telemedicine
Call for locations and appointments: (855) 699-3639
[855-MY-ZENDY] | Zendyhealth.com
See their remedies under Leg Pain

Arizona

Advanced Ankle & Foot
Dr. Jessica Prebish, Podiatrist
2915 E Baseline Rd #103, Gilbert, AZ 85234
Appointments: (480) 962-4281 | advancedanklefoot.com
See their remedies under Ingrown Toenail

Mayo Clinic, Phoenix/Scottsdale, AZ
Appointments: (800) 446-2279 | Mayoclinic.org
See further details under Minnesota below

Redirect Health Medical & Surgical Centers
Janice Johnston, M.D., Chief Medical Officer
13430 N. Scottsdale Road, Suite 200, Scottsdale, AZ 85254
Appointments: (888) 407-7928 | redirecthealth.com
See their remedies under Muscle Pain

San Tan Allergy & Asthma | S. Reed Shimamoto, M.D., Allergy, Immunology, and Pediatrics
4840 E. Indian School Rd., Phoenix, AZ 85018
4915 E Baseline Rd Ste 112, Gilbert, AZ 85234-2966
Appointments: (480) 526-7788 | santanallergy.com
See their remedies under Allergies

Arkansas

Fayetteville Diagnostic Clinic
Michael A. Eckles, M.D., Pulmonary Medicine
3344 N Futrall Dr., Fayetteville, AR 72703
Appointments: (479) 582-7330 | mana.md
See their remedies under Insomnia

California

Allergy Partners of the Central California Coast
Daniel More, M.D., Allergist
220 S Palisade Drive, Suite 102, Santa Maria, CA 93454
Also in San Luis Obispo and Pismo Beach, CA
Appointments: (805) 543-2744 | allergypartners.com
See their remedies under Mosquito Bites

Cedars-Sinai Primary Adult Care Clinic
Christopher Almario, M.D., Gastroenterology
8723 Alden Dr #290, Los Angeles, CA 90048
Appointments: (310) 423-7785 | cedars-sinai.org
See their remedies under Constipation

Cedars-Sinai Spine Center, Los Angeles
Neel Anand, M.D., Orthopaedics
444 S San Vicente Blvd, Ste 901, Los Angeles, CA 90048
Appointments: (310) 423-9779 | cedars-sinai.org
See their remedies under Sciatica

The Doctors of Saint John's
Daniel S. Ganjian, M.D., Pediatrics
1821 Wilshire Blvd, Suite 100, Santa Monica, CA 90403
Appointments: (310) 829-4403 | providence.org
See their remedies under Diaper Rash

Kaiser Permanente Walnut Creek Medical Center
Dr. Elaine Hanh Le, Family Medicine
1425 S Main St, Walnut Creek, CA, 94596
Appointments: (925) 295-4000 | kaiserpermanente.org
See their remedies under HIV/AIDS (Part I) and Snakebites

MemorialCare Medical Group, Long Beach
Catherine D. Gritchen, M.D., Pediatrics
2110 N Bellflower Blvd, Long Beach, CA 90815
Appointments: (877) 696-3622 | memorialcare.org
See their remedies under Diaper Rash

Mission Heritage Medical Group
William Chapin Shiel, Jr., M.D., Rheumatology
26732 Crown Valley Pkwy, Suite 151, Mission Viejo, CA
92691 Appointments: (949) 364-6000 | vitals.com
See their remedies under Athlete's Foot

Nordland Oral Microsurgical Institute
W. Peter Nordland, DMD, Periodontics
850 Prospect Street, Suite 7, La Jolla, CA 92037
Appointments: (858) 459-7374 | oralplasticsurgery.com
See their remedies under Bee And Wasp Stings

Permanente Medicine, Oakland Medical Center
Donna Deng, M.D., Urology
4th Floor, 3600 Broadway, Oakland, CA 94611
Appointments: (510) 752-6789 | kaiserpermanente.org
See their remedies under Urinary Tract Infection

Providence Saint John's Health Center
Elyse J. Rubenstein, M.D., Rheumatology
1328 16th Street, Santa Monica, CA 90404
Appointments: (310) 256-2425 | providence.org
See their remedies under Arthritis

Sansum Clinic Pediatrics, Santa Barbara
Pediatrics | Daniel Brennan, M.D.
51 Hitchcock Way, Santa Barbara, CA 93105
Appointments: (805) 563-6211| Sansumclinic.org
See their remedies under Mosquito Bites

The Skin & Wellness Center
Nili Alai, M.D., Dermatology
26081 Merit Cir, Suite 109, Laguna Hills, CA 92653
Appointments: (949) 582-7699 | castleconnolly.com
See their remedies under Dandruff

Stanford Health Care | Niraj Sehgal, M.D.,
Chief Medical Officer, Hospital Medicine
300 Pasteur Dr, Stanford, CA 94305
Multiple locations in California; see website
Appointments: (650) 723-5462 | stanfordhealthcare.org
See their remedies under Bursitis

Sutter Health
Dr. Kacy A. Church M.D., Endocrinologist
1501 Trousdale Dr., Building B, 3rd Floor, Burlingame, CA
94010 | Appointments: (650) 652-8282 | sutterhealth.org
See their remedies under Diabetes

Talbert Medical Group
Dr. Gary William Cole, Dermatology
19066 Magnolia St., Huntington Beach, CA 92646 |
Appointments: (714) 698-0068 | caloptima.org
See their remedies under Athlete's Foot

UC Davis Health | George R. Thompson, M.D.,
Internal Medicine, Infectious Diseases
4301 X St., Sacramento, CA 95817
Appointments: (800) 282-3284 | health.ucdavis.edu
See their remedies under Athlete's Foot

UC Davis Health Infectious Diseases Clinic
Natascha Tuznik, D.O., Infectious Diseases
4860 Y St., Sacramento, CA 95817
Appointments: (800) 482-3284 | health.ucdavis.edu
See their remedies under Motion Sickness

UC Davis Medical Center
Dr. Steven D. Brass, M.D., Neurologist
1300 West 7th Street, Verdi, CA 90732
Appointments: (310) 514-5410 | doximity.com
See their remedies under Jet Lag

UCSF Health | Joshua Adler, M.D., Internist
1701 Divisadero St., Suite 500, San Francisco, CA 94115
Appointments: (415) 353-7999 | ucsfhealth.org
See their remedies under Flu (Influenza)

UCSF Health
Michelle A. Albert, M.D., Cardiologist
535 Mission Bay Blvd. South, San Francisco, CA
Appointments: (415) 353-2873 | ucsfhealth.org
See their remedies under Stress

Colorado

Foot and Ankle Center of the Rockies
Dr. Daniel J. Hatch, Podiatric Medicine
Denver, Longmont, and Greely, CO
Appointments: (303) 321-4477 (Denver) | facrockies.com
See their remedies under Foot Odor

MedNOW Clinics, Primary Care Medical Services
Dr. Nathan Moore, Family Medicine
15101 E. Iliff Avenue, Suite 140, Aurora, CO 80014
Also in Washington Park, Lakewood, Denver, Englewood

Appointments: (720) 878-7055 | mednowclinics.com
See their remedies under Rectal Itch & Anal Fissures

Prime Health Denver
Dr. Soyona Rafatjah, Family Medicine
6001 W. 16th Ave, Lakewood, CO 80214
Appointments: (303) 335-9092 | primehealthdenver.com
See their remedies under Irritable Bowel Syndrome

Connecticut

Connecticut Children's | Patricia Pinto-Garcia,
M.D., Pediatric and Adolescent Med.
282 Washington Street, Hartford, CT 06106
Appointments: (860) 545-8272 | hartfordhospital.org
See their remedies under High Cholesterol

MidState Medical Center
Laurence Gopal Nair, M.D., Pulmonary Medicine
455 Lewis Avenue, Suite 206, Meriden, CT 06451
Appointments: (203) 238-9446 | midstatemedical.org
See their remedies under Emphysema

Yale Dermatology, Middlebury | Brett King, M.D.
1625 Straits Turnpike, Suite 211, Middlebury, CT 06762
Appointments: (203) 577-1050 | medicine.yale.edu
See their remedies under Hair Loss

Delaware

Delaware Advanced Vein Center | Dr. Anthony
Alfieri, DO, Cardiologist and Vein Specialist
39 Omega Dr, Bldg G, Newark, DE 19713
Also with offices in Glasgow and Wilmington, DE
Appointments: (302) 722-6550 |
delawareadvancedveincenter.com
See their remedies under Phlebitis

Nemours Children's Hospital | Dr. Melanie L.
Pitone, M.D., Pediatric Emergency Medicine
1600 Rockland Road, Wilmington, DE, 19803
Appointments: (302) 651-4000 | nemours.org
See their remedies under Cuts And Scrapes

District of Columbia

GW Medical | Cathleen Clancy, M.D., Internal
Medicine, Emergency Med., Medical Toxicology
2150 Pennsylvania Ave NW, #5, cWashington, DC 20037
Appointments: (202) 741-3000 | gwdocs.com
See their remedies under Stingray stings

Florida

Advanced Dermatology and Cosmetic Surgery
Mark Kaufmann, M.D.
Pembroke Pines, Aventura, and Weston FL
Appointments: (866) 400-3376 | advancedderm.com
See their remedies under Corns and Calluses, Frostbite,
Hives, and Rashes

AdventHealth Medical Group
Chetan K. Patel, M.D., Spine Surgery
711 E Altamonte Dr., Altamonte Springs, FL 32701
Appointments: (407) 303-5452 | adventhealth.com
See their remedies under Backache

Baumann Cosmetic and Research Institute
Dr. Leslie Baumann, M.D., Cosmetic Dermatology
7257 NE 4th Avenue Miami, FL 33138
Appointments: (305) 532-5552 | lesliebaumannmd.com
See their remedies under Rosacea

REMEMBER: Most of these providers treat many more conditions beyond those listed here. Check their websites or give them a call to see if their services are a fit for your needs.

Doctors Urgent Care
David Dean, M.D., Medical Director
7620 Gunn Hwy, Suite 170, Tampa, FL 33625; also Citrus
Park, Palm Harbor, Odessa/Trinity | Appointments
(Tampa): (813) 475-6525 yourdoctorsurgentcare.com
See their remedies under Jellyfish Stings

Fifth Avenue Palm Beach | Marie Hayag, M.D.
1411 North Flagler Dr, West Palm Beach, FL 33401
Appointments: (212) 722.2055 | mariehayagmd.com
See their remedies under Oily Hair and Skin

HCA Florida Brandon Hospital
Michael L. Davis, M.D., Family Medicine
119 Oakfield Dr, Brandon, FL 33511
Appointments: (813) 681-5551 | hcafloridahealthcare.com
See their remedies under Erectile Dysfunction

Holy Cross Health | John P. Cunha, D.O.
4725 N. Federal Hwy., Ft Lauderdale, FL 33308
Appointments: (954) 492-5753 | holy-cross.com
See their remedies under Black Eye

Klement Family Dental
Stephen M. Klement, DMD
7650 38th Ave N, St. Pete. FL 33710
Appointments: (727) 344-9740 | Stpetedentist.com
See their remedies under Tooth Pain

Mayo Clinic, Jacksonville, FL | Chrisandra L.
Shufelt, M.D., Women's Health Specialist
Appointments: (904) 953-0853 | Mayoclinic.org
See their remedies under Hot Flashes
See further details under Minnesota below

MedFast Urgent Centers | David Williams, DO
490 Centre Lake Dr NE # 200, Palm Bay, FL 32907
Urgent care clinics in Brevard Co. and Edgewater, FL
Appointments: (321) MEDFAST | medfastcare.com
See their remedies under Scratches, Bites, And Stings

Riverchase Dermatology
Lucy Chen, M.D., Dermatologist
1111 Kane Concourse, Suite 100, Bay Harbor Is., FL 33154
Appointments: (800) 591-3376 | riverchasedermatology.com
See their remedies under Ingrown Hair

Sand Lake Dermatology Center
Allison Arthur, M.D., Dermatologist
7335 W. Sand Lake Road, #200, Orlando, FL 32819
Appointments: (407) 352-8553 | sandlakedermatology.com
See their remedies under Acne

Georgia

Cleaver Medical Group Dermatology
Dr. Stephanie Gardner, M.D., Dermatologist
6300 Hospital Parkway, Suite 375, Johns Creek, GA 30097
Appointments: (770) 800-3455 | cleavermedicalgroup.com
See their remedies under Fire Ant Stings

Dr. Nicholas Jones, M.D., FACS, Plastic Surgeon
3280 Howell Mill Road NW, Suite 200, Atlanta, GA 30327
Appointments: (404) 882-8044 | drnipandtuck.com
See their remedies under Wrinkles

Piedmont Heart Institute Vascular Surgeons
Dr. Patrick Mell Battey, M.D.
95 Collier Road Northwest, Suite 2045, Atlanta, GA 30309
Appointments: (404) 605-5110 | piedmont.org
See their remedies under Flu (Influenza)

Idaho

Full Circle Health, Inc. | Dr. Kathleen Michele Romito, M.D., Family Medicine
3673 Stone Creek Way, Boise, ID 83703
Appointments: (208) 861-3673 | stlukesonline.org
See their remedies under Acne

Intermountain Healthcare
J.P. Valin, M.D., Chief Clinical Officer
36 S State Street, Salt Lake City, Utah 84111
See website for locations in Idaho and Utah
Appointments: (866) 877-4325
intermountainhealthcare.org
See their remedies under Bursitis

Saint Alphonsus Health System
Patrice Burgess, M.D., Family Medicine
10255 W Overland Rd, Boise, ID 83709
Appointments: (208) 302-5600 | saintalphonsus.org
See their remedies under Athlete's Foot

Illinois

Advocate Trinity Hospital
Dr. Angela M. Bell, M.D., Internist
1653 W Congress Pkwy, Chicago, IL 60612
Appointments: (312) 942-5000 | advocatehealth.com
See their remedies under Phlebitis

The Derm Institute of Chicago
Jordan C. Carqueville, M.D., Dermatologist
737 North Michigan Ave., Chicago, IL 60611
Appointments: (312) 319-1978 | carquevillemd.com
See their remedies under Acne

Pinnacle Dermatology | Owen Kramer, M.D.
103 Haven Rd, Suite 7, Elmhurst, IL 60126
Appointments: (630) 832-2111 | pinnacleskin.com
See their remedies under Diabetes

Mark S. Travis, M.D., Geriatric Medicine, Internal Medicine, Nephrology
1211 S Prairie Avenue, Chicago, IL 60605
Appointments: (312) 939-5090 | md.com
See their remedies under Fatigue

Indiana

Indiana Sleep Center | Abhinav Singh, M.D.
701 East County Line Road, Greenwood, IN 46143
Appointments: (317) 887 6400 | indianasleepcenter.com
See their remedies under Night Sweats

Iowa

Health System Emergency Physicians
Timothy R. Gutshall, M.D.
1301 Pennsylvania Ave., Suite 417, Des Moines, IA 50316
Appointments: (515) 263-5684 | md.com
See their remedies under High Cholesterol

Iowa Retina Consultants
Christopher L. Haupert, M.D., Ophthalmologist
1501 50th Street, Suie 133, West Des Moines, IA 50266
Appointments: (515) 222-6400 | iowaretina.com
See their remedies under Eyestrain

University of Iowa Hospitals & Clinics
Mary S. Stone, M.D., Dermatologist
200 Hawkins Drive, Iowa City, IA 52242
Appointments: (800) 777-8442 | uihc.org
See their remedies under Dry Skin and Winter Itch

Kansas

All About Vision | Shane Kannarr, OD, Optometry
2521 N. Broadway, Pittsburg, KS 66762
Also: Girard and Fort Scott, KS
Appointments: (620)-235-1737 | kannarreyecare.com
See their remedies under Black Eye

East Wichita Dentist | Dr. David Koepsel
Preventive, cosmetic, and restorative dentistry
8150 E. Douglas Ave, Wichita, KS 67206
Appointments: (316) 686-7395 | eastwichitadentist.com
See their remedies under Denture Discomfort

Post Rock Family Medicine | Beth Oller, M.D.
1210 N Washington, Plainville, KS 67663
Also offices in Stockton and Palco, KS

Appointments: (785) 434-2622 | postrock.us
See their remedies under Heat Exhaustion/Heat Stroke, Black Eye

University of Kansas Medical Center
Nancy Hammond, M.D., Neurology
4000 Cambridge Street, Kansas City, KS 66160
Appointments: (913) 588-1227 | kansashealthsystem.com
See their remedies under Dizziness

Kentucky

Norton Healthcare
Dr. Steven Heilman, M.D., Emergency Medicine
1 Audubon Plaza Dr, Louisville, KY 40217
Appointments: (502) 636-7111 | nortonhealthcare.com
See their remedies under Tick Bites

Louisiana

Allure Enhancement Center
Dr. Cindy Cobb, Doctorate in Nursing Practice
500 Juliette Place, Lafayette, LA 70506
Appointments: (337) 222-3539 | allureenhancement.com
See their remedies under Age Spots, Dry Skin And Winter Itch, and Hair Loss

LSU Health, Shreveport
Thomas Arnold, M.D., Emergency Medicine
1501 Kings Highway, Shreveport, LA 71103
Appointments: (318) 626-0050 | lsuhs.edu
See their remedies under Bee And Wasp Stings

Ochsner LSU Health Shreveport
Pat Bass, M.D., Internal Medicine and Pediatrics
1023 Provenance Place Blvd, Shreveport, Louisiana 71106
Appointments: (318) 626-0100 | ochsnerlsuhs.org
See their remedies under Asthma

Maryland

Anne Arundel Medical Group | Robert M. Verklin, Jr., M.D., Orthopedics and Sports Med.
Annapolis, Bowie, Millersville, Odenton, & Pasadena, MD
Appointments: (410) 268-8862 | osmc.net
See their remedies under Athlete's Foot

Johns Hopkins Community Physicians
Dr. Charlene Gamaldo, M.D., Sleep Medicine
11085 Little Patuxent Pkwy, Columbia, MD 21044
Appointments: (410) 715-1060 | hopkinsmedicine.org
See their remedies under Insomnia

Johns Hopkins Medicine | Meredith Christine McCormack, M.D. Pulmonology & Critical Care
1800 Orleans St., Baltimore, MD 21287
Appointments: (410) 550-5864 | hopkinsmedicine.org
See their remedies under Asthma

Johns Hopkins Medicine
Paul Bennett Rothman, M.D., Rheumatology
600 N Wolfe St, Baltimore, MD 21287
Appointments: (410) 955-3052 | hopkinsrheumatology.org
See their remedies under Blisters

Maryland Center for Complete Dentistry
Jonathan Silverman, DDS
23 Crossroads Drive, Owings Mills, MD 21117
Appointments: (443) 222-0399 | saveteeth.com
See their remedies under Bad Breath

University of Maryland Medical System
Sharleen St. Surin-Lord, M.D.
1400 Mercantile Lane, Suite 110, Largo, MD 20774
Appointments: (301) 773-7546 | umms.org
See their remedies under Poison Ivy And Oak

Massachusetts

Boston Medical Center | Kevin Wilson, M.D., Pulmonary, Allergy, Sleep & Critical Care
725 Albany St., Boston, MA 02118
Appointments: (617) 638-7480 | bumc.bu.edu
See their remedies under Boils

Granite Chiropractic | Drs. Sarah & Adrian Granite
333 Elm Street, Suite 120, Dedham, MA 02026
Appointments: (781) 467-0088
granitefamilychiropractic.com | *See their remedies under Physical Activity and Nutrition, Part I*

Michigan

Cornerstone Medical Group
Jasneet Bhullar, M.D., Colon & Rectal Surgery
46591 Romeo Plank, Macomb Township, MI 48044
Also with locations in Southfield and Rochester Hills
Appointments: (586) 226-6120 | cornerstonemedgroup.com
See their remedies under Rectal Itch & Anal Fissures

Spectrum Health
Randall Meisner, M.D., Gastroenterology
4100 Lake Dr SE, Grand Rapids, MI 49546
Appointments: (616) 267-7414 | spectrumhealth.org
See their remedies under Diarrhea

Minnesota

Allina Health
Hsieng Su, M.D., Chief Medical Executive
2925 Chicago Ave., Minneapolis, MN 55407
Appointments: (888) 425-5462 | allinahealth.org
See their remedies under Sunburn

Hennepin Healthcare
Jing (Jenny) Liu, M.D., Dermatology
715 South 8th Street, Minneapolis, MN 55404
Appointments: (612) 873-6963 | hennepinhealthcare.org
See their remedies under Dandruff

Mayo Clinic, Rochester, MN
Summer V. Allen, M.D., Family Medicine
Edward T. Creagan, M.D., Oncology
Colin L. Driscoll, M.D., Otolaryngology
Bradley C. Leibovich, M.D., Urology
Donald D. Hensrud, M.D., Internal Medicine
Darrell S. Pardi, M.D., Gastroenterology
John H. Pemberton, M.D., Colon/Rectal Surg.
Darrell S. Pardi, M.D., Gastroenterology and
Hepatology
Sandhya Pruthi, M.D., Family Physician
Laura Walker, M.D., Emergency Medicine
Appointments: (507) 538-3270 | mayoclinic.org
*See their remedies under Cancer, Common Cold, Diabetes,
Diarrhea, Diverticulosis/Diverticulitis, Earwax, Hair Loss,
Hiccups, Incontinence, Knee Pain, Laryngitis, Overweight
and Obesity (Part I), Poison Ivy And Oak, Raynaud's
Syndrome, Rectal Itch & Anal Fissures, Spider Bites,
Tachycardia*

Missouri

BJC HealthCare
Kenneth A. Hacker, M.D., General Surgery
4901 Forest Park Avenue, St. Louis, MO 63108
Appointments: (888) 906- 2961 | doctors.bjc.org
See their remedies under Bad Breath

Missouri Orthopedics & Advanced Sports
Medicine | Dr. David Irvine
621 S. New Ballas Road, St. Louis, MO 63141
845 N. New Ballas Court, Creve Coeur, MO 63141
Appointments: (314) 567-5850 | mosportsmed.com
See their remedies under Tendonitis

Missouri Vein Specialists | Scott Darling, DO
Comprehensive Venous Disease Treatment
26 S. Village Dr. (291 Hwy), Liberty, MO 64068
Appointments: (816) 792-3400 |
missouriveinspecialists.com
See their remedies under Restless Legs

St. Louis Dermatology & Cosmetic Medicine
Lawrence E. Samuels, M.D.
222 S Woods Mill Rd, Chesterfield, MO 63017
Appointments: (314) 576-7343 | saintlouisderm.com
See their remedies under Raynaud's Syndrome

St. Luke's Medical Group, Heart and Vascular
Institute | Ronald Leidenfrost, M.D.
232 S Woods Mill Rd, Chesterfield, MO 63017
Appointments: (314) 434-1500 | stlukes-stl.com
See their remedies under Chest Pain

Nebraska

Williamsburg Dental | Michael Kotopka, DDS
1265 S. Cotner Blvd. #1, Lincoln, NE 68510
Appointments: (402) 858-9405 | williamsburgdentalllc.com
See their remedies under Gingivitis

Nevada

Silverado Family Dental | Dr. R. Garth Harris
9777 S. Bermuda Road, Las Vegas, NV 89183
Appointments: (702) 699-5551 | silveradofamilydental.com
See their remedies under Denture Discomfort

New Hampshire

Dartmouth Hitchcock Medical Center
Eric D. Shah, M.D., Gastroenterology, Hepatology
1 Medical Center Dr, Lebanon, NH 03766
Appointments: (603) 650-5262 | dartmouth-hitchcock.org
See their remedies under Irritable Bowel Syndrome

New Jersey

Chilton Medical Center
Dr. Eric Perez, M.D., Emergency Medicine
97 West Pkwy, Pompton Plains, NJ 07444
Appointments: (973) 831-5000 | atlantichealth.org
See their remedies under Jet Lag

Hackensack Meridian Health | Michael J.
Cunningham, M.D., Orthopedic Surgery
301 Church Street, Suite B, Aberdeen, NJ 07747
Appointments: (732) 264-5454 |
hackensackmeridianhealth.org
See their remedies under Carpal Tunnel Syndrome

Image Dermatology P.C. | Dr. Jeanine B. Downie
51 Park Street, Montclair, NJ 07042
Appointments: (973) 509-6900 | imagedermatology.com
See their remedies under Nail Problems

Stiles Dental Care, Dr. William H. Stiles
25 North Main Street, Medford, NJ 08055
Appointments: (609) 654-0033 | medfordsmiles.com
See their remedies under Canker Sores

New York

Blum Center for Health | Susan Blum, M.D.
Preventive Medicine and Chronic Disease
Danielle Greenman, M.D. Functional Medicine
34 Rye Ridge Plaza, Rye Brook, NY 10573
Appointments: (914) 652-7800 | blumcenterforhealth.com
See their remedies under Arthritis and Diabetes

Columbia University Irving Medical Center
Dr. Daichi Shimbo, Cardiovascular Disease
622 W. 168th St, New York, NY 10032
Appointments: (212) 342-1273 | doctors.columbia.edu
See their remedies under Anger

Fifth Avenue Aesthetics | Marie Hayag, M.D.
875 Fifth Avenue #1CDE, New York, NY 10065
Appointments: (212) 722.2055 | mariehayagmd.com
See their remedies under Oily Hair and Skin

**Firshein Center | Richard Firshein, D.O.,
Integrative Medicine & Family Medicine**
1226 Park Ave, New York, NY 10128
Appointments: (212) 860-0282 | firsheincenter.com
See their remedies under Asthma

**Hospital for Special Surgery
Theodore R. Fields, M.D., Rheumatology**
535 East 70th St., 8th Fl., New York, NY 10021
Appointments: (212) 606-1286 | hss.edu
See their remedies under Gout

**Integrative Cardiology Center of Long Island
Regina Druz, M.D., Cardiovascular Disease and
Internal Medicine**
121 Jericho Tpke Mineola, NY 11501
Appointments: (516) 619-3888 | Iccli.com
See their remedies under Tachycardia

**LM Medical NYC
Dr. Morgan Rabach, Dermatologist**
33 5th Avenue #1B, New York, NY 10003
Appointments: (212) 777-2272 | Lmmedicalnyc.com
See their remedies under Acne

**Laser & Skin Surgery Center Of New York
Dr. Blair Murphy-Rose, Dermatologist**
317 East 34th Street, New York, NY 10016
Appointments: (212) 941-5055 | laserskinsurgery.com
See their remedies under Ingrown Hair

**Memorial Sloan Kettering Cancer Center
Yen-Nien (Jason) Hou, Herb Information Center**
New York, NY
Information: (833) 920-3234 | mskcc.org
See their remedies under Cancer

**Natural Eye Care
Dr. Marc Grossman, Optometrist, Acupuncturist**
3 Paradies Lane, New Paltz, NY 12561
Appointments: (845) 475-4158 | naturaleyecare.com
See their remedies under Dry Eyes

**NYU Langone Health
Dr. Amina Abdeldaim, M.D., Allergist
Kathryn A. Colby, M.D., PhD., Eye Specialist**
60 E 56th St, Fl 7, New York, NY 10022
Appointments: (646) 470-1151 | nyulangone.org
See their remedies under Allergies and Conjunctivitis

**RMA of New York | Tia Jackson-Bey, M.D.,
Reproductive Endocrinologist**
Offices in Manhattan, Brooklyn and Westchester, NY
Appointments: (212) 756-5777 | rmany.com
See their remedies under Constipation

**St. Barnabas Hospital
David Perlstein, M.D., Pediatrics**
4422 Third Avenue, Bronx, NY 10457
Appointments: (718) 960-9071| sbhny.org
See their remedies under Black Eye

**Soho Skin & Laser Dermatology PC
Dr. Laurie J. Polis, Dermatologist**
197 Grand St Ste 3E, New York, NY 10013
Appointments: (212) 431-1600 | Mountsinai.org
See their remedies under Age Spots

**Treiber Dermatology Associates,
Leah Ansell, M.D., Dermatology**
175 Purchase Street, Rye, NY 10580
Appointments: (914) 967-2153 | treiberderm.com
See their remedies under Corns and Calluses

**Dr. Amy Wechsler Dermatology, Board-Certified
in both Dermatology and Psychiatry**
45 East 85th Street, New York, NY 10028
Appointments: (212) 396-2500 | dramywechsler.com
See their remedies under Nail Problems

**White Plains Hospital
Michael Menna, DO, Emergency Medicine**
41 E. Post Rd., White Plains, NY 10601
Appointments: (914) 681-0600 | wphospital.org
See their remedies under Cat Bites

Dr. Joshua Zeichner, Dermatologist
234 East 85th Street, New York, NY 10028
Appointments: (212) 731-3311 | zeichnerdermatology.com
See their remedies under Acne

North Carolina

**Atrium Health Primary Care, Cabarrus Family
Medicine | Amber Anderson, DO, Family Med.**
4315 Physicians Blvd., Harrisburg, NC 28075
Appointments: (704) 455-6521 | atriumhealth.org
See their remedies under Seasonal Affective Disorder

**Duke Endocrinology Clinic
Kenneth W. Lyles, M.D., Geriatrics**
30 Duke Medicine Cir, Durham, NC 27710
Appointments: (919) 668-5360 | dukehealth.org
See their remedies under Osteoporosis

**Lake Norman Oral & Facial Surgery
Raymond J. Haigney II, DDS**
9727 Northcross Center Ct., Huntersville, NC 28079
Appointments: (704) 286-1567 | lakenormanofs.com
See their remedies under TMJ

**Leigh Brain & Spine
Cosmas Leigh, D.C., Chiropractor
Trish Leigh, Ph.D., Certified Brain Health Coach**
6110 Falconbridge Road, Chapel Hill, NC 27517
Appointments: (919) 401-9933 | leighbrainandspine.com
See their remedies under Foot Pain

*For omissions, updates, or corrections, please share
caregiver's street address, website, and appointment
telephone number with info@trustedremedies.com.*

Ohio

Cleveland Clinic
Steven Gordon, M.D., Infectious Disease Specialist
David M. Lang, M.D., Allergy and Immunology
Jeremy Lipman, M.D., Colorectal Surgery
Francis Papay, M.D., Dermatology
Stephen Sayles III, M.D., Emergency Medicine
Troy Woodard, M.D., Otolaryngology
9500 Euclid Avenue, Cleveland, OH 44195
Appointments: (216) 444-6900 | my.clevelandclinic.org
See their remedies under Allergies, Boils, Dog Bites,
Earwax, Hemorrhoids, and Irritable Bowel Syndrome

Oregon

Kaiser Permanente Hillsboro Medical Office
Judith Lynn Marcin, M.D., Family Medicine
5373 E Main St, Cornelius, OR
Appointments: (503) 547-1254 | kaiserpermanente.org
See their remedies under Ulcers

Providence Heart Clinic – St. Vincent
James Beckerman, M.D., Cardiologist
9427 SW Barnes Road, Portland, OR 97225
Appointments: (503) 216-1661| providence.org
See their remedies under Chest Pain

Pennsylvania

BergerHenry ENT Specialty Group
Alan S. Berger, M.D., Ear, Nose, and Throat
Willow Grove, PA and other Philadelphia area offices
Appointments: (215) 830-8620 | bergerhenryent.com
See their remedies under Dry Mouth

Legg Counseling and Consulting Services, LLC
Timothy Legg, Ph.D., Psychologist
1418 Main St, Peckville, PA 18452
Appointments: (570) 489-4357 | leggcounseling.com
See their remedies under Mental Health

Geisinger Medical Center | Jonathan Edward
Spahr, MD, Pediatric Pulmonology
100 North Academy Avenue, Danville, PA 17822
Appointments: (800-275-6401 | providers.geisinger.org
See their remedies under Environmental Quality (Part I)

Hospital of University of Pennsylvania
Dr. Mariell L. Jessup, M.D., Cardiologist
3400 Spruce St Philadelphia, PA 19104
Appointments: (215) 615-4949 | pennmedicine.org
See their remedies under High Blood Pressure

Jefferson Health
Nancy DeAngelis, CRNP, Adult Psychiatry
1245 Highland Avenue, Abington, PA 19001
Appointments: (215) 481-3133 | abingtonhealth.org
See their remedies under Anxiety

Jefferson Health
Bruce A. Meyer, M.D., Obstetrics/Gyn
925 Chestnut Street, Philadelphia, PA 19107
Appointments: (215) 503-8691 | jefferson.edu
See their remedies under Anxiety

Penn Medicine Lancaster General Health
John J. Eichenlaub, M.D., Obstetrics/Gyn
2128 Embassy Drive, Lancaster, PA 17603
Appointments: (717) 509-5090 | PennMedicine.org
See their remedies under Hot Flashes

Penn State Health | Sankar Bandyopadhyay,
M.D., Neurology, Neuromuscular Medicine
30 Hope Dr, Hershey, PA 17033
Appointments: (800) 243-1455 | pennstatehealth.org
See their remedies under Motion Sickness

Philadelphia Hand to Shoulder Center
A. Lee Osterman, M.D., Hand Surgery
950 Pulaski Drive, King of Prussia, PA 19406
Appointments: (800) 385-7472 | Hand2shouldercenter.com
See their remedies under Arthritis

South Carolina

CENTA Medical Group | William Giles, M.D.,
Facial Plastic and Reconstructive Surgery
Offices in Lexington and Columbia, SC
Appointments: (803) 256-2483 | Centamedical.com
See their remedies under Laryngitis

McLeod Health
Christopher G. Cunningham, Vascular Surgery
107 McLeod Health Blvd, Myrtle Beach, SC 29579
Appointments: (843) 366-3755 | mcleodhealth.org
See their remedies under Leg Pain

Midlands Oral & Maxillofacial Surgery
James Lemon, DMD
1755 St. Julian Place, Columbia, SC 29204
Appointments: (803) 254-2972 | midlandsoms.com
See their remedies under Fire Ant Stings

Tennessee

Elite Sports Medicine + Orthopedics | Burton F.
Elrod, M.D., Orthopedic Surgery, Sports Medicine
Offices in Nashville and Franklin, TN
Appointments: (615) 324-1600 | eliteorthopaedic.com
See their remedies under Sprains

Southern Plastic & Reconstructive Surgical
Institute | Nathan Brought, D.O., Plastic Surgery
4601 Carothers Parkway, Franklin, TN 37067
Appointments: (615) 724.9818 | sprsi.com
See their remedies under Scars

Threlkeld Infectious Disease | Dr. Daniel Murrell
6029 Walnut Grove Road, Suite C002, Memphis TN 38120
Appointments: (901) 685-3490 | medicalofmemphis.com
See their remedies under HIV/AIDS in Part I

Texas

Collin County ENT (Ear, Nose, and Throat)
Keith E. Matheny, M.D., Otolaryngology
8380 Warren Pkwy, Suite 504, Frisco, TX 75034
Appointments: (972) 596-4005 | collincountyent.com
See their remedies under Nosebleed

Corpus Christi Allergy Associates
Jurairat J. Molina, M.D., Allergist
5402 S Staples Street, Corpus Christi, TX 78411
Appointments: (361) 882-3487 | corpuschristiallergy.com
See their remedies under Mosquito Bites

Dallas Allergy & Asthma Center
Lara M. Gross, M.D., Allergy/Immunology
5499 Glen Lakes Drive, Dallas, TX 75231
Appointments: (214) 691-1330 | daac-prc.com
See their remedies under Allergies

Digestive Health Associates of Texas
Jay N. Yepuri, M.D., Gastroenterologist
1600 Central Drive, Suite 155, Bedford, TX 76022
Appointments: (817) 267-8470 | dfwgidoctor.com
See their remedies under Lactose Intolerance

First Eye Care DFW | Craig C. Hughes, OD
751 Mid Cities Blvd, Ste A, Hurst, TX, 76054
Also with offices in Keller and Roanoke, TX
Appointments: (817) 656-2020 | firsteyecaredfw.com
See their remedies under Night Blindness

Houston Methodist
Marc L. Boom, M.D., Geriatric Medicine
6550 Fannin St Ste 1101, Houston, TX, 77030
Appointments: (713) 441-2750 | houstonmethodist.org
See their remedies under Heartburn

M.D. Anderson Tobacco Treatment Program
Maher Karam-Hage, M.D.
1155 Pressler St, Houston, TX 77030
Appointments: (866) 245-0862 | mdanderson.org
See their remedies under Tobacco (Part I)

Medical City Healthcare | Joseph Parra, M.D.,
Chief Medical Officer, Hospitalist
13155 Noel Rd., Suite 2000, Dallas, TX 75240
Appointments: (844) 671-4204 | medicalcityhealthcare.com
See their remedies under Bursitis, Burns, Chapped Lips

Physicians Premier ER, Texas Freestanding
Emergency Rooms | Dr. David Kenyon, M.D.
Corpus Christi, San Antonio, and Brazos Valley, TX
Appointments (San Antonio): (210) 337-0911
mdpremier.com | *See their remedies under Cuts & Scrapes*

Prime Urgent Care | Dr. Niharika Mehra, D.O.
2510 Smith Ranch Rd, Pearland, TX 77584
Also Missouri City and Sugar Land, TX
Appointments: (713) 340-3111 | primeuc.com
See their remedies under Dizziness

Texas A&M Health Family Care
Dr. Jason McKnight, M.D., Primary Care
Dr. Susan Roberman, M.D., Primary Care
2900 E. 29th St., Ste. 200, Bryan, TX 77802
Appointments: (979) 776-8440 | stlukeshealth.org
See their remedies under Cough

UT Health San Antonio | Tom Patterson, M.D.,
Internal Medicine/Infectious Disease
8300 Floyd Curl Dr., San Antonio, TX 78229
Appointments: (210) 450-9000 | uthscsa.edu
See their remedies under Allergies

UT Physicians Center for Autoimmunity
Dr. Maureen D. Mayes, M.D., Rheumatologist
6410 Fannin Street, Suite 450, Houston, TX, 77030
Appointments: (713) 486-3100 | utphysicians.com
See their remedies under Raynaud's Syndrome

REMEMBER: Most of these providers treat many more conditions beyond those listed here. Check their websites or give them a call to see if their services are a fit for your needs.

University of Texas Medical Branch
Sally Robinson, M.D., Complex Care, Pediatric
2785 Gulf Freeway South, League City, TX 77573
Appointments: (409) 772-3695 | utmbhealth.com
See their remedies under Diaper Rash

Urology Clinics of North Texas
Gregory Robert Thoreson, M.D., Urologist
3417 Gaston Avenue, Dallas, TX 75246
Appointments: (214) 826-6021 | urologyclinics.com
See their remedies under Erectile Dysfunction

Women's Health Specialists | Marc Wilson, M.D.
323 North Bonnie Brae Street, Denton, TX 76201
Appointments: (940) 202-0301 | pro-lifeobgyn.com
See their remedies under Menopause

Utah
Intermountain Healthcare
J.P. Valin, M.D., Chief Clinical Officer
See website for locations in Idaho and Utah
Appointments: (866) 877-4325
intermountainhealthcare.org
See their remedies under Bursitis

Intermountain LDS Hospital
Dr. Stephen L. Barlow, M.D., Internist
4646 W Lake Park Blvd, Salt Lake City, UT 84120

Appointments: (801) 442-6126 | md.com
See their remedies under Headache

Mountain Peaks Family Practice
Robert Durrans, M.D., Sports Medicine, Adult
Medicine, Wellness Care, and Mental Health
501 East 770 North, Orem, UT 84097
Appointments: (801) 724-9840 |
mountainpeaksfamilypractice.com
See their remedies under Splinters

Virginia

Crowell Reconstructive Surgery
Michael W. Hasz, M.D., Spine Surgeon
1860 Town Center Dr, Ste 180, Reston, VA 20190
Appointments: (703) 936-9474 | hcavirginia.com
See their remedies under Neck Pain

District Endocrine
Anis Rehman, M.D., Endocrinology
1916 Opitz Blvd, Woodbridge, VA 22191
Appointments: (703) 214-9773 | districtendocrine.com
See their remedies under Earache And Ear Infection

Foot and Ankle Clinic of the Virginias
Dr. Timothy Donatelli, Podiatric Medicine
10 locations in Virginia and W. Virginia
See website for details: drfootpain.com
See their remedies under Blisters

Dr. Paul Henny, DDS
Affordable, Fine, Health-Centered Dentistry
1213 Corporate Circle, SW, Roanoke, VA 24018
Appointments: (540) 774-1577 | paulhennydds.com
See their remedies under Bad Breath

Rose Wellness | Andrew David Shiller, M.D.,
Integrative Medicine Physician
2944 Hunter Mill Rd, Suite 101, Oakton, VA 22124
Appointments: (833) ROSEWEL | rosewellness.com
See their remedies under Premenstrual Syndrome

Sentara Healthcare | Don Martin, M.D.,
Internal Medicine and Rheumatology
2509 Pleasant Run Dr, Harrisonburg, VA 22801
Appointments: (540) 689-5700 | sentara.com
See their remedies under Arthritis

Washington

Foot & Ankle Center of Washington | Dr. Douglas
S. Hale and Dr. Lawrence Z. Huppin, Podiatrists
600 Broadway #220, Seattle, WA 98122
Appointments: (206) 344-3808 | footankle.com
See their remedies under Shin Splints

Seattle Children's Hospital | Jeff Sperring, M.D.,
CEO, Pediatrics, Hospital Medicine
4800 Sand Point Way NE, Seattle, WA 98105

Appointments: (206) 987-2000 | seattlechildrens.org
See their remedies under Jellyfish Stings

University of Washington Medicine
Susan D. Reed M.D., MPH, MS
325 Ninth Avenue, Seattle, WA 98104
Appointments: (206) 744-3367 | obgyn.uw.edu
See their remedies under Menopause

Vantage Radiology & Diagnostic Services
Philip Lund, M.D., President
Auburn, Renton, and other Seattle WA area offices
Appointments: (253) 661-1700 | vrads.com
See their remedies under Varicose Veins

West Virginia

Foot and Ankle Clinic of the Virginias
Dr. Timothy Donatelli, Podiatric Medicine
10 clinics in W. Virginia and Virginia
See website for locations: drfootpain.com
See their remedies under Blisters

Wisconsin

American Family Children's Hospital
Dipesh Navsaria, M.D., Urgent Care (Pediatrics)
2402 Winnebago Street, Madison, WI
Appointments: (608) 242-6845 | uwhealth.org
See their remedies under Cough

SSM Health
Dr. David Rebedew, Geriatric Medicine
515 22nd Street, Monroe, WI, 53566
Appointments: (608) 324-3200 | ssmhealth.com
See their remedies under Overweight and Obesity in Part I

CANADA

Advance Eye Care Center, Saskatchewan
Dr. Myles Bokinac and Dr. Rhea Anderson
Offices in Regina and Grenfell
Appointments: (306) 992-3010 | Advanceeyecarecenter.com
See their remedies under Dry Eyes

For omissions, updates, or corrections, please share caregiver's street address, website, and appointment telephone number with info@trustedremedies.com

YOUR 4 FREE EBOOKS!

Thank you for purchasing the **PHYSICIANS' DIRECTORY OF TRUSTED REMEDIES**. Use it in good health! Please accept these **Four Free Bonus eBooks** (pdf's) with our compliments; simply use the QR scan codes below to access your free gifts. Each is also available as a paperback on Amazon for under $10.

HOW TO SCAN: Select the camera or your phone or other device. Hold your device so that one QR code appears in the viewfinder. Your device reads the code and shows a notification. Tap the notification to open the eBook. Repeat for each.

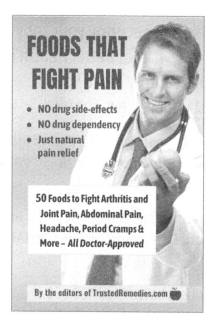

MAKE YOUR IMPACT, LEAVE A REVIEW!

1. Scan the code.   2. Click the stars.   3. Post your review!

5.0  ⌄   Write a customer review

You've taken a wise step to start improving your health yourself by securing your copy of this directory ... *congratulations!* Now help share the good news that better health is possible without risky fads, folklore, or over-reliance on drugs. Simply leave your honest review on Amazon; just scan the code above and post your review. Thanks!

- **Let's reduce the number of tragic strokes.** 3 out of 5 stroke victims are dehydrated at the time of their stroke. That's one of the 101 reasons we published *WATER CURES: 101 Little-Known Health Remedies Using Only Water* [paperback or eBook].

- **Seniors can avoid or delay dementia.** Doctors say we can all take specific steps to reduce our risk for dementia. That's why we've published *15 Trusted Remedies to Prevent Dementia: Cognitive Decline Is Not Inevitable* [paperback, eBook].

- **Let's help people reduce the suffering of chronic pain.** Opioid painkillers have killed 400,000 Americans in the last 5 years. Even over-the-counter pain pills can have harmful side effects. And none of these drugs even address the root causes of pain. That's why we wrote *FOODS THAT FIGHT PAIN: 50 Foods To Fight Arthritis and Joint Pain, Abdominal Pain & More* [paperback, eBook].

- **We can bring hope and comfort in trying times.** Fire, hospital, and military chaplains offer words of comfort in times of sickness and loss. We share over 40 expressions of hope in *CHAPLAINS' PRAYERS FOR HEALTH AND HEALING* [paperback, eBook].

- **We can replace risky folklore and celebrity-driven "health hacks"** with doctor-trusted home remedies. Losing 10,000 people a year to social media "health hacks" is not acceptable. That's why we published the *PHYSICIANS' DIRECTORY OF TRUSTED REMEDIES: 1,000+ Doctor-Approved Home Remedies for 145 Leading Health Concerns.*

Join Trusted Remedies Publishing on our mission to help others live simpler, healthier lives. Post your honest review of this directory on Amazon today!

Made in the USA
Monee, IL
05 November 2024

69400885R00157